THE WORLD ALMANAC
FOR KIDS
2011

WORLD ALMANAC® BOOKS
An Imprint of Infobase Publishing

THE WORLD ALMANAC®
ALMANAC®

FOR KIDS

2011

Project Management: Robert Famighetti
New Content: RJF PUBLISHING

Contributors: Emily Dolbear, Brian Fitzgerald, Richard Hantula, Lisa M. Herrington, Amanda Hudson, William A. McGeveran
Photo Research: Edward A. Thomas

Design: BILL SMITH GROUP
Chief Creative Officer: Brian Kobberger
Project Manager: Allison Harm
Design: Brock Waldron, Jennifer Basilio, Tamara English, Faith Hutchinson, Geron Hoy
Production: Rob Duverger, Bob Horvath, Steve Scheluchin, Mie Tsuchida

INFOBASE PUBLISHING
Editorial Director: Laurie E. Likoff
Senior Editor: Sarah Janssen
Project Editor: Edward A. Thomas

World Almanac® Books
An imprint of Infobase Publishing
132 West 31st Street
New York NY 10001

Hardcover	Paperback
ISBN-13: 978-1-60057-135-0	ISBN-13: 978-1-60057-136-7
ISBN-10: 1-60057-135-2	ISBN-10: 1-60057-136-0

For Library of Congress cataloging information, please contact the publisher.

The World Almanac® for Kids is available at special discounts when purchased in bulk quantities for businesses, associations, institutions, or sales promotions. Please call our Special Sales Department in New York at (212) 967-8800 or (800) 322-8755.

You can find The World Almanac® for Kids on the World Wide Web at http://www.worldalmanac.com

Book printed and bound by RR Donnelley, Crawfordsville, IN
Date printed: July 2010
Printed in the United States of America

RRD BSG 10 9 8 7 6 5 4 3 2 1

The addresses and content of Web sites referred to in this book are subject to change. Although The World Almanac® for Kids carefully reviews these sites, we cannot take responsibility for their content.

CONTENTS

FACES & PLACES 6

ANIMALS 22

ART 34

BIRTHDAYS 38

BOOKS 44

BUILDINGS 50

CALENDAR 56

CRIME 64

DISASTERS 66

ENERGY 72

ENVIRONMENT 78

FASHION 86

GAMES 90

GEOGRAPHY 92

HEALTH 100

HOMEWORK HELP 108

INVENTIONS 112

LANGUAGE 114

3

MILITARY
120

MONEY
124

MOVIES & TV
128

MUSIC & DANCE
132

MYTHOLOGY
136

NATIONS
138

Maps Showing Nations of the World
140
Facts About Nations
152

NATIVE AMERICANS
178

NUMBERS
182

POPULATION
186

PRIZES & CONTESTS
192

RELIGION
196

SCIENCE
200

SPACE
210

SPORTS
220

Olympics
222
Auto Racing
229
Baseball
230
Basketball
232
Football
234
Golf
237
Gymnastics
237
Ice Hockey
238
Soccer
239
Tennis
240
X Games
241

TECHNOLOGY & COMPUTERS
242

TRANSPORTATION
246

TRAVEL
250

UNITED STATES
256

2008 Election
264
Presidents
270
First Ladies
277
Time Line
279
They Made
History
287
Map of the U.S.
288
How the States
Got Their Names
290
Facts About
the States
292
Washington,D.C.
309

VOLUNTEERING
310

WEATHER
312

WEIGHTS &
MEASURES
314

WORLD HISTORY
318

Middle East
318
Africa
320
Asia
322
Europe
324
Australia
327
The Americas
328
Then & Now
330
Women in
History
332

ANSWERS
334

INDEX
337

PHOTO
CREDITS
349

In the News

SURGE FORWARD

The United States announced plans to send 30,000 more troops to Afghanistan by fall 2010, to join the fight against the Taliban.

REACHING NEW HEIGHTS

The world's new tallest building, the Burj Khalifa, officially opened on January 4, 2010. The giant skyscraper in Dubai, United Arab Emirates, is more than twice as tall as the Empire State Building.

HELPING HAITI

Aid poured in from around the world after a deadly earthquake rocked Haiti on January 12, 2010. About 230,000 people in the poor Caribbean nation lost their lives in the disaster.

A FRESH START

U.S. President Barack Obama and Russian President Dmitri Medvedev signed a new Strategic Arms Reduction Treaty (START) in April 2010. Each country agreed to reduce its number of nuclear warheads by about one-third over seven years.

In the News

SHUTTLE SHUTDOWN

In April 2010, space shuttle *Discovery* transported astronauts to the International Space Station. It was the 131st mission for the shuttle fleet, which was scheduled to be retired later in the year.

EVERYONE COUNTS

The 2010 U.S. census got underway in March. Held every ten years, the census is an attempt to count all Americans. In April, thousands of census workers began to go door-to-door to help people complete their census forms.

THE DOCTOR IS IN

In March 2010, President Obama signed a historic law intended to provide health-care coverage to millions of Americans. The law passed after a year of heated debate between supporters and opponents in Congress and across the country.

THE BIG SPILL

On April 20, 2010, an oil rig in the Gulf of Mexico exploded and caught fire, killing 11 workers. Millions of gallons of oil spilled into the Gulf and threatened wildlife and industry along the coast of Louisiana and other states.

Television

WIPEOUT ZONE

Wipeout returned for a third season filled with wild obstacle courses, along with a video game that allowed fans to play at home.

GLEEFUL RETURN

After a long break, *Glee*'s first season returned—with more drama, humor, and elaborate song-and-dance routines.

NEW IDOL
Lee DeWyze (left) beat out runner-up Crystal Bowersox in the ninth season of *American Idol*.

TRUE LOVE
Fans tuned in for a second season of laughs with star Keke Palmer on *True Jackson, VP*.

DANCING DOLL
Nicole Scherzinger and partner Derek Hough took home the first-place trophy on *Dancing with the Stars*.

Movies

IRON MAN RETURNS
Star Robert Downey Jr. suited up
for more adventure as Tony Stark
in *Iron Man 2.*

3-D DRAGON

Fans and critics cheered *How to Train Your Dragon*, which featured the voices of Jay Baruchel and America Ferrera.

ECLIPSE OF THE HEART

Bella was forced to choose between Edward (right) and Jacob (left) in *Eclipse*, the third movie in the Twilight series.

Movies

THE NEW KID
Jackie Chan and Jaden Smith charmed audiences in a remake of *The Karate Kid*.

SUCCESS STORY
Lotso, Buzz, and Woody came to life in *Toy Story 3*, shown in 3-D.

MAD FOR ALICE

Johnny Depp played the Mad Hatter in a 3-D update of *Alice in Wonderland*.

AMAZING *AVATAR*

Moviegoers all over the world lined up to see the groundbreaking special effects in *Avatar*.

Music

KEYS TO SUCCESS
The fourth album from Alicia Keys, *The Element of Freedom*, went platinum in early 2010.

BIEBER BONANZA
Justin Bieber's first full album, *My World 2.0*, debuted at number-one on the Billboard 200 chart in March 2010.

GOING SOLO

Nick Jonas took a break from his brothers to create an album, *Who I Am*, with his band Nick Jonas and the Administration.

CARRIE ON

Carrie Underwood had another huge hit with her third album, *Play On*.

Sports

Olympic Heroes

AIR TIME

At the 2010 Winter Olympics in Vancouver, Canada, snowboarder Shaun White soared (and twisted and spun) past the competition to win his second straight Olympic gold medal in the halfpipe.

PRECIOUS MEDAL

Skier Lindsey Vonn overcame a painful shin injury to win gold in downhill skiing.

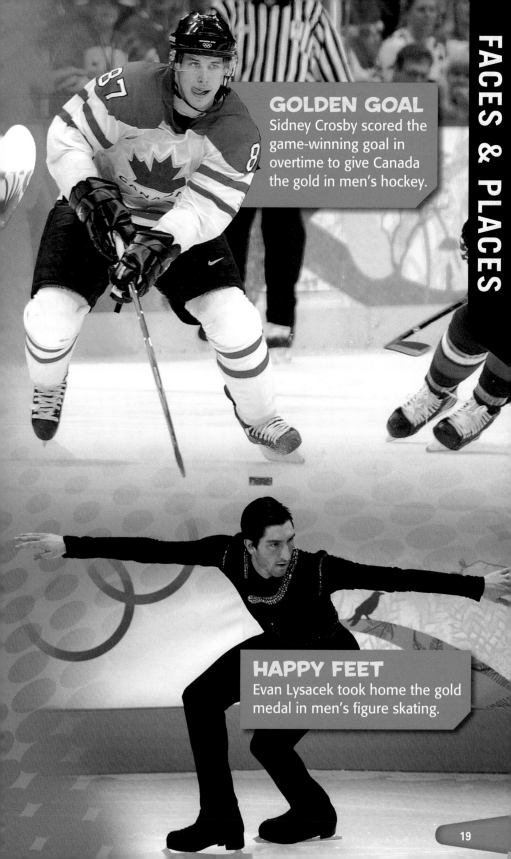

GOLDEN GOAL
Sidney Crosby scored the game-winning goal in overtime to give Canada the gold in men's hockey.

HAPPY FEET
Evan Lysacek took home the gold medal in men's figure skating.

Sports

COOL BREES
Quarterback Drew Brees threw for two touchdowns in the New Orleans Saints' 31–17 victory in Super Bowl XLIV.

BACK ON TOP
Kobe Bryant (holding trophy) and the Los Angeles Lakers topped the rival Boston Celtics to win their second consecutive NBA title.

78 AND COUNTING

Tina Charles (in white uniform) led the University of Connecticut to its second straight perfect season. The Huskies stretched their unbeaten streak to 78 games with a win over Stanford in the 2010 championship game.

GIMME FIVE!

In January 2010, Serena Williams won her record fifth Australian Open singles title. She also teamed up with big sister Venus to win the doubles championship.

Animals

Which breed of dog is the most popular? → page 28

Furry or scaly, creepy or crawly, schoolbus-sized or microscopic—animals fascinate people of all stripes. Here are some facts about the Animal Kingdom.

WEIRD ANIMAL FACTS

STRAWBERRY POISON ARROW FROG

This tiny poisonous frog—about the size of a fingernail—is found in the rain forests of Central America. Also called the strawberry poison dart frog, it has bright red coloring that warns predators that it is toxic.

Frogs and other amphibians are not usually known for their parenting skills. But strawberry poison arrow frog mothers go to great lengths for their offspring. Once her tadpoles hatch on the forest floor, the mother carries her offspring one by one into the treetops. Her trips often take her 100 feet off the ground. She places each tadpole into a pool of rain water that gathers in a leaf. The tadpoles are much safer in the trees than they would be on the ground. The mother returns to each pool every few days to bring food.

ANTS AND APHIDS

Species within an ecosystem depend on one another for survival. Sometimes, however, odd couples can be found. When animals of different species form a relationship that benefits all involved, it's called **mutualism**. Ants and aphids have this kind of relationship.

Aphids are insects that feed on plants. As part of digestion, they produce a sugary waste called honeydew. Ants will protect and take care of aphids in return for honeydew, which they eat. They will even carry aphids into their nest so they will survive through the winter.

LIFE ON EARTH

This time line shows how life developed on Earth. The earliest life forms are at the bottom of the chart. The most recent are at the top of the chart.

Years Ago		Animal Life on Earth
Cenozoic	10,000 to present	Human civilization develops.
	1.8 million to 10,000	Large mammals like mammoths, saber-toothed cats, and giant ground sloths develop. Modern human beings evolve. This era ends with an ice age.
	65 to 1.8 million 	Ancestors of modern-day horses, zebras, rhinos, sheep, goats, camels, pigs, cows, deer, giraffes, elephants, cats, dogs, and primates begin to develop.
Mesozoic	144 to 65 million 	In the Cretaceous period, new dinosaurs appear. Many insect groups, modern mammal and bird groups also develop. A global extinction of most dinosaurs occurs at the end of this period.
	206 to 144 million 	The Jurassic is dominated by giant dinosaurs. In the late Jurassic, birds evolve.
	248 to 206 million 	In the Triassic period, marine life develops again. Reptiles also move into the water. Reptiles begin to dominate the land areas. Dinosaurs and mammals develop.
Paleozoic	290 to 248 million	A mass extinction wipes out 95% of all marine life.
	354 to 290 million 	Reptiles develop. Much of the land is covered by swamps.
	417 to 354 million 	The first trees and forests appear. The first land-living vertebrates, amphibians, and wingless insects appear. Many new sea creatures also appear.
	443 to 417 million 	Coral reefs form. Other animals, such as the first known freshwater fish, develop. Relatives of spiders and centipedes develop.
	542 to 443 million 	Animals with shells (called trilobites) and some mollusks form. Primitive fish and corals develop. Evidence of the first primitive land plants.
Precambrian	3.8 billion to 542 million	First evidence of life on Earth. All life is in water. Early single-celled bacteria and achaea appear, followed by multi-celled organisms, including early animals.
	4.6 billion	Formation of Earth.

ANIMAL KINGDOM

The world has so many animals that scientists looked for a way to organize them into groups. A Swedish scientist named Carolus Linnaeus (1707–1778) worked out a system for classifying both animals and plants. We still use it today.

The Animal Kingdom is separated into two large groups—animals with backbones, called **vertebrates**, and animals without backbones, called **invertebrates**.

These large groups are divided into smaller groups called **phyla**. And phyla are divided into even smaller groups called **classes**. The animals in each group are classified together when their bodies are similar in certain ways.

Vertebrates
Animals with Backbones

FISH	Swordfish, tuna, salmon, trout, halibut, goldfish

AMPHIBIANS	Frogs, toads, mud puppies
REPTILES	Turtles, alligators, crocodiles, lizards
BIRDS	Sparrows, owls, turkeys, hawks
MAMMALS	Kangaroos, opossums, dogs, cats, bears, seals, rats, squirrels, rabbits, chipmunks, porcupines, horses, pigs, cows, deer, bats, whales, dolphins, monkeys, apes, humans

Invertebrates
Animals without Backbones

PROTOZOA	The simplest form of animals
COELENTERATES	Jellyfish, hydra, sea anemones, coral
MOLLUSKS	Clams, snails, squid, oysters
ANNELIDS	Earthworms
ARTHROPODS	
Crustaceans	Lobsters, crayfish
Centipedes and Millipedes	
Arachnids	Spiders, scorpions
Insects	Butterflies, grasshoppers, bees, termites, cockroaches
ECHINODERMS	Starfish, sea urchins, sea cucumbers

HOMEWORK TIP

How can you remember the animal classifications from most general to most specific? Try this sentence:

King **P**hilip **C**ame **O**ver **F**rom **G**reat **S**pain.

K = Kingdom; **P** = Phylum; **C** = Class; **O** = Order; **F** = Family; **G** = Genus; **S** = Species

PARASITES AMONG US

A PARASITE is an organism that usually lives on or in another organism, called a **host**. Parasites usually feed off their host. It's gross to think about, but parasites are everywhere! A common example of a parasite is a flea that feeds on the blood of a pet dog or cat. But there are many other types of common parasites. Here are some examples.

TAPEWORMS live inside animals and people. They usually live in the intestines, because they find their way into a host by being eaten—when food that is raw or that has not been cooked properly is consumed. Tapeworms are flat, like tape, and have hooks or suckers on their heads that allow them to latch on to the slimy surface of the intestines. They absorb digested food, which can deprive the host of nourishment.

TICKS are external parasites. This means that they latch on to the outside of a host, rather than living inside the host like a tapeworm. They are often found in tall grasses and shrubs, and they can latch on to a host as it walks by. Ticks attach themselves by digging their heads into the host's skin. Then they fill with blood as they feed. Ticks can be very dangerous to humans and pets, since some types of ticks carry diseases, such as Lyme disease.

Parasites Q&A

Are all parasites harmful? No. According to one estimate, the average American carries about two pounds of parasites in his or her body. Most of these parasites do not cause problems. Scientists are starting to learn that some may even be helpful.

How can harmful parasites be avoided? To avoid many types of internal parasites, make sure that food is washed and cooked properly. Wash all fruits and vegetables before eating, and wash your hands after handling raw meat. Parasites thrive in water—never drink from ponds or lakes, and change your pet's water often.

Are all parasites visible to the naked eye? No. Many can be seen only under a microscope. Dirty water is filled with these types of parasites.

did you Know? *The disease malaria—common in parts of Africa, Asia, and other tropical areas—is caused by a tiny parasite called* Plasmodium, *which is carried by a type of mosquito. People can be infected by the parasite and become ill if they are bitten by a mosquito carrying* Plasmodia.

BIGGEST, SMALLEST, FASTEST

IN THE WORLD

WORLD'S BIGGEST ANIMALS

Marine mammal: Blue whale (100 feet long, 200 tons)

Heaviest land mammal: African bush elephant (12 feet high, 4–7 tons)
Tallest land mammal: Giraffe (18 feet tall)

Reptile: Saltwater crocodile (20–23 feet long, 1,150 pounds)

Heaviest snake: Green anaconda (16–30 feet, 550 pounds)
Longest snake: Reticulated python (26–32 feet long)

Fish: Whale shark (40–60 feet long, 10–20 tons)

Bird: Ostrich (9 feet tall, 345 pounds) ----------→

Insect: Stick insect (15 inches long)

WORLD'S FASTEST ANIMALS

Marine mammal: Killer whale and Dall's
porpoise (35 miles per hour)

Land mammal: Cheetah (70 miles per hour)

Fish: Sailfish (68 miles per hour, leaping)

Bird: Peregrine falcon
(200 miles per hour)

Insect: Dragonfly (35 miles
per hour) ----------→

Snake: Black mamba (14 miles per hour)

WORLD'S SMALLEST ANIMALS

Mammal: Bumblebee bat
(1.1–1.3 inches)

Fish: *Paedocypris progenetica* or stout
infantfish (0.31–0.33 inches)

Bird: Bee hummingbird
(1–2 inches) ----------→

Snake: Thread snake and
brahminy blind snake (4.25 inches)

Lizard: Jaragua sphaero and Virgin Islands
dwarf sphaero (0.63 inch)

Insect: Fairyfly (0.01 inch)

HOW FAST DO ANIMALS RUN?

This table shows how fast some animals can go on land. A snail can take more than 30 hours just to go 1 mile. But humans at their fastest are still slower than many animals. The human record for fastest speed for a recognized race distance is held by Usain Bolt, who set a new world record in 2009 in the 100-meter dash of 9.58 seconds, for an average speed of about 23 miles per hour.

MILES PER HOUR	
Cheetah	70
Pronghorn antelope	60
Elk	45
Ostrich	40
Rabbit	35
Giraffe	32
Grizzly bear	30
Elephant	25
Wild turkey	15
Crocodile	10
Tiger beetle	5.5
Snail	0.03

HOW LONG DO ANIMALS LIVE?

Most animals do not live as long as humans do. A monkey that's 14 years old is thought to be old, while a person at that age is still considered young. The average life spans of some animals in the wild are shown here. An average 10-year-old boy in the U.S. can expect to live to be about 75.

Galapagos tortoise	100+ years	Dog (domestic)	13 years
Blue whale	80 years	Camel (bactrian)	12 years
Alligator	50 years	Pig	10 years
Chimpanzee	50 years	Deer (white-tailed)	8 years
African elephant	35 years	Kangaroo	7 years
Bottlenose dolphin	30 years	Chipmunk	6 years
Horse	20 years	Guinea pig	4 years
Tiger	16 years	Mouse	3 years
Lobster	15 years	Opossum	1 year
Cat (domestic)	15 years	Worker bee	6 weeks
Tarantula	15 years	Adult housefly	1–3 weeks

BATS: FACT OR FICTION?

Many people are afraid of bats. These small flying mammals can look scary, and most kinds leave their homes only at night. But bats are useful to humans in many ways. They eat insects and help pollinate plants. Learn the facts about these unusual animals.

Fact or fiction? Bats are flying rodents.
Fiction. Like rodents, bats are mammals, but bats and rodents are not closely related to each other. Recent evidence has shown that bats are more closely related to primates (the group of animals that includes monkeys, apes, and humans).

Fact or fiction? Bats carry rabies.
Fact. All bats do not carry the disease rabies, but a very small percentage of them do. Because the disease can be transferred to humans, scientists who study bats get shots before working with the animals. These shots make it easier to treat rabies.

Fact or fiction? Flying bats can get tangled in human hair.
Fiction. Many kinds of bats see very well in the dark, and many use echolocation to fly and hunt at night. This means the bats send out sounds that bounce off even tiny objects, such as insects, and create an echo that the bats can hear. The echo tells the bats where an object is located. It is easy for a bat to avoid a large object like a human. Also, most bats are afraid of people, and they would not go near one intentionally.

Fact or fiction? Vampire bats commonly drink human blood.
Fiction. Three types of bats are known as "vampire bats," but they almost never bite humans. These bats—common, white-winged, and hairy-legged vampire bats—almost always consume animal blood.

WHAT ARE GROUPS OF ANIMALS CALLED?

Here are some (often odd) names for animal groups:

BEARS: *sleuth* of bears	**KITTENS:** *kindle* or *kendle* of kittens
CATS: *clowder* of cats	**LEOPARDS:** *leap* of leopards
CATTLE: *drove* of cattle	**MONKEYS:** *troop* of monkeys
CROCODILES: *bask* of crocodiles	**MULES:** *span* of mules
CROWS: *murder* of crows	**NIGHTINGALES:** *watch* of nightingales
FISH: *school* or *shoal* of fish	**OWLS:** *parliament* of owls
FLIES: *swarm* or *cloud* of flies	**OYSTERS:** *bed* of oysters
FOXES: *skulk* of foxes	**PEACOCKS:** *muster* of peacocks
GIRAFFES: *tower* of giraffes	**RAVENS:** *unkindness* of ravens
HARES: *down* of hares	**SHARKS:** *shiver* of sharks
HAWKS: *cast* of hawks	**SQUIRRELS:** *dray* or *scurry* of squirrels
HYENAS: *cackle* of hyenas	**TURTLES:** *bale* of turtles
JELLYFISH: *smack* of jellyfish	**WHALES:** *pod* of whales

PETS AT THE TOP

Here are some of the most popular pets in the United States and the approximate number of each pet:

1. Freshwater fish:
171,700,000

2. Cats:
93,600,000

3. Dogs:
77,500,000

4. Small animals:
15,900,000

5. Birds:
15,000,000

6. Reptiles:
13,630,000

7. Equine:
13,300,000

8. Saltwater fish:
11,200,000

Source: American Pet Products Manufacturers Association's
2009/2010 National Pet Owners Survey

PETS Q&A

Which breed of dog was the most popular in the U.S. in 2010? The Labrador retriever. According to the American Kennel Club, the Labrador retriever has been the most popular breed of dog in the U.S. for many years.

Can cats see in the dark? No. Cats see very well in dim light and near-darkness, but like most animals, they need a little bit of light to see. In a completely dark room, a cat will use its whiskers and sense of smell to find its way.

True or false? Dogs and cats are color-blind. False. Dogs and cats can see in color, though not all the colors humans can see. For example, dogs can see blues but not greens.

WHICH PET IS RIGHT FOR YOU?

Freshwater fish (like goldfish), cats, and dogs—in that order—are the three most popular pets in the United States. If your family has decided to get a pet, how can you decide which type will be the best fit for you?

Freshwater **fish** are an excellent option if you live in a small space or if any family members suffer from allergies. Some people think that fish require very little work and care, but this is not necessarily the case. Fish do not need to be walked or taken on regular trips to a veterinarian, but responsible fish owners keep the bowl or tank very clean and research which types of fish can share a living space. Even a simple goldfish in a bowl can be a big commitment—a goldfish may live for 10 years!

Cats are very popular pets, and with good reason. They can be playful and affectionate, but they are independent in many ways. Most cats use a litter box indoors, and they keep clean by licking themselves. But cats must be taken to a veterinarian at least once a year, and cats with claws often tear furniture or clothing. Many people are allergic to cats, so it is important for all family members to spend time with a cat before bringing one home.

Dogs are well-known for being loyal and loving to their owners. But of all the popular pets, dogs require the most work. Puppies often take many months to be housebroken, or trained to relieve themselves only outside. Adult dogs need daily exercise, and many breeds require regular grooming. Dogs are often given to animal shelters by owners who are overwhelmed by the need to care for them. Once your family has decided to get a dog, animal shelters are a great place to start your search!

ENDANGERED

When a species becomes extinct, the variety of life on Earth is reduced. In the world today, many thousands of known species of animals and plants are in danger of becoming extinct. Humans have been able to save some endangered animals and are working to save more.

Some Endangered Animals

Indus River Dolphin Indus River dolphins, also known as bhulan, live in the Indus River, in Pakistan. The Indus River dolphin is one of the world's most endangered aquatic mammals. This unusual, blind dolphin could once be found throughout the entire Indus River system. It is estimated that there are about 1,000 left, in one small section of the river.

Reasons for population decline:
• Fishing methods, including use of nets and hooks, that indirectly harmed dolphins
• Loss of habitat due to increased development
• Pollution

Giant Panda Humans have been trying to save the giant panda population for many years. The animals can be found in the wild only in China, and they must eat large amounts their primary food source—bamboo—every day. In the 1970s and 1980s, much of the bamboo habitat was destroyed by logging. Giant pandas also have a very low birth rate, and they rarely reproduce in captivity. It is estimated that only 1,600 pandas currently live in the wild.

Reasons for population decline:
• Habitat loss due to deforestation
• Low rate of reproduction
• Hunting by humans

Tibetan Antelope Tibetan antelopes live in the harsh climate of the Tibetan plateau, in Asia. The antelopes are covered in layers of fur that keep them warm and dry. The bottom layer, or undercoat, is known as shahtoosh. The wool woven from this fur is used to make expensive shawls. Demand for the wool has pushed the Tibetan antelope to near extinction.

Reasons for population decline:
• Hunting by humans
• Loss of habitat due to increased development

SPECIES

Success Stories

American Alligator Alligator-skin products were once very popular in the United States and Europe. This business led to widespread hunting of alligators, and by 1967 the American alligator was listed as an endangered species. Once the animal was protected under U.S. law, hunting was outlawed and efforts were made to protect its habitat. By 1987, the population had bounced back, and the American alligator was removed from the endangered species list.

Bald Eagle The bald eagle is the national bird and symbol of the United States. In 1967, the bird was added to the U.S. government's endangered species list. A pesticide called DDT, used to kill insects, was preventing eagle eggs from developing and hatching properly. Strict laws were put into place, providing for harsh penalties for anyone who harmed the birds. In 1972, use of DDT was banned in the United States. The bald eagle population responded quickly. The bird is no longer considered an endangered species.

Siberian Tiger Also known as the Amur tiger, this powerful big cat was on the brink of extinction in 1940. At that time, perhaps only about 40 remained in the wild. Thanks to conservation efforts—including laws that made it illegal to hunt tigers in Russia—the tiger population began to grow. The animals are still endangered, but there are now an estimated 450 in the wild.

HOW TO HELP ENDANGERED SPECIES

VISIT A NATURE RESERVE. There are nature reserves and national parks all over the United States. In these places, animals are protected. Many of these parks and reserves have special tours for kids, where you can learn more about threatened species in your area.

RECYCLE. Many animals lose their habitats when trees are cut down—and most paper is made from trees. Recycle as much paper as you can. If your school does not recycle, find out if you can help start a program.

CONTACT LAWMAKERS. The World Wildlife Fund keeps track of laws that may affect endangered species. This information can be found on the organization's website, www.worldwildlife.org, along with ways to contact your local representatives to urge them to take action to protect endangered species.

CREATURES OF THE DEEP

Though scientists have been studying underwater creatures for many years, they are always making new discoveries about life in the deepest parts of the ocean. The deep sea is the largest habitat on Earth, but it is a difficult one for humans to study. At depths below 3,300 feet, the water is extremely cold and pitch black. The pressure from the water above would crush humans and most other animals. But some creatures have adapted—often in surprising ways—and live comfortably in these deep waters. These creatures are divided into three groups.

Microorganisms make up the largest group of deep-sea life forms. Many of these organisms have just one cell, and they provide food for the other creatures. In some areas, they are so common that they group together in huge formations that look like rugs.

Invertebrates are creatures without backbones. Many types of worms, crabs, and sponges—all invertebrates—live on the deep-sea floor. They often live at hydrothermal vents. These vents shoot out water that is warmer than the rest of the deep sea and that is rich in minerals and other chemicals. The giant tube worm is one of the invertebrates that can be found at these vents. These worms can grow to as much as 5 feet long.

Fish are the only creatures with backbones found in the deep sea. These fish must be able to withstand the pressure at these depths. Because the water is so dark, many fish have features that produce light. They also digest their food very slowly, to help them survive in a place where food is scarce. Many of these fish, like the common fangtooth (see photo at top of page), have long teeth that help grab onto large prey. These teeth are not meant for chewing— the fish swallows its food whole.

Giant tube worms ▶

THE WORLD ALMANAC FOR KIDS

ON THE JOB:

VETERINARIAN

A veterinarian, or vet, is a physician for animals.

What do veterinarians do?

There are more than 90,000 veterinarians in the United States, according to the American Veterinary Medical Association. Most of these vets care for small pets such as cats and dogs. Others care for large farm animals, including horses, sheep, and cattle. These vets usually make house calls! Vets also do research for companies that make food or medicine for animals. The U.S. government even hires vets to be food inspectors. These vets help make sure that the meat and poultry we eat are safe. Some adventurous vets work in zoos and circuses.

Would you like to be a veterinarian?

If you are thinking about being a veterinarian, here are some questions to ask yourself:

1. Do you like animals and want to help them?
2. Can you imagine staying calm when an animal is hurt or scared?
3. Are you interested in science?
4. Would you be comfortable dealing with blood and giving shots?
5. Do you like working with people, too?

If your answer to these questions is "yes," a career as a veterinarian could be for you!

How can you become a veterinarian?

To be a vet, you must have a Doctor of Veterinary Medicine (DVM) degree. Getting this degree takes a lot of hard work. After four years of college, students must be accepted to a veterinary school. There are only 28 veterinary schools in the United States—compared to 131 medical schools—so it can be difficult to be accepted to one. It takes four years to graduate from veterinary school. Students spend three of these years learning about animals, diseases, and medicines. They spend the last year working with an established vet in an animal hospital or clinic. Here they can work with patients and their families. Some vets take more time to become specialists in a specific area—such as animal cancer or allergies. Some vets even specialize in animal dentistry. It takes two to five more years to become a specialized veterinarian. Specialized or not, all vets must continue to learn throughout their careers. There are always new medicines and treatments to study.

How can you get started?

If you think you might want to be a vet, you can learn from your own pets. Read about them and learn how their bodies work. You can also learn from other people's pets. You might walk your neighbor's dog or feed a friend's cat when the friend is away. Vets have to be comfortable with different types of animals. Get in touch with your local animal shelter and find out how you can help as a volunteer. Many animal shelters have homeless dogs and cats who would love some special attention.

Art

What is a graphic designer? ➔ page 37

ART Q&A

HOW OLD IS ART?
Art goes back to our earliest records of human life. See the cave paintings on the next page for an example.

IS ARTISTIC TALENT SOMETHING YOU ARE BORN WITH OR SOMETHING YOU CAN LEARN?

Learning to draw is a skill like writing or playing a sport. Some people are naturally more talented, but anyone can learn to draw. Even people with severe physical disabilities can make masterpieces.

WHEN I SEE A PAINTING IN A MUSEUM, WHAT MIGHT I SAY ABOUT IT?

Look at the painting without thinking too hard about it. How does it make you feel? Happy, sad, confused, silly? Study the painting and try to discover the colors, shapes, and textures that create those feelings in you.

Look at the information card next to the work of art. Usually, it will tell you who painted it, when it was made, and what media (materials) were used. You can compare it to other works of art by the same artist, from the same time, or in the same medium.

WHAT IS ART?

The answer is up for debate. People who study this question are studying aesthetics (ess-THET-ics), which is a kind of philosophy. Usually art is something that an artist interprets for an audience. Art reveals something that you can see, that then makes you think and feel.

DIFFERENT KINDS OF ART

Throughout history, artists have painted pictures of nature (called landscapes), pictures of people (called portraits), and pictures of flowers in vases, food, and other objects (known as still lifes). Today many artists create pictures that do not look like anything in the real world. These are examples of abstract art.

Photography, too, is a form of art. Photos record both the commonplace and the exotic and help us look at events in new ways.

Sculpture is a three-dimensional form made from clay, stone, metal, or other material. Sculptures can be large, like the Statue of Liberty. Some are realistic. Others have no form you can recognize.

Artists work with many materials. For example, some beautiful works of art are created in glass. Some artists today use computers and video screens to create their art.

ART ALL-STARS

These works of art helped change the
way we see the world around us.

Lascaux (13,000–15,000 B.C.)

Lascaux is a cave in France. It contains some of the
earliest known cave art. The cave was discovered in 1940
by four teenagers. The images found on the cave walls
consist of handprints and animals such as bison, deer,
horses, and cattle. It is believed that the paintings may
have been part of a ritual to help make a successful hunt.

CLAUDE MONET (1840–1926)
White Nenuphars (1899)

The French painter Claude Monet was one of the leading
artists who painted in the style known as Impressionism. The
Impressionist painters did not try to achieve a sharp, realistic
image as you would find in a photograph. They were more
interested in how light affects colors and shape, and they used
small strokes of pure color to show how light changes the way
things look. Monet settled in the tiny town of Giverny, near
Paris, in 1883, and there he built a large Japanese garden, which he painted many
times. Many of these paintings show the large water lilies called nenuphars.

LOUIS COMFORT TIFFANY (1848–1933)
A Wooded Landscape in Three Panels (c. 1905)

Louis Comfort Tiffany worked in the style known as Art
Nouveau (French for "new art"). The style arose as a
reaction to the stiff, realistic art popular in the 1800s.
Art Nouveau emphasized long, flowing, curved lines
and imaginative representations of nature. Tiffany is
particularly known for his work in glass, which he used
for lamps, vases, tableware, and home decoration. His
stained-glass panels of nature scenes—using brilliant,
rich colors—are beautiful and creative works of art.

DOROTHEA LANGE (1895–1965)
Migrant Mother (1936)

Dorothea Lange knew even when she was a child that she wanted to be
a photographer. Left with a limp after a bout with polio and having been
abandoned by her father, she understood suffering, and she wanted to record
other people's pain and to convey their humanity. During the Great Depression
of the 1930s, Lange toured migrant workers' camps and the poorest towns
across the United States. Her photos record for all time what she saw. In this
famous portrait of a migrant woman and her three children, viewers can see
the woman's worried expression and the deep emotional pain in her eyes.

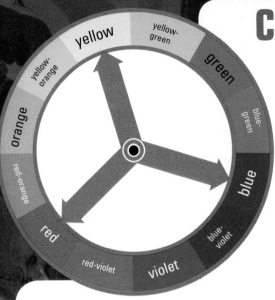

COLOR WHEEL

Primary colors The most basic colors are RED, YELLOW, and BLUE. They're called primary because you can't get them by mixing any other colors. In fact, the other colors are made by mixing red, blue, or yellow. Arrows on this wheel show the primary colors.

Secondary colors ORANGE, GREEN, and VIOLET are the secondary colors. They are made by mixing two primary colors. You make orange by mixing yellow and red, or green by mixing yellow and blue. On the color wheel, GREEN appears between BLUE and YELLOW.

Tertiary colors When you mix a primary and a secondary color, you get a tertiary, or intermediate, color. BLUE-GREEN and YELLOW-GREEN are intermediate colors.

This color wheel shows how colors are related to each other.

More Color Terms

VALUES The lightness or darkness of a color is its value. Tints are light values made by mixing a color with white. **PINK** is a tint of **RED**. Shades are dark values made by mixing a color with black. **MAROON** is a shade of **RED**.

COMPLEMENTARY COLORS

Contrasting colors that please the eye when used together are called complementary colors. These colors appear opposite each other on the wheel and don't have any colors in common. RED is a complement to GREEN, which is made by mixing YELLOW and BLUE.

ANALOGOUS COLORS

The colors next to each other on the wheel are from the same "family." BLUE, BLUE-GREEN, and GREEN all have BLUE in them and are analogous colors.

COOL COLORS
Cool colors are mostly GREEN, BLUE, and PURPLE. They make you think of cool things like water and can even make you feel cooler.

WARM COLORS
Warm colors are mostly RED, ORANGE, and YELLOW. They suggest heat and can actually make you feel warmer.

THE WORLD ALMANAC FOR KIDS

ON THE JOB:
GRAPHIC DESIGNER

Graphic designers, or graphic artists, use art to provide information to people.

What Do Graphic Designers Do?

Working with special computer software and using pictures, abstract designs, and different styles of type, graphic designers determine the look of the things we see every day all around us—books and magazines, websites, brochures, packaging for items we buy in stores, posters, advertising billboards, and pretty much anything that involves art. When you are in a restaurant and look at the menu, remember that someone had to design the menu: choose the colors, the typefaces, and any pictures and decide how big the words should be and how they should be arranged on each page. That person was probably a graphic designer.

▲ *A graphic designer created this book cover. The designer chose the colors and the picture and decided how the words and the image should be arranged.*

What Talents and Education Do You Need?

Graphic designers have to be creative people who have good ideas about how to present information and how to make it look attractive and eye-catching. Most people in this field have a college degree. They must also keep up on the latest changes in computer software. As more and more people shop online, graphic designers who can create attractive ads and computer animations for the Internet will have an edge in finding jobs.

Where Do Graphic Designers Work?

As a graphic designer, you might work for a large advertising or design firm or for a publishing company. Some people prefer to work as free-lance artists, which means that they are not employed by one company. They work on their own and get contracts from many different companies to work on particular projects. Being a graphic designer gives you a lot of opportunity to be creative, to work on different kinds of projects, and to work in the setting you like best.

Birthdays

What is an "Echo Boomer"? → page 42

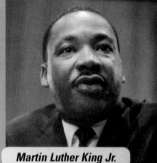

Martin Luther King Jr.

JANUARY
Birthstone: Garnet

1 J.D. Salinger, author, 1919
2 Heather O'Reilly, soccer player, 1985
3 Eli Manning, football player, 1981
4 Isaac Newton, physicist/ mathematician, 1643
5 Alvin Ailey, choreographer, 1931
6 Early Wynn, baseball player, 1920
7 Liam Aiken, actor, 1990
8 Stephen Hawking, physicist, 1942
9 Dave Matthews, musician, 1967
10 Jake Delhomme, football player, 1975
11 Mary J. Blige, singer, 1971
12 Christiane Amanpour, journalist, 1958
13 Orlando Bloom, actor, 1977
14 Dave Grohl, musician, 1969
15 Rev. Martin Luther King Jr., civil rights leader, 1929
16 Sade, singer, 1959
17 Jim Carrey, actor, 1962
18 Mark Messier, hockey player, 1961
19 Edgar Allan Poe, writer, 1809
20 Buzz Aldrin, astronaut, 1930
21 Hakeem Olajuwon, basketball player, 1963
22 Sir Francis Bacon, philosopher, 1561
23 John Hancock, revolutionary leader, 1737
24 Mischa Barton, actress, 1986
25 Alicia Keys, singer, 1981
26 Wayne Gretzky, hockey player, 1961
27 Wolfgang Amadeus Mozart, composer, 1756
28 Elijah Wood, actor, 1981
29 Adam Lambert, singer, 1982
30 Christian Bale, actor, 1974
31 Justin Timberlake, singer, 1981

FEBRUARY
Birthstone: Amethyst

1 Langston Hughes, poet, 1902
2 Bob Marley, singer, 1945
3 Elizabeth Blackwell, first woman physician, 1821
4 Rosa Parks, civil rights activist, 1913
5 Hank Aaron, baseball player, 1934
6 Ronald Reagan, 40th president, 1911
7 Frederick Douglass, abolitionist, 1817
8 Ted Koppel, journalist, 1940
9 Travis Tritt, singer, 1963
10 Emma Roberts, actress, 1991
11 Taylor Lautner, actor, 1992
12 Abraham Lincoln, 16th president, 1809
13 Grant Wood, artist, 1891
14 Drew Bledsoe, football player, 1972
15 Matt Groening, cartoonist, 1954
16 Jerome Bettis, football player, 1972
17 Chaim Potok, novelist, 1929
18 Molly Ringwald, actress, 1968
19 Amy Tan, author, 1952
20 Ansel Adams, photographer, 1902
21 Jennifer Love Hewitt, actress, 1979
22 Edna St. Vincent Millay, poet, 1892
23 Dakota Fanning, actress, 1994
24 Steve Jobs, computer innovator, 1955
25 Sean Astin, actor, 1971
26 Marshall Faulk, football player, 1973
27 Josh Groban, singer, 1981
28 Lemony Snicket (Daniel Handler), author, 1970
29 Ja Rule, rapper, 1976

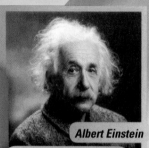

Albert Einstein

MARCH
Birthstone: Aquamarine

1 Justin Bieber, singer, 1994
2 Dr. Seuss, author, 1904
3 Jessica Biel, actress, 1982
4 Landon Donovan, soccer player, 1982
5 Eva Mendes, actress, 1974
6 Elizabeth Barrett Browning, poet, 1806
7 Laura Prepon, actress, 1980
8 Marcia Newby, gymnast, 1988
9 Bow Wow, actor/rapper, 1987
10 Carrie Underwood, singer, 1983
11 Benji and Joel Madden, musicians, 1979
12 Edward Albee, playwright, 1928
13 Percival Lowell, astronomer, 1855
14 Albert Einstein, physicist/ Nobel laureate, 1879
15 Ruth Bader Ginsburg, U.S. Supreme Court justice, 1933
16 Lauren Graham, actress, 1967
17 Mia Hamm, soccer player, 1972
18 Queen Latifah, rapper/actress, 1970
19 Bruce Willis, actor, 1955
20 Spike Lee, filmmaker, 1957
21 Matthew Broderick, actor, 1962
22 Reese Witherspoon, actress, 1976
23 Jason Kidd, basketball player, 1973
24 Peyton Manning, football player, 1976
25 Danica Patrick, racecar driver, 1982
26 Keira Knightley, actress, 1985
27 Mariah Carey, singer/actress, 1970
28 Vince Vaughn, actor, 1970
29 Sam Walton, Wal-Mart founder, 1918
30 Vincent Van Gogh, artist, 1853
31 Cesar Chavez, labor leader, 1927

Taylor Lautner

APRIL
Birthstone: Diamond

1 Phil Niekro, baseball player, 1939
2 Hans Christian Andersen, author, 1805
3 Amanda Bynes, actress, 1986
4 Robert Downey Jr., actor, 1965
5 Booker T. Washington, educator, 1856
6 Paul Rudd, actor, 1969
7 Jackie Chan, actor, 1954
8 Taylor Kitsch, actor, 1981
9 Kristen Stewart, actress, 1990
10 John Madden, sportscaster, 1936
11 Jason Varitek, baseball player, 1972
12 Beverly Cleary, author, 1916
13 Thomas Jefferson, 3rd president, 1743
14 Abigail Breslin, actress, 1996
15 Emma Watson, actress, 1990
16 Kareem Abdul-Jabbar, basketball player, 1947
17 Jennifer Garner, actress, 1972
18 Alia Shawkat, actress, 1989
19 Kate Hudson, actress, 1979
20 Tito Puente, musician, 1923
21 Queen Elizabeth II, British monarch, 1926
22 Robert J. Oppenheimer, physicist, 1904
23 Andruw Jones, baseball player, 1977
24 Kelly Clarkson, singer, 1982
25 Ella Fitzgerald, singer, 1917
26 Kane, WWE wrestler, 1967
27 Samuel Morse, inventor, 1791
28 Harper Lee, author, 1926
29 Uma Thurman, actress, 1970
30 Kirsten Dunst, actress, 1982

Sally Ride

MAY
Birthstone: Emerald

1 Tim McGraw, musician, 1967
2 Dwayne "The Rock" Johnson, actor/wrestler, 1972
3 Sugar Ray Robinson, boxer, 1921
4 Dawn Staley, basketball player/coach 1970
5 Brian Williams, journalist, 1959
6 Martin Brodeur, hockey player, 1972
7 Johannes Brahms, composer, 1833
8 Enrique Iglesias, singer, 1975
9 Rosario Dawson, actress, 1979
10 Bono, musician/activist, 1960
11 Salvador Dali, artist, 1904
12 Tony Hawk, skateboarder, 1968
13 Robert Pattinson, actor, 1986
14 Miranda Cosgrove, actress, 1993
15 L. Frank Baum, author, 1856
16 Janet Jackson, singer/actress 1966
17 Sugar Ray Leonard, boxer, 1956
18 Tina Fey, actress/comedian, 1970
19 Malcolm X, militant civil rights activist, 1925
20 Stan Mikita, hockey player, 1940
21 John Muir, naturalist, 1838
22 Sir Arthur Conan Doyle, author, 1859
23 Margaret Wise Brown, author, 1910
24 Tracy McGrady, basketball player, 1979
25 Stacy London, TV personality, 1969
26 Sally Ride, astronaut, 1951
27 Chris Colfer, actor, 1990
28 Jim Thorpe, Olympic champion, 1888
29 Andre Agassi, tennis champion, 1970
30 Manny Ramirez, baseball player, 1972
31 Walt Whitman, poet, 1819

JUNE
Birthstone: Pearl

1 Morgan Freeman, actor, 1937
2 Freddy Adu, soccer player, 1989
3 Anderson Cooper, journalist, 1967
4 Angelina Jolie, actress, 1975
5 Richard Scarry, author/illustrator, 1919
6 Cynthia Rylant, author, 1954
7 Michael Cera, actor, 1988
8 Kanye West, musician, 1977
9 Natalie Portman, actress, 1981
10 Maurice Sendak, author/illustrator, 1928
11 Diana Taurasi, basketball player, 1982
12 Anne Frank, diary writer, 1929
13 William Butler Yeats, poet, 1865
14 Harriet Beecher Stowe, author, 1811
15 Neil Patrick Harris, actor, 1973
16 Kerry Wood, baseball player, 1977
17 Venus Williams, tennis player, 1980
18 Sir Paul McCartney, musician, 1942
19 Paula Abdul, singer/TV personality, 1962
20 Nicole Kidman, actress, 1967
21 Prince William of Great Britain, 1982
22 Meryl Streep, actress, 1949
23 Clarence Thomas, U.S. Supreme Court justice, 1948
24 Solange Knowles, singer/actress, 1986
25 Sonia Sotomayor, U.S. Supreme Court justice, 1954
26 Babe Didrikson Zaharias, Olympic champion, 1914
27 Tobey Maguire, actor, 1975
28 John Elway, football player, 1960
29 Theo Fleury, hockey player, 1968
30 Michael Phelps, Olympic champion, 1985

Ella Fitzgerald

Neil Patrick Harris

Shaun White

AUGUST
Birthstone: Peridot

1 Francis Scott Key, composer/lawyer, 1779
2 Isabel Allende, writer, 1942
3 Tom Brady, football player, 1977
4 Barack Obama, 44th president, 1961
5 Neil Armstrong, astronaut, 1930
6 Andy Warhol, artist, 1928
7 Charlize Theron, actress, 1975
8 Roger Federer, tennis player, 1981
9 Eric Bana, actor, 1968
10 Antonio Banderas, actor, 1960
11 Stephen Wozniak, computer pioneer, 1950
12 Ann M. Martin, author, 1955
13 Alfred Hitchcock, filmmaker, 1899
14 Halle Berry, actress, 1966
15 Ben Affleck, actor, 1972
16 Steve Carell, actor, 1963
17 Robert De Niro, actor, 1943
18 Meriwether Lewis, explorer, 1774
19 Bill Clinton, 42nd president, 1946
20 Demi Lovato, actress/singer, 1992
21 Stephen Hillenburg, SpongeBob creator, 1961
22 Bill Parcells, football coach, 1941
23 Julian Casablancas, singer, 1978
24 Rupert Grint, actor, 1988
25 Tim Burton, director, 1958
26 Branford Marsalis, musician, 1960
27 Alexa Vega, actress, 1988
28 Jack Black, actor, 1969
29 Lea Michele, actress, 1986
30 Andy Roddick, tennis player, 1982
31 Chris Tucker, actor, 1972

Selena Gomez

JULY
Birthstone: Ruby

1 Missy Elliott, rapper, 1971
2 Lindsay Lohan, actress, 1986
3 Tom Cruise, actor, 1962
4 Neil Simon, playwright, 1927
5 P. T. Barnum, showman/circus founder, 1810
6 George W. Bush, 43rd president, 1946
7 Michelle Kwan, figure skater, 1980
8 John D. Rockefeller, industrialist, 1839
9 Tom Hanks, actor, 1956
10 Jessica Simpson, singer/actress, 1980
11 E.B. White, author, 1899
12 Topher Grace, actor, 1978
13 Harrison Ford, actor, 1942
14 Matthew Fox, actor, 1966
15 Rembrandt van Rijn, artist, 1606
16 Will Farrell, actor, 1967
17 Donald Sutherland, actor, 1935
18 Kristin Bell, actress, 1980
19 Edgar Degas, artist, 1834
20 Sir Edmund Hillary, Everest climber, 1919
21 "CC" Sabathia, baseball player, 1980
22 Selena Gomez, actress/singer, 1992
23 Daniel Radcliffe, actor, 1989
24 Jennifer Lopez, actress/singer, 1969
25 Ray Billingsley, cartoonist, 1957
26 Sandra Bullock, actress, 1964
27 Alex Rodriguez, baseball player, 1975
28 Beatrix Potter, author, 1866
29 Allison Mack, actress, 1982
30 Jaime Pressley, actress, 1977
31 J. K. Rowling, author, 1965

SEPTEMBER
Birthstone: Sapphire

1 Conway Twitty, country singer, 1933
2 Keanu Reeves, actor, 1964
3 Shaun White, Olympic snowboarder, 1986
4 Beyoncé Knowles, singer/actress, 1981
5 Rose McGowan, actress, 1973
6 Mark Chesnutt, singer, 1963
7 Evan Rachel Wood, actress, 1987
8 Latrell Sprewell, basketball player, 1970
9 Charlie Stewart, actor, 1993
10 Bill O'Reilly, TV personality, 1949
11 Ludacris, rapper, 1977
12 Benjamin McKenzie, actor, 1978
13 Roald Dahl, author, 1916
14 Nas, rapper, 1973
15 Prince Harry of Great Britain, 1984
16 Alexis Bledel, actress, 1981
17 Rasheed Wallace, basketball player, 1974
18 Lance Armstrong, cyclist, 1971
19 Jim Abbott, baseball player, 1967
20 Red Auerbach, basketball coach, 1917
21 Hiram Revels, first black U.S. senator, 1822
22 Tom Felton, actor, 1987
23 Ray Charles, musician, 1930
24 Paul Hamm, gymnast, 1982
25 Will Smith, actor/rapper, 1968
26 Serena Williams, tennis player, 1981
27 Avril Lavigne, singer, 1984
28 Hilary Duff, actress/singer, 1987
29 Kevin Durant, basketball player, 1988
30 Elie Wiesel, author, 1928

Neil Armstrong

OCTOBER
Birthstone: Opal

1 William Boeing, founder of Boeing Company, 1881
2 Mohandas Gandhi, activist, 1869
3 Ashlee Simpson, singer, 1984
4 Alicia Silverstone, actress, 1976
5 Parminder Nagra, actress, 1975
6 Olivia Thirlby, actress, 1986
7 Simon Cowell, television personality, 1959
8 R. L. Stine, author, 1943
9 Brandon Routh, actor, 1979
10 Maya Lin, sculptor and architect, 1960
11 Michelle Trachtenberg, actress, 1985
12 Hugh Jackman, actor, 1968
13 Ashanti, singer, 1980
14 Usher, singer, 1978
15 Elena Dementieva, tennis player, 1981
16 John Mayer, musician, 1977
17 Mae Jemison, astronaut, 1956
18 Wynton Marsalis, musician, 1961
19 Ty Pennington, TV personality, 1965
20 Snoop Dogg, rapper/actor, 1971
21 Dizzy Gillespie, trumpet player, 1917
22 Ichiro Suzuki, baseball player, 1973
23 Tiffeny Milbrett, soccer player, 1972
24 Brian Vickers, racecar driver, 1983
25 Pablo Picasso, artist, 1881
26 Jon Heder, actor, 1977
27 Teddy Roosevelt, 26th president, 1858
28 Bill Gates, computer pioneer, 1955
29 Winona Ryder, actress, 1971
30 John Adams, 2nd president, 1735
31 Juliette Gordon Low, Girl Scouts' founder, 1860

Maya Lin

Condoleezza Rice

NOVEMBER
Birthstone: Topaz

1 Coco Crisp, baseball player, 1979
2 Nelly, rapper, 1974
3 Walker Evans, photographer, 1903
4 Sean Combs (Diddy), producer/rapper, 1969
5 Johnny Damon, baseball player, 1973
6 John Philip Sousa, composer, 1854
7 Marie Curie, scientist/Nobel laureate, 1867
8 Parker Posey, actress, 1968
9 Nick Lachey, singer, 1973
10 Ellen Pompeo, actress, 1969
11 Leonardo DiCaprio, actor, 1974
12 Ryan Gosling, actor, 1980
13 Rachel Bilson, actress, 1981
14 Condoleezza Rice, American statesperson, 1954
15 Zena Grey, actress, 1988
16 Maggie Gyllenhaal, actress, 1977
17 Rachel McAdams, actress, 1978
18 Owen Wilson, actor, 1968
19 Larry Johnson, football player, 1979
20 Joe Biden, 47th vice president, 1942
21 Jena Malone, actress, 1984
22 Jamie Lee Curtis, actress, 1958
23 Miley Cyrus, singer/actress, 1992
24 Katherine Heigl, actress, 1978
25 Donovan McNabb, football player, 1976
26 Charles Schulz, cartoonist, 1912
27 Bill Nye, "The Science Guy," 1955
28 Jon Stewart, TV host, 1962
29 Louisa May Alcott, author, 1832
30 Mark Twain, author, 1835

DECEMBER
Birthstone: Turquoise

1 Sarah Silverman, actress/comedienne, 1970
2 Lucy Liu, actress, 1967
3 Amanda Seyfried, actress, 1985
4 Tyra Banks, model/TV personality, 1973
5 Walt Disney, cartoonist/filmmaker, 1901
6 Otto Graham, football player/coach, 1921
7 Larry Bird, basketball player/coach, 1956
8 AnnaSophia Robb, actress, 1993
9 Felicity Huffman, actress, 1962
10 Raven, actress, 1985
11 Mos Def, actor/rapper, 1973
12 Edvard Munch, artist, 1863
13 Taylor Swift, singer, 1989
14 Vanessa Hudgens, actress/singer, 1988
15 Adam Brody, actor, 1979
16 Ludwig van Beethoven, composer, 1770
17 Sean Patrick Thomas, actor, 1970
18 Brad Pitt, actor, 1963
19 Jake Gyllenhaal, actor, 1980
20 Rich Gannon, football player, 1965
21 Ray Romano, actor/comedian, 1957
22 Diane Sawyer, journalist, 1945
23 Alge Crumpler, football player, 1977
24 Ryan Seacrest, DJ/TV personality, 1974
25 Clara Barton, American Red Cross founder, 1821
26 Marcelo Rios, tennis player, 1975
27 Carson Palmer, football player, 1979
28 Denzel Washington, actor, 1954
29 Jude Law, actor, 1972
30 LeBron James, basketball player, 1984
31 Val Kilmer, actor, 1959

Clara Barton

Talkin' 'Bout Your Generation

Do you ever feel like your parents don't really get your slang or the clothes and music you like? Ever feel like you don't really get the stuff they like either? Maybe it's because you're from different generations.

A generation usually spans about 20 years. Not everyone agrees on which years each generation covers, but the labels can be helpful in describing the shared experiences and popular culture of a group of the population.

iGeneration (born about 2001 and after)

- About 14% of the U.S. population, or around 41 million people in 2008
- First generation to grow up with a lifelong use of communications technology such as the Internet, cell phones, and digital cameras
- First Americans to grow up with widespread equality between sexes at work and home

Generation Y (born about 1980–2000)

- Also known as "Millennials" or "Echo Boomers"
- About 28% of the U.S. population, or around 84 million people in 2008
- First generation to grow up fluent in digital technology

Generation X (born about 1965–1979)

- About 21% of the U.S. population, or around 63 million people in 2008
- Born during the so-called "Baby Bust," a drop in birthrates after the Baby Boom
- The best-educated generation in U.S. history up to that time, with women educated in equal numbers to men.

Baby Boomers (born about 1946–1964)

- About 25% of the population, or around 77 million people in 2008
- The "Baby Boom" began right after World War II, as millions of soldiers returned home
- Witnessed the civil rights and women's rights movements, as well as the Vietnam War

MOST POPULAR NAMES

Boys (born 1900)	Girls (born 1900)	Boys (born 2000)	Girls (born 2000)	Boys (born 2009)	Girls (born 2009)
1. John	1. Mary	1. Jacob	1. Emily	1. Jacob	1. Isabella
2. William	2. Helen	2. Michael	2. Hannah	2. Ethan	2. Emma
3. James	3. Anna	3. Ethan	3. Madison	3. Michael	3. Olivia
4. George	4. Margaret	4. Joshua	4. Ashley	4. Alexander	4. Sophia
5. Charles	5. Ruth	5. Daniel	5. Sarah	5. William	5. Ava

What's Your Sign?

ASTROLOGY is a study of the positions of celestial bodies—such as the sun, moon, planets, and stars—that looks to find connections between these bodies and things that happen on Earth. Most scientists do not believe that there are connections, and astrology is often called a "pseudoscience" or "superstition." Still, many people enjoy learning about astrology and using it for entertainment.

THE ZODIAC is very important to people who follow astrology. The zodiac is a belt-shaped section of the sky that has been divided into twelve constellations. A constellation is a cluster of stars that can be seen from Earth. Astrologers give special meaning to these constellations. They believe that every person is influenced by one of these twelve constellations—or twelve signs—depending on his or her birthday. For example, a person born between July 23 and August 22 is a Leo. Leos are said to be confident and generous, but stubborn.

A HOROSCOPE is a prediction about a person's future based on his or her astrological sign. Daily or monthly horoscopes can be found in many newspapers and magazines, in print or online, and on other websites.

SIGNS OF THE ZODIAC

Here are the twelve signs of the zodiac, with the approximate date span for each one and the symbol commonly used to represent it.

Aries
March 21 –
April 19
RAM

Taurus
April 20 –
May 20
BULL

Gemini
May 21 –
June 20
TWINS

Cancer
June 21 –
July 22
CRAB

Leo
July 23 –
August 22
LION

Virgo
August 23 –
September 22
MAIDEN

Libra
September 23 –
October 22
SCALES

Scorpio
October 23 –
November 21
SCORPION

Sagittarius
November 22 –
December 21
ARCHER

Capricorn
December 22 –
January 19
GOAT

Aquarius
January 20 –
February 18
WATER CARRIER

Pisces
February 19 –
March 20
FISHES

Books

What is parchment made from? → page 48

BOOK AWARDS, 2010

Newbery Medal
For the author of the best children's book
2010 winner: *When You Reach Me* by Rebecca Stead

Michael L. Printz Award
For excellence in literature written for young adults
2010 winner: *Going Bovine* by Libba Bray

Caldecott Medal
For the artist of the best children's picture book **2010** winner: *The Lion and the Mouse* written and illustrated by Jerry Pinkney

Coretta Scott King Award
For artists and authors whose works encourage expression of the African American experience

2010 winners:
Author Award: *Bad News for Outlaws* by Vaunda Micheaux Nelson

Illustrator Award: *My People* Illustrated by Charles R. Smith Jr.

NEW BOOK SPOTLIGHT

Alchemy and Meggy Swann (2010), by Karen Cushman, is set in the 1500s in London. It tells the story of a young disabled girl who is sent there to help her father, an alchemist, even though they have never met. She is forced to rely on herself and her inner strength to make a success of her new life.

Famous Authors FOR KIDS

Author	Try the Book
Beverly Cleary (1916–) lived in a town so small it didn't have a library when she was a child. Later, she worked as a librarian before she became a writer. She has written more than 30 books, including the popular *Ramona* series, and has won many awards.	*Strider*
C.S. Lewis (1898–1963), born Clive Staples Lewis, fought in World War I and later taught at Oxford University. The British author belonged to a literary group called The Inklings, whose members included J. R. R. Tolkien, author of *The Lord of the Rings*.	*The Lion, the Witch, and the Wardrobe* (the first book in the Narnia series)
 **Christopher Paolini** (1983–) began writing *Eragon* when he was 15. He read many fantasy and science fiction books and wanted to see if he could write one himself. By the time he was 20, *Eragon* was a bestseller. He and his younger sister Angela—who inspired the character of "Angela the herbalist" in his books—were home-schooled by their parents.	*Eragon* (the first book in the *Inheritance* series)
Gary Paulsen (1939–) worked a variety of jobs—including as an engineer, construction worker, and truck driver—before realizing he wanted to be a writer. His dedication to writing has led him to produce more than 175 books for children and adults. Three of his books have received the Newbery Honor award. In addition to writing, Paulsen trains dogs for the Iditarod sled race in Alaska, rides horses, and sails.	*The Brian Saga: Hatchet, The River, Brian's Winter,* and *Brian's Return*
 **J.K. Rowling** (1965–), whose initials stand for Joanne Kathleen, is the British author of the world-famous Harry Potter series. The idea for Harry Potter came to her suddenly during a train trip. She spent the next five years making an outline of the story and writing it out before *Harry Potter and the Sorcerer's Stone* was published.	*Harry Potter and the Sorcerer's Stone* (the first book in the Harry Potter series)
Judy Blume (1938–) started writing books when she was at home caring for her young children. Her books for children and teenagers have sold more than 80 million copies. Using humor and honest discussions of what it's like to be young, books like *Are You There, God? It's Me, Margaret* draw the reader into the character's lives and feelings.	*Otherwise Known as Sheila the Great*

BOOKS TO TRY

There are two major types of literature: fiction and nonfiction. A **fiction** book includes people, places, and events that might be inspired by reality but are mainly from an author's imagination. **Nonfiction** is about real things that actually happened or exist. Nonfiction may be about a person's life, an event in history, or how something works.

Within these two groups there are smaller subgroups called genres (ZHAN-ruz).

Fiction

Mysteries, Thrillers, and Horror

These adventure stories will keep you up late, as you follow a main character who must uncover a secret.

Try These *Bunnicula,* by Deborah and James Howe; *The House With a Clock in Its Walls,* by John Bellairs

Fantasy and Science Fiction

This genre is one of the most popular for teen readers. You've heard of the Harry Potter books, but there are thousands of books for kids and teens in this genre.

Try These *The Hobbit,* by J.R.R. Tolkien; *The Little Prince,* by Antoine de Saint-Exupery

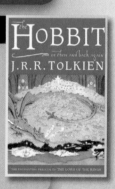

Realistic Fiction

Do you like stories that might have happened to you? Realistic fiction is about real-life situations that teens and kids deal with every day.

Try These *A Crooked Kind of Perfect,* by Linda Urban; *Tales of a Fourth Grade Nothing,* by Judy Blume

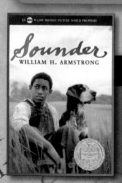

Historical Fiction

If you think history is just about facts, this is the genre for you. Authors take exciting historical events and put the most interesting fictional characters right in the middle of them.

Try These *My Brother Sam Is Dead,* by James Lincoln Collier and Christopher Collier; *Sounder,* by William H. Armstrong

Myths and Legends

These made-up stories go way back. Some are from nineteenth-century America; others are from ancient Greece and Africa.

Try These *The People Could Fly: American Black Folktales*, told by Virginia Hamilton; *D'Aulaires' Book of Greek Myths*, by Edgar and Ingri D'Aulaire

Graphic Novels, Comics, and Manga

Check out these books and series that use drawings and text to tell complicated stories.

Try These *Gettysburg: The Graphic Novel*, by C. M. Butzer; *Diary of a Wimpy Kid*, by Jeff Kinney

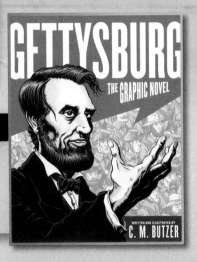

Nonfiction

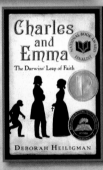

Biographies, Autobiographies, and Memoirs

Do you like reading all about the details of a real person's life? This genre is for you.

Try These *Charles and Emma: The Darwins' Leap of Faith*, by Deborah Heiligman; *Lincoln: A Photobiography*, by Russell Freedman

History

Books in this genre can be about an event, an era, a country, or even a war.

Try This *Blizzard: The Storm That Changed America*, by Jim Murphy

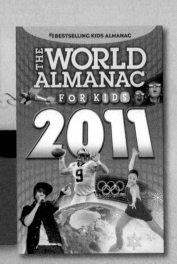

Reference

Books that supply facts and practical information on one topic or many, including almanacs, atlases, dictionaries, and encyclopedias

Try This *The World Almanac for Kids*

All About ...
BOOKS

If a Roman emperor wanted to read a book, he had to unroll it. Books were written on long scrolls (kind of like a roll of paper towels) that you unrolled as you went along. This was clumsy, especially if you were looking for a certain passage. Around A.D. 100 the codex was invented. It was made up of a stack of pages stitched together at the side and protected by a cover. The codex was easier to carry around, to store, and to search through. Books we read today look something like a codex.

In the Middle Ages books were made by monks who copied them by hand onto prepared animal skins called parchment. The monks often decorated the pages with beautiful color illustrations called "illuminations." Books were scarce and very expensive, and few people who were not priests or monks could read.

A big change came with the use of paper and printing, which were first invented in China. Paper came into Europe through the Muslim world and was common by the 14th century. Johann Gutenberg of Germany perfected printing in the 1450s. Once books no longer had to be copied by hand and could be printed on paper, they became less expensive and reading became more common.

At first, books were still not easy to make and not cheap. Each letter was on a separate piece of type, and a typesetter had to put each letter into place individually. Once all the letters for the page were in place, they were covered with ink and printed, one page at a time, by hand on a press. By the 19th century, however, steam-powered presses could print out hundreds of pages at a time. Another invention was the linotype machine, which stamped out individual letters and set them up much faster than a typesetter could. Now books had become truly affordable, and the skill of reading was something that everyone was expected to learn. Today, with the use of computers, books can be easily transferred into electronic files, and read as e-books.

WHO AM I?

I was born in 1812 in Portsmouth, England. When I was two, my family moved to London. Ten years later, my father was put in prison because our family couldn't pay its debts. I was sent to work in a blacking factory (a factory where shoe polish was made), putting labels on jars. I later wrote about the misery of this experience in my book *David Copperfield*. Eventually, I was able to go back to school, and I worked for a time as a newspaper reporter. My first book, *Sketches by Boz*, was published in 1836, and from that time I wrote many books, edited a magazine, and gave many public readings. In my books, I often showed the poverty and misery of everyday people who were working in filthy factories for very low pay, and I showed the cruelty of many factory owners. My works were tremendously popular, and I became a very successful writer. One of my most beloved tales, *A Christmas Carol*, tells of a miser who learns to see the error of his ways thanks to three spirits who visit him on Christmas Eve.

Answer: Charles Dickens

new ways to read

E-Books and E-Readers

More and more people today are reading their books in electronic form rather than on paper. There are several versions of e-book readers available, including the Kindle, from Amazon.com; the Sony Reader; and the Nook, from Barnes & Noble.

All e-readers allow you to download books from the Internet wirelessly, and you can also download magazines, newspapers, blogs, and other material to read and view. You can control how bright the screen is, how large the type is, and other aspects of how each page looks on the screen. On some machines, you turn the page by using a page button, and on others, you change the page by running your finger across the screen.

Some e-readers have a keyboard. This lets you add your own comments to the page as you read it. Others readers use a touch screen, so you type from virtual letters on the screen. There are e-readers that let you access some websites. And there are some that let you get books as audio files, and the reader will read the book out loud to you!

Tablets for Reading and More

A new form of computer, halfway between a traditional netbook computer and a smart phone, is on the market. Called a tablet computer, it works as an e-reader but also lets you access the Internet, play music, write and send e-mails, and play videos. Apple's iPad tablet computer came out in April 2010, and others were on the way. And who knows what's next?

Buildings

When was the first elevator used? ➔ page 51

TALLEST BUILDINGS IN THE WORLD

Here are the world's tallest buildings, with the year each was completed. Heights listed here don't include antennas or other outside structures.

Burj Khalifa (Khalifa Tower)
Dubai, United Arab Emirates (2010)
Height: 162 stories, 2,717 feet

Taipei 101
Taipei, Taiwan (2004)
Height: 101 stories, 1,667 feet

World Financial Center
Shanghai, China (2008)
Height: 101 stories, 1,614 feet

Petronas Towers 1 & 2
Kuala Lumpur, Malaysia
(1998) Height: each building is
88 stories, 1,483 feet

Greenland Financial Center
Nanjing, China (2009)
Height: 69 stories, 1,476 feet

Willis Tower
(formerly Sears Tower)
Chicago, Illinois (1974)
Height: 110 stories, 1,450 feet

✳ Burj Khalifa

The Burj Khalifa (Khalifa Tower), which was officially opened on January 4, 2010, is the world's tallest building. A slender shaft built of aluminum-covered round sections set on top of one another, the building has an observation deck on the 124th floor, as well as 24,348 windows. It houses apartments, corporate offices, restaurants, a fitness center, and a luxury hotel. The building can hold up to 35,000 people. Outside the tower is a large park. The tower holds many world records besides its height. For example, it has the world's highest mosque (on the 158th floor) and the world's highest swimming pool (on the 76th floor). The lavish opening ceremonies, which were broadcast on TV, included a huge fireworks display.

WORLD'S TALLEST WHEN BUILT

Great Pyramid of Giza, Egypt
Built c. 2250 B.C. Height: 480 feet

Cologne Cathedral, Germany
Built 1248-1880. Height: 515 feet

Washington Monument, Washington
Built 1848-84. Height: 555 feet

Eiffel Tower, Paris, France
Built 1887-89. Height: 984 feet

Chrysler Building, New York, NY
Built 1930. Height: 1,046 feet ▶

Empire State Building, New York, NY
Built 1931. Height: 1,250 feet

Ostankino Tower, Moscow, Russia
Built 1963-67. Height: 1,771 feet

A Short History of Tall Buildings

For most of history, people built tall structures to honor gods, kings, and other powerful leaders, not as places to live. Building tall required lots of wealth and workers. But the biggest challenge was gravity. Each part of a wall had to support everything above it. Building higher required thicker walls at the base. Too many windows would weaken the building. The Great Pyramid required an area equal to 10 football fields and more than 2 million massive stone blocks. The Washington Monument, the last entirely stone structure to reach a record height, has walls 15 feet thick at its base.

By the 1880s, three **key factors in the evolution of tall buildings** were in place:

1. A NEED FOR SPACE Crowded cities had less space for building, and land got expensive. To create more space, buildings had to go up instead of out.

2. BETTER STEEL PRODUCTION Mass-producing steel meant more of it was available for construction. Long vertical **columns** and horizontal girders could be joined to form a strong cube-like grid that was lighter than a similar one made of stone or brick. Weight was also directed down the columns to a solid **foundation**, usually underground, instead of to walls.

3. THE ELEVATOR Tall buildings need elevators! The first elevator, powered by steam, was installed in a New York store in 1857. Electric elevators came along in 1880.

As buildings got taller, a new problem sprang up—**wind**. Too much movement could damage buildings or make the people inside uncomfortable. Some tall buildings, like New York's Citicorp Center, actually have a counter-weight near the top. A computer controls a 400-ton weight, moving it back and forth to lessen the building's sway.

In California and Japan, **earthquakes** are a big problem, and special techniques are needed to make tall buildings safer from quakes.

IT'S NOT ALL ABOUT... TALL!

When it comes to buildings, the tall ones grab people's attention. But many other buildings are interesting and fun to look at. Here are a few really cool buildings.

THE GUGGENHEIM MUSEUM, Bilbao, Spain

This stunning building, which houses a collection of modern art, was designed by the Canadian-American architect Frank Gehry. Its exterior is composed of many curved titanium panels that look as if they have been piled up at random. Since Bilbao is a port, the building was given a shape resembling that of a ship. The museum opened in 1997.

THE GLASS HOUSE, New Canaan, Connecticut

When architect Philip Johnson designed his own home in 1949, he created something beautiful and unique. What makes this house special is the structure: it is a steel frame with outside walls made of clear glass. This makes the house totally see-through. (Johnson did enclose the bathroom in brick!)

NATIONAL AQUATICS CENTER, Beijing, China

The "Water Cube" was built for the 2008 Olympic Games swimming and diving competitions. It's made to look natural and random, like soap bubbles or plant cells. The walls and roof are made of thousands of steel polygons fitted with inflated Teflon (plastic) bubbles. The bubbles make a greenhouse, capturing solar energy to heat the pools. Rain cleans the bubbles while the roof catches rainwater, which is reused inside. Each bubble has skin as thin as a pen tip but each could hold the weight of a car.

SYDNEY OPERA HOUSE, Sydney, Australia

Though it looks like a giant sea creature rising out of Sydney Harbor, architect Joern Utzon had the sections of an orange in mind when he designed this building. Finished in 1973, the shells are made of more than 2,000 concrete sections held together by 217 miles of steel cable. The roof cover—bolted on in 4,240 sections—is covered with 1.5 million ceramic tiles.

COLOSSEUM
Rome, Italy; 70-80 A.D.

The Colosseum, built during the reign of the Roman emperor Vespasian, was used for gladiator fights and other public events, such as re-enactments of great land and sea battles and the presentation of classical plays. It could hold 50,000 people and was built of stone. Marble was used to decorate the inside. The Colosseum had 80 entrances. The arches in the structure used to hold statues. Over the centuries, the Colosseum has been used as a cemetery and as a castle. Some of its stones were removed and used in other buildings. Today it is a huge tourist attraction.

DOME OF THE ROCK
Jerusalem, Israel; 687

The Dome of the Rock is the oldest Islamic monument still standing. A shrine, it was built over a rock sacred to both Muslims and Jews. Its 25-meter dome is covered with gold. Because the structure is considered the center of the Earth for the Arabs who built it, there are exits leading north, east, south, and west.

FORBIDDEN CITY
Beijing, China; 1406-1420

This was the exclusive home for emperors of the Ming and Qing dynasties for 492 years. The palace grounds are the world's largest (178 acres). It was "forbidden" because people could not enter without the emperor's permission. The palace itself contains thousands of wooden chambers and great halls that cover 37 acres. Every roof is yellow, the color of Chinese royalty.

THE TAJ MAHAL
Agra, India; c. 1632-1653

The Taj Mahal was built by the Mughal emperor Shah Jahan as a mausoleum (a kind of above-ground tomb) for his dead wife. Its design includes elements of Islamic, Persian, and Indian styles. The Taj Mahal became a United Nations World Heritage Site in 1983 because of its great beauty and its importance as perhaps the finest example of Indian architecture.

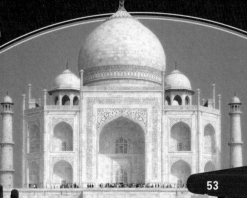

BRIDGES

There are four main bridge designs: beam, arch, truss, and suspension or cable-stayed.

BEAM

The beam bridge is the most basic kind. A log across a stream is a simple style of beam bridge. Highway bridges are often beam bridges. The span of a beam bridge, or the length of the bridge without any support under it, needs to be fairly short. Long beam bridges need many supporting poles, called piers.

ARCH

You can easily recognize an arch bridge, because it has arches holding it up from the bottom. The columns that support the arches are called abutments. Arch bridges were invented by the ancient Greeks.

TRUSS

The truss bridge uses mainly steel beams, connected in triangles to increase strength and span greater distances.

SUSPENSION

On suspension bridges, the roadway hangs from smaller cables attached to a pair of huge cables running over two massive towers. The ends of the giant cables are anchored firmly into solid rock or huge concrete blocks at each end of the bridge. The weight of the roadway is transferred through the cables to the anchors. On a cable-stayed bridge, the cables are attached directly from the towers (pylons) to the deck.

Word Scramble

Can you unscramble the letters and come up with the names of important buildings discussed in this section?

LSILWI ETWRO

ATJ HALMA

HEMGIGUGNE SUMEMU

IDFEOBRDN YICT

ANSWERS ON PAGES 334–336.

PARTS OF A SUSPENSION BRIDGE

Anchorage Main cables are attached here, adding strength and stability

Deck Surface of the bridge

Main cable Primary load-bearing cables, secured by anchorages

Pier Supports for pylons

Pylon Tower supports that hold up cables and decks

Suspender cable Vertical cables that hold up the deck

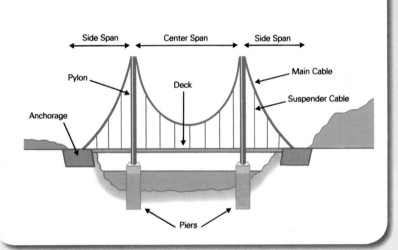

DAM FACTS

Dams are built to control the flow of rivers. They can provide water for drinking or farming, prevent flooding, and create electricity. The first dams were embankment dams built thousands of years ago out of walls of rocks and dirt to prevent flooding or to make lakes called reservoirs for irrigation. Today, most dams are made of concrete. "Hydroelectric" dams are used to generate electricity by channeling the force of rivers and waterfalls into tunnels in the dam to move enormous machines called turbines.

Hoover Dam in Nevada

Calendar

Which day celebrates our planet? → page 58

CALENDAR BASICS

Holidays and calendars go hand in hand. Using a calendar, you can see what day of the week it is and look for the next special day. Calendars divide time into days, weeks, months, and years. According to our calendar, also known as the Gregorian calendar, a year is the time it takes for one revolution of Earth around the Sun: 365¼ days. To make things easier, we add an extra day, February 29, in "leap years," every 4 years.

THE NAMES OF THE MONTHS

January	named for the Roman god Janus, guardian of gates (often shown with two faces, looking backward and forward)
February	named for Februalia, a Roman time of sacrifice
March	named for Mars, the Roman god of war (the end of winter meant fighting could begin again)
April	"aperire," Latin for "to open," as in flower buds
May	named for Maia, the goddess of plant growth
June	"Junius," the Latin word for the goddess Juno
July	named after the Roman ruler Julius Caesar
August	named for Augustus, the first Roman emperor
September	"septem," Latin for seven (the Roman year began in March)
October	"octo," the Latin word for eight
November	"novem," the Latin word for nine
December	"decem," the Latin word for ten

Other Calendars

The **Gregorian calendar** is used by the United States and much of the rest of the world. But some nations and religions use other calendars.

Islamic Calendar The Islamic calendar is used by Muslim people around the world. Twelve lunar months, each beginning with the new Moon, make up the year. The year is 354 days long (355 days in leap years). Al-Hijra/Muharram (Islamic New Year) in Islamic year 1433 will fall on November 26, 2011.

Jewish Calendar The Jewish calendar has months of 29 and 30 days, and its years are either 12 or 13 months long. It is a lunar-solar calendar, which means its months are lunar, but its years adjust to the movement of Earth around the Sun. It is the official calendar in Israel and is used as a religious calendar by Jewish people worldwide. Rosh Hashanah (New Year) in the year 5772 begins at sundown on September 28, 2011, on the Gregorian calendar.

Chinese Calendar The Chinese calendar is a lunar-solar calendar that runs on a 60-year cycle. Within the cycle, years are given one of twelve animal designations: Rat, Ox, Tiger, Rabbit, Dragon, Snake, Horse, Sheep, Monkey, Rooster, Dog, and Pig. On February 3, 2011, the Year of the Rabbit starts.

HOLIDAY HIGHLIGHTS

Each month brings new chances to celebrate famous people, historic events, and special occasions. On federal holidays, U.S. government offices are closed as are many schools and businesses. There are also other holidays that might not mean a day off from school, but they are still enthusiastically celebrated. Holidays marked with an asterisk (*) are federal holidays.

JANUARY 2011

January is National Oatmeal Month and National Skating Month. Learn how to ice skate—for free—at events at participating ice rinks nationwide. Grab a bowl of oatmeal beforehand for a nutritious way to stay warm from the inside out.

* January 1: New Year's Day
Until the year 1753, New Year's Day was celebrated on March 25 every year. When the Gregorian calendar was adopted in 1582, the date was switched to January 1.

* January 17: Martin Luther King Jr. Day
Martin Luther King Jr. Day takes place on the third Monday in January. The holiday honors the famous civil rights leader who was born on January 15, 1929.

FEBRUARY 2011

February is Black History Month and American Heart Month. Learn about the contributions of some important African Americans who changed history. See if your school is sponsoring a "Jump Rope for Heart" event.

February 2: Groundhog Day
On February 2, thousands of people gather in the small town of Punxsutawney, Pennsylvania, to see if Punxsutawney Phil will see his shadow. According to legend, if the famous groundhog sees his shadow, winter will last six more weeks. If he doesn't, spring will come early.

February 3: Chinese New Year
The year 4709 begins on February 3 according to China's traditional lunar-solar calendar. The celebration lasts for 15 days, ending with the Lantern Festival.

February 14: Valentine's Day
Valentine's Day is mostly a way to celebrate those you care about—people have been exchanging Valentine cards with loved ones since the 1500s.

* February 21: Presidents' Day
Observed on the third Monday in February, Presidents' Day honors George Washington and Abraham Lincoln. Both presidents were born in February. George Washington was born on February 22, 1732, and Abraham Lincoln was born on February 12, 1809.

MARCH 2011

March is Women's History Month. From science to sports, discover some of history's leading ladies. March is also National Nutrition Month. It is a good time to learn how to eat well and stay fit all year long.

March 17: St. Patrick's Day
This day celebrates the patron saint of Ireland. Many people, especially those with Irish heritage, consider St. Patrick's Day a time to remember their ancestors and eat traditional Irish foods.

March 20: First Day of Spring
Today marks the first day of spring in the Northern Hemisphere. Also known as the Vernal Equinox, the first day of spring is observed when the center of the Sun appears directly above the Earth's equator.

APRIL 2011

April is National Humor Month and National Poetry Month. Be sure to laugh at any pranks on April Fools' Day, then try telling a new joke every day during the month. Visit the library for books of poetry (try *Where the Sidewalk Ends*, by Shel Silverstein), then try writing some of your own.

April 1: April Fools' Day
People have been celebrating April Fools' Day with pranks and gags for more than 400 years. Have fun tricking your family or friends, but make sure that none of your pranks are cruel or harmful.

April 22: Earth Day
First celebrated on this date in 1970, Earth Day has been an occasion to bring attention to environmental issues ever since. Contact the Earth Day Network, *www.earthday.org*, for events near you if your school doesn't have anything planned. As little as making a commitment to recycle can make a difference.

MAY 2011

May is National Bike Month. Give up that car ride and bike instead. Biking is good for the environment. It's also a good way to stay fit. Before you jump on your bike, be sure to wear a helmet to stay safe.

May 5: Cinco de Mayo

Mexicans remember May 5, 1862, when Mexico defeated the French army in the Battle of the Puebla.

May 8: Mother's Day

Since 1914, Mother's Day has been celebrated on the second Sunday of May. Each year, more than 155 million cards are bought and given to moms across the United States. And that doesn't even include the special homemade cards that moms receive!

* May 30: Memorial Day

Originally celebrated in honor of members of the military who died during the Civil War, Memorial Day now honors all men and women who have died while serving in the U.S. military. It falls on the last Monday in May.

JUNE 2011

June is Great Outdoors Month. Be sure to get outside and get active at special events, from National Boating and Fishing Week to the Great American Backyard Campout, to celebrate the Great Outdoors.

June 14: Flag Day

Celebrated on June 14, this day remembers the adoption of the first version of the Stars and Stripes by the Continental Congress in 1777. Flag Day is not an official federal holiday, but many communities hold celebrations to honor the American flag.

June 19: Juneteenth

Juneteenth, also known as Emancipation Day, celebrates a military order on June 19, 1865, that formally completed the freeing of the slaves. People all over the country—especially in Texas, where it is a state holiday—spend Juneteenth celebrating freedom.

June 19: Father's Day

This day that celebrates fathers falls on the third Sunday in June.

June 21: First Day of Summer

The first day of summer in the Northern Hemisphere is observed on the Summer Solstice, when the Sun rises and sets the farthest north on the horizon and daylight hours are longest.

JULY 2011

July is Cell Phone Courtesy Month. This month reminds the 233 million cell phone users in the United States to be more aware of how cell phone use in public places affects other people.

July 1: Canada Day

Canada Day (called Dominion Day until 1982) celebrates the creation of the Dominion of Canada on July 1, 1867. Like the Fourth of July in the United States, Canada Day is celebrated with parades and fireworks.

* July 4: Independence Day

Commonly known as the Fourth of July, this federal holiday marks the anniversary of the signing of the Declaration of Independence on July 4, 1776. Americans celebrate with picnics, parades, barbecues, and fireworks.

July 14: Bastille Day

This holiday commemorates the beginning of the French Revolution by the storming of the Bastille, an event that eventually led to the formation of modern France.

AUGUST 2011

August is American Adventures Month and Happiness Happens Month. Celebrate vacations in North, South, and Central America, by going on one of your own or remembering a fun vacation you've taken in the past. Happiness Happens Month encourages people to appreciate happiness.

August 7: Friendship Day

Celebrated on the first Sunday in August, this special day honors friendship.

August 26: Women's Equality Day

This holiday remembers the day that the 19th Amendment to the Constitution was ratified to grant women the right to vote.

SEPTEMBER 2011

September is Library Card Sign-Up Month and Hispanic Heritage Month (September 15–October 15). If you don't already have a library card, now is the time to get one. And take advantage of the library to learn about the 500-year-old roots of Hispanic culture in the Americas.

* September 5: Labor Day
A federal holiday celebrated on the first Monday in September, Labor Day celebrates workers with a day off in their honor. Labor Day has its roots in the late 19th-century labor movement, when workers began to organize to demand shorter hours and fairer pay. It was made a federal holiday in 1894.

September 11: National Grandparents' Day
Celebrated on the Sunday after Labor Day, Grandparents' Day honors grandparents and the knowledge they pass on.

September 16: Constitution or Citizenship Day
Constitution Day celebrates the rights and responsibilities of U.S. citizens. It usually takes place on September 17, the date of the signing of the U.S. Constitution in 1787. Because that date falls on a weekend in 2011, the holiday is being observed on the 16th.

September 23: First Day of Autumn
Today is the first day of autumn, or fall, in the Northern Hemisphere. Also known as the Autumnal Equinox, the first day of fall occurs when the center of the Sun appears directly above the Earth's equator.

OCTOBER 2011

October is National Dental Hygiene Month and National Popcorn Poppin' Month. When you snack on popcorn this month, experiment by adding your own flavors or spices to the wholesome treat. If you get a kernel stuck in your teeth (or just eat too much Halloween candy!), brush and floss extra carefully.

* October 10: Columbus Day
Celebrated on the second Monday in October, Columbus Day marks Christopher Columbus's landing on an island in the Bahamas, then thought of as the New World, in 1492.

October 31: Halloween
Halloween always falls on the last day of October. A holiday similar to Halloween has been celebrated since at least the seventh century. Today, global customs vary as much as costumes do, but trick-or-treating remains the most common way to celebrate in the United States.

NOVEMBER 2011

November is National American Indian Heritage Month. Learn about Native Americans and their roles in American history.

November 8: Election Day

The first Tuesday after the first Monday in November, Election Day is a mandatory holiday in some states.

* November 11: Veterans Day

On this special day, Americans honor U.S. veterans—men and women who have served in the armed forces. Veterans Day originally marked the "eleventh hour of the eleventh day of the eleventh month" in 1918. This is when World War I battles came to an end according to the conditions of an armistice (an agreement to stop fighting) signed earlier that morning.

* November 24: Thanksgiving

Every year on the fourth Thursday in November, Americans take the day to honor the people, events, and things in their lives for which they are thankful. Tradition calls for a big meal, shared with friends and family, along with watching the televised Thanksgiving Day parade and football.

DECEMBER 2011

December is National Drunk and Drugged Driving Prevention Month. Impaired driving causes an injury every two minutes and a death every half hour. Contribute something to raise awareness of the danger of drunk and drugged driving this month.

December 22: First Day of Winter

The first day of winter, in the Northern Hemisphere, is observed on the Winter Solstice, when the Sun rises and sets the farthest south on the horizon and daylight hours are shortest. Get outside for your favorite winter activity. Don't worry if the days seem short—they'll be getting longer from this day on leading up to summer.

December 31: New Year's Eve

This day isn't technically a holiday, but you'll still find a lot of people celebrating the end of one year and the beginning of the next. Get a head start on making your New Year's resolutions before you go to bed.

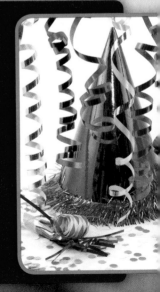

MORE DAYS TO CELEBRATE

Mark your calendar! Here are some exciting and unusual days you don't want to miss:

January 17: Kid Inventors' Day
What do water skis, earmuffs, and the Popsicle have in common? They were all invented by kids! Celebrate young minds on the birthday of Ben Franklin, who invented the first swim fins at age 12.

February 6: Super Bowl XLV
The year's biggest game is the grand finale of the NFL season. More than 106.5 million people tuned in to Super Bowl XLIV in 2010, making it the most-watched TV program of all time.

March 3: National Anthem Day
O say, can you see... "The Star-Spangled Banner," written by Francis Scott Key during the War of 1812, officially became the U.S. national anthem on March 3, 1931.

April 29: National Arbor Day
Give a tree a hug today. Arbor Day, observed each year on the last Friday in April, encourages people to plant and care for trees. For ideas on how to celebrate, visit *www.arborday.org.*

May 1: Mother Goose Day
It's rhyme time! Celebrate your favorite Mother Goose nursery rhymes, from *Jack and Jill* to *Humpty Dumpty.*

June 15: Nature Photography Day
Today is a day to get focused, so grab a camera and look for opportunities to capture the great outdoors in all its natural beauty.

July 17: National Ice Cream Day
Let's all scream for ice cream! Also known as "Sundae Sunday," National Ice Cream Day celebrates America's popular dessert on the third Sunday in July.

August 19: National Aviation Day
Up, up, and away! The Wright brothers (Wilbur and Orville) made history in 1903 with the first self-powered flights in a heavier-than-air aircraft. In recognition of flight, people celebrate National Aviation Day on Orville's birthday.

September 16: Mayflower Day
Destination: America! This day commemorates the anniversary of the *Mayflower's* departure from Plymouth, England, in 1620 with 102 passengers and a small crew.

October 16: Dictionary Day
Calling all wordsmiths! Learn a new word today in honor of the birthday of Noah Webster, the father of the American dictionary.

November 21: World Hello Day
Say hello to ten people today. Since 1973, the goal of the day has been to encourage world leaders to strive for peace through communication.

December 31: Make Up Your Mind Day
This is no day for indecisiveness. Make up your mind to follow those New Year's resolutions!

Crime

How might a forensic entomologist help solve a crime? → page 64

FORENSICS:
USING SCIENCE TO SOLVE CRIMES

Any use of scientific procedures to help resolve legal issues can be called **forensics**. But the word is often used to refer specifically to the scientific analysis of evidence in order to solve a crime.

Checking Fingerprints: Some forensic methods have been used for a long time—for example, gathering fingerprints at a crime scene in order to compare them with prints of known individuals on file. Technological advances have made this traditional method more effective and simpler to use. Certain chemicals can help expose a fingerprint to view, and modern computer networks make it easier to build and quickly access large collections of fingerprints stored in databases.

Checking a crime scene

Identifying Guns: With certain types of guns, when a bullet goes through the gun barrel, it picks up markings that are distinctive for the gun. Investigators compare these markings with those on file from known guns, in hopes of identifying the gun that fired the bullet.

Analyzing DNA Evidence: DNA, or genetic, evidence can be very helpful in identifying individuals. Except in identical twins, every person's DNA is unique. Investigators often gather it from sources such as blood, saliva, and skin. To make an identification, they compare the DNA pattern in the sample they collect with those registered in large DNA databases.

DNA lab work

Using Chemistry: Many chemistry techniques are valuable aids in solving crimes. For example, an investigator may apply a chemical such as luminol at a crime scene to make hidden bloodstains visible. Well-equipped crime labs use sophisticated techniques to find out the makeup of unknown substances found at a crime scene.

did you Know?

Crime investigators sometimes call on the help of various experts. Fans of TV crime shows know about the **toxicologist**, who specializes in drugs and poisons, and the **pathologist**, a doctor specializing in the changes disease and injury can make in the body. A **forensic anthropologist** can analyze human remains such as bones. A **forensic dentist** can help identify unknown persons by matching teeth patterns with dental records. **Forensic entomologists**, experts in insects, can use their knowledge of the life cycles of bugs that feed on corpses to help identify the time of death.

LEGAL PROCESS

In the U.S., the federal and state governments have their own courts. The **federal courts**, or U.S. courts, hear cases such as those involving disputes between states. **State courts** hear other types of cases. Most of the legal work in this country occurs at the state level.

Different states organize their court systems differently. Below is a description of how a typical criminal case might proceed after a judge has determined there was sufficient reason to arrest a suspect (the person accused of a crime).

1 Grand jury. Citizens with no connection to the case review evidence and decide if there is enough to **indict**, or charge, the defendant with a crime.

2 Arraignment. A judge tells the defendant what crimes he or she has been charged with by the grand jury. The defendant can plead guilty, not guilty, or no contest. (No contest means the person will not fight the charges but does not admit to being guilty.)

3 Trial. A prosecutor presents evidence of the defendant's guilt. A defense attorney represents the defendant's best interests. Witnesses may testify about what they know. A jury listens to all the evidence and arguments. The judge makes sure everyone follows the rules.

Juvenile court cases follow different procedures from those used for adults. Juveniles are usually defined as those under 18. The top age for juveniles in the justice system varies from 15 to 17, depending upon the laws of the state. Juvenile cases are determined by a juvenile court judge. Sentencing options may include a fine, community service, restitution, placement in a group or foster home, probation, or referral for treatment.

4 Deliberations. Jury members discuss the evidence and try to agree on a **verdict**, or decision about the defendant's guilt. They must agree that the defendant is not guilty or is guilty "beyond a reasonable doubt." If they cannot agree, the defendant may receive a trial before a new jury.

5 Conviction and sentencing. If the defendant is found guilty, the judge sentences the person, or says how he or she will be punished.

6 Appeal. The defendant may appeal a guilty verdict to an **appellate court**, which may agree or disagree with the original verdict. It may send the case back to the lower court for a new trial.

What do storm chasers do? → page 71

Hurricanes

Hurricane Categories

1: 74-95 mph
2: 96-110 mph
3: 111-130 mph
4: 131-155 mph
5: over 155 mph

Hurricanes—called typhoons or cyclones in the Pacific—are Earth's biggest storms. When conditions are right, they form over the ocean from collections of storms and clouds known as tropical disturbances. Strong winds create a wall of clouds and rain that swirl in a circle around a calm center called the **eye**.

The eye develops as **warm, moist air** is forced upward in the storm by **denser, cooler air**. From the outer edge of the storm to the inner eye, the pressure drops and wind speeds rise sharply, creating swirling **convection currents** around the eye. If wind speeds reach 39 mph, the storm is named. If wind speeds top 74 mph, the storm is called a **hurricane**.

Convection currents — Eye — Cool dense air — Warm moist air — Hurricane winds and rain

Hurricanes can be up to 300 miles wide. On land, the storm can snap trees and tear buildings apart. Strong winds blowing toward shore can create a rise in the ocean water called a **storm surge**. It can combine with heavy rains to cause flooding and massive damage.

For the Atlantic Ocean, Caribbean Sea, and Gulf of Mexico, hurricane season runs from June 1 to November 30. Most hurricanes happen in August, September, and October, when the oceans are warmest.

Notable U.S. Hurricanes

Date	Location	What Happened?	Deaths
Sept. 8, 1900	Galveston, TX	Category 4 storm flooded the island with 15-foot waves.	8,000+
Sept. 19, 1938	NY, CT, RI, MA	"The Long Island Express," with storm surges rising 10-25 feet, caused $306 million in damages.	600+
Aug. 24-26, 1992	FL, LA	Hurricane Andrew swept across the Gulf of Mexico, leaving 250,000 homeless.	65
Aug. 25-29, 2005	LA, MS, AL, GA, FL	Hurricane Katrina, with 175 mph winds and a 25-foot high storm surge, caused about $125 billion in damage.	1,833

Hurricane Names

The U.S. began using women's names for hurricanes in 1953 and added men's names in 1979. When all letters (except Q, U, X, Y, and Z) are used in one season, any additional storms are named with Greek letters. Six Greek letters were needed to name 2005 storms.

2011 Atlantic Hurricane Names: Arlene, Bret, Cindy, Don, Emily, Franklin, Gert, Harvey, Irene, Jose, Katia, Lee, Maria, Nate, Ophelia, Philippe, Rina, Sean, Tammy, Vince, Whitney

Tornado Categories

WEAK
EF0: 65-85 mph
EF1: 86-110 mph

STRONG
EF2: 111-135 mph
EF3: 136-165 mph

VIOLENT
EF4: 166-200 mph
EF5: over 200 mph

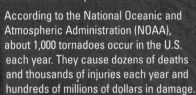

Tornadoes

Tornadoes are rapidly spinning columns of air. They form when winds change direction, speed up, and spin around in or near a thunderstorm. They can also spin off from hurricanes.

Tornadoes can happen any time that the weather is right, but they are more common between March and July. They can happen in any state, but strong tornadoes touch down most often in the U.S. southeast or central plains.

According to the National Oceanic and Atmospheric Administration (NOAA), about 1,000 tornadoes occur in the U.S. each year. They cause dozens of deaths and thousands of injuries each year and hundreds of millions of dollars in damage.

Tornadoes are measured by how much damage they cause. In February 2007, the U.S. began using the Enhanced Fujita (EF) Scale (at left) to measure tornadoes. The EF-Scale provides an estimate of a tornado's wind speed based on the amount of damage. If a tornado doesn't hit anything, it may be hard to classify it.

Wind speeds are difficult to measure directly, because measuring instruments can be destroyed in more violent winds. The highest wind speed ever recorded—318 mph—was taken in May 1999 in an Oklahoma tornado.

did you know?

The state with the highest average number of tornadoes is Texas. Between 2004 and 2009, an average of almost 147 tornadoes a year were reported in Texas.

U.S. Tornado Records (since record keeping began in 1950)

YEAR: The 1,819 tornadoes reported in 2004 topped the previous record of 1,424 in 1998.

MONTH: In May 2003, there were a total of 543 tornadoes, easily passing the old record of 399 set in June 1992.

TWO-DAY PERIOD: On April 3 and 4, 1974, 147 tornadoes touched down in 13 states, causing more than 300 deaths.

For more information on storms and weather, go to the NOAA Education page: *www.education.noaa.gov/cweather.html*

EARTHQUAKES

There are thousands of earthquakes each year. Most are small, but about 1 in 500 causes damage. Some quakes are incredibly powerful and destructive, such as the one in Haiti in January 2010. After the earthquake in Chile in February 2010, scientists reported that the entire city of Concepcion shifted 10 feet to the west.

▲ *Collapsed buildings in Haiti after the January 2010 earthquake*

WHAT CAUSES EARTHQUAKES?

To understand earthquakes, imagine Earth as an egg with a cracked shell. The cracked outer layer (the eggshell) is called the **lithosphere**, and it is divided into huge pieces called **plates** (see map). The plates are constantly moving away from, toward, or past one another. Earthquakes result when plates collide or scrape against each other. The cracks in the lithosphere are called **faults**. Many quakes occur along these fault lines.

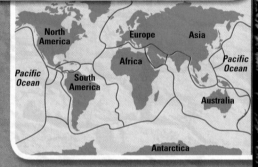

MAJOR EARTHQUAKES

These earthquakes are among the largest and most destructive in the past 50 years.

Year	Location	Magnitude	Deaths (estimated)
1960	near Chile	9.5	5,000
1970	Northern Peru	7.8	66,000
1976	Tangshan, China	8.0	255,000
1988	Soviet Armenia	7.0	55,000
1989	United States (San Francisco area)	7.1	62
1990	Western Iran	7.7	40,000
1994	United States (Los Angeles area)	6.8	61
1995	Kobe, Japan	6.9	5,502
1999	Western Turkey	7.4	17,200
2001	Western India	7.9	30,000
2004	Sumatra, Indonesia	9.0	225,000
2005	Pakistan and India	7.6	80,000
2008	Sichuan, China	7.9	87,652
2010	Haiti	7.0	230,000
2010	Chile	8.8	700

VOLCANOES

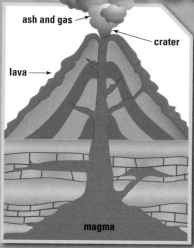

ash and gas
crater
lava
magma

A volcano is a mountain or hill (**cone**) with an opening on top known as a **crater**. Hot melted rock (**magma**), gases, and other material from inside Earth mix together and rise up through cracks and weak spots. When enough pressure builds up, the magma can escape, erupting through the crater. Magma is called **lava** when it reaches the air. Lava may be hotter than 2,000°F. The cone of a volcano is often made of layers of lava and ash that have erupted, then cooled.

Some islands, like the Hawaiian Islands, are really the tops of undersea volcanoes.

Where Is the Ring of Fire?

The hundreds of active volcanoes near the edges of the Pacific Ocean make up what is called the **Ring of Fire.** They mark the boundary between the plates under the Pacific Ocean and the plates under the surrounding continents. (Earth's plates are explained on page 68, with the help of a map.) The Ring of Fire runs from Alaska, along the west coast of South and North America, to the southern tip of Chile. The ring also runs down the east coast of Asia, starting in the far north. It continues down past Australia.

Some Famous Volcanic Eruptions

Year	Volcano (place)	Deaths (estimated)
79	Mount Vesuvius (Italy)	16,000
1586	Kelut (Indonesia)	10,000
1792	Mount Unzen (Japan)	14,500
1815	Tambora (Indonesia)	10,000
1883	Krakatau, or Krakatoa (Indonesia)	36,000
1902	Mount Pelée (Martinique)	28,000
1980	Mount St. Helens (U.S.)	57
1982	El Chichón (Mexico)	1,880
1985	Nevado del Ruiz (Colombia)	23,000
1986	Lake Nyos (Cameroon)	1,700
1991	Mount Pinatubo (Philippines)	800

TSUNAMIS

Tsunami (pronounced *tsoo-NAH-mee*) comes from two Japanese words: "tsu" (harbor) and "nami" (wave). These huge waves are sometimes called tidal waves, but they have nothing to do with the tides.

The strongest tsunamis happen when a big part of the sea floor lifts along a fault (see page 68), pushing up a huge volume of water. The resulting waves are long and low, and might not even be noticed in deep water. They move at speeds of up to 500 miles per hour. As they near shore, they slow down and the great energy forces the water upward into big waves.

On December 26, 2004, a magnitude-9.0 earthquake off the Indonesian island of Sumatra triggered a tsunami in the Indian Ocean. The tsunami hit 12 countries. An estimated 225,000 people were killed, and 1.6 million were left homeless.

MAJOR DISASTERS

Here are some other disasters the world has faced.

Hindenburg *disaster*

Aircraft Disasters

Date	Location	What Happened?	Deaths
May 6, 1937	Lakehurst, NJ	German zeppelin (blimp) *Hindenburg* caught fire as it prepared to land.	36
Aug. 12, 1985	Japan	Boeing 747 jet collided with Mt. Osutaka. Japan's worst single-aircraft disaster in history.	520
March 27, 1977	Tenerife, Canary Islands	Two Boeing 747s collide on the runway of Los Rodeos airport.	582
Sept. 11, 2001	New York, NY; Arlington, VA; Shanksville, PA	Two hijacked planes crashed into the World Trade Center, one into the Pentagon, one went down in a PA field.	Nearly 3,000

Explosions and Fires

Date	Location	What Happened?	Deaths
June 15, 1904	New York City	*General Slocum,* wooden ship carrying church members up the East River, caught fire.	1,021
March 25, 1911	New York City	Triangle Shirtwaist Factory caught fire. Workers were trapped inside.	146
Nov. 28, 1942	Boston, MA	Fire swept through the Coconut Grove nightclub; patrons panicked. Deadliest nightclub fire in U.S. history.	146
Dec. 3, 1984	Bhopal, India	A pesticide factory explosion spread toxic gas; worst industrial accident in history.	15,000

Rail Disasters

Date	Location	What Happened?	Deaths
Jan. 16, 1944	León Prov., Spain	Train crashed in the Torro Tunnel.	500
March 2, 1944	Salerno, Italy	Passengers suffocated when train stalled in tunnel.	521
June 6, 1981	Bihar, India	Train plunged off of a bridge into the river; India's deadliest rail disaster ever.	800

Ship Disasters

Date	Location	What Happened?	Deaths
April 14, 1912	near Newfoundland	Luxury liner *Titanic* collided with iceberg.	1,503
May 7, 1915	Atlantic Ocean, near Ireland	British steamer *Lusitania* torpedoed and sunk by German submarine.	1,198
Jan. 30, 1945	Baltic Sea	Liner *Wilhelm Gustloff* carrying German refugees and soldiers sunk by Soviet sub. Highest death toll for a single ship.	9,000

Other Disasters

Date	Location	What Happened?	Deaths
Aug. 1931	China	Vast flooding on the Huang He River. Highest known death toll from a flood.	3,700,000
1984	Africa (chiefly Ethiopia)	Several years of severe drought caused one of the worst modern famines.	800,000
April 1986	Chernobyl, USSR (now Ukraine)	Explosions at a nuclear power plant leaked radioactive material. 135,000 people were exposed to harmful levels of radiation.	31
Summer 2003	Europe	A severe summer heat wave swept across Europe.	35,000
Feb. 2006	The Philippines	Landslide on Leyte Island buries a village.	1,000

THE WORLD ALMANAC FOR KIDS
ON THE JOB:
STORM CHASERS

What do storm chasers do?

Storm chasers study the most dangerous weather up close. In the United States, most storm chasers track tornadoes in the Midwest. Some study hurricanes and other major storms.

Why do they do it?

Some people chase tornadoes as a hobby. Some take photographs of the storms that they then sell. Many storm chasers are **meteorologists** (scientists who study weather). They want to learn how to better predict when and where tornadoes will strike.

What do they use?

Storm chasing can be very dangerous. Some storm chasers use strong all-weather vehicles to put themselves as close as possible to a tornado (or perhaps drive into the eye of a hurricane). Most use special high-tech radar and GPS systems to help track a storm's movement.

Do you want to be a storm chaser?

Scientists who study storms usually get a college degree in meteorology or a related branch of science. Many of them go on to get a doctorate in meteorology.

Energy

What is biomass made from? → page 73

Energy can take many forms. Heat, light, and electricity are forms of energy. The Sun's warmth is energy in the form of heat. We extract energy from natural resources and put it to use, providing heat, electricity, and mechanical power. Some resources—like sunlight, water, and wind—will always be around or—like biomass—will always be made by nature. These are renewable resources. Nonrenewable resources, like fossil fuels and uranium, are not naturally replenished.

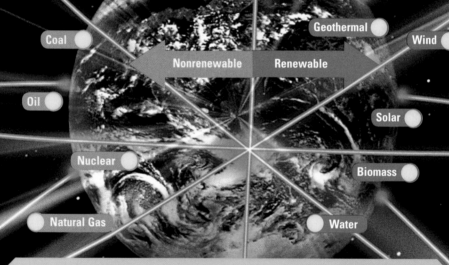

Coal

Geothermal

Wind

Nonrenewable ← → Renewable

Oil

Solar

Nuclear

Biomass

Natural Gas

Water

Who Produces and Uses the MOST ENERGY?

The United States produces about 15% of the world's energy—more than any other country—but it also uses 21% of the world's supply. The table on the left lists the world's top ten energy producers and the percent of the world's production that each nation was responsible for in 2007. One of these countries—Saudi Arabia—is the world's largest oil producer. The table on the right lists the world's top energy users and the percent of the world's energy that each nation consumed that same year.

TOP ENERGY PRODUCERS		TOP ENERGY USERS	
United States	15%	United States	21%
China	15%	China	16%
Russia	11%	Russia	6%
Saudi Arabia	5%	Japan	5%
Canada	4%	India	4%
India	3%	Germany	3%
Iran	3%	Canada	3%
Australia	2%	France	2%
Indonesia	2%	Brazil	2%
Norway	2%	South Korea	2%

SOURCES OF ENERGY

Where Does Energy Come From?

Nonrenewable resources come in limited supply. The "fossil fuels" **coal, oil,** and **natural gas** are the most common. Those are the decayed remains of ancient animals and plants, many of which lived long before the dinosaurs. Such fossil fuels took millions of years to form and, if we run out, will take millions more for new supplies to be made. **Uranium**, the element that is split to power U.S. nuclear reactors, is more abundant than silver. However, U-235, the type of uranium used for fuel in nuclear power plants, is relatively rare.

Uranium and coal are mined, either by digging huge pits or making tunnels that go deep underground. Oil and gas are pumped from wells drilled into the ground, sometimes at the bottom of the ocean. Oil fresh from the ground is called crude. It is sent to a refinery where it is separated into different types of fuel like gasoline, diesel, jet fuel, and other petroleum products. Natural gas consists mostly of methane. It also includes such gases as propane and butane, which are removed during refining.

Renewable sources of energy will never run out. We can find many by just looking around. The force of moving water, such as a river or waterfall, can create **hydropower**. It is one of the oldest sources of energy. **Ocean energy** uses the motion of the tides or the power of breaking waves to produce energy. The Sun's light can be converted into **solar power**. Steady winds can be used to spin giant propellers, generating **wind power**. **Biomass** is renewable material made from plants or animals. This material, including wood or garbage, can be burned to make energy. Heat from the Earth's mantle, called **geothermal energy**, can be collected at natural hot springs where hot magma boils surface water.

How Do We Power Homes?

The most common uses of energy in the home are to control heating and cooling and provide electricity for lighting and appliances.

Most electricity is generated at power stations by wheel-shaped engines called **turbines**. Water and wind can be used to push turbines, but usually a turbine is pushed with steam. Water is heated into steam by burning biomass or fossil fuels, by splitting uranium atoms during nuclear fission, or by using the heat of sunlight. More than two-fifths of America's electricity is generated from burning coal. But two-thirds of the energy stored in coal is lost when it is burned. Natural steam from hot springs can be used to spin turbines, but natural hot springs are rare.

Some homes have solar "collectors" that capture the Sun's energy for use in heating water. Also used in homes are solar panels, made of solar cells that convert sunlight directly into electricity. Many people have natural gas, the most widely used energy source in American homes, delivered to their home through pipes. Gas stoves burn natural gas, which can also power home furnaces and hot water heaters.

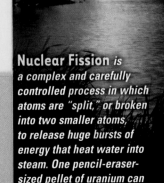

Nuclear Fission *is a complex and carefully controlled process in which atoms are "split," or broken into two smaller atoms, to release huge bursts of energy that heat water into steam. One pencil-eraser-sized pellet of uranium can produce as much energy as 1,780 pounds of coal.*

Renewable Energy in Action:

Washington state is the nation's biggest producer of hydroelectricity and gets about 70 percent of its power from renewable resources. The Grand Coulee Dam, which spans the Columbia River in northern Washington, is the biggest hydroelectric dam in the U.S.

Iceland gets most of its heat from geothermal sources. Water is boiled in hot springs by underground heat and piped into buildings like a giant radiator. Geothermal and hydropower sources provide 99% of the country's electricity.

Producing Electricity: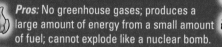

Nuclear Fission

Pros: No greenhouse gases; produces a large amount of energy from a small amount of fuel; cannot explode like a nuclear bomb.

Cons: Creates dangerous nuclear waste that takes thousands of years to become safe; accidents might contaminate large areas (like Chernobyl) with radiation; expensive.

Hydroelectric

Pros: Does not pollute or heat the water or air; no waste products, runs nonstop; very inexpensive.

Cons: Massive dams are expensive and difficult to build; alters the environment around the dam; can affect fish migratory patterns.

Biomass

Pros: Reduces trash in landfills; cuts down on release of methane; plants, such as corn for ethanol, are a renewable resource.

Cons: Burning some trash releases toxins and some greenhouse gases into the air; leaves ash; plants require large farms and specific climate conditions; could raise food prices.

Wind

Pros: Clean; land for wind farms can be used for other purposes like farming; can be built offshore.

Cons: Wind farms take up a lot of space; can kill birds if placed in migratory paths; require winds of at least 12 to 14 mph; can be noisy.

Solar

Pros: No pollution; little maintenance required.

Cons: Solar panels are expensive and take up a lot of space; energy can't be gathered when the Sun isn't shining; manufacturing the solar cells produces waste products.

Solar-powered home

Fossil Fuels
(primarily coal)

Pros: Affordable because equipment is in wide use; needs smaller space to generate power compared to most other sources.

Cons: Limited supply; major contributor to global warming; causes chemical reactions that create acid rain and smog; releases pollutants that cause breathing problems like asthma, can harm land and pollute water.

WHERE DOES **U.S. ENERGY** COME FROM?

In 2009, about 83% of the energy used in the U.S. came from fossil fuels, mainly petroleum, natural gas, or coal. The rest came mostly from nuclear power, renewable resources such as hydroelectric power, geothermal, solar, and wind energy, and from alternative fuels such as biomass (including wood, animal waste, and fuels made from plant materials).

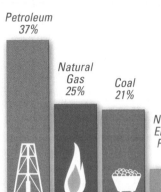

Petroleum 37%

Natural Gas 25%

Coal 21%

Nuclear Electric Power 9%

Hydro-power 3%

Other Renewable and Alternative Sources 5%

ENERGY QUIZ

Are you energy savvy? Can you answer these questions about where energy comes from and how it is used?

1 What country produces the most energy?
- A. Saudi Arabia
- B. Russia
- C. United States
- D. Canada

2 What country produces the most oil?
- A. Saudi Arabia
- B. Russia
- C. United States
- D. Canada

3 Which of the following is a fossil fuel?
- A. uranium
- B. natural gas
- C. biomass
- D. geothermal energy

4 When coal is burned, how much of the energy that it contains is lost?
- A. one-half
- B. one-fourth
- C. four-fifths
- D. two-thirds

5 What country gets almost all of its energy from geothermal sources and hydropower?
- A. Chile
- B. Iceland
- C. Japan
- D. Ethiopia

6 Which of the following is used in nuclear power plants?
- A. fullerenes
- B. uranium
- C. coal
- D. methane

ANSWERS ON PAGES 334–336.

Offshore oil rig

"Greener" Cars, Cleaner Air

More than 600 million motor vehicles, most of them passenger cars, fill the world's roads. Nearly all of these vehicles burn fossil fuels, mainly gasoline or diesel fuel, putting gases and dust particles into the air. The gases and particles that come out of a vehicle's tail pipe are called **emissions**, and some of them are harmful to people's health. Some emissions contribute to **smog** and other types of air pollution. Some, such as carbon dioxide, are known as **greenhouse gases**, which promote global warming. The 21st century has seen a surge of interest in reducing the harmful emissions from cars and trucks in order to reduce harm to the environment. More and more "green" cars, offering reduced or even zero emissions, have come on the market. Additional models are in the works.

ELECTRIFYING!

One way to deal with the emission problem is to replace gasoline or diesel fuel with some other power source for cars—such as electricity. **Electric cars** don't give off any emissions at all. They first appeared at the end of the 19th century but failed to catch on, largely because the batteries they used had a very limited capacity. Batteries are better today, and electric cars are beginning to make a comeback. But the batteries they need are expensive. For example, the Tesla Roadster, a zippy sports car, first appeared on the road in 2008. The initial model could go as fast as 125 miles per hour and could travel as far as 240 miles on a single charge. But it had more than 6,800 batteries and cost more than $100,000.

Tesla Roadster

Batteries are not the only possible source of electricity. A lot of effort has been devoted, for example, to studying **hydrogen fuel cells** as a means of powering cars. These devices, when provided with a supply of hydrogen, can make the hydrogen combine with oxygen, a process that yields electricity and a very nonpolluting by-product: water. A few hydrogen fuel cell vehicles have been built, but this technology is not yet ready for use in mass-produced cars.

Hybrid Cars

A popular approach to dealing with automobile emissions in recent years has been not to eliminate them but to reduce them. Carmakers brought out vehicles called **hybrid cars** that feature both a gasoline (or diesel) engine and an electric motor. The two power sources work together to make the vehicle go, and its fossil fuel consumption is much less than in a traditional vehicle.

The first hybrid car to go on sale in the U.S. was the little Honda Insight in December 1999. Seventeen of them were sold that month. Ten years later there were more than 20 models of hybrid cars on the U.S. market. By the end of 2009, more than 1.6 million hybrids had been sold in the U.S. The popular Toyota Prius accounted for about half of that total.

CLEANER-BURNING CARS

Carmakers have also brought out nonelectric, fuel-burning cars that are less polluting than those of the past. Some of these vehicles reduce emissions by using alternative fuels, such as biofuels or the relatively clean-burning fossil fuel natural gas. Also, engines in many modern gasoline and diesel cars are simply more efficient and run more cleanly. They offer better fuel economy (and thus a lower rate of emissions per mile). In fact, the 2010 World Green Car title went to the BlueMotion models in Volkswagen's Polo, Passat, and Golf lines.

ON THE JOB:
"GREEN" JOBS in the
ENERGY INDUSTRY

ENERGY

The energy industry includes the production, distribution, and sale of fuels and other useful forms of energy, such as electricity.

What Makes a Job "Green"?

The industry includes a big grab bag of different jobs. The ones that help the environment in some way are considered "green." They include jobs connected with renewable energy sources—such as solar, wind, or geothermal energy. Producing energy from these sources causes less harm to the environment than using fossil fuels. Some jobs relating to fossil fuels can also be regarded as green—such as jobs helping to lessen emissions from fossil fuel production and use and jobs involving natural gas, which is cleaner than coal or oil. Nuclear power poses risks of its own to the environment, but it doesn't produce the emissions that fossil fuels do. So nuclear power industry jobs are also sometimes said to be green.

Growing Opportunities

The green sector of the energy industry offers lots of job opportunities. Because of mounting worries about the harmful effects of fossil fuels, along with concern over the fact that they will eventually run out, the green sector is expanding. In the U.S. it already is large. In 2006, nearly 200,000 people worked in just the branch dealing with renewable energy sources, according to a United Nations study.

Plenty of Choices

Green jobs draw on a huge range of skills. Among the many different workers involved in solar power, for example, are scientists and engineers who develop new solar cells and find new uses for them, planners of solar power plants, solar power plant operators, workers who manufacture solar cells and panels, home and business solar panel installers, and solar panel salespeople.

A worker installs solar panels on a building.

Education and Training

Many green jobs begin with apprenticeships or some other form of on-the-job training. Some jobs require applicants to already have a college degree and/or certification by a government body or some other organization. Others don't. Even when not required, a college degree, specialized training, and certification can often be a help in landing a position. People applying for jobs as solar electric system installers, for example, have a good head start if they have passed the relevant exams given by the North American Board of Certified Energy Practitioners.

For more information on green careers, see
http://www.greenenergyjobs.com/career-guide

Environment

Where does garbage go? ➔ page 82

HOME SWEET BIOME

A "biome" is a large natural area that is home to certain types of plants. The animals, climate, soil, and even the amount of water in the region also help distinguish a biome. There are many kinds of biomes in the world. But the following types cover most of Earth's surface.

Forests

Forests cover about one-third of Earth's land surface. Pines, hemlocks, firs, and spruces grow in the cool **evergreen forests** farthest from the equator. These trees are called **conifers** because they produce cones.

Temperate forests tend to have warm, rainy summers and cool, snowy winters. They often are home to **deciduous trees** (which lose their leaves in the fall and grow new ones in the spring), such as maple, oak, beech, and poplar. Mixtures of deciduous trees and evergreens also occur, and some temperate forests are primarily coniferous. Areas where temperate forests can be found include the United States, southern Canada, southern Chile, Europe, Asia, eastern Australia, and New Zealand.

Still closer to the equator are the **tropical rain forests**, home to the greatest variety of plants on Earth. Typically, more than 80 inches of rain fall each year. Tropical trees stay green all year. They grow close together, shading the ground. There are several layers of trees. The top, **emergent layer** has trees that can reach 200 feet in height. The **canopy**, which gets lots of sunlight, comes next, followed by the **understory**. The **forest floor**, covered with roots, gets little sunlight. Many plants cannot grow there.

Tropical rain forests are found mainly in Central America, South America, Africa, Southeast Asia, and Australia and nearby islands. They once covered as much as 12% of Earth's land surface or nearly 7 million square miles. Today, because of destruction by humans, fewer than 2.5 million square miles of rain forest remain. Half the plant and animal species in the world live there. The Amazon rain forest is the world's largest tropical rain forest. It covers more than 2 million square miles—roughly two-thirds the size of the United States.

When forests are burned, carbon dioxide is released into the air. This adds to the **greenhouse effect** (see page 84). As forests are destroyed, the precious soil is easily washed away by the heavy rains. To help bolster conservation efforts, the United Nations has named 2011 the International Year of Forests.

Emergent Layer

Canopy

Understory

Forest Floor

78

Tundra

Tundra, the coldest biome, is a treeless plain. In the Arctic tundra—located in the northernmost regions of North America, Europe, and Asia surrounding the Arctic Ocean—the temperature rarely rises above 50°F. Water in the ground freezes the subsoil solid (permafrost) so plant and tree roots can't dig down. Most plants are mosses and lichens without roots. In some areas, the top layer of soil thaws for about two months each year. This may allow wildflowers or small shrubs to grow. Alpine tundra is located on top of the world's highest mountains (such as the Himalayas, Alps, Andes, and Rockies). Plants and low shrubs may be found here, and patches of permafrost may occur. Tundra is also found on outer parts of Antarctica and nearby islands.

What Is the Tree Line? On mountains there is an altitude above which trees will not grow. This is the **tree line** or **timberline**.

Deserts

The driest areas of the world are the **deserts**. Hot or cold (Antarctica has desert), they receive less than 10 inches of rain in a year. Many contain an amazing number of plants that store water in thick bodies or roots deep underground. Rain can spur fields of wildflowers to spontaneously bloom. Shrubby sagebrush and spiny cacti are native to dry regions of North and South America. Prickly pear, barrel, and saguaro cacti can be found in the southwestern United States. Date palms grow in desert oases of the Middle East and North Africa.

Monument Valley, Arizona

Grasslands

Savanna, Uganda

Areas that are too dry to have green forests, but not dry enough to be deserts, are **grasslands**. The most common plants are grasses. Cooler grasslands are found in the Great Plains of the United States and Canada, in the steppes of Europe and Asia, and in the pampas of Argentina. Drier grasslands called steppes have short grasses and are used for grazing cattle and sheep. In **prairies**, characterized by tall grasses, there is a little more rain. Wheat, rye, oats, and barley grow there. The warmer grasslands, called **savannas**, are found in central and southern Africa, Venezuela, southern Brazil, and Australia. Most savannas have moist summers and cool, dry winters.

Marine

Covering more than two-thirds of Earth's surface, marine regions are the largest biome. The marine biome includes the **oceans, coastal areas, tidal zones,** and **coral reefs**. Reefs are found most often in relatively shallow warm waters. Like tropical rain forests, reefs are home to thousands of species of plant and animal life. Australia's Great Barrier Reef is the largest in the world.

Great Barrier Reef, Australia

WATER, WATER EVERYWHERE

Earth is the water planet. More than two-thirds of its surface is covered with water, and every living thing on it needs water to live. Scientists looking for life on other planets start by looking for water. Water is not only part of our daily life (drinking, cooking, cleaning, bathing); it makes up 75% of our brains and about 60% of our whole bodies! Humans can survive for about a month without food, but only for about a week without water. People also use water to produce power, to irrigate farmland, and for recreation.

HOW MUCH IS THERE TO DRINK?

About 97% of the world's water is salt water in the oceans and inland seas, which can be drunk only after special treatment. Another 2% of the water is frozen in ice caps and glaciers. Half of the 1% left is too far underground to be reached. That leaves only 0.5% for all the people, plants, and animals on Earth.

WHERE DOES DRINKING WATER COME FROM?

Most smaller cities and towns get their freshwater from **groundwater**—melted snow and rain that seeps deep into the ground and is drawn out from wells. Larger cities usually rely on lakes or rivers (and reservoirs) for their water. Areas of the world with little freshwater sometimes use a process called desalination (removing salt from seawater) for drinking water. But this process is slow and expensive.

THE WATER CYCLE

Water is special. It's the only thing on Earth that exists naturally in **all three normal physical states**: solid (ice), liquid, and gas (water vapor). Although the water cycle has no starting or ending point, it is driven by the Sun.

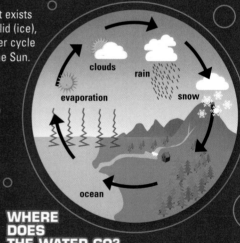

clouds · rain · evaporation · snow · ocean

HOW DOES WATER GET INTO THE AIR?

Heat from the Sun causes surface water in oceans, lakes, swamps, and rivers to turn into water vapor. This is called **evaporation**. Ice and snow can also **sublimate** (go from solid to gas with no liquid stage) into water vapor. Plants release water vapor into the air as part of the process called **transpiration**. Animals release a little bit when they breathe and when they perspire.

HOW DOES WATER COME OUT OF THE AIR?

Warm air holds more water vapor than cold air. As the air rises into the atmosphere, it cools and the water vapor **condenses**—changes back into tiny water droplets. These droplets form clouds. As the drops get bigger, gravity pulls them down as **precipitation** (rain, snow, sleet, fog, and dew are all types of precipitation). Precipitation, which falls mostly as rain, is the main route for water's return to Earth.

WHERE DOES THE WATER GO?

Depending on where the precipitation lands, it can: **1.** evaporate back into the atmosphere, **2.** run off into streams and rivers, **3.** be absorbed by plants, **4.** soak down into the soil as groundwater, or **5.** fall as snow on a glacier and be trapped as ice for thousands of years. Snowpack from winter snow in the mountains often melts in the spring and flows into streams as snowmelt.

WHY WE NEED WETLANDS

Wetlands are—you guessed it—wet lands. They are wet (covered with water, or with water at or near the surface) for at least part of every year. Bogs, swamps, and marshes are wet most of the year. Prairie potholes are wet for only part of the year. Wetlands also include fens, wet meadows, vernal pools, playa lakes, and pocosins.

Wetlands have at least three important functions:

▶ **Storing water.** They absorb water like giant sponges and hold it in, releasing it slowly. During floods an acre of wetland can hold in up to 1.5 million gallons of water. As a result, wetlands help to control floods.

▶ **Cleaning up water.** They slow down water flow and let harmful sediments drop to the bottom. Plant roots and tiny organisms remove human and animal waste.

▶ **Providing habitats.** They are home to huge numbers of plants, fish, and wildlife. More than one-third of all threatened and endangered species in the U.S. live only in wetlands.

There are fewer than 100 million acres of wetlands in the contiguous 48 states, less than half of what there were in 1600. Wetlands are lost when people drain and fill them in for farmland, dam them up to form ponds and lakes, or pave and build up surrounding areas.

Wetlands, Florida

WATER WOES

Pollution: Polluted water can't be used for drinking, swimming, or watering crops, nor can it provide a good habitat for plants and animals. Even fish caught in polluted waters may be inedible if they contain high levels of toxins (poisons), such as mercury. Major sources of water pollutants are sewage, chemicals from factories, fertilizers and pesticides, and landfills that leak. In general, anything that anyone dumps on the ground finds its way into the water cycle. The United Nations promotes March 22 each year as "World Water Day" to remind people of the need to protect precious freshwater.

Overuse: Using water faster than nature can pass it through the hydrological cycle can create other problems. When more water is taken out of lakes and reservoirs (for drinking, washing, watering lawns, and other uses) than is put back in, the water levels begin to drop. Combined with lower than normal precipitation, this can be devastating. In some cases, lakes become salty or dry up completely.

Oil Spill Disaster: An explosion of an oil rig in the Gulf of Mexico in April 2010 resulted in the worst oil spill ever in U.S. waters. Tens of millions of gallons of oil were released into the Gulf, contaminating coastal waters of several states.

WHERE GARBAGE GOES

The disposal of garbage is a serious issue. The problem is that we now produce more garbage than our natural environment can absorb. And many modern products, such as television sets and mobile phones, have parts that may never fully break down. The piles of garbage keep growing, and we add more to them every year.

What We Throw Out*

Metal
8%

Plastic
17%

Food and Yard Waste
26%

Rubber and Leather
4%

Other Trash
24%

Paper
21%

*2008, after recycling

WHAT HAPPENS TO THINGS WE THROW AWAY?

Landfills

About half of our trash goes to places called landfills. A **landfill** (or dump) is a low area of land that is filled with garbage. Most modern landfills are lined with a layer of plastic or clay to try to keep dangerous liquids from seeping into the soil and groundwater supply. The number of landfills is one-fourth of what it was in 1988, but they're much larger.

The Problem with Landfills

Because of the unhealthy materials many of them contain, landfills do not make good neighbors. But where can we dispose of waste? How can hazardous waste—that is, material that can poison air, land, and water—be disposed of in a safe way?

Incinerators

One way to get rid of trash is to burn it. Trash is burned in a furnace-like device called an **incinerator** to make energy. Incinerators burned a fifth of landfill-bound trash in 2007.

The Problem with Incinerators

Leftover ash and smoke from burning trash like rubber tires may contain harmful chemicals, called **pollutants**, including greenhouse gases. Pollutants can make it hard for some people to breathe. They can harm plants, animals, and people.

did you Know? *In 2000, humans produced 13.9 billion tons of garbage, more than 2.2 tons per person. By 2050, we will probably produce 29.4 billion tons. That's a lot of garbage.*

Reduce, Reuse, Recycle

Reducing garbage helps protect the environment. Avoid buying overly packaged goods. Reuse products. Buy durable and recyclable products or products made of recycled materials.

	TO REDUCE WASTE	TO RECYCLE
Paper	Use both sides of the paper. Use cloth towels instead of paper towels.	Recycle newspapers, magazines, comic books, and junk mail.
Plastic	Wash food containers and store leftovers in them. Reuse plastic bags.	Return soda bottles to the store. Recycle other plastics.
Glass	Keep bottles and jars to store other things.	Recycle glass bottles and jars.
Clothes	Give clothes to younger relatives or friends. Donate clothes to thrift shops.	Cut unwearable clothing into rags to use instead of paper towels.
Metal	Keep leftovers in storage containers instead of wrapping them in foil. Use glass or stainless steel pans instead of disposable pans.	Recycle aluminum foil, pans, and trays, and steel cans and containers. Return wire hangers to the dry cleaner.
Food/Yard Waste	Cut the amount of food you throw out. Try saving leftovers for snacks or meals later on.	Make a compost heap using food scraps, leaves, grass clippings, and the like.
Batteries	Use rechargeable batteries for toys and games, radios, music players, and flashlights.	Find out about your town's rules for recycling or disposing of batteries.

What Is Made From RECYCLED MATERIALS?

▶ *From* RECYCLED PAPER we get newspapers, cereal boxes, wrapping paper, cardboard containers, and insulation.

▶ *From* RECYCLED PLASTIC we get soda bottles, tables, benches, bicycle racks, cameras, backpacks, carpeting, shoes, and clothes.

▶ *From* RECYCLED STEEL we get steel cans, cars, bicycles, nails, and refrigerators.

▶ *From* RECYCLED GLASS we get glass jars and tiles.

▶ *From* RECYCLED RUBBER we get pencil cases, computer mousepads, shoe soles, bulletin boards, floor tiles, playground equipment, and speed bumps.

BIG $AVINGS

Producing an aluminum can from recycled material can save enough energy to run a television for three hours.

What Is GLOBAL WARMING?

What is the Greenhouse Effect?

Global warming is a gradual increase in the average temperature at Earth's surface. Earth reflects back into space about 30% of the Sun's rays that reach it. Some rays are absorbed by Earth's surface and converted into heat energy. The heat radiates from the surface, and some of it escapes into space. But some is prevented from escaping by **greenhouse gases** in the atmosphere. The most common greenhouse gases are water vapor, carbon dioxide, methane, nitrous oxide, ozone, and fluorinated gases. Most greenhouse gases occur naturally, and they help to make life on Earth possible. Without this natural **greenhouse effect**, Earth would be about 60° colder than it is today.

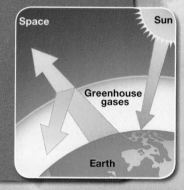

Why Are Greenhouse Gases Increasing?

Since the mid-1700s, humans have been releasing more and more greenhouse gases into the atmosphere. Mostly these additions have come from burning fossil fuels—like coal, natural gas, and oil—which produce carbon dioxide. Factories, farms, and landfills also give off greenhouse gases. Deforestation adds to the problem, because trees absorb carbon dioxide.

There is more carbon dioxide and methane in the atmosphere today than has been normal for the last 650,000 years, trapping more of the Sun's energy. The decade from 2000 to 2009 was the warmest recorded since good temperature records began in 1880. Scientists find it very likely that humans are the primary cause of this global warming.

Where Greenhouse Gases Come From in the U.S.*

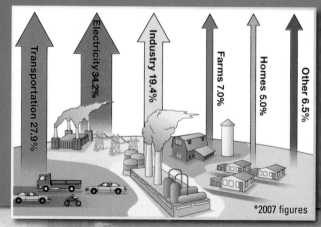

Transportation 27.9%
Electricity 34.2%
Industry 19.4%
Farms 7.0%
Homes 5.0%
Other 6.5%

*2007 figures

How Do We Know about Global Warming?

Worldwide records of climate have been kept since around the mid-1800s. They show global increases in air and ocean temperatures, a rise in sea level, and melting glaciers. Today, weather balloons, ocean buoys, and satellites provide even more information.

Scientists drill thousands of feet into ice caps in Antarctica and Greenland to remove ice core samples. The layers of ice and air pockets trapped in them can be read like a timeline of climate change over the past 800,000 years.

What Will Happen?

Rising Sea Levels: Scientists have created computer climate models that identify patterns and make predictions. In the short run, average temperatures may go up or down in a given year. But in the long run, current estimates predict that they will rise. In fact, by the year 2100, Earth's average temperature may increase at least 2°F and oceans will rise 7 inches. The worst-case scenarios suggest that Earth could warm by more than 11°F and sea levels could rise 2 feet or more.

A piece of a glacier falls into the sea.

As Earth warms, sea levels rise:

- Water expands slightly as it warms.

- The ice sheet covering Greenland and the Arctic Sea are melting. Also, chunks of ice (icebergs) are breaking away from ice sheets in Antarctica and Greenland.

- Glaciers and permafrost are melting in non-polar regions, producing more groundwater.

- As ice melts, it exposes darker land or sea, which is less reflective and absorbs more heat.

Melting Polar Ice: The Arctic region may warm up more than many other places because of the albedo effect, or a surface's power to reflect light. Ice reflects the Sun's rays. With less ice on Earth, more of the Sun's heat will be absorbed by the oceans. Warmer water raises sea levels and melts ice faster.

Changing Water Cycle: Warmer air affects the water cycle (see page 80). More water evaporates, and the atmosphere can hold more water vapor. Places with plenty of water will have more rain and floods. But in places where water is scarce, evaporation will dry out the land even more. Vapor will take more time to condense, meaning less rain and more droughts.

Rising sea levels already threaten some coastal settlements and small Pacific islands.

Many scientists believe that warmer oceans will lead to more intense tropical cyclones (also called hurricanes and typhoons).

As environments change, animals must find new homes or they may become extinct. Warmer global climates will allow disease-carrying creatures like mosquitoes to spread to new places.

Fashion

Which fashion designer created the "little black dress"? → page 88

Take a trip through fashion history since the year 1900. What style do you like the best? It's a modern trend for the fashion-forward, especially kids, to borrow from past decades and make their own special styles.

1900s:

THE EDWARDIAN ERA

Women: Formal females favored custom-made dresses, tight corsets, lots of lace, and feathered hats.

Men: High society gents wore tailored wool suits, straw boater hats, and narrow shoes.

1920s:

THE ROARING TWENTIES

Women: Flappers had short, sleek hair and wore drop-waist sequined dresses and fancy costume jewelry.

Men: Distinguished men wore pastel-colored shirts, and silk ties that were secured with tie pins.

1940s:

MAKE DO AND MEND

Women: During World War II, Rosie the Riveter styles (such as blue jeans and drainpipe trousers) were practical and patriotic. Stockings were a luxury.

Men: Materials were scarce during the war. Pillowcases and parachutes were used to make clothing. Instead of wool, suits were made of wood pulp and had fake pockets.

1960s:

FLOWER POWER

Women: A groovy chick would look mod in a bright-colored dress, blue eye shadow, white go-go boots, and long hair.

Men: A hippie guy might wear bell-bottom jeans, a paisley shirt, and a leather vest. Funky peace signs and flower patches were popular.

1970s:

.... DISCO DAYS

Women: Girls were staying alive in hot pants, polyester pantsuits, bell-bottoms, and platform shoes.
Men: Mr. Disco wore polyester bell-bottoms, brightly colored shirts, and gold chains on the dance floor.

1990s:

ANYTHING GOES

Women: Inspired by the era of grunge music, girls wore big black boots by Dr. Martens, hooded sweatshirts, and layered T-shirts.
Men: Grungy guys kept themselves warm in lumberjack flannels and their money secure with trucker chain wallets. The hip-hoppers, on the other hand, warmed up in puffy athletic jackets and sneakers.

2000s:

FROM HIP-HOP TO *GOSSIP GIRL* ....

Women: Girls start the decade in low-rise jeans, tight T-shirts with bare midriffs, and bell-bottoms. As the decade continued, girls turned to fashions from teen dramas such as television's *Gossip Girl*, adopting its glamorous yet funky styles.

Men: Hip-hop guys kept a beat in baggy pants, gold chains, and athletic gear. The *Gossip Girl* boys brought back prep-school fashions with their blazers, striped ties, and loafers.

2010s:

GOOD DEALS, CLEAN PLANET

Women: As the U.S. economy takes a tumble, girls begin re-thinking the luxurious styles of the 2000s. Recessionista becomes a popular term to describe a girl who can look fashionable on a budget. High-end designers such as Eugenia Kim and Jean Paul Gaultier create affordable clothing for chains like Target.
Men: Men's clothing takes on a more relaxed, natural style. In addition to looking for good deals, both girls and guys want environmentally friendly clothing. More stores and online retailers begin to offer options made with recycled and organic materials.

Some Famous
Fashion Designers

COCO CHANEL

The future designer was born in 1883, a time when there were not many career options available for women. She was raised in an orphanage in France, where she learned how to sew. She was born Gabrielle Chanel but earned the nickname "Coco" in her brief career as a singer. In 1910, she opened a hat shop in Paris. She would eventually expand to more stores—and start designing her own clothes. Her creations became very popular. One of her best-known styles is a collarless women's suit, introduced in 1925, that is still seen today. She is also given credit for creating the "little black dress"—before Chanel, black had traditionally been worn only by women in mourning.

Coco Chanel ▲

STELLA MCCARTNEY

Born in 1971, Stella McCartney is the daughter of singer/songwriter and former Beatle Paul McCartney and his wife Linda. Surrounded by rock stars and other celebrities from the very beginning, Stella was always familiar with fashion. Stella began designing her own clothing as a teenager, and at age 15, she was hired as an intern with designer Christian Lacroix. Her design career took off from there. Linda McCartney was an animal-rights activist, and Stella has followed in her footsteps. She is a committed vegetarian who uses no fur or leather in her designs. Today, Stella McCartney designs both high-end clothing for celebrities and also more affordable fashions sold in stores like H&M and the Gap.

◄ *Actress Amanda Seyfried wearing a Stella McCartney design*

JAY-Z

Originally named Shawn Corey Carter, Jay-Z was born in Brooklyn, New York, in 1969. He rose to rap stardom in the 1990s. In 1999, Jay-Z expanded his career into fashion design. With partner Damon Dash, he created the clothing company Rocawear. The clothing was inspired by hip-hop culture and sold in department stores. Though Jay-Z sold the rights to the brand in 2007, he kept a stake in the company and continues to oversee the company's products and marketing. Today, Rocawear is extremely successful, with annual sales of about $700 million.

Jay-Z ▶

THE WORLD ALMANAC FOR KIDS — ON THE JOB:

FASHION **DESIGNER**

What does a fashion designer do? A fashion designer creates the designs for clothing and accessories, such as bags or shoes. There are fashion designers working all over the world today. A few designers work for themselves, creating clothing or accessories that will sell with their own labels. These are the famous designers that are featured in fashion magazines. It is much more common, however, for a designer to work for a large clothing manufacturer. At these companies, designers often work in teams, helping to design clothes that will eventually sell in retail stores.

Would you like to be a fashion designer? If you are thinking about being a fashion designer, here are some questions to ask yourself:

1. Do you like clothing, even if it is designed for a different gender or age group?

2. Are you creative?

3. Are you interested in art, especially drawing?

4. Can you handle receiving criticism about your work?

5. Do you like working with people as part of a team?

If your answer to these questions is "yes," a career as a fashion designer could be for you!

▲ *Sketches by designer Meredith Evans*

How can you become a fashion designer? There are many different ways to become a fashion designer. Some famous designers got their start by working in clothing stores. Others had connections to the industry through a famous parent or friend. A few have found an audience through TV shows like *Project Runway*. For most people, though, the best way to start a design career is with a college education. A few schools specialize in fashion—many others offer fine arts degrees that provide a solid foundation for clothing design. College courses can teach advanced drawing skills, which will help a designer share ideas for clothing. Because the design industry can be very competitive, it is best to have a college degree.

How can you get started? If you think you might want to be a fashion designer, you can start by learning more about fashion. Read fashion magazines—found at most libraries—to find out about current designs. Read books about fashion design and biographies of famous designers to learn more about the industry. Develop your own personal style by mixing in unique details that appeal to you. Search out used clothing stores to find bargains on unusual vintage styles. Remember that fashion is about creating your own kind of art, not just following the latest trends!

Games

What is the best-selling home video game of all time? → page 90

Kids are spending more time playing video games than ever before. On average, American kids ages 8 to 18 spent 1 hour 13 minutes a day playing video games in 2009, according to the Kaiser Family Foundation. That is 24 minutes more daily gaming time than in 2004. The increase is due mainly to the popularity of "on the go" gaming on cell phones and handheld players.

GAME ON!

Percent of video game time played on each platform:

CELL PHONES: **23%**

HANDHELD PLAYERS (Nintendo DS, Sony PSP): **29%**

HOME CONSOLES (Wii, PlayStation 3, Xbox 360): **49%**

Note: Percentages do no 100% because of roundir Kaiser Family Foundatior

TOP SELLERS

Since launching the Nintendo Entertainment System (NES) in 1985, Nintendo has created dozens of memorable titles—including the five top-selling games of all time. Each game came bundled with a Nintendo console at some point during its record-setting run.

Game	Console	U.S. Release	Units Sold*
Wii Sports	Wii	2006	62.78 million
Super Mario Bros.	NES	1985	40.24 million
Pokémon Red / Green / Blue	Game Boy	1998	31.37 million
Tetris	Game Boy	1989	30.26 million
Duck Hunt	NES	1985	28.31 million

*Through May 2010; sales figures are worldwide. Source: VGChartz

GAME SPOTLIGHT: TETRIS

One of the simplest games remains among the most popular: *Tetris*. Players have been trying to fit its falling puzzle pieces together for more than 25 years. Created by Russian programmer Alexey Pajitnov in 1984, *Tetris* soon conquered the gaming world. As games moved from home consoles to handhelds to phones, *Tetris's* popularity grew. Today, it is the best-selling mobile game ever, with more than 100 million paid downloads.

GAMING TIMELINE

1972
The Magnavox Odyssey is the first commercial home video-game console. The system has no sound.

1975
The home version of Atari's *Pong* debuts. It features two lines (or paddles) that players use to hit a dot back and forth.

1977
The Atari VCS (later renamed the 2600) is the first popular system to feature cartridges for different games.

1980
The pie-shaped pellet-eating character Pac-Man chomps its way into arcades.

1985
Known as Famicom in Japan, the Nintendo Entertainment System invades the United States.

1989
Nintendo's first handheld game system, Game Boy, is a huge hit.

1994
The Entertainment Software Rating Board (ESRB) creates rating standards for video games.

1995
Sony releases its popular PlayStation, which uses CD-Roms instead of cartridges.

2001
Home computer giant Microsoft gets into the action with the Xbox.

2004
The Nintendo DS (dual-screen) ushers in a new era of handheld gaming.

2006
Nintendo Wii changes gaming with the introduction of wand-like controllers.

2008
Nintendo *Wii Fit* features a balance board that allows users to exercise as they play.

WHAT'S NEXT?

Among the most awaited new games are the latest sequels to some all-time classics.

Final Fantasy XIV: Released in the U.S. in March 2010, *Final Fantasy XIII* sold more than 1 million copies in its first week. The next installment will be a massively multiplayer online role-playing game (MMORPG), which will allow gamers to face off against (or team up with) players around the world.

Madden NFL 11: The latest installment of the hard-hitting football game promises to be the most lifelike yet. Simulations conducted by the game's makers have correctly predicted six of the last seven Super Bowl winners—including the New Orleans Saints in 2010.

Geography

How many people live in Antarctica? → page 97

SIZING UP THE EARTH

The word "geography" comes from the Greek word *geographia*, meaning "writing about the Earth." It was first used by the Greek scholar Eratosthenes, who was head of the great library of Alexandria in Egypt. Around 230 B.C., when many people believed the world was flat, he did a remarkable thing. He calculated the circumference of the Earth. His figure of about 25,000 miles was close to the modern measurement of 24,901 miles!

Actually, the Earth is not perfectly round. It's flatter at the poles and bulges out a little at the middle. This bulge around the equator is due to Earth's rotation. Although Earth seems solid to us, it is really slightly plastic, or flexible. As the Earth spins, material flows toward its middle, piling up and creating a slight bulge. The Earth's diameter is 7,926 miles at the equator, but only 7,900 miles from North Pole to South Pole. The total surface area of the Earth is 196,940,000 square miles.

GEOGRAPHY 1 2 3

Longest Rivers
1. Nile (Egypt and Sudan)—4,160 miles
2. Amazon (Brazil and Peru)—4,000 miles
3. Chang (China)—3,964 miles (formerly called the Yangtze)

Tallest Mountains
1. Mount Everest (Tibet and Nepal)—29,035 feet
2. K2 (Kashmir)—28,250 feet
3. Kanchenjunga (India and Nepal)—28,208 feet

Biggest Islands
1. Greenland (Atlantic Ocean)—840,000 square miles
2. New Guinea (Pacific Ocean)—306,000 square miles
3. Borneo (Pacific Ocean)—280,100 square miles

Biggest Desert Regions
1. Sahara Desert (North Africa)—3.5 million square miles
2. Australian Deserts—1.3 million square miles
3. Arabian Peninsula—1 million square miles

Biggest Lakes
1. Caspian Sea (Europe and Asia)—143,244 square miles
2. Superior (U.S. and Canada)—31,700 square miles
3. Victoria (Kenya, Tanzania, Uganda)—26,828 square miles

Highest Waterfalls
1. Angel Falls (Venezuela)—3,212 feet
2. Tugela Falls (South Africa)—2,800 feet
3. Monge Falls (Norway)—2,540 feet

READING A MAP

▶ **DIRECTION** Maps usually have a **compass rose** that shows you which way is north. On most maps, like this one, it's straight up. The compass rose on this map is in the upper left corner.

▶ **DISTANCE** As you can see, the distances on a map are much shorter than the distances in the real world. The **scale** shows you how to estimate the real distance. This map's scale is in the lower left corner.

▶ **PICTURES** Maps usually have little pictures or symbols to represent real things like roads, towns, airports, or other points of interest. The map **legend** (or **key**) tells what they mean.

▶ **FINDING PLACES** Rather than use latitude and longitude to locate features, many maps, like this one, use a grid system with numbers on one side and letters on another. An index, listing place names in alphabetical order, gives a letter and a number for each. The letter and number tell you in which square to look for a place on the map's grid. For example, Landisville can be found at A-1 on this map.

▶ **Using the map** People use maps to help them travel from one place to another. What if you lived in East Petersburgh and wanted to go to the Hands-on-House Children's Museum? First, locate the two places on the map. East Petersburgh is C1, and the Hands-on House Children's Museum is E1. Next, look at the roads that connect them and decide on the best route. (There could be several different ways to go.) One way is to travel east on Route 722, then southeast on Valley Road until you see the Children's Museum.

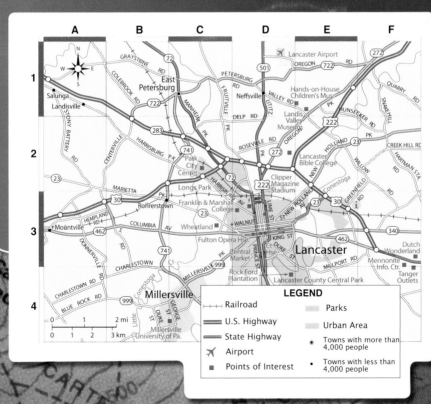

Note.

The asterisk ✱ between t
of S.t Helena denotes the
hitherto ascertained , be

Early Exploration

AROUND 1000	**Leif Ericson**, from Iceland, explored "Vinland," which may have been the coasts of northeast Canada and New England.
1271–95	**Marco Polo** (Italian) traveled through Central Asia, India, China, and Indonesia.
1488	**Bartolomeu Dias** (Portuguese) explored the Cape of Good Hope in southern Africa.
1492–1504	**Christopher Columbus** (Italian) sailed four times from Spain to America and started colonies there.
1497–98	**Vasco da Gama** (Portuguese) sailed farther than Dias, around the Cape of Good Hope to East Africa and India.
1513	**Juan Ponce de León** (Spanish) explored and named Florida.
1513	**Vasco Núñez de Balboa** (Spanish) explored Panama and reached the Pacific Ocean.
1519–21	**Ferdinand Magellan** (Portuguese) sailed from Spain around the tip of South America and across the Pacific Ocean to the Philippines, where he died. His expedition continued around the world.
1519–36	**Hernán Cortés** (Spanish) conquered Mexico, traveling as far west as Baja California.
1527–42	**Alvar Núñez Cabeza de Vaca** (Spanish) explored the southwestern United States, Brazil, and Paraguay.
1532–35	**Francisco Pizarro** (Spanish) explored the west coast of South America and conquered Peru.
1534–36	**Jacques Cartier** (French) sailed up the St. Lawrence River to the site of present-day Montreal.
1539–42	**Hernando de Soto** (Spanish) explored the southeastern United States and the lower Mississippi Valley.
1603–13	**Samuel de Champlain** (French) traced the course of the St. Lawrence River and explored the northeastern United States.
1609–10	**Henry Hudson** (English), sailing from Holland, explored the Hudson River, Hudson Bay, and Hudson Strait.
1682	**Robert Cavelier, sieur de La Salle** (French), traced the Mississippi River to its mouth in the Gulf of Mexico.
1768–78	**James Cook** (English) charted the world's major bodies of water and explored Hawaii and Antarctica.
1804–06	**Meriwether Lewis and William Clark** (American) traveled from St. Louis along the Missouri and Columbia rivers to the Pacific Ocean and back.
1849–59	**David Livingstone** (Scottish) explored Southern Africa, including the Zambezi River and Victoria Falls.

arrows, describe the velocity of the   *Extent of Polar Ice*
Currents in Nautical Miles in 24 h.rs   *Floating Islands of Ice*

SOME FAMOUS EXPLORERS

These explorers, and many others, risked their lives on trips to explore faraway and often unknown places. Some sought fame. Some sought fortune. Some just sought challenge. All of them increased people's knowledge of the world.

CHRISTOPHER COLUMBUS

(1451–1506), Italian navigator who sailed for Spain. He had hoped to find a fast route to Asia by going west from Europe. Instead he became the first European (other than the Vikings) to reach America, landing in the Bahamas in October 1492.

FERDINAND MAGELLAN (1480–1521),

Portuguese navigator and explorer who set sail from Spain in 1519, seeking a western route to the Spice Islands of Indonesia. He became the first European to cross the Pacific Ocean, but was killed by natives in the Philippines. However, because he passed the easternmost point he had reached on an earlier voyage, he is recognized as the first person to circumnavigate the Earth.

MERIWETHER LEWIS (1774–1809) and WILLIAM CLARK

(1770–1838), American soldiers and explorers. In 1804–06 they led an expedition across the American West and back. Aided by a Shoshone woman, Sacagawea, they gained knowledge of the huge Louisiana Territory that the United States had bought from France.

MARY HENRIETTA KINGSLEY (1862–1900),

British explorer. At a time when women were discouraged from traveling into remote regions, she made two trips to West Africa, visiting areas never seen by Europeans. She studied and wrote about the customs and natural environment.

MATTHEW HENSON (1866–1955),

the first famous African-American explorer. As an assistant to explorer Robert Peary (1856–1920), he traveled on seven expeditions to Greenland and the Arctic region. In April 1909, Peary and Henson became the first to reach, or nearly reach, the North Pole. (Recent research suggests they may have fallen short by about 30 to 60 miles.) ▼

ROALD AMUNDSEN

(1872–1928), Norwegian polar explorer. Amundsen was the first person to fly over the North Pole in a dirigible (a large balloon-like aircraft that can be steered), and he was the first person to reach the South Pole, which he reached by dog sled on December 14, 1911. Amundsen was also the first person to reach both the North and South Poles.

JACQUES COUSTEAU

(1910–1997), French undersea explorer and environmentalist. He helped invent the Aqualung, allowing divers to stay deep underwater for hours, and made award-winning films of what he found there.

MAE C. JEMISON

(1956–), was the first African-American woman in space. She is a medical doctor and also has training in engineering. Jemison flew on the space shuttle *Endeavour* in September 1992, serving as Mission Specialist.

BENEDICT ALLEN

(1960–), British explorer. He has published nine books about his journeys, through remote and extreme environments. While studying in New Guinea, he participated in a secret ceremony that left many scars on his body.

For a site about explorers with lots of useful links, try
www.kidinfo.com/American_History/Explorers.html

LOOKING AT OUR WORLD

THINKING GLOBAL

Shaped like a ball or sphere, a globe is a model of our planet. Like Earth, it's not perfectly round. It is an oblate spheroid (called a "geoid") that bulges a little in the middle.

In 1569, Gerardus Mercator found a way to project the Earth's curved surface onto a flat map. One problem with a Mercator map (like the one on page 97) is that land closer to the poles appears bigger than it is. Australia looks smaller than Greenland on this type of map, but in reality it's not.

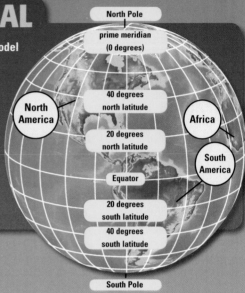

North Pole

prime meridian (0 degrees)

40 degrees north latitude

North America

Africa

20 degrees north latitude

South America

Equator

20 degrees south latitude

40 degrees south latitude

South Pole

LATITUDE AND LONGITUDE

Imaginary lines that run east and west around Earth, parallel to the equator, are called **parallels**. They tell you the **latitude** of a place, or how far it is from the equator. The equator is at 0 degrees latitude. As you go farther north or south, the latitude increases. The North Pole is at 90 degrees **north latitude**. The South Pole is at 90 degrees **south latitude**.

Imaginary lines that run north and south around the globe, from one pole to the other, are called **meridians**. They tell you the degree of **longitude**, or how far east or west a place is from the prime meridian (0 degrees).

Which Hemispheres Do You Live In?

Draw an imaginary line around the middle of Earth. This is the **equator**. It splits Earth into two halves called **hemispheres**. The part north of the equator, including North America, is the **northern hemisphere**. The part south of the equator is the **southern hemisphere**.

An imaginary line called the **Greenwich meridian** or **prime meridian** divides Earth into east and west. It runs north and south around the globe, passing through the city of Greenwich in England. North and South America are in the **western hemisphere**. Africa, Asia, and most of Europe are in the **eastern hemisphere**.

THE TROPICS OF CANCER AND CAPRICORN

If you find the equator on a globe or map, you'll often see two dotted lines running parallel to it, one above and one below (see pages 150–151). The top one marks the Tropic of Cancer, an imaginary line marking the latitude (about 23°27' North) where the sun is directly overhead on June 21 or 22, the beginning of summer in the northern hemisphere.

Below the equator is the Tropic of Capricorn (about 23°27' South). This line marks the sun's path directly overhead at noon on December 21 or 22, the beginning of summer in the southern hemisphere. The area between these dotted lines is the tropics, where it is consistently hot because the sun's rays shine more directly than they do farther north or south.

THE SEVEN CONTINENTS AND FIVE OCEANS

ASIA

Area: 11,948,911 square miles
2010 estimated population: 4,133,000,000
Highest pt.: Mt. Everest (Nepal/Tibet) 29,035 ft
Lowest pt.: Dead Sea (Israel/Jordan) −1,348 ft

OCEANIA (including Australia)

Area: 3,253,542 square miles
2010 estimated population: 35,000,000
Highest pt.: Jaya, New Guinea 16,500 ft
Lowest pt.: Lake Eyre, Australia −52 ft

INDIAN OCEAN

26,469,500 square miles
13,002 feet avg. depth

ARCTIC OCEAN

5,427,000 square miles
3,953 feet avg. depth

EUROPE

Area: 8,815,510 square miles
2010 estimated population: 728,000,000
Highest pt.: Mt. Elbrus (Russia) 18,510 ft
Lowest pt.: Caspian Sea −92 ft

AFRICA

Area: 11,508,043 square miles
2010 estimated population: 1,013,000,000
Highest pt.: Mt. Kilimanjaro (Tanzania) 19,340 ft
Lowest pt.: Lake Assal (Djibouti) −512 ft

SOUTHERN OCEAN

7,848,300 square miles
14,750 feet avg. depth

ATLANTIC OCEAN

29,637,900 square miles
12,880 feet avg. depth

ANTARCTICA

Area: 5,405,430 square miles
2010 population: no permanent residents
Highest pt.: Vinson Massif 16,864 ft
Lowest pt.: Bently Subglacial Trench −8,327 ft

NORTH AMERICA

Area: 8,234,599 square miles
2010 estimated population: 540,000,000
Highest pt.: Mt. McKinley (AK) 20,320 ft
Lowest pt.: Death Valley (CA) −282 ft

SOUTH AMERICA

Area: 6,731,004 square miles
2010 estimated population: 397,000,000
Highest pt.: Mt. Aconcagua (Arg.) 22,834 ft
Lowest pt.: Valdes Peninsula (Arg.) −131 ft

PACIFIC OCEAN

60,060,700 square miles
13,215 feet avg. depth

N E W S

WHAT'S INSIDE THE EARTH?

Starting at the Earth's surface and going down you find the **lithosphere**, the **mantle**, and then the **core**.

The lithosphere, the rocky crust of the Earth, extends for about 60 miles.

The dense, heavy inner part of the Earth is divided into a thick shell, the mantle, surrounding an innermost sphere, the core. The mantle extends from the base of the crust to a depth of about 1,800 miles and is mostly solid.

Then there is the Earth's core. It has two parts: an inner sphere of scorchingly hot, solid iron almost as large as the moon and an outer region of molten iron. The inner core is much hotter than the outer core. The intense pressure near the center of Earth squeezes the iron in the inner core into a solid ball nearly as hot as the surface of the Sun. Scientists believe the core formed billions of years ago during the planet's fiery birth. Iron and other heavy elements sank into the planet's hot interior while the planet was still molten. As this metallic soup cooled over millions of years, crystals of iron hardened at the center.

In 1996, after nearly 30 years of research, it was found that, like the Earth itself, the inner core spins on an axis from west to east, but at its own rate, outpacing the Earth by about one degree per year.

lithosphere

mantle — about 1,800 miles

outer core — about 1,300 miles

core — about 1,500 miles

◤ HOMEWORK TIP

There are three types of rock:

1 IGNEOUS rocks form from underground magma (melted rock) that cools and becomes solid. Granite is an igneous rock made from quartz, feldspar, and mica.

2 SEDIMENTARY rocks form on low-lying land or the bottom of seas. Layers of small particles harden into rock such as limestone or shale over millions of years.

3 METAMORPHIC rocks are igneous or sedimentary rocks that have been changed by chemistry, heat, or pressure (or all three). Marble is a metamorphic rock formed from limestone.

CONTINENTAL DRIFT

The Earth's landmasses didn't always look the way they do now. The continents are always in motion. It was only in the early 20th century, though, that a geologist named Alfred Lothar Wegener came up with the theory of continental drift. Wegener got the idea by looking at the matching rock formations on the west coast of Africa and the east coast of South America. He named the enormous continent that existed more than 250 million years ago Pangaea. The maps below show how the continents have moved since then. They are still moving, athough most move no faster than your fingernails grow—about 2 inches a year.

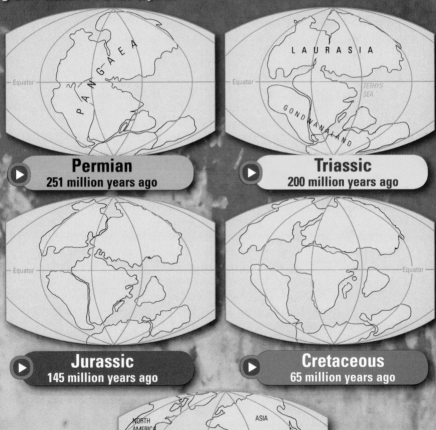

▶ **Permian**
251 million years ago

▶ **Triassic**
200 million years ago

▶ **Jurassic**
145 million years ago

▶ **Cretaceous**
65 million years ago

▶ **Present Day**

Health

What is the epidermis? ➡ page 107

KIDS' HEALTH ISSUES

ALLERGIES

Our immune systems protect us from harmful substances. Certain people's immune systems, however, try to fight off even harmless substances. Common **allergens**—the substances people are allergic to—include pollen and peanuts. If a person inhales, eats, or touches an allergen, he or she might have an allergic reaction. The person might look as if he or she has a cold or have trouble breathing. In severe cases, a person can die from an allergic reaction.

ASTHMA

Asthma is a condition that makes breathing difficult. Allergens, polluted air, vigorous exercise, or stress can trigger an asthma attack. During an attack, the airways narrow and can't carry as much air to the lungs.

An asthma attack might last up to a few hours. After one attack, another might not occur until hours, days, or years later. Asthma can't be cured, but people can take medication to prevent or treat attacks. They can also avoid things that trigger an attack. About 9% of American kids, or 7 million, have asthma.

EATING DISORDERS

About 8 million teenagers in the United States have an eating disorder. Some have **anorexia nervosa**, a condition in which the person has an overwhelming desire to be thin. **Anorexics** skip meals and drastically reduce the amount of food they eat. They lose so much weight that they endanger their health. About 5 percent of anorexics die from the disorder.

Other teenagers suffer from **bulimia nervosa**, also known as bulimia. **Bulimics** alternate between bingeing, when they eat huge amounts of food, and purging, when they empty their bodies of everything they've eaten. Unlike anorexics, who are significantly underweight, most bulimics are of normal or above-normal weight.

OBESITY

Generally, someone who is significantly overweight is considered obese. Since 1980, obesity rates have tripled among kids in the United States. Nearly one in three kids today is overweight or obese. When people eat more calories than they burn off through physical activity, their bodies store the extra calories as fat. Being obese can lead to health problems, such as heart disease and diabetes.

To help fight obesity, First Lady Michelle Obama launched the Let's Move campaign in 2010. The program encourages kids to eat a healthful diet and to get in shape. For more information, visit **www.LetsMove.gov.**

Michelle Obama encourages kids to eat well and stay active.

THE FOOD PYRAMID

To help kids stay healthy, the U.S. government has designed a food pyramid. The pyramid shows kids how to pick nutritious foods and reminds them that it's important to stay active. The colors on the pyramid represent the five different food groups, plus oils. Some stripes are wider than others. You should eat more foods from food groups with the wider stripes. The person climbing the stairs encourages you to get your daily exercise, such as walking your pet, running, playing a sport, or riding your bike.

Grains	Vegetables	Fruits	Milk	Meat & Beans
Make half your grains whole	Vary your veggies	Focus on fruits	Get your calcium-rich foods	Go lean with protein

🜄**Oils** Oils are not a food group, but you need some for good health. Get your oils from fish, nuts, and liquid oil such as corn oil, soybean oil, and canola oil.

★ **Find your balance between food and fun**   ★ **Fats and sugars — know your limits**

MyPyramid.gov STEPS TO A HEALTHIER YOU

To figure out what you should be eating, based on your age, gender, and activity level, use the calculator online at *www.mypyramid.gov.*

For example, an active girl between the ages of 9 and 13 should eat between 1,800 and 2,200 calories daily, including:

Fruits	1.5-2 cups	Meat & Beans	5-6 ounces
Vegetables	2.5-3 cups	Milk	3 cups
Grains	6-7 ounces	Oils	5-6 teaspoons

YOUR BODY

Know What Goes Into It

NUTRITION FACTS: KNOWING HOW TO READ THE LABEL

Every food product approved by the Food and Drug Administration (FDA), whether it's a can of soup or a bag of potato chips, has a label that describes the nutrients derived from that product. For instance, the chips label on this page shows the total calories, fat, cholesterol, sodium, carbohydrate, protein, and vitamin content per serving.

A serving size is always defined (here, it is about 12 chips or 28 grams). This label shows that there are 9 servings per container. Don't be fooled by the calorie count of 140—these are calories per serving and not per container. If you ate the entire bag of chips, you would have eaten 1,260 calories!

Nutrition Facts

Serving Size 1 oz. (28g/About 12 chips)
Servings Per Container About 9

Amount Per Serving		
Calories 140		Calories from Fat 60
		% Daily Value*
Total Fat 7g		**11%**
Saturated Fat 1g		**5%**
Trans Fat 0g		
Cholesterol 0mg		**0%**
Sodium 170mg		**7%**
Total Carbohydrate 18g		**6%**
Dietary Fiber 1g		**4%**
Sugars less than 1g		
Protein 2g		

Vitamin A 0%	•	Vitamin C 0%
Calcium 2%	•	Iron 2%
Vitamin E 4%	•	Thiamin 2%
Riboflavin 2%	•	Vitamin B6 4%
Phosphorus 6%	•	Magnesium 4%

* Percent Daily Values are based on a 2,000 calorie diet. Your daily values may be higher or lower depending on your calorie needs:

		Calories:	2,000	2,500
Total Fat	Less than		65g	80g
Sat Fat	Less than		20g	25g
Cholesterol	Less than		300mg	300mg
Sodium	Less than		2,400mg	2,400mg
Total Carbohydrate			300g	375g
Dietary Fiber			25g	30g

Calories per gram:
Fat 9 • Carbohydrate 4 • Protein 4

Why You Need To Eat:

Fats are needed to help kids grow and to stay healthy. Fats contain nine calories per gram—the highest calorie count of any type of food. So you should limit (but not avoid) intake of fatty foods. Choose unsaturated fats, like the fat in nuts, over saturated fats and trans fats, like the fat in doughnuts.

Carbohydrates are a major source of energy for the body. Simple carbohydrates are found in white sugar, fruit, and milk. Complex carbohydrates, also called starches, are found in bread, pasta, and rice.

Cholesterol is a soft, fat-like substance produced by your body. It's also present in animal products such as meat, cheese, and eggs but not in plant products. Cholesterol helps with cell membrane and hormone production, but there are two main types. Bad cholesterol, or LDL, gets stuck easily in blood vessels, which can lead to a heart attack or stroke. Good cholesterol, or HDL, helps break down bad cholesterol.

Proteins help your body grow and make your immune system stronger. Lean meats and tofu are good options.

Vitamins and Minerals are good for all parts of your body. For example, vitamin A, found in carrots, promotes good vision; calcium, found in milk, helps build bones; and vitamin C, found in fruits, helps heal cuts.

SOME LOW-FAT FOODS

Bananas
Oatmeal
Plain popcorn
Apples
Sunflower seeds
Lentils

SOME FATTY FOODS

Ice cream
Cheeseburgers
Buttered popcorn
Chocolate candy
Potato chips

HAVE **FUN** GETTING FIT

Why Work Out?

Exercise is a great way to prevent obesity and improve health. Children should get at least 60 minutes of exercise every day. But keep in mind that exercise should be fun. You can play soccer, ride a bike, dance, swim, or play catch with a friend. Look at the table below to see how many calories you'll burn up every minute doing different kinds of exercise.

HOW TO WORK OUT

▶ Begin with a five-minute warm-up! Warm-up exercises heat the body up, so that muscles become soft, limber, and ready for more intense activity. Warm-up exercises include jumping jacks, walking, and stretching.

▶ After warming up, do an activity that you like, such as running or playing basketball with your friends. This increases your heart rate.

▶ After working out, cool down for 5 to 10 minutes. Cooling down is like a reverse warm-up. It lets your heart rate slow gradually. Walking is an example of a cool-down activity. Afterward, do some stretching. This helps your muscles remove waste, such as lactic acid, that your muscles make when you exercise. Also remember to drink plenty of water during and after your exercise.

▶ Building up strength through your workouts can be very beneficial. This doesn't mean you should lift the heaviest weights possible! It's better to do more lifts using light weights (1/2 lb or 1 lb) than fewer lifts with very heavy weights. Give your body time to recover between strength workouts.

ACTIVITY

ACTIVITY	CALORIES PER MINUTE
Racquetball	10
Jogging (6 miles per hour)	8
Martial arts	8
Playing basketball	7
Playing soccer	6
Bicycling (10-12 miles per hour)	5
Raking the lawn	4
Skating or rollerblading (easy pace)	4
Swimming (25 yards per minute)	3
Walking (3 miles per hour)	3
Yoga	3
Playing catch	2

did you Know?

It's becoming easier for people with all kinds of disabilities to take part in physical activities. Many groups across the U.S. help out by providing information and chances to compete. Special equipment uses the latest materials (such as light plastics) and improved design to let people with disabilities hold their own in almost any activity.

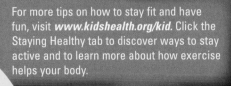

For more tips on how to stay fit and have fun, visit ***www.kidshealth.org/kid.*** Click the Staying Healthy tab to discover ways to stay active and to learn more about how exercise helps your body.

Body Basics

Your body is made up of many parts. Even though we are all individuals, our bodies share similar structures. These structures make up different systems in the body.

CIRCULATORY SYSTEM In the circulatory system, the **heart** pumps **blood**. Blood travels through tubes, called **arteries**, to all parts of the body. Blood carries oxygen and food that the body needs to stay alive. **Veins** carry blood back to the heart.

DIGESTIVE SYSTEM The digestive system moves food through the **esophagus**, **stomach**, and **intestines**. As food passes through, some of it is broken down into tiny particles called **nutrients**. Nutrients enter the bloodstream and are carried to all parts of the body. The digestive system changes whatever food isn't used into waste that is eliminated from the body.

ENDOCRINE SYSTEM

The endocrine system includes **glands**. There are two kinds of glands. **Exocrine** glands produce liquids such as sweat and saliva. **Endocrine** glands produce chemicals called **hormones**. Hormones control body functions like growth.

NERVOUS SYSTEM

The nervous system enables us to think, feel, move, hear, and see. It includes the **brain**, the **spinal cord**, and **nerves** throughout the body. Nerves in the spinal cord carry signals between the brain and the rest of the body. The brain has three major parts. The **cerebrum** controls thinking, speech, and vision. The **cerebellum** is responsible for physical coordination. The **brain stem** controls the respiratory, circulatory, and digestive systems.

RESPIRATORY SYSTEM The respiratory system allows us to breathe. Air enters the body through the nose and mouth. It goes through the **windpipe**, or **trachea**, to two tubes called **bronchi**, which carry air to the **lungs**. Oxygen from the air is absorbed by tiny blood vessels in the lungs. The blood then carries oxygen to the heart, from where it is sent to the body's cells.

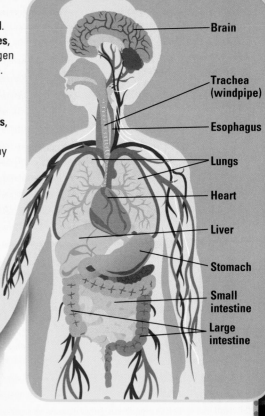

- Brain
- Trachea (windpipe)
- Esophagus
- Lungs
- Heart
- Liver
- Stomach
- Small intestine
- Large intestine

What the Body's Systems Do

MUSCULAR SYSTEM Muscles are made up of elastic fibers. There are three types of muscle: **skeletal**, **smooth**, and **cardiac**. Skeletal muscles help the body move—they are the large muscles we can see. Smooth muscles are found in our digestive system, blood vessels, and air passages. Cardiac muscle is found only in the heart. Smooth and cardiac muscles are **involuntary** muscles—they work without us having to think about them.

REPRODUCTIVE SYSTEM Through the reproductive system, adult human beings are able to create new human beings. Reproduction begins when a man's **sperm** cell fertilizes a woman's **egg** cell.

URINARY SYSTEM This system, which includes the **kidneys**, cleans waste from the blood and regulates the amount of water in the body.

IMMUNE SYSTEM The immune system protects your body from diseases by fighting against certain outside substances, or **antigens**. This happens in different ways. For example, white blood cells called **B lymphocytes** learn to fight viruses and bacteria by producing **antibodies** to attack them. Sometimes, as with **allergies**, the immune system makes a mistake and creates antibodies to fight a substance that's really harmless.

SKELETAL SYSTEM The skeletal system is made up of **bones** that hold the body upright. It also gives your body its shape, protects your organs, and works with your muscles to help you move. Babies are born with 350 bones. By adulthood, some of the bones have grown together for a total of 206.

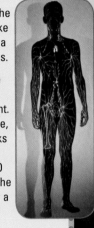

Brain Power

The typical human brain only weighs about three pounds. But it's like the control center of the body, responsible for making sure everything functions properly. Different parts of the brain do different things.

Right hemisphere of cerebrum
- Controls left side of body
- Location of things relative to other things
- Recognizes faces
- Music
- Emotions

Left hemisphere of cerebrum
- Controls right side of body
- Ability to understand language and speech
- Ability to reason
- Numbers

Cerebrum

Brain stem
Regulates vital activities like breathing and heart rate

Cerebellum
Controls coordination, balance

THE 5 SENSES

Your senses gather information about the world around you. The five senses are **hearing, sight, smell, taste,** and **touch**. You need senses to find food, resist heat or cold, and avoid situations that might be harmful. Your ears, eyes, nose, tongue, and skin sense changes in the environment. Nerve receptors send signals about these changes to the brain, where the information is processed.

HEARING

1

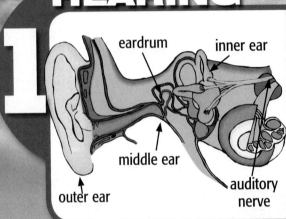

eardrum

inner ear

middle ear

auditory nerve

outer ear

The human ear is divided into three parts—the outer, middle, and inner. The **outer ear** is mainly the flap we can see on the outside. Its shape funnels sound waves into the **middle ear**, where the eardrum is located. The **eardrum** vibrates when sound waves hit it, causing three tiny bones behind it to vibrate as well. These vibrations are picked up in the **inner ear** by tiny filaments of the **auditory nerve**. This nerve changes the vibrations into nerve impulses and carries them to the brain.

did you Know? *The smallest bones in the human body are found in the ear. Located in the middle ear, the hammer, anvil, and stirrup are full size when you are born. The bones are so tiny that all three could fit on a penny together!*

SIGHT

2

The **lens** of the eye is the first stop for light waves, which tell you the shapes and colors of things around you. The lens focuses light waves onto the **retina**, located on the back wall of the eye. The retina has light-sensitive nerve cells. These cells translate the light waves into patterns of nerve impulses that travel along the **optic nerve** to your brain, where an image is produced. So in reality, all the eye does is collect light. It is the brain that actually forms the image.

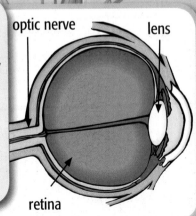

optic nerve

lens

retina

SMELL

3

In our noses are nerve cells called **olfactory receptors**. Tiny mucus-covered hairs from these receptors detect chemicals in the air. These chemicals make what we call odor, or scent. This information then travels along the **olfactory nerves** to the brain. Nerves from the olfactory receptors connect with the **limbic system**, the part of the brain that deals with emotions. That's why we tend to like or dislike a smell right away. The smell can leave a strong impression on our memory, and very often a smell triggers a particular memory.

TASTE

4

Taste buds are the primary receptors for taste. They are located on the surface and sides of the tongue, on the roof of the mouth, and at the back of the throat. These buds can detect five qualities—**sweet** (like sugar), **sour** (like lemons), **salty** (like chips), **bitter** (like coffee), and **umami** or savory flavors (like meat). Taste signals come together with smell signals in the same part of your brain. That's why you need both senses to get a food's full flavor.

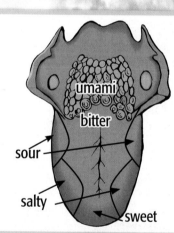

umami

bitter

sour

salty

sweet

TOUCH

5

Your sense of touch allows you to feel temperature, pain, and pressure. These environmental factors are all sensed by nerve fibers located in the **epidermis**, the outer layer of skin, and the **dermis**, the second layer of skin, throughout the body. As with all the other senses, nerves send information to the brain through the nervous system.

Homework Help

What's the difference between "capitol" and "capital"? ➡ page 109

If you need to study for an exam or write a research paper, there are helpful hints in this chapter.

In other chapters, you can find lots of information on topics you may write about or study in school. **Facts About Nations,** pages 152–177, and **Facts About the States,** pages 292–309, are good places to look. For math tips and formulas, look up the chapter on **Numbers**. For good books to read, and write about, see the **Books** chapter.

HOMEWORK TIP

Plus, there are many other study and learning tips throughout the book. Look for the **"Homework Tip"** icon!

THOSE TRICKY TESTS

GETTING READY

Being prepared for a test can relieve some of your jitters and can make test taking a lot easier! Here are some tips to help you get ready.

▶ Take good notes in class and keep up with assignments, so you don't have to learn material at the last minute! Just writing down the notes helps you remember the information.

▶ Make a study schedule and stick to it! Don't watch TV or listen to distracting music while studying.

▶ Start reviewing early if you can—don't wait until the night before the test.

▶ Go over the headings, summaries, and questions in each chapter to review key points. Read your notes and highlight the most important topics.

▶ Take study breaks so you can concentrate and stay alert.

▶ Get a good night's sleep and eat a good breakfast before the test.

THE BIG EVENT

Follow these suggestions for smooth sailing during test time:

▶ Take a deep breath and relax! That will help calm your nerves.

▶ If you are allowed, skim through the entire exam so you know what to expect and how long it may take.

▶ As you start each part of the exam, read directions carefully.

▶ Read each question carefully before answering. For a multiple-choice question, check every possible answer before you decide on one. The best answer could be the last one.

▶ Don't spend too much time on any one question. Skip hard questions and go back to them at the end.

▶ Keep track of time so you can pace yourself. Use any time left at the end to go back and review your answers. Make sure you've written the answer you meant to select.

WHICH ONE DO I USE?

When you need to write answers for a school assignment or write a research paper, you'll want to be careful to use words correctly. There are many examples in English of two words (or even three) that sound alike but that mean different things. Words that sound alike but have different meanings are called **homonyms**. It's important to use the right word so that anyone who reads what you've written can understand what you want to say. Here are a few of the most common homonyms.

Its/It's

Its is a possessive. That means that it shows ownership. For example:

Each room is decorated in its own color.

It's, on the other hand, is a contraction of *it is*. For example:

It's time to leave for school.

Affect/Effect

These two words are often confused. *Affect* is a verb that means *to change* or *to influence*. Here's an example:

Our picnic was affected by the rain.

Effect is a noun that means *result* or *impact*. For example:

What *effect* did the rain have on your picnic?

Principal/Principle

Here's another pair of words that often confuse people. *Principal* means *most important*. For example:

What are the *principal* products of France?

The head of a school is also usually called a *principal*.

A *principle*, on the other hand, is a standard or rule that people use to live by. Here's an example:

An important *principle* stated in the Declaration of Independence is that all men are created equal.

Compliment/Complement

Compliment and *complement* are two very different words. A compliment is a flattering remark:

He paid me a nice *compliment* about my new dress.

To *complement* something means to *complete* it or to *supply a needed portion* of it. Here's an example:

My partner's work on the research paper complemented my own efforts.

They're/There/Their

This time we have three words that sound the same but mean different things. *They're* is a contraction of *they are*:

They're coming to visit at noon.

There refers to a place and means the opposite of *here*.

Put the dishes over *there*.

Finally, the third form, *their*, is a possessive adjective and means *belonging to them*.

Where are *their* coats?

Capital/Capitol

This pair is a bit tricky. *Capital* means the city where a state or country has its government.

The *capital* of the United States is Washington, D.C.

Capitol, on the other hand, is the name for the building where members of the government meet.

The U.S. *Capitol* is the building where Congress meets in Washington, D.C.

Got that? The U.S. *Capitol* is in the *capital* city of Washington, D.C.

HOW TO WRITE A
RESEARCH PAPER

Doing Research

To start any research paper or project, the first thing to do is research.

▶ **Encyclopedias are a good place to start.** They can give you a good overview of the subject.

▶ **The electronic catalog** of your school or public library will probably be your main source for finding books and articles about your subject. A librarian can help show you how this works.

▶ You can also use **the Internet** as a research tool (see opposite page).

▶ As you read each source, **write down the facts and ideas** that you may need. Include the title and author for each source and the page numbers or the web site and address for the web page where you found the particular information.

Writing It Down

The next step is to organize your facts. **Develop a rough outline** of your ideas in the order in which they'll appear. Then, write a draft of your paper. It should contain three main parts:

INTRODUCTION The paper's introduction, or first paragraph, explains your topic and your point of view on it. It should draw readers into the paper and let them know what to expect.

BODY The body of the paper develops your ideas. Use specific facts, examples, and details to make your points clear and convincing. Use separate paragraphs for each new idea and use words and phrases that link one paragraph to the next so your ideas flow smoothly.

CONCLUSION Summarize your main points in the final paragraph, or conclusion.

Showing Your Sources

You may need to do a **bibliography** at the end of your paper. This is a list of all the sources you used to prepare the report. Here are some guidelines for how to cite commonly used types of sources.

FOR A BOOK: Author. *Title*. City Published: Publisher, Year.
> Fitzgerald, Stephanie. *Wind Power*. New York: Chelsea Clubhouse, 2010.

FOR A MAGAZINE ARTICLE: Author. "Article Title." *Magazine Title*, Date of Issue, Pages.
> Dunn, Robert R. "Dune Buggies." *Natural History*, September 2009, 38–39.

FOR ONLINE (INTERNET): Author. "Entry Title." *Book Title*. City Published: Publisher, Year. *Database Name*. Database Company. URL (date accessed).
> Longshore, David. "Hurricane Katrina." *Encyclopedia of Hurricanes, Typhoons, and Cyclones,* New ed. New York: Facts On File, Inc., 2008. *American History Online*. Facts On File, Inc. http://www.fofweb.com/activelink2.asp? ItemID=WE5 2&DataID=2&iPin=EAFP019&SingleRecord=True (accessed April 30, 2009).

RESEARCH ON THE INTERNET

Using Library Resources

Your school or public library is a great place to start. It probably has a list (catalog) of its books and of periodicals (newspapers and magazines) available from computers at the library, or even from home over the Internet through your library's web site. You can search using **keywords** (words that describe your subject) in three basic ways: by **author**, by **title**, or by **subject**.

For example, doing a subject search for "Benjamin Franklin" will give you a list of books and articles about him, along with their locations in the library.

Your library may also subscribe to online reference databases that companies create especially for research. These are accessible over the Internet and could contain almanacs, encyclopedias, reference books, other nonfiction books, or collections of articles. You can access these databases from the library, and maybe even from home from your library's web site.

When you write your report, don't copy directly from books, articles, or the Internet—that's **plagiarism**, a form of cheating. Keep track of all your **sources**—the books, articles, and web sites you use—and list them in a **bibliography**. (See page 110 for some examples.)

Why shouldn't I just search the Internet?

The library's list may look just like other information on the Internet. But these sources usually have been checked by experts. This is not true of all the information on the Internet. It could come from almost anybody, and it may not be trustworthy.

When can I use the Internet?

The Internet is still a great way to look things up. You can find addresses or recipes, listen to music, or find things to do. You can look up information on hobbies or musical instruments, or read a magazine or newspaper online.

If you search the Internet on your own, make sure the web site you find is reliable. A U.S. government site or a site produced by a well-known organization or publication is usually your best bet.

Using a Search Engine

The best way to find web sites is to use a search engine. Here are some helpful ones:

Yahoo Kids (kids.yahoo.com)
Kidsclick (www.kidsclick.org)

Start by typing one or two search terms—words that describe your topic. The search engine scans the Internet and gives you a list of sites that contain them. The results appear in a certain order, or **rank**. Search engines use different ways of measuring which web sites are likely to be the most helpful. One way is by counting how many times your search terms appear on each site. The site that's listed first may not have what you want. Explore as many of the sites as possible.

Inventions

When was the digital camera invented? → page 112

Invention TIME LINE

YEAR	INVENTION	INVENTOR (COUNTRY)
105	paper	Cai Lun (China)
1440s	printing press/movable type	Johann Gutenberg (Germany)
1590	2-lens microscope	Zacharias Janssen (Netherlands)
1608	telescope	Hans Lippershey (Netherlands)
1616	reflecting telescope	Niccolo Zucchi (Italy)
1714	mercury thermometer	Gabriel D. Fahrenheit (Germany)
1752	lightning rod	Benjamin Franklin (U.S.)
1783	parachute	Sebastien Lenormand (France)
1800	electric battery	Alessandro Volta (Italy)
1804	steam locomotive	Richard Trevithick (England) ▶
1837	telegraph	Samuel F. B. Morse (U.S.) , Charles Wheatstone & William F. Cooke (England)
1842	anesthesia (ether)	Crawford W. Long (U.S.)
1870s	telephone*	Antonio Meucci (Italy), Alexander G. Bell (U.S.)
1879	practical light bulb	Thomas A. Edison (U.S.)
1886	automobile (gasoline)	Karl Benz (Germany)
1892	moving picture viewer	Thomas A. Edison & William K. Dickson (U.S.)
1895	X-ray	Wilhelm Roentgen (Germany)
1897	diesel engine	Rudolf Diesel (Germany)
1902	air conditioning	Willis Carrier (U.S.)
1922	insulin	Frederick G. Banting & Charles Best (Canada)
1923	television**	Vladimir K. Zworykin (U.S.)
1926	liquid-fuel rocket engine	Robert H. Goddard (U.S.)
1928	tape recorder	Fritz Pfleumer (Germany)
1928	penicillin	Alexander Fleming (Scotland)
1933	FM radio	Edwin Armstrong (U.S.)
1938	Frisbee	Fred Morrison (U.S.)
1939	jet airplane	Hans von Ohain (Germany)
1942	electronic computer	John V. Atanasoff & Clifford Berry (U.S.)
1955	Velcro®	George de Mestral (Switzerland)
1957	digital image	Russell Kirsch (U.S.)
1957	laser***	Gordon Gould (U.S.)
1971	CAT scanner	Godfrey N. Hounsfield (England)
1973	personal computer	André Thi Truong (France)
1975	digital camera	Steven Sasson (U.S.) ▶
1989	World Wide Web	Tim Berners-Lee (England)
2007	iPhone	Apple (U.S.) ▶
2009	3D digital camera	Fujifilm (Japan)

* Meucci developed a type of telephone (early 1870s); Bell received a patent for a telephone in 1876.

** Others who helped invent the television in the 1920s were Philo T. Farnsworth and John Baird.

*** First working laser built in 1960 by Theodore Maiman.

CURRENT Inventions

AN ELECTRONICS REVOLUTION

If you could go back in time to the 1980s, you'd be amazed at what you saw. More exactly, at what you didn't see. Many of the ways people today play games, listen to music, watch TV and movies, communicate, study, and work didn't exist then. Or if they did, they existed only in simple, sometimes experimental forms. The use of electronics has grown at a fantastic pace since then, made possible by a slew of discoveries and inventions.

Inventors came up with new materials for electronic devices, improvements in old materials, new forms of wireless linkups, new ideas for using the Internet, and new ways of storing, displaying, and using information.

Actually, information was key to many of these developments. Information—whether words, or numbers, or pictures, or whatever—is represented by electronic signals. Scientists and engineers keep developing better and faster ways of processing such signals. More and more information can be handled by smaller and smaller devices.

Smaller but More POWERFUL

Because of this miniaturization trend, little pieces of equipment can now carry enormous computing power. Today's tiny digital cameras do many more things, and do them better, than the film cameras that everyone once used.

The same is true of cell phones. Cell phones were rare in the 1980s. Those that existed looked like bricks compared to today's small phones. Almost all mobile phones today take advantage of efficient digital technology. Many are "smart" phones that carry powerful computer chips and can do things—surf the Web, handle e-mail, show videos, play music, and run games, among dozens of other applications—unthinkable in a phone just 20 or 25 years ago.

▲ *Computer chips*

Thanks to advances in chips, people now enjoy such conveniences as robot vacuum cleaners, highly computerized cars, digital video recorders, digital televisions, electronic readers such as Amazon's Kindle, portable media players such as Apple's iPod, and laptop computers far more powerful than the biggest desktop machines of the 1980s.

did you Know?

Back in the 1960s, one of the founders of the computer chip company Intel made a bold prediction about the chip industry and the basic signal-handling components called transistors. He said chips would improve so fast that every couple of years the number of transistors they could accommodate would double. The man was Gordon E. Moore, and his prediction is now known as **Moore's law**. Early transistors were quite big. But they kept getting smaller. In the past couple of decades, chip designers have managed to keep pace with Moore's law, and this has paid off in a big way for electronic devices.

Gordon E. Moore

Language

How do you count to three in Chinese?➜ page 115

TOP LANGUAGES

More people speak some form (dialect) of Chinese than any other language in the world. Spanish ranks as the second most common native, or first, language. The table below and the map show the languages with at least 100 million native speakers.*

*2008 estimates

LANGUAGE	KEY PLACES WHERE SPOKEN	NATIVE SPEAKERS
Chinese	China, Taiwan	1,213 million
Spanish	Latin America, Spain	329 million
English	U.S., Canada, Britain, Australia	328 million
Arabic	Middle East, North Africa	221 million
Hindi	India	182 million
Bengali	Bangladesh, India	181 million
Portuguese	Portugal, Brazil	178 million
Russian	Russia	144 million
Japanese	Japan	122 million

Which LANGUAGES Are SPOKEN in the UNITED STATES?

Most Americans speak English at home. But since the beginning of American history, immigrants have come to the U.S. from all over the world. Many have brought other languages with them.

"¡Hola!" That's how more than 34 million Spanish-speaking Americans say "hi" at home.

The table at the right lists the most frequently spoken languages in the U.S., according to a 2008 Census Bureau report.

LANGUAGE USED AT HOME	SPEAKERS 5 YEARS AND OLDER
1 Speak only English	227,365,509
2 Spanish, Spanish Creole	34,559,894
3 Chinese	2,465,761
4 Tagalog (Philippines)	1,488,385
5 French	1,332,633
6 Vietnamese	1,225,036
7 German	1,122,014
8 Korean	1,051,641
9 Russian	864,069
10 Arabic	786,210
11 Italian	782,097
12 African languages	742,375
13 Other Asian languages	705,199
14 Portuguese, Portuguese Creole	661,437
15 Other Indic languages	652,929
16 French Creole	646,109
17 Polish	619,567
18 Hindi	560,112
19 Japanese	439,883
20 Other Indo-European languages	446,682

LANGUAGE EXPRESS

Ciao!
(Italian)

Hello!
(English)

Konnichiwa!
(Japanese)

Surprise your friends and family with words from other languages.

English	Italian	French	German	Chinese
January	gennaio	janvier	Januar	yi-yue
February	febbraio	février	Februar	er-yue
March	marzo	mars	Marz	san-yue
April	aprile	avril	April	si-yue
May	maggio	mai	Mai	wu-yue
June	giugno	juin	Juni	liu-yue
July	luglio	juillet	Juli	qi-yue
August	agosto	août	August	ba-yue
September	settembre	septembre	September	jiu-yue
October	ottobre	octobre	Oktober	shi-yue
November	novembre	novembre	November	shi-yi-yue
December	dicembre	decembre	Dezember	shi-er-yue
blue	azzurro	bleu	blau	lan
red	rosso	rouge	rot	hong
green	verde	vert	grün	lu
yellow	giallo	jaune	gelb	huang
black	nero	noir	schwarz	hei
white	bianco	blanc	weiss	bai
Happy birthday!	Buon compleanno!	Joyeux anniversaire!	Glückwunsch zum Geburtstag!	Sheng-ri kuai le!
Hello!	Ciao!	Bonjour!	Hallo!	Ni hao!
Good-bye!	Arrivederci!	Au revoir!	Auf Wiedersehen!	Zai-jian!
fish	pesci	poisson	Fisch	yu
bird	uccello	oiseau	Vogel	niao
horse	cavallo	cheval	Pferd	ma
one	uno	un	eins	yi
two	due	deux	zwei	er
three	tre	trois	drei	san
four	quattro	quatre	vier	si
five	cinque	cinq	fünf	wu

did you Know?

The longest word in the English language that contains only one vowel is: Strengths.

The only two common words in the English language that end in "gry" are: Angry and hungry.

Two words in the English language that have no true rhymes are: Orange and silver.

¡SAY IT EN ESPAÑOL!

After English, Spanish is the most commonly spoken language in the U.S. More than 34 million people speak Spanish at home. That's more than 10 percent of all people in the U.S.

Pronouncing Spanish Words

In Spanish, the vowels only make one type of sound. The sound each vowel makes in Spanish is the same sound it makes in the English words at right.

Also, if you see the letters *j*, *g*, or *x* followed by a vowel, pronounce them like the English *h*. So, *frijoles* (beans) sounds like free-HOLE-lehs. *México* sounds like MAY-hee-co. The *h* in Spanish is always silent. So *hermano* (brother) sounds like er-MAN-o.

A	w**a**ter
E	b**e**t
I	f**ee**t
O	sl**ow**
U	t**u**be

Try pronouncing the Spanish on this page.

Sister Languages

There are some words that sound alike in both Spanish and English. These are called cognates. See if you can guess each kid's answer to the question:

What do you want to be when you grow up?

Julio	Yo quiero ser *músico*.
Maria	Un dia, yo quisiera ser *autora*.
Juan	Yo quiero ser *banquero*.
Olivia	Un dia, yo quisiera ser *arquitecta*.
Andrés	Yo quiero ser *piloto*.

Answers: Julio—musician; Maria—author; Juan—banker; Olivia—architect; Andrés—pilot.

Basic Spanish Phrases

Hello	Hola
Good-bye	Adiós
How are you?	¿Cómo estás?
Please	Por favor
Thank you	Gracias
What is your name?	¿Cómo te llamas?

Food Next time you're having dinner, ask your father to pass the *jugo*.

Salad **Ensalada**

Juice **Jugo**

Shrimp **Camarones**

Rice **Arroz**

Chicken **Pollo**

Paella Traditional Rice Dish

Your Body
Es Su Cuerpo

Use your *boca* to say these parts of the body (*cuerpo*). Use your *cabeza* to remember how to say them!

Head	Cabeza
Ears	Orejas
Eyes	Ojos
Hair	Cabello

Face	Cara
Mouth	Boca
Neck	Cuello

| Arm | Brazo |
| Hand | Mano |

| Belly | Barriga |

| Leg | Pierna |
| Knee | Rodilla |

| Foot | Pie |

Numbers

1	uno	6	seis
2	dos	7	siete
3	tres	8	ocho
4	cuatro	9	nueve
5	cinco	10	diez

Joke en Español

Patient: *Doctor, doctor, no puedo recordar nada.*
(Doctor, doctor, I can't remember anything.)

Doctor: *Vaya, y desde cuando tiene usted este problema?*
(Wow, and how long have you had this problem?)

Patient: *¿Qué problema?* (What problem?)

117

THE ENGLISH LANGUAGE

Facts About English

- According to the *Oxford English Dictionary*, the English language contains between 250,000 and 750,000 words. (Some people count different meanings of the same word as separate words and include all obscure technical terms.)

- The most frequently used letters of the alphabet are *e, t, a,* and *o,* in that order.

- The 30 most common words in the English language are: *the, of, and, a, to, in, is, that, it, was, he, for, as, on, with, his, be, at, you, I, are, this, by, from, had, have, they, not, or, one.*

New Words

English is always changing as new words are born and old ones die out. Many new words come from the fields of electronics and computers, from the media, or from slang.

cardioprotective: serving to protect the heart

frenemy: one who pretends to be a friend but is in fact an enemy

locavore: one who eats foods grown locally whenever possible

ollie: a skateboarding or snowboarding maneuver in which the board rises off the ground

staycation: a vacation spent at home or nearby

vlog: a blog that contains video material

In Other Words: SIMILES

Similes are comparisons of two dissimilar things that use "as" or "like." Here are some to wrap your brain around:

fast as lightning = "moves quickly." Lightning travels speedily through the sky, in the same way that a person might act in a rapid way.

graceful as a swan = "smooth and elegant." Swans are admired for their long necks and the way they quietly glide through the water. Ballerinas are often compared to swans, with their extended, smooth movements on the stage.

strong as an ox = "stronger than most people." Oxen are cattle that are trained to pull very heavy loads.

GETTING TO THE ROOT

Many English words and parts of words can be traced back to Latin or Greek. If you know the meaning of parts of a word, you can probably guess what it means. A root (also called a stem) is the part of the word that gives its basic meaning but can't be used by itself. Roots need other word parts to complete them: either a prefix at the beginning, or a suffix at the end, or sometimes both. The following tables give some examples of Latin and Greek roots, prefixes, and suffixes.

LATIN

root	basic meaning	example
-alt-	high	altitude
-dict-	to say	dictate
-port-	to carry	transport
-scrib-/ -script-	to write	prescription
-vert-	turn	invert

prefix	basic meaning	example
de-	away, off	defrost
in-/im-	not	invisible
non-	not	nontoxic
pre-	before	prehistoric
re-	again, back	rewrite
trans-	across, through	transatlantic

suffix	basic meaning	example
-ation	(makes verbs into nouns)	invitation
-fy/-ify	make or cause to become	horrify
-ly	like, to the extent of	highly
-ment	(makes verbs into nouns)	government
-ty/-ity	state of	purity

GREEK

root	basic meaning	example
-anthrop-	human	anthropology
-bio-	life	biology
-dem-	people	democracy
-phon-	sound	telephone
-psych-	soul	psychology

prefix	basic meaning	example
anti-/ant-	against	antisocial
auto-	self	autopilot
biblio-/ bibl-	book	bibliography
micro-	small	microscope
tele-	far off	television

suffix	basic meaning	example
-graph	write, draw, describe, record	photograph
-ism	act, state, theory of	realism
-ist	one who believes in, practices	capitalist
-logue/ -log	speech, to speak	dialogue
-scope	see	telescope

Military

Who founded the Coast Guard? → page 123

American Revolution

George Washington

Why? The British king sought to control American trade and tax the 13 colonies without their consent. The colonies wanted independence from Great Britain.

Who? British vs. Americans with French support

When? 1775–1783

Result? The colonies gained independence.

War of 1812

Why? Britain interfered with American commerce and forced American sailors to join the British navy.

Who? Britain vs. United States

When? 1812–1814

Battle of Lake Erie

Result? There was no clear winner. The U.S. unsuccessfully invaded Canada, a British colony. The British burned Washington, D.C., and the White House but were defeated in other battles.

Mexican War

Why? The U.S. annexed Texas. It also sought control of California, a Mexican province.

Who? Mexico vs. United States

When? 1846–1848

Result? Mexico gave up its claim to Texas and ceded to the U.S. California and all or part of six other Western states.

Civil War

Why? Eleven Southern states seceded from the U.S. The U.S. fought to keep them.

Who? Confederacy vs. Union

When? 1861–1865

Civil War soldier

Result? The United States remained a unified country. Slavery was abolished.

Spanish-American War

Why? The Americans supported Cuban independence from Spain.

Who? United States vs. Spain

When? 1898

Result? Spain handed the Philippines, Guam, and Puerto Rico over to the U.S. Cuba became independent.

The wreck of the U.S.S. Maine

did you Know? In 1814, First Lady Dolley Madison fled the White House just hours before the British arrived. She had been preparing a large dinner party, and she left the food on the table. So the British feasted—and then set fire to the White House.

did you Know? The U.S. battleship Maine exploded in Havana harbor on January 25, 1898, when a mine was set off underneath the ship. The cry "Remember the Maine!" helped fuel the war fever in the U.S.

World War I

Why? Colonial and military competition between European powers.

Who? Allies (including the U.S., Britain, France, Russia, Italy, and Japan) vs. Central Powers (including Germany, Austria-Hungary, and Turkey)

When? 1914–1918 (U.S. entered in 1917)

Result? The Allies defeated the Central Powers. An estimated 8 million soldiers and close to 10 million civilians were killed.

World War II

U.S. troops land in France on D-Day, June 6, 1944

Why? The Axis sought world domination.

Who? Axis (including Germany, Italy, and Japan) vs. Allies (including the U.S., Britain, France, and the Soviet Union). The U.S. did not enter the war until Japan attacked Pearl Harbor in 1941.

When? 1939–1945 (U.S. dropped atomic bombs on Hiroshima and Nagasaki in August 1945.)

Result? The Allies defeated the Axis. The Holocaust (the Nazi effort to wipe out the Jews and other minorities) was stopped. The U.S. helped rebuild Western Europe and Japan. The Soviet Union set up Communist governments in Eastern Europe.

did you know? *After the war ended, many German leaders were tried for war crimes and crimes against humanity.*

Korean War

Why? North Korea invaded South Korea. In many ways, the conflict was part of the Cold War between the Communist and non-Communist nations.

Who? North Korea with support from China and the Soviet Union vs. South Korea backed by the United States and its allies

When? 1950–1953

Result? The war ended in a stalemate. Korea remains divided.

did you know? *The U.S. still has about 28,000 troops stationed in South Korea.*

Vietnam War

Why? Communists (Viet Cong) backed by North Vietnam attempted to overthrow South Vietnam's government.

Who? North Vietnam with support from the Soviet Union and China vs. South Vietnam with support from the U.S. and its allies

When? 1959–1975

Result? The U.S. withdrew its troops in 1973. In 1975, South Vietnam surrendered. Vietnam became a unified Communist country.

Persian Gulf War

Why? Iraq invaded and annexed Kuwait. It refused to withdraw despite United Nations demands.

Who? Iraq vs. U.S.-led coalition

When? 1991

Result? The coalition drove out Iraqi forces from Kuwait.

A-10A Thunderbolt II ground attack plane flying during the Persian Gulf War, 1991

Where Are We Now?

Afghanistan War

Why? The U.S. demanded that Afghanistan's Taliban regime turn over Osama bin Laden, the man who planned the 9/11 terrorist attacks in 2001. The Taliban claimed not to know bin Laden's whereabouts.

Who? Taliban vs. Afghani forces, supported by the U.S. and its allies.

When? 2001–

Result? The Taliban was driven from power but in recent years regained control over large parts of the country. In response, President Barack Obama increased U.S. troop strength to nearly 100,000 by mid-2010.

did you Know? MRAPs (mine-resistant ambush-protected vehicles) are heavily armored tanks that protect soldiers from roadside bombs, which are responsible for most of the U.S. and allied military casualties in both Afghanistan and Iraq.

Iraq War

Why? The U.S. accused Iraq of hiding weapons of mass destruction (WMDs) and supporting terrorists.

Who? Iraq vs. United States, Great Britain, and their allies

When? 2003–

Result? Saddam Hussein's government was toppled. Hussein was captured, put on trial, and hanged. No WMDs were found. The U.S. has begun withdrawing its troops and hopes to have all combat forces out of Iraq in 2010.

TOP ⑩ NATIONS WITH LARGEST ARMED FORCES*

1.	China	2,185,000	6.	South Korea	687,000
2.	United States	1,540,000	7.	Pakistan	617,000
3.	India	1,281,000	8.	Iraq	577,000
4.	North Korea	1,106,000	9.	Iran	523,000
5.	Russia	1,027,000	10.	Turkey	511,000

*Figures are for 2009. Source: The Military Balance/International Institute for Strategic Studies

All About ⟩⟩ SERVICE ACADEMIES

The United States has five service academies to train officers for the U.S. armed services. They are the U.S. Merchant Marine Academy (Kings Point, NY); the U.S. Military Academy (West Point, NY); the U.S. Naval Academy (Annapolis, MD); the U.S. Coast Guard Academy (New London, CT); and the U.S. Air Force Academy (Colorado Springs, CO). Students at all of the academies earn a college degree when they finish their training. After they graduate, they must serve in the military.

West Point is the oldest of the academies. It was founded in 1802. The Continental Army had built a fort on the spot in 1778, during the American Revolution. West Point, like all the other academies, accepted only men for much of its history, but in 1976 all the service academies started accepting women.

Annapolis was founded in 1845. During the Civil War, most of its students served in either the Confederate or the Union armed forces, and the school itself moved for a time to Newport, Rhode Island. The famous Navy song "Anchors Aweigh" was written by the leader of the school's band and dedicated to the class of 1907.

The Coast Guard was founded by Alexander Hamilton in 1790. Its job is to protect the U.S. coast from invasion, to protect the environment, and to maintain the nation's waterways. It can stop ships that are bringing illegal drugs or undocumented immigrants into the country. Students at the **Coast Guard Academy**, which opened in 1876, study how to handle a ship, as well as science, math, and engineering.

The **Merchant Marine Academy**, which opened in 1943, trains people to operate ships that transport both passengers and cargo in peacetime. When the country is at war, merchant marine ships transport cargo and supplies to troops serving overseas.

The youngest academy is the **Air Force Academy**, which opened in 1954. Enrollment grew quickly after the Vietnam War, in which the Air Force played a major role. Students learn to be pilots, receive all kinds of military training, and study academic subjects.

IT'S NOT JUST ABOUT FIGHTING WARS

Members of the U.S. armed forces do a lot more than fight wars. They play a big role in disaster relief. For example, after the terrible earthquake in Haiti in January 2010, the U.S. military took control of the country's main airport; brought in tons of food, water, and medical supplies; and ferried in disaster relief teams that looked for survivors and helped them to get to hospitals and relief centers (see photo at right).

Armed forces units also led the relief efforts after Hurricane Katrina destroyed much of the city of New Orleans and caused major damage along the Gulf Coast in 2005. Military units were in the same area in 2010, helping in the clean-up after an offshore oil rig exploded and large amounts of oil leaked into the Gulf of Mexico.

Money

How much is $1 worth in Japan? → page 127

World's Ten Richest People*

Name	Age	Country	Industry	Worth (in billions)
Carlos Slim Helú	70	Mexico	Communications	$53.5
Bill Gates	54	United States	Software (Microsoft)	53.0
Warren Buffett	79	United States	Investments	47.0
Mukesh Ambani	52	India	Manufacturing – Oil	29.0
Lakshmi Mittal	59	United Kingdom	Manufacturing – Steel	28.7
Lawrence Ellison	65	United States	Data Management – Oracle	28.0
Bernard Arnault	61	France	Luxury goods – LVMH	27.5
Eike Batista	53	Brazil	Mining, oil	27.0
Amancio Ortega	74	Spain	Fashion	25.0
Karl Albrecht	90	Germany	Retail – Aldi	23.5

*As of March 2010 (Source: www.forbes.com)

World's Youngest Billionaires*

Name	Age	Country	Industry	Worth (in billions)
Sergey Brin	35	United States	Technology – Google	$12
Larry Page	36	United States	Technology – Google	12
Sheikh Mansour Bin Zayed Al Nahayan	39	Abu Dhabi	Family, Investments	4.9
John Arnold	35	United States	Hedge Fund Manager	2.7
Prince Albert von Thurn und Taxis	25	Germany	Diversified Investments	2.1
Kenneth Griffin	40	United States	Hedge Fund Manager	1.5
Chu Lam Yiu	39	China	Industrialist	1.5
William Ding	38	China	Industrialist	1.1
Jerry Yang	40	United States	Technology – Yahoo	1.1
Andrey Melnichenko	37	Russia	Industrialist	1.0

*As of March 2010 (Source: www.forbes.com)

New gold-colored dollar coins honoring the nation's presidents are now being circulated. The U.S. Mint is making one-dollar coins that show the faces of the presidents. The coins are being released in the order in which the presidents served in office. The Mint plans to issue four presidential $1 coins per year through 2016.

The George Washington dollar coin was the first. It was released on February 15, 2007. Coins with Presidents John Adams, Thomas Jefferson, and James Madison were also released in 2007. In 2008, the coins honored Presidents James Monroe, John Quincy Adams, Andrew Jackson, and Martin Van Buren.

Tails

The coins released in 2009 featured William Henry Harrison, John Tyler, James K. Polk, and Zachary Taylor. The 2010 coins portrayed Millard Fillmore, Franklin Pierce, James Buchanan, and Abraham Lincoln.

In addition to new presidential dollars, the U.S. Mint introduced a new design for the back of the Lincoln penny in 2010. This new design shows the Union shield. It has 13 vertical strips and has a horizontal bar going across the top that contains the words "E pluribus unum" ("out of many, one"). The stripes represent the 13 original colonies, and the horizontal bar symbolizes their union into one country. The design also has a scroll (going across the shield) with the words "one cent" on it, and the words "United States of America" appear above the shield.

The U.S. Mint also released the first of its new national park quarters in 2010. The first quarters honor Yellowstone National Park, Hot Springs National Park, Yosemite National Park, Grand Canyon National Park, and Mount Hood National Park.

For more information on all these coins, visit the U.S. Mint's website at
www.usmint.gov

The U.S. $1 Bill: AN OWNER'S MANUAL

Everybody knows that George Washington is on the U.S. one-dollar bill, but did you ever wonder what all that other stuff is?

Plate position
Shows where on the 32-note plate this bill was printed.

The Treasury Department seal: The balancing scales represent justice. The pointed stripe across the middle has 13 stars for the original 13 colonies. The key represents authority.

Plate serial number
Shows which printing plate was used for the face of the bill.

Serial number
Each bill has its own.

Federal Reserve District Number
Shows which district issued the bill.

Secretary of the Treasury signature

Treasurer of the U.S. Signature

Series indicator (year note's design was first used)

(Since 1949, every Treasurer of the U.S. has been a woman.)

Federal Reserve District Seal
The name of the Federal Reserve Bank that issued the bill is printed in the seal. The letter tells you quickly where the bill is from. Here are the letter codes for the 12 Federal Reserve Districts:

A: Boston	**G:** Chicago
B: New York	**H:** St. Louis
C: Philadelphia	**I:** Minneapolis
D: Cleveland	**J:** Kansas City
E: Richmond	**K:** Dallas
F: Atlanta	**L:** San Francisco

Front of the Great Seal of the United States: The bald eagle is the national bird. The shield has 13 stripes for the 13 original colonies. The eagle holds 13 arrows (symbol of war) and an olive branch (symbol of peace). Above the eagle is the motto "E Pluribus Unum," Latin for "out of many, one," and a constellation of 13 stars.

Plate serial number
Shows which plate was used for the back.

Back of the Great Seal of the United States:
The pyramid symbolizes something that lasts for ages. It is unfinished because the U.S. is always growing. The eye, known as the "Eye of Providence," probably comes from an ancient Egyptian symbol. The pyramid has 13 levels; at its base are the Roman numerals for 1776, the year of American independence. "Annuit Coeptis" is Latin for "God has favored our undertaking." "Novus Ordo Seclorum" is Latin for "a new order of the ages." Both phrases are from the works of the Roman poet Virgil.

WORLD CURRENCY

Most countries have their own currency. Sometimes two countries call their currency by the same name, but the money usually has different designs and may have different values. Most currency is decorated with cultural symbols and pictures of important people in the country's history. The designs are colorful and interesting, and they also make it harder to counterfeit the money.

An exchange rate is the price of a country's currency in terms of another. For example, one U.S. dollar cost, or could buy, 6.83 yuan in China in March 2010. These rates are based on a country's economy, the value of products it makes and buys, and inflation, the increase in how much money is needed to buy goods.

When people want to buy goods or services from someone in another country, they need to exchange their money for, or buy, some of the other country's currency.

THE EURO

For most of their histories, countries in Europe, like countries around the world, all had their own currencies. France, for example, used the franc. Germany's currency was called the mark, and Italy's was called the lira. Because Europe is so small and because many European countries wanted to make it easier for companies in one country to do business with companies in other countries, an organization was formed to find ways to eliminate barriers to trade. This organization, now called the European Union (EU), decided, among other things, to create one currency that could be used by many countries.

The euro, whose symbol is €, became the official currency of 12 EU members on January 1, 2002. Today, it is used by 16 EU countries, called the Eurozone: Austria, Belgium, Cyprus, Finland, France, Germany, Greece, Ireland, Italy, Luxembourg, Malta, the Netherlands, Portugal, Slovakia, Slovenia, and Spain. The euro is also now used by agreement in six other countries as well.

HOW MUCH IS A DOLLAR WORTH?

In March 2010, here is about how much one dollar could buy of 12 other currencies:

0.67	British pounds		92.68	Japanese yen
1.02	Canadian dollars		12.49	Mexican pesos
6.83	Chinese yuan		29.52	Russian rubles
0.75	euros		3.75	Saudi Arabian riyals
45.40	Indian rupees		1,142.45	South Korean won
3.73	Israeli new shekels		1.54	Turkish lira

Movies & TV

Which actor will be playing the Green Lantern in 2011? → page 129

MOVIE & TV FACTS

A Good Run Before *The Simpsons*, *The Flintstones* held the record for TV's longest running prime-time animated series. The cartoon, about two Stone Age families, lasted six seasons, from 1960 to 1966. *The Simpsons*, which has been on air since 1989, will begin its 22nd season in late 2010.

Giving Credit *The Lord of the Rings: The Return of the King* (2003) has one of the longest closing credits of any movie. Hundreds of people, including a horse makeup artist, are listed in the credits, which last for nearly 10 minutes.

New Record *Avatar* broke records in 2010, claiming the top spot as the highest-grossing film of all time. It was a bittersweet victory for director James Cameron—the record had previously been held by his 1997 film *Titanic*.

Avatar ▼

ALL-TIME TOP ANIMATED MOVIES*			ALL-TIME TOP MOVIES*		
1	*Shrek 2* (2004)	$436.7	1	*Star Wars* (1977)	$461.0
2	*Finding Nemo* (2003)	339.7	2	*Shrek 2* (2004)	436.7
3	*Shrek the Third* (2007)	322.7	3	*E.T. the Extra-Terrestrial* (1982)	435.0
4	*The Lion King* (1994)	312.9	4	*Star Wars: Episode I— The Phantom Menace* (1999)	431.1
5	*Up* (2009)	293.0	5	*Finding Nemo* (2003)	339.7
6	*Shrek* (2001)	267.7	6	*Alice in Wonderland* (2010)	331.1
7	*The Incredibles* (2004)	261.4	7	*Shrek the Third* (2007)	322.7
8	*Monsters, Inc.* (2001)	255.9	8	*Harry Potter and the Sorcerer's Stone* (2001)	317.6
9	*Toy Story 2* (1999)	245.9	9	*The Lion King* (1994)	312.9
10	*Cars* (2006)	244.1	10	*Star Wars: Episode II—Attack of the Clones* (2002)	310.7

Source: © 2010 by Rentrak Corporation. Rankings are for movies rated G or PG. *Avatar* is not included because it was rated PG-13.
*Through May 2010. Gross in millions of dollars based on box office sales in the U.S. and Canada.

TOP TV SHOWS IN 2009–10

AGES 6–11

NETWORK
1. *American Idol,* Tuesday
2. *American Idol,* Wednesday
3. *FOX NFL Sunday*
4. *CBS NFL Sunday*
5. *Survivor: Samoa*

CABLE
1. *iCarly Movie: iQuit iCarly*
2. *SpongeBob Squarepants: Truth or Square*
3. *Good Luck Charlie*
4. *Meet the Robinsons*
5. *iCarly Movie: iFight Shelby Marx*

▲ *American Idol*

AGES 12–17

NETWORK
1. *American Idol,* Tuesday
2. *American Idol,* Wednesday
3. *FOX NFL Sunday*
4. *Family Guy*
5. *CBS NFL Sunday*

CABLE
1. *iCarly Movie: iQuit iCarly*
2. *Starstruck*
3. *NFL on ESPN*
4. *Make It or Break It*
5. *High School Musical 3*

Source: The Nielsen Group; September 21, 2009, to April 18, 2010

did you Know?

The year 2010 was an important one for women filmmakers. Until 2010, only three women had ever been nominated for an Academy Award in the Best Director category. None of them had won. Kathryn Bigelow broke the streak when she was given the award for directing The Hurt Locker. In an odd twist of fate, her ex-husband, James Cameron, had been nominated in the same category—for directing Avatar.

HITTING THEATERS

IN THE SECOND HALF OF 2010

▶ Fans of the Step Up movies will be putting on glasses for *Step Up 3-D,* the third movie in the dance-filled series. (August)

▶ Two wolves, voiced by Hayden Panettiere and Justin Long, form an unlikely friendship in *Alpha and Omega.* (October)

▶ *Harry Potter and the Deathly Hallows: Part I* brings the Hogwarts crew together for the seventh movie in the beloved series. (November)

▶ *Tangled,* an animated update of the Rapunzel story, features the voices of Mandy Moore and Zachary Levi. (November)

▶ Lucy and Edmund Pevensie return to Narnia in *The Chronicles of Narnia: The Voyage of the Dawn Treader.* (December)

...AND IN 2011

▶ Johnny Depp returns as Captain Jack Sparrow in *Pirates of the Caribbean: On Stranger Tides,* due in May. ▼

▶ Ryan Reynolds suits up for *Green Lantern,* coming in June.

▶ The final installment in the Harry Potter series, *Harry Potter and the Deathly Hallows: Part II,* hits theaters in July.

▶ Stars Robert Pattinson and Kristen Stewart will be reunited for the fourth movie in the Twilight series, *Breaking Dawn,* due in November.

BOOKS TO FILM

Movie: *Alice in Wonderland* (2010)
Books: *Alice's Adventures in Wonderland* (1865); *Through the Looking-Glass and What Alice Found There* (1871) by Lewis Carroll

Movie adaptations of *Alice* usually take bits and pieces from two of Lewis Carroll's books. The most recent *Alice in Wonderland*, released in 2010, was directed by Tim Burton and starred Johnny Depp as the Mad Hatter. The movie was shown in 3-D, and it wowed audiences with its bright colors and unusual-looking characters.

Fans of Lewis Carroll's books could spot many places where the story had been changed for the movie. Alice is a child in the books, but in the movie she is 19 years old and trying to avoid getting married. Instead of Wonderland, the magical world is called Underland. Moviegoers were not bothered by the changes—*Alice in Wonderland* was a huge hit.

Movie: *Where the Wild Things Are* (2009)
Book: *Where the Wild Things Are* (1963) by Maurice Sendak

Many people wondered how director Spike Jonze would bring Maurice Sendak's beloved book to the screen. *Where the Wild Things Are* was published in 1963 and has fans of all ages all over the world—but the book is only ten sentences long, made up of mostly wordless illustrations. How could it be made into a full-length movie?

Several filmmakers attempted to make an animated movie, but the concept never quite worked. Jonze worked with author Dave Eggers on a screenplay, and Jonze took advice from Maurice Sendak throughout the process. The film followed the original story of a young boy named Max and a group of "wild things," but the movie added many more details. It used a combination of human actors and puppets created by Jim Henson's Creature Shop, and it was well-received by fans and critics. Maurice Sendak was thrilled with the final product, saying "I've never seen a movie that looked or felt like this."

WHERE THE WILD THINGS ARE

STORY AND PICTURES BY MAURICE SENDAK

Movie: *Harry Potter and the Deathly Hallows* (2010 and 2011)
Book: *Harry Potter and the Deathly Hallows* (2007)

Each of the books in the tremendously popular Harry Potter series by J. K. Rowling has been or will be made into a movie. The seventh book, more than 700 pages long, has been split into two films. All of the movies have also been very popular.

Harry Potter Retrospective

1 *Harry Potter and the Sorcerer's Stone* (book: 1997; movie: 2001)

2 *Harry Potter and the Chamber of Secrets* (book: 1998; movie: 2002)

3 *Harry Potter and the Prisoner of Azkaban* (book: 1999; movie: 2004)

4 *Harry Potter and the Goblet of Fire* (book: 2000; movie: 2005)

5 *Harry Potter and the Order of the Phoenix* (book: 2003; movie: 2007)

6 *Harry Potter and the Half-Blood Prince* (book: 2005; movie: 2009)

7 *Harry Potter and the Deathly Hallows* (book: 2007; movies: 2010 and 2011)

Harry Potter and the Deathly Hallows: Part I

Movie: *Eclipse* (2010)
Book: *Eclipse* (2007)

Stephenie Meyer is the author of four books, known as the Twilight series, about Bella Swan, a girl who falls in love with a vampire named Edward Cullen. Like the Harry Potter books, each of Meyer's Twilight books has been or will be made into a movie. Fans of the books can easily spot changes made for the films, but for the most part, the movies follow the book plots closely.

The Twilight Series

1 *Twilight* (book: 2005; movie: 2008)

2 *New Moon* (book: 2006; movie: 2009)

3 *Eclipse* (book: 2007; movie: 2010)

4 *Breaking Dawn* (book: 2008; movie: 2011)

Eclipse

MOVIES & TV SCRAMBLE

Unscramble these words to find the name of a movie or TV show.

yCaril

gnFiidn eNom

scEiple

cmreAina odll

rSat rsaW

ielcA ni doanedWrnl

tvAaar

heT smipSsno

myFial uyG

enlagTd

ANSWERS ON PAGES 334–336

Music & Dance

What are pointe shoes? → page 135

TOP ALBUMS OF 2009

1. *Fearless* . . . . Taylor Swift
2. *I am...Sasha Fierce* . . . . Beyoncé ▶
3. *Dark Horse.* . . . . Nickelback
4. *Twilight* . . . . Soundtrack
5. *Hannah Montana: The Movie* . . . Soundtrack
6. *Circus* . . . . Britney Spears
7. *808s & Heartbreak* . . . . Kanye West
8. *The Fame* . . . . Lady Gaga
9. *Relapse* . . . . Eminem
10. *The E.N.D.* . . . . The Black Eyed Peas

Source: *Billboard 200*/The Nielsen Company

All About ≫ American Idol

American Idol is a popular television reality competition show. The program's goal is to discover the best singer in the country. Auditions are held in various cities across the United States. The show's judges select a group of semifinalists who sing each week on the program. The judges offer comments after each performance. Then the viewing public votes by phone or text message to decide who advances or who goes home. The results are announced the following night. Eventually, only two finalists are left to compete for the title of American Idol. In 2010, the winner was **Lee DeWyze**. Winners from previous seasons are Kelly Clarkson, Ruben Studdard, Fantasia Barrino, Carrie Underwood, Taylor Hicks, Jordin Sparks, David Cook, and Kris Allen. Many of the runners-up and other contestants have gone on to successful musical and acting careers, including Adam

TAYLOR SWIFT

Born: December 13, 1989, in Wyomissing, Pennsylvania

Albums: *Taylor Swift* (2006), *Fearless* (2008)

Country-pop singer Taylor Swift grew up in Pennsylvania. She was drawn to performing from a very young age. When she was 11, she sang "The Star-Spangled Banner" before a Philadelphia 76ers basketball game. Two years later, Taylor's family moved to Nashville, Tennessee, where she was quickly signed to a record deal. She insisted on singing songs she had written herself. Her first album, *Taylor Swift*, was released when she was just 16 years old. The album featured five hit singles, including "Our Song," and earned Taylor a Grammy nomination for Best New Artist. Taylor's second album, *Fearless*, was released two years later. It was an even bigger success than her first, earning Taylor eight more Grammy nominations—and four Grammy wins. While Taylor was accepting an MTV Video Music award for Best Female Video ("You Belong with Me") in September 2009, Kanye West came to the stage and took the microphone from her. He told the audience that Beyoncé should have received the award. The crowd booed him, and a stunned Taylor did not finish her speech. The incident did not hold her back—at the end of the year, it was announced that *Fearless* was the Billboard 200 best-selling album of 2009. Taylor made her feature-film acting debut at the beginning of 2010 in *Valentine's Day* and planned to release a third album by the end of the year.

USHER

Born: October 14, 1978, in Dallas, Texas

Albums: *Usher* (1994), *My Way* (1997), *8701* (2001), *Confessions* (2004), *Here I Stand* (2008), *Raymond v. Raymond* (2010)

Usher Raymond IV spent his early childhood in Chattanooga, Tennessee, where he loved to sing in the church choir. His family moved to Atlanta, Georgia, where he would have more career opportunities. At age 13, Usher competed on the television talent show *Star Search*, and he was signed to a record deal. His first album, *Usher*, featured several songs that were produced by Sean "P. Diddy" Combs. His second album, *My Way*, made Usher a household name with hits including "You Make Me Wanna." It also earned him his first Grammy nomination. Over the next few years, he would win many awards, and he also took on several acting roles. In 2004, he had a string of hits from his album *Confessions*, which would go on to sell more than 20 million copies. Usher also works as a producer, and he owns his own record label. In 2009, he began introducing a promising new talent—Justin Bieber—to the world. Usher's own career shows no signs of slowing down. His sixth studio album, *Raymond v. Raymond*, was released in 2010.

MUSICAL INSTRUMENTS

There are many kinds of musical instruments. Instruments in an orchestra are divided into four groups, or sections: string, woodwind, brass, and percussion.

PERCUSSION INSTRUMENTS Percussion instruments make sounds when they are struck. They include drums, cymbals, triangles, gongs, bells, and xylophones. Keyboard instruments, like the piano, are sometimes included in percussion instruments.

BRASSES Brass instruments are hollow inside. They make sounds when air is blown into a mouthpiece. The trumpet, French horn, trombone, and tuba are brasses.

WOODWINDS Woodwinds are cylindrical and hollow inside. They make sounds when air is blown into them. The clarinet, flute, oboe, bassoon, and piccolo are woodwinds.

STRINGS Stringed instruments make sounds when the strings are either stroked with a bow or plucked with the fingers. The violin, viola, cello, bass, and harp are used in an orchestra. The guitar, banjo, and mandolin are other stringed instruments.

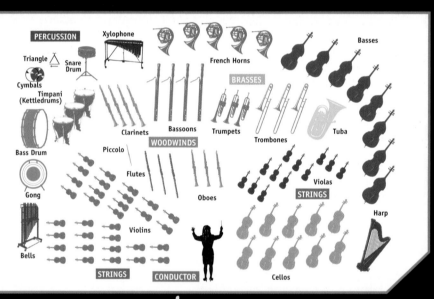

Unusual MUSICAL INSTRUMENTS

◄ The Aeolian Wind Harp, also called a harmonic harp, is an ancient musical instrument that is played by the wind. It dates back to ancient Greece and is named for the Greek god of the wind, Aeolus. It is designed to play only pure harmonic tones. Changes in wind velocity create higher or lower harmonics at louder or softer volumes. Aeolian wind harps are still hand-crafted today.

The Sea Organ is a musical instrument that is played by the sea. It was created by Nikoa Basic in 2005. The Sea Organ is a pipe organ with 35 organ pipes built under concrete along the shores of Zadar, Croatia. Sea water and wind movements push air through the pipes to create a variety of random, beautiful musical sounds.

DANCING with the STARS

Dancing with the Stars is a television reality-competition show that pairs a celebrity with a professional ballroom dancer. The professional dancer teaches the celebrity how to perform various ballroom dances.

Each pair dances live on the show every week. The dancers receive scores from three professional dance judges. Program viewers may also cast their votes by calling a toll-free number, online at the ABC website, or by text messaging. The judges' scores and the viewer votes are combined to create a score. The pair with the lowest score is eliminated from the competition each week.

The winners of the show's 10th season were Nicole Scherzinger (lead singer of the Pussycat Dolls) and professional dancer Derek Hough. It was the second win for Hough, who won the 7th season with partner Brooke Burke.

All About >> Dance Classes

Dance classes are a great way to have fun, stay healthy (dancing can be great exercise), and make new friends. In some areas, there are organizations that offer free classes. If that's not an option, many dance studios will at least allow you to take a free class, to see if this something you might be interested in, before signing up. No matter what kind of dancing appeals to you, there are probably classes offered in it. Here are just a few types of dance classes that might be available near you:

BALLET is a formal type of dancing, usually performed to classical music. Beginning classes will often teach stretching exercises, the five basic positions of ballet, and simple movements. Ballet dancers begin with flat shoes. Some dancers eventually use pointe shoes, which allow them to dance on the tips of the toes. But dancing "en pointe" takes lots of practice and help from a trained instructor.

TAP dancing requires a special kind of shoes that make a tapping sound on a dance floor. Beginning tap dancing classes will teach basic steps—these steps are eventually combined to create more complicated routines. Tap dancing usually moves at a faster pace than ballet.

JAZZ dance is less formal than either ballet or tap, though it may use similar steps and moves. It does not require any special equipment and usually has a relaxed dress code. Jazz dance routines may be unpredictable—they can start slow, then have bursts of energy. Beginning classes may focus on stretching and learning how to find the beat in different types of music.

Mythology

What name did the Romans give to the Greek god Zeus? → page 136

MYTHS OF THE GREEKS

As the ancient Greeks went about their daily lives, they believed that a big family of gods and goddesses was watching over them from Mount Olympus. Farmers planting crops, sailors crossing the sea, and poets writing verses thought that these powerful beings could help or harm them. Stories of the gods and goddesses are called **myths**.

After the Romans conquered Greece in 146 B.C., they adopted Greek myths but gave Roman names to the main gods and goddesses. Except for Earth, the planets in our solar system are named after Roman or Greek gods.

The family of Greek and Roman gods and goddesses was large. Their family tree would have more than 50 figures on it. The deities listed are the Olympian gods, the most important of the gods, who lived on Mount Olympus. Those with * are children of Zeus (Jupiter).

Greek Name	Roman Name	Description
Aphrodite	Venus	Goddess of beauty and of love
*Apollo	Apollo	God of prophecy, music, and medicine
*Ares	Mars	God of war; protector of the city
*Artemis	Diana	Goddess of the Moon; and of the Hunt
*Athena	Minerva	Goddess of wisdom and of war
Cronus	Saturn	Father of Zeus (Jupiter), Poseidon (Neptune), Hades (Pluto), Hera (Juno), and Demeter (Ceres)
Demeter	Ceres	Goddess of crops and harvest, sister of Zeus (Jupiter)
*Dionysus	Bacchus	God of wine, dancing, and theater
Hades	Pluto	Ruler of the Underworld, brother of Zeus (Jupiter)
Hephaestus	Vulcan	God of fire
Hera	Juno	Queen of the gods, wife of Zeus (Jupiter), goddess of marriage
*Hermes	Mercury	Messenger god, had winged helmet and sandals
Poseidon	Neptune	God of the sea and of earthquakes, brother of Zeus (Jupiter)
Zeus	Jupiter	Sky god (grandson of Uranus), ruler of gods and mortals

Greek & Roman Gods

MAKING SENSE of the WORLD

Unlike folklore or fables, myths were once thought to be true. Most ancient peoples explained many things in nature by referring to gods and heroes with superhuman qualities. To the Greeks a rough sea meant that POSEIDON was angry. Lightning was THOR'S hammer in Norse mythology. Egyptians worshipped the sun god RE, who sailed across the sky in a ship each day. In Japan, AMATERASU was the Shinto sun goddess who gave light to the land. Her brother SUSANOO was the storm god who ruled the sea.

There are even stories of gods or heroes who chose brain over brawn to get what they wanted. COYOTE was wild and cunning, a true trickster for many Native American tribes throughout the West. He was usually a loner and was never simply good or bad. ANANSI was a spider in the stories of the Akan tribes of West Africa. The tiny spider used his wits to capture the hornet, python, and leopard. In return the sky god NYAME let him own every story ever told.

Myths have remained popular long after people knew they weren't real because the stories hold important life lessons and morals for cultures around the world. Myths have also inspired countless stories and works of art.

Re

Greek & Roman Heroes

Besides stories about the gods, Greek and Roman mythology has many stories about other heroes with amazing qualities.

- ODYSSEUS, the king of Ithaca, was a hero of the Trojan War in the epic poem the *Iliad*. It was his idea to build a huge wooden horse, hide Greek soldiers inside, and smuggle them into the city of Troy to capture it. The long poem the *Odyssey* is the story of his long and magical trip home after the war.

- PANDORA was the first woman created by the Greek gods. Zeus ordered Hephaestus to create a beautiful woman out of earth. All the Olympian gods gave her gifts. Hera's gift was curiosity. When Pandora was finished, she received a box which she was never to open. But because of her curiosity, Pandora could not resist. She opened the box and released all the evil spirits into the world.

- JASON and the Argonauts set out on a quest to find the golden fleece so that Jason could reclaim his rightful throne. Among the Argonauts were Herakles and Orpheus. After many adventures and with the help of Medea, Jason slew the Minotaur and claimed the fleece. He later betrayed

Medea and eventually died when a beam from his ship, the Argo, fell off and hit him on the head.

Hercules

The most popular hero was Herakles, or **Hercules**. The most famous of his deeds were his 12 labors. They included killing the **Hydra**, a many-headed monster, and capturing the three-headed dog **Cerberus**, who guarded the gates of the Underworld. Hercules was so great a hero that the gods granted him immortality. When his body lay on his funeral pyre, Athena came and carried him off to Mount Olympus in her chariot.

Nations

Which country is bigger in land area, Canada or China? → page 156

GOVERNMENTS

Among the world's 195 independent nations there are various kinds of governments.

Totalitarianism In **totalitarian** countries, the rulers have strong power, and the people have little freedom. Elections are controlled, so that people do not have a real choice. North Korea is an example of a totalitarian country.

Monarchy A **monarchy** is a country headed by a king or queen (or occasionally by a ruler with a different title), who usually has inherited the title from a parent or other relative. There still are some monarchies in the world today. The United Kingdom (Great Britain) is one.

Democracy The word **democracy** comes from the Greek words *demos* ("people") and *kratos* ("rule"). In modern democracies, people govern themselves through the leaders they choose in elections. The United States and many other countries are democracies. Some monarchies, like the United Kingdom, are also democracies because the main decisions are actually made by elected leaders.

The European Union (EU)
The EU is an organization of 27 member countries, with more than 500 million people. The EU sets many common policies for its members. People and goods can usually move easily from one EU country to another. Many EU countries share a common currency, the euro.

EU Members

1. Austria*	15. Latvia
2. Belgium*	16. Lithuania
3. Bulgaria	17. Luxembourg*
4. Cyprus*	18. Malta *
5. Czech Republic	19. Netherlands*
6. Denmark	20. Poland
7. Estonia	21. Portugal*
8. Finland*	22. Romania
9. France*	23. Slovakia*
10. Germany*	24. Slovenia*
11. Greece*	25. Spain*
12. Hungary	26. Sweden
13. Ireland*	27. United Kingdom
14. Italy*	

* People in these countries use the euro.

A COMMUNITY OF NATIONS

The **United Nations (UN)** was started in 1945 after World War II. The first members were 51 nations, 50 of which met in San Francisco, California. They signed an agreement known as the UN Charter. The UN now has 192 members. Only three independent nations—Kosovo, Taiwan, and Vatican City—are not members.

The UN emblem shows the world surrounded by olive branches of peace.

HOW THE UN IS ORGANIZED

→ **GENERAL ASSEMBLY** **What It Does:** Discusses world problems, admits new members, appoints the secretary-general, decides the UN budget. **Members:** All UN members; each country has one vote.

→ **SECURITY COUNCIL** **What It Does:** Handles questions of peace and security. **Members:** Five permanent members (China, France, the United Kingdom, Russia, and the United States) who must all vote the same way before certain proposals can pass; ten elected by the General Assembly to two-year terms. In 2010, the ten temporary members were Austria, Japan, Mexico, Turkey, and Uganda (terms ending December 31, 2010) and Bosnia and Herzegovina, Brazil, Gabon, Liberia, and Nigeria (terms ending December 31, 2011).

→ **ECONOMIC AND SOCIAL COUNCIL** **What It Does:** Deals with issues related to economic development, population, education, health, and human rights. **Members:** 54 member countries elected to three-year terms.

→ **INTERNATIONAL COURT OF JUSTICE (WORLD COURT)** located in The Hague, Netherlands. **What It Does:** UN court for disputes between countries. **Members:** 15 judges, each from a different country, elected to nine-year terms.

→ **SECRETARIAT** **What It Does:** Carries out the UN's day-to-day operations. **Members:** UN staff, headed by the secretary-general.

For more information, e-mail *inquiries@un.org*, write to: Public Inquiries Unit, Dept. of Public Information, United Nations, Room GA-57, New York, NY 10017; or go to *www.un.org*

did you Know? Since 1948 the UN has operated more than 60 "peacekeeping missions" to help keep peace and order in trouble spots around the world. Lightly armed UN troops, with their blue helmets, can be found today in many parts of Africa, the Middle East, and elsewhere, often joined by aid workers, human rights monitors, and others.

Other UN Agencies

The UN also runs a number of special agencies that perform humanitarian work. They include the Food and Agriculture Organization, the World Health Organization, and the World Bank.

AUSTRALIA 140
PACIFIC ISLANDS 141
NORTH AMERICA 142
SOUTH AMERICA 144
ANTARCTICA 145
EUROPE 146
ASIA 148
AFRICA 150

Maps showing the continents and nations of the world appear on pages 140–151. Flags of the nations appear on pages 152–177. A map of the United States appears on pages 288–289.

AUSTRALIA

⊛ National Capital

★ State Capital

• Other City

1:40,886,000

0   250   500 mi

0   250   500 km

Two-Point Equidistant Projection

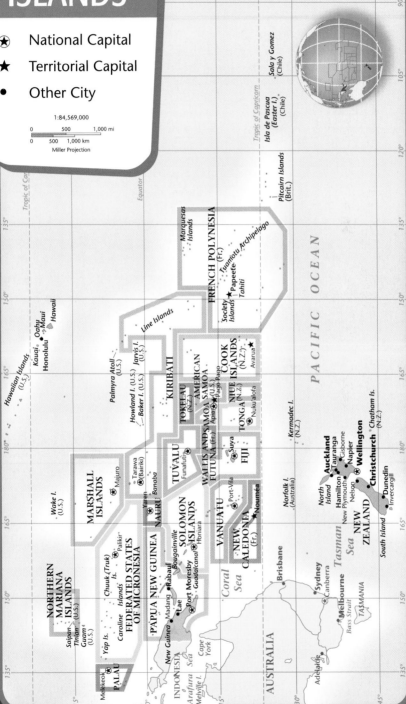

PACIFIC ISLANDS

⊛ National Capital

★ Territorial Capital

● Other City

1:84,569,000

0 — 500 — 1,000 mi
0 — 500 — 1,000 km

Miller Projection

Tropic of Cancer

Tropic of Capricorn

Equator

Sala y Gomez (Chile)

Isla de Pascua (Easter I.) (Chile)

Pitcairn Islands (Brit.)

Marquesas Islands

FRENCH POLYNESIA (Fr.)

Tuamotu Archipelago

Society Islands ★ Papeete Tahiti

PACIFIC OCEAN

Line Islands

Hawaiian Islands (U.S.)

Kauai Oahu Maui
Honolulu Hawaii

Palmyra Atoll (U.S.)

Howland I. (U.S.)
Baker I. (U.S.)

Jarvis I. (U.S.)

KIRIBATI

TOKELAU (N.Z.)

AMERICAN SAMOA (U.S.)
Pago Pago

SAMOA ⊛ Apia

COOK ISLANDS (N.Z.)
Avarua ★

Wake I. (U.S.)

MARSHALL ISLANDS

Majuro ⊛

Tarawa ⊛ (Bairiki)

Banaba

NAURU ⊛

TUVALU
Funafuti ⊛

WALLIS AND FUTUNA (Fr.)

NIUE (N.Z.)

TONGA ⊛ Nuku'alofa

Suva ⊛

FIJI

Kermadec I. (N.Z.)

NORTHERN MARIANA ISLANDS
Saipan ★ (U.S.)
Tinian (U.S.)
Guam (U.S.)

Chuuk (Truk)
Caroline Islands
Palikir ★

FEDERATED STATES OF MICRONESIA

Yap Is.

Yaren

SOLOMON ISLANDS
Honiara ⊛
Guadalcanal

Bougainville

Rabaul
PAPUA NEW GUINEA
Madang
Lae
Port Moresby ⊛

VANUATU
Port-Vila ⊛

NEW CALEDONIA (Fr.)
Nouméa ★

Norfolk I. (Australia)

North Island
Auckland
Tauranga
Hamilton Gisborne
New Plymouth Napier
Nelson ⊛ Wellington
Christchurch Chatham Is. (N.Z.)
Dunedin
Invercargill
South Island

NEW ZEALAND

Melekeok ⊛ PALAU

INDONESIA
New Guinea
Arafura Sea
Melville I.

Cape York

Coral Sea

Brisbane

AUSTRALIA

Adelaide

Sydney
Canberra ⊛

Melbourne
Tasman Sea
Bass Strait
TASMANIA

SWEDEN

NORWAY

UNITED KINGDOM

ICELAND

Arctic Circle

Denmark Strait

Cape Farewell

Tasiilaq

Greenland Sea

Svalbard (Nor.)

NEWFOUNDLAND AND LABRADOR

St. Anthony
Island of Newfoundland

St. Pierre & Miquelon (Fr.)

St. John's

Corner Brook

Happy Valley Goose Bay

Anticosti I.

P.E.I.

GREENLAND (KALAALLIT NUNAAT) (Den.)

Nuuk

Labrador Sea

Hebron

QUEBEC

Schefferville

Labrador City

Sept-Îles

Nord

Baffin Bay

Davis Strait

Pangnirtung

Ungava Peninsula

CANADIAN SHIELD

Cape Morris Jessup

Knud Rasmussen Land

Qaanaaq (Thule)

Grise Fiord

Arctic Bay

Pond Inlet

Baffin Island

Iqaluit

Povungnituk

Belcher Is.

James Bay

North Pole

Alert

Ellesmere I.

Hudson Strait

Repulse Bay

Hudson Bay

Moosonee

Chibougamau

Arctic Ocean

Queen Elizabeth Islands

Resolute

Southampton I.

Churchill

York Factory

Cambridge Bay

NUNAVUT

Kugluktuk

Victoria I.

Holman

CANADA

MANITOBA

Thompson

Flin Flon

L. Winnipeg

Winnipeg

Beaufort Sea

Banks I.

Sachs Harbour

Great Bear L.

Déline

Yellowknife

Uranium City

La Ronge

Prince Albert

SASK.

Inuvik

Fort McPherson

Mackenzie

Great Slave L.

Ft. Simpson

Ft. Smith

Hay River

Athabasca

La Loche

McMurray

Edmonton

Saskatoon

NORTHWEST TERRITORIES

ALBERTA

GREAT

Point Barrow

Barrow

Fort Yukon

Dawson

Mayo

Watson Lake

Peace River

Prince George

Jasper

ROCKY

Calgary

Kozebue

Fairbanks

YUKON

Carmacks

Whitehorse

BRITISH COLUMBIA

Williams Lake

Fraser

RUSSIA

Point Hope

BROOKS RANGE

Yukon

ALASKA

ALASKA RANGE

Mt. McKinley 6,194 m (20,320 ft.)

Anchorage

Skagway

Juneau

Sitka

COAST MOUNTAINS

Prince Rupert

Ketchikan

Kitimat

Queen Charlotte Is.

Vancouver I.

Vancouver

Nome

Bethel

Kenai

Seward

Valdez

Yakutat

Mt. Logan 5,959 m (19,551 ft.)

Kodiak

Gulf of Alaska

Bering Strait

Arctic Circle

Bering Sea

142

NATIONS

NORTH AMERICA

⊛ National Capital

★ Territorial Capital

• Other City

1:39,978,000

0   350   700 mi

0   350   700 km

Azimuthal Equal Area Projection

143

Map labels

BRAZIL

VENEZUELA

COLOMBIA

PANAMA

COSTA RICA

NICARAGUA

HONDURAS

BELIZE

GUATEMALA

EL SALVADOR

ATLANTIC OCEAN

PACIFIC OCEAN

Caribbean Sea

Gulf of Mexico

Bay of Campeche

Gulf of California

Straits of Florida

Bermuda (Brit.)

BARBADOS

GUADELOUPE (Fr.)

ANTIGUA & BARBUDA

DOMINICA

MARTINIQUE (Fr.)

ST. LUCIA

ST. VINCENT & THE GRENADINES

GRENADA

TRINIDAD & TOBAGO

Bonaire (Neth.)

Curaçao (Neth.)

Aruba (Neth.)

ST. KITTS & NEVIS

VIRGIN IS. (U.S., Brit.)

PUERTO RICO (U.S.)

San Juan

TURKS & CAICOS IS. (Brit.)

DOMINICAN REPUBLIC

Santo Domingo

HAITI

Port-au-Prince

CUBA

Santiago de Cuba

Havana

THE BAHAMAS

Nassau

JAMAICA

Kingston

CAYMAN IS. (Brit.)

Belmopan

Tegucigalpa

Managua

San José

Panama City

Guatemala City

San Salvador

Mérida

YUCATAN PENINSULA

Campeche

Villahermosa

Tuxtla Gutiérrez

Oaxaca

Veracruz

Acapulco

Orizaba Pk. (18,405 ft) 5,610 m

MEXICO

Mexico City

Puebla

León

Guadalajara

San Luis Potosí

Monterrey

SIERRA MADRE ORIENTAL

SIERRA MADRE OCCIDENTAL

Torreón

Durango

Mazatlán

La Paz

BAJA CALIFORNIA

Tijuana

Mexicali

Nogales

Ciudad Obregón

Hermosillo

Chihuahua

Ciudad Juárez

El Paso

Rio Grande

UNITED STATES

San Antonio

Austin

Houston

Dallas

TEXAS

Shreveport

Baton Rouge

New Orleans

LA.

Jackson

MISS.

Mobile

ALA.

Birmingham

Memphis

TENN.

Nashville

KY.

Louisville

Atlanta

GA.

Savannah

Jacksonville

St. Petersburg

Tampa

Miami

FLA.

APPALACHIAN MTS.

N.C.

Raleigh

Charlotte

S.C.

VA.

Richmond

W. VA.

OHIO

Columbus

Cincinnati

IND.

Indianapolis

St. Louis

MO.

ARK.

Little Rock

OKLA.

Oklahoma City

Wichita

KANSAS

Kansas City

NEB.

Omaha

IOWA

Des Moines

ILL.

Chicago

Milwaukee

MICH.

Detroit

Cleveland

Pittsburgh

PENN.

Toronto

Buffalo

Rochester

Lake Ontario

Lake Michigan

Minneapolis

Minnesota

S. DAK.

Rapid City

Platte

Cheyenne

WYO.

Casper

COLORADO

Denver

Arkansas

Colorado Plateau

NEW MEXICO

Albuquerque

Phoenix

ARIZONA

UTAH

Salt Lake City

Great Salt L.

NEVADA

Reno

Las Vegas

Snake

Pocatello

Boise

Great Basin

CALIF.

Sacramento

San Francisco

Santa Barbara

Los Angeles

San Diego

SIERRA NEVADA

Fresno

Mt. Whitney 4,418 m (14,494 ft.)

Eureka

COAST RANGES

Tropic of Cancer

New York City

Philadelphia

Baltimore

Washington, D.C.

MARYLAND

DELAWARE

NEW JERSEY

CONN.

R.I.

MASS.

MAINE

N.H.

VT.

Colorado

MONTANA

ROCKY MOUNTAINS

MOUNTAIN STATES

OHIO

Columbus

Colorado

Mississippi

Legend

- ✪ National Capital
- ★ Territorial Capital
- • Other City

1:29,277,000

0   250   500   750 mi
0   250   500   750 km

Azimuthal Equal Area Projection

CARIBBEAN SEA

TRINIDAD AND TOBAGO

PACIFIC OCEAN

Equator

PANAMA

Panama City

COLOMBIA

Santa Marta
Barranquilla
Cartagena
Sincelejo
Montería
Coro
Maracaibo
Cabimas
Valencia
Valera
Valledupar
Mérida
Cúcuta
San Cristóbal
Bucaramanga
Barrancabermeja
Medellín
Manizales
Pereira
Armenia
Ibagué
Cali
Palmira
Popayán
Pasto
Buenaventura
Tunja
✪ Bogotá
Villavicencio
Neiva

VENEZUELA
Caracas ✪
Maracay
Barquisimeto
San Fernando de Apure
Puerto Ayacucho
Cumaná
El Tigre
Maturín
Ciudad Bolívar
Ciudad Guayana

L. Maracaibo
LLANOS
Orinoco R.
ANDES
MTS.
Magdalena R.

GUYANA
Georgetown ✪
New Amsterdam

SURINAME
Paramaribo ✪

FRENCH GUIANA (Fr.)
Kourou
Cayenne ★

GUIANA HIGHLANDS

Boa Vista

Negro R.

AMAZON BASIN

SELVAS

Manaus

Macapá
Marajó I.
Santarém
Belém

Amazon R.

Putumayo R.

ECUADOR
Quito ✪
Esmeraldas
Portoviejo
Ambato
Chimborazo 6,310 m. (20,702 ft.) ▲
Guayaquil
Machala
Cuenca
Tumbes
Talara
Sullana
Piura
Cajamarca

PERU
Iquitos
Yurimaguas
Cruzeiro do Sul
Benjamin Constant

Marañón R.
Ucayali R.
Juruá R.
Purus R.

Trujillo
Chimbote
Mt. Huascarán ▲ 6,768 m. (22,205 ft.)
Chiclayo
Huánuco
Cerro de Pasco
Pucallpa
Rio Branco
Porto Velho

Callao ✪
Lima
Ica
Huancayo
Ayacucho
Cusco
Puno
Arequipa
Tacna
Arica
Iquique

Huancavélica

L. Titicaca

Guajará-Mirim
Madeira R.
Guaporé R.
Mamoré R.
Beni R.

BOLIVIA
Cobija
Puerto Maldonado
Juliaca
Riberalta
Trinidad
La Paz ✪
Oruro
Cochabamba
Sucre ✪
Potosí
Santa Cruz

ALTIPLANO
L. Poopó
CHACO

BRAZIL
BRAZIL

MATO GROSSO PLATEAU
Cuiabá
Corumbá
Campo Grande

Paraguay R.

Tocantins R.
Xingú R.
Tapajós R.
Araguaia R.
São Francisco R.

Teresina
Imperatriz
São Luís
Parnaíba
Juàzeiro do Norte
Fortaleza
Natal
João Pessoa
Recife
Maceió
Aracaju
Salvador
Ilhéus
Itabuna
Feira de Santana
Vitória da Conquista
Montes Claros
Governador Valadares
Campina Grande

BRAZILIAN HIGHLANDS

Gurupi
Anápolis
Goiânia
Brasília ✪
Uberlândia
São José do Rio Prêto
Ribeirão
Belo

Vitória

SERT

ATLANTIC OCEAN

South Polar Region

Cape Horn
Drake Passage
South Shetland Is.
South Orkney Is.

ATLANTIC OCEAN

SOUTHERN OCEAN

Billingshausen Sea

Weddell Sea

Riiser Larsen Ice Shelf
Fimbul Ice Shelf

Antarctic Pen.

Alexander I.

Thurston I.

Ellsworth Land

Vinson Massif 4,897 m (16,067 ft.)

Ronne Ice Shelf
Berkner I.
Filchner Ice Shelf

ELLSWORTH MTS.

Queen Maud Land

Amundsen Sea

Siple I.

Marie Byrd Land

PENSACOLA MTS.

+South Pole

ANTARCTICA

Enderby Land

PRINCE CHARLES MTS.

ROCKEFELLER PLATEAU

QUEEN MAUD MTS.

AMERICAN HIGHLAND

Amery Ice Shelf

Ross Ice Shelf
Roosevelt I.
Ross I.

TRANSANTARCTIC MTS.

Prydz Bay

West Ice Shelf

Ross Sea

McMurdo Sound
PRINCE ALBERT MTS.

Davis Sea

Shackleton Ice Shelf

Cape Adare

Wilkes Land

Cape Poinsett

Scott Island

Balleny Is.

SOUTHERN OCEAN

INDIAN OCEAN

ATLANTIC OCEAN

Cabo Frio
Joinville
Florianópolis
Porto Alegre
Passo Fundo
Caxias do Sul
Pelotas
Santa Maria
Ciudad del Este
Santo Tomé
Encarnación
Posadas
Rivera
Melo
Montevideo
Minas
URUGUAY
Paysandú
Salto
Río de la Plata
Santo
Formosa
Resistencia
Corrientes
Curuzú Cuatiá
Concordia
Paraná
La Plata
Avellaneda
Mar del Plata
Asunción
Paraná R.
Uruguay R.
San Miguel de Tucumán
Santiago del Estero
Santa Fe
Rosario
Junín
Buenos Aires
Santa Rosa
Catamarca
La Rioja
Río Cuarto
Córdoba
San Juan
Mendoza
San Rafael
Neuquén
Bahía Blanca
Punta Alta
Viedma
Valdés Peninsula
Rawson
Comodoro Rivadavia
ARGENTINA
PATAGONIA
San Carlos de Bariloche
Esquel
Trelew
Río Gallegos
Falkland Is. (Islas Malvinas) (Brit.) (claimed by Arg.)
Stanley
Strait of Magellan
Tierra del Fuego
Ushuaia
Cape Horn
Punta Arenas
Puerto Montt
Osorno
Valdivia
Temuco
Concepción
Talcahuano
Chillán
Talca
Rancagua
San Bernardo
Santiago
Valparaíso
Viña del Mar
Mt. Aconcagua 6,960 m (22,834 ft.)
CHILE
La Serena
Copiapó
Mt. Ojos del Salado 6,880 m (22,572 ft.)
ANDES MTS.
Chiloé I.
Los Chonos Archipelago
Taitao Peninsula
San Félix I. (Chile)
San Ambrosio I. (Chile)
Juan Fernández Is. (Chile)

EUROPE

⊛ National Capital

• Other City

1:22,107,000

| 0 | 250 | 500 mi |
| 0 | 250 | 500 km |

Azimuthal Equal Area Projection

Reykjavik ⊛   Akureyri
ICELAND

Norwegian   *Sea*

Faroe Is.
(Den.)

Shetland Is.
(Brit.)

Orkney
Is.

Hebrides

Trondheim

Troms

Bodø

K

Sundsvall

NORWAY

Bergen

SWEDEN

Oslo ⊛   Uppsala
Stavanger

Stockholm ⊛
Linköping

Gotland

Skagerrak   Göteborg

Glasgow
Edinburgh

Belfast

Dublin ⊛

IRELAND
Cork

Liverpool
Manchester

Birmingham

Cardiff
Bristol

Portsmouth

Land's End

English Channel

Channel Is.
(Brit.)

Le Havre

Brest

Nantes

UNITED KINGDOM
Newcastle
(GREAT BRITAIN)
Leeds
Sheffield

*Irish
Sea*

Jutland   Århus

Öland

Copenhagen ⊛ Helsingborg
DENMARK   Odense   Malmö

*North
Sea*

Gdańsk

Hamburg   Szczecin

NETHERLANDS
Amsterdam ⊛

Bremen

Hannover

Elbe

London
Rotterdam

Antwerp
Brussels ⊛
Lille
BELGIUM   Liège

Rouen

LUXEMBOURG
Paris ⊛   Luxembourg ⊛

Strasbourg

Essen
Cologne
Bonn

Frankfurt

GERMANY

Leipzig

Mannheim

FRANCE
Dijon

Bern ⊛   Zurich

Berlin ⊛

Poznań

Oder

Dresden

Ł

Wroc

Prague ⊛
CZECH REP.
Brno

SLOVA

Katowic

Ostrav

Munich

Stuttgart

Danube

Linz

LIECHTENSTEIN
AUSTRIA
Graz

SLOVENIA
Ljubljana ⊛

Vienna ⊛ Bratislav

HUNG.
Budap
Pécs
Zagreb

*ATLANTIC
OCEAN*

Cape Finisterre

Vigo

Porto

Bilbao

Gijón

Valladolid

*Bay
of
Biscay*

Bordeaux

Loire

Toulouse

PYRENEES

Rico de Aneto
3404 m
(11,168 ft)

Zaragoza

Ebro

Lyon

Geneva
SWITZERLAND

Mt. Blanc
4807 m
(15,771 ft)

ALPS

Milan
Turin

Verona

Po

CROATIA
SAN
MARINO

Genoa
Bologna

Florence

Venice

APENNINES

DINARIC

BOSNIA &
HERZEGOV
Sarajevo

Marseille

Nice

Nantes

PORTUGAL
Lisbon ⊛

Badajoz

IBERIAN

Tagus

Madrid ⊛

PENINSULA

Valencia

Córdoba

SPAIN

Palma

Alicante

Granada

Cádiz

Málaga

Strait of
Gibraltar

GIBRALTAR
(Brit.)

ANDORRA

Barcelona

Balearic Sea

Majorca

Minorca

Balearic Is.
(Sp.)

Toulon

Corsica
(Fr.)

Sardinia
(It.)

Ligurian Sea

MONACO

Elba

VATICAN
CITY

Sea

⊛**Rome**

ITALY

Naples

Salerno

Cagliari

*Tyrrhenian
Sea*

Palermo

Catania

Sicily

Split

Adriatic

ALPS

Dubrovnik

MONTENE
Podgori

Bari

Co

*Ioni
Se*

Mt. Etna
3323 m
(10,902 ft)

Cape
St. Vincent
Sevilla

Mediterranean

Algiers

MOUNTAINS

ATLAS

Rabat
Casablanca

MOROCCO

ATLAS

ALGERIA

Tunis

TUNISIA

Valletta ⊛
MALTA

Sea

146

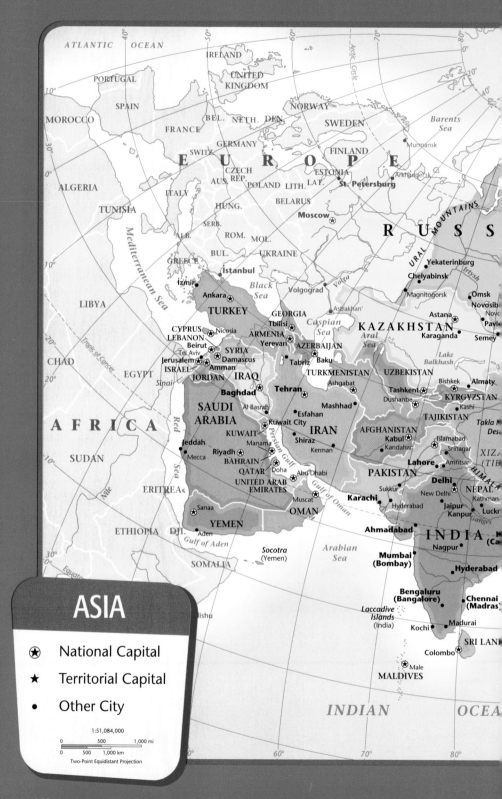

ATLANTIC OCEAN

IRELAND

PORTUGAL

UNITED
KINGDOM

20°

SPAIN

10°

BEL. NETH. DEN.

NORWAY

Barents
Sea

MOROCCO

FRANCE

GERMANY

SWEDEN

SWITZ.

FINLAND

Murmansk

30°

40°

0°

E U R O P E

CZECH
REP.

ESTONIA

Arkhangel'sk

ALGERIA

ITALY

AUS.

POLAND LITH. LAT.

St. Petersburg

TUNISIA

HUNG.

BELARUS

Moscow

R U S S

URAL MOUNTAINS

ALB.

SERB.

ROM.

MOL.

BUL.

UKRAINE

10°

GREECE

Istanbul

Yekaterinburg

İzmir

Black
Sea

Volgograd

Chelyabinsk

Irtysh

LIBYA

Mediterranean Sea

Ankara

TURKEY

GEORGIA

Caspian
Sea

Astrakhan'

Magnitogorsk

Omsk
Novosib

CYPRUS

Nicosia

Tbilisi

KAZAKHSTAN

Astana

Novo

20°

Tropic of Cancer

LEBANON

ARMENIA

Aral
Sea

Karaganda

Pavl

Beirut

Tel Aviv

SYRIA

Yerevan

AZERBAIJAN

Semey

CHAD

EGYPT

Jerusalem

Damascus

Baku

Tabriz

TURKMENISTAN

UZBEKISTAN

Lake
Balkhash

20°

ISRAEL

Amman

Ashgabat

Bishkek

Almaty

Sinai

JORDAN

IRAQ

Tehran

Tashkent

KYRGYZSTAN

Baghdad

Mashhad

Dushanbe

Kashi

AFRICA

Red Sea

SAUDI
ARABIA

Al-Basrah

Esfahan

TAJIKISTAN

Takla N
Des

Kuwait City

Nile

KUWAIT

IRAN

AFGHANISTAN

Islamabad

XIZ
(TIB

10°

SUDAN

Jeddah

Manama

Shiraz

Kabul

Kandahar

Srinagar

Mecca

Riyadh

Kerman

Lahore

Amritsar

HIMALA

BAHRAIN

QATAR

Doha

PAKISTAN

Delhi

NEPAL

ERITREA

Sanaa

UNITED ARAB
EMIRATES

Abu Dhabi

Gulf of Oman

Karachi

Sukkur

New Delhi

Kathman

Muscat

Hyderabad

Jaipur

Kanpur

Luckr

ETHIOPIA

DJI.

Aden

YEMEN

OMAN

Ahmadabad

Ganges

30°

Gulf of Aden

Socotra
(Yemen)

Arabian
Sea

I N D I A

(Ca

Nagpur

SOMALIA

Equa

Mumbai
(Bombay)

Hyderabad

Bengaluru
(Bangalore)

Chennai
(Madras)

ishu

Laccadive
Islands
(India)

Kochi

Madurai

SRI LAN

Colombo

Male

MALDIVES

INDIAN

OCEA

ASIA

⊛ National Capital

★ Territorial Capital

• Other City

1:51,084,000

0   500   1,000 mi

0   500   1,000 km

Two-Point Equidistant Projection

n Pole

CTIC
EAN

180°
160°
140°
120°

*Chukchi
Sea*

*East
Siberian
Sea*

*Bering
Sea*

ALASKA

80°
70°
60°
50°
40°

170°

*Laptev
Sea*

KAMCHATKA
PENINSULA

Magadan

180°

Anadyr

Yakutsk

Petropavlovsk-
Kamchatskiy

*Sea of
Okhotsk*

170°
30°

I B E R I A

Sakhalin

*Kuril
Islands*
(Russia)

varsk   Bratsk

*Lake
Baikal*   Chita

Komsomolsk
na Amure

Khabarovsk

Blagoveshchensk

Sapporo

160°

Irkutsk   Ulan-Ude

Harbin

Changchun

Vladivostok

JAPAN

Sendai

*Sea of
Japan
(East Sea)*

Ulaanbaatar

MONGOLIA

Shenyang

Pyongyang

N. KOREA

Tokyo

Yokohama

Kyoto

GOBI DESERT

Beijing

Dalian

Seoul

Kobe   Osaka

ANG

Hohhot

Tianjin

S. KOREA

Hiroshima

20°

Jinan

Qingdao

Taiyuan

*Yellow
Sea*

Nagasaki

Lanzhou

Zhengzhou

Xi'an

Nanjing

Shanghai

*East
China
Sea*

PACIFIC
OCEAN

HINA

Wuhan

150°

Chengdu

Changsha

Wenzhou

Okinawa (Japan)

hasa

Chongqing

Fuzhou

Ryukyu Islands

AN

Xiamen

Taipei

10°

Guangzhou

TAIWAN

*Philippine
Sea*

ADESH

Kunming

Nanning

Hong Kong

aka

Macao

LUZON

Hanoi

*Gulf
of
Tonkin*

Mandalay

LAOS

Nay Pyi Taw

Manila

PHILIPPINES

MYANMAR
(BURMA)

Vientiane

Da Nang

*South
China
Sea*

angon
goon)

THAILAND

VIETNAM

Cebu

MINDANAO

Bangkok

CAMBODIA

*Sulu
Sea*

Davao

Andaman
Sea

Phnom
Penh

Ho Chi Minh City

Kota Kinabalu

Bandar Seri Begawan

*Celebes
Sea*

Manado

NEW GUINEA

*Gulf of
Thailand*

BRUNEI

MALAYSIA

Kuching

BORNEO

*Banda
Sea*

*Arafura
Sea*

Medan

Kuala
Lumpur

Kuching

SINGAPORE

Singapore

I N D O N E S I A

SUMATRA

Padang

Banjarmasin

Makassar

Dili

*Timor
Sea*

TIMOR-
LESTE

Palembang

*Java
Sea*

Jakarta

Kupang

AUSTRALIA

Bandung

JAVA

Surabaya

100°   110°   120°   130°   140°

INDIAN OCEAN

Antsiranana
Toamasina
MADAGASCAR
COMOROS
Moroni
Antananarivo
Fianarantsoa
Toliara

Tropic of Capricorn

Mtwara
Nacala-
Porto
Nampula
Quelimane
MOZAMBIQUE

Mozambique Channel

Mombasa
Nairobi
Kilimanjaro
5895 m (19,340 ft)
Tanga
Zanzibar
Dar es Salaam
SERENGETI
PLAIN
Arusha
Mwanza
Dodoma
TANZANIA
Tabora
Mbeya
MALAWI
Lilongwe
Lake
Nyasa
Beira
Inhambane

Kigali
RWANDA
BURUNDI
Bujumbura
Bukavu
Kananga
Mbuji-Mayi
DEMOCRATIC
REPUBLIC OF
THE CONGO
KATANGA
Kolwezi
Likasi
Lubumbashi
GREAT RIFT VALLEY
L. Tanganyika
L. Mweru
PLATEAU
Kabwe
Kitwe
Ndola
ZAMBIA
Lusaka
L. Kariba
Livingstone
Chipata
Blantyre
Harare
Mutare
ZIMBABWE
Bulawayo
Francistown
Maputo
Mbabane
SWAZILAND
Newcastle
Pietermaritzburg
Durban
East London
Port Elizabeth

Pretoria
Johannesburg
Klerksdorp
Kimberley
Bloemfontein
LESOTHO
Maseru
SOUTH
AFRICA
BOTSWANA
KALAHARI
DESERT
Gaborone
Cape
Agulhas

CONGO
Brazzaville
Franceville
Kinshasa
Matadi
Tshikapa
Kikwit
Kasai
ANGOLA
Malanje
Huambo
Menongue
Kwango
NAMIBIA
NAMIB DESERT
Grootfontein
Windhoek
Walvis Bay
Lüderitz
Orange
Cape Town
Cape of Good Hope

Port-
Gentil
Pointe-Noire
Cabinda
(Ang.)
Luanda
Lobito
Benguela
Namibe

ATLANTIC

OCEAN

ASCENSION
(Brit.)

ST. HELENA
(Brit.)

AFRICA

⊛ National Capital

• Other City

1:39,550,000

0   250   500   750 mi
0   250   500   750 km
Azimuthal Equal Area Projection

Facts About Nations

Here are basic facts about each of the world's 195 independent nations. The color of the heading for each country tells you what continent it belongs in. The population is an estimate for 2010. The area includes both land and inland water. The language entry gives official languages and other common languages.

Afghanistan

Capital: Kabul
Population: 29,121,286
Area: 250,001 sq mi (647,500 sq km)
Language: Afghan Persian (Dari), Pashtu
Did You Know? More than half the men and nearly nine out of ten women in Afghanistan cannot read and write.

VILLAGE IN AFGHANISTAN

Albania

Capital: Tirana
Population: 3,659,616
Area: 11,100 sq mi (28,748 sq km)
Language: Albanian, Greek
Did You Know? Almost all Albanians are descended from the Illyrians, who lived in the area in ancient times.

Algeria

Capital: Algiers (El Djazair)
Population: 34,586,184
Area: 919,595 sq mi (2,381,740 sq km)
Language: Arabic, French, Berber dialects
Did You Know? Algeria's desert region contains large "sand seas" called *ergs*, which feature constantly shifting dunes up to 2,000 feet high.

Andorra

Capital: Andorra la Vella
Population: 84,525
Area: 181 sq mi (468 sq km)
Language: Catalan, French, Castilian
Did You Know? Tiny Andorra is ruled by two "co-princes" from neighboring countries: the president of France and the bishop of Urgel in Spain.

Angola

Capital: Luanda
Population: 13,068,161
Area: 481,354 sq mi (1,246,700 sq km)
Language: Portuguese, African languages
Did You Know? Angola is one of the world's leading suppliers of diamonds.

Antigua & Barbuda

Capital: St. John's
Population: 86,754
Area: 171 sq mi (443 sq km)
Language: English
Did You Know? On Aug. 1, 1834, Antigua became the first of the British Caribbean colonies to free its slaves.

COLOR KEY

- Africa
- Asia
- Australia
- Europe
- North America
- Pacific Islands
- South America

Argentina

Capital: Buenos Aires
Population: 41,343,201
Area: 1,068,302 sq mi (2,766,890 sq km)
Language: Spanish, English, Italian, German, French
Did You Know? Ushuaia, at the tip of Argentina, attracts many tourists. It is the world's southernmost city and lies about 700 miles from Antarctica.

Armenia

Capital: Yerevan
Population: 2,966,802
Area: 11,484 sq mi (29,743 sq km)
Language: Armenian, Russian
Did You Know? Armenia considers itself the first country to have formally adopted Christianity as a state religion, in the year 301.

Australia

Capital: Canberra
Population: 21,515,754
Area: 2,967,909 sq mi (7,686,850 sq km)
Language: English, Aboriginal languages
Did You Know? Australia is home to more than 50 million kangaroos; there are twice as many kangaroos as people.

Austria

Capital: Vienna
Population: 8,214,160
Area: 32,382 sq mi (83,870 sq km)
Language: German, Slovene, Croatian, Hungarian
Did You Know? Austria's most popular foods include wiener schnitzel, a tasty veal dish, and apple strudel, one of many delicious desserts.

Azerbaijan

Capital: Baku
Population: 8,303,512
Area: 33,436 sq mi (86,600 sq km)
Language: Azeri, Russian, Armenian
Did You Know? Azerbaijan became an independent nation in 1991, when the Soviet Union broke up.

The Bahamas

Capital: Nassau
Population: 310,426
Area: 5,382 sq mi (13,940 sq km)
Language: English, Creole
Did You Know? Columbus first set foot in America when he landed on an island in the Bahamas, probably Watling Island, on October 12, 1492.

Bahrain

Capital: Manama
Population: 738,004
Area: 257 sq mi (665 sq km)
Language: Arabic, English, Farsi, Urdu
Did You Know? Groundwater and treated seawater are the only sources of freshwater in Bahrain.

BEACH IN AUSTRALIA

Bangladesh

Capital: Dhaka
Population: 158,065,841
Area: 55,599 sq mi (144,000 sq km)
Language: Bangla, English
Did You Know? The saltwater crocodile, found mainly in India and Bangladesh, can measure more than 20 feet long.

Barbados

Capital: Bridgetown
Population: 285,653
Area: 166 sq mi (431 sq km)
Language: English
Did You Know? Considered one of the Seven Wonders of Barbados, the grapefruit is believed to have been developed in Barbados from other fruits.

Belarus

Capital: Minsk
Population: 9,612,632
Area: 80,155 sq mi (207,600 sq km)
Language: Belarusian, Russian
Did You Know? Contamination from the 1986 Chernobyl nuclear power plant explosion, in neighboring Ukraine, continues to affect Belarus. High numbers of children have been diagnosed with cancer. Many people are unemployed because land that was contaminated could no longer be farmed.

Belgium

Capital: Brussels
Population: 10,423,493
Area: 11,787 sq mi (30,528 sq km)
Language: Dutch, French, German
Did You Know? Belgium produces about 170,000 tons of chocolate every year, supporting about 300 chocolate makers and more than 2,000 shops.

Belize

Capital: Belmopan
Population: 314,522
Area: 8,867 sq mi (22,966 sq km)
Language: English, Spanish, Mayan, Garifuna, Creole
Did You Know? Belize Barrier Reef is the second largest coral reef system (a diverse underwater habitat) in the world.

Benin

Capital: Porto-Novo (constit.); Cotonou (admin.)
Population: 9,056,010
Area: 43,483 sq mi (112,620 sq km)
Language: French, Fon, Yoruba
Did You Know? Most of present-day Benin was part of the Kingdom of Abomey for almost 300 years, until the area came under French control around 1900.

Bhutan

Capital: Thimphu
Population: 699,847
Area: 18,147 sq mi (47,000 sq km)
Language: Dzongkha, Tibetan dialects
Did You Know? After Bhutan's king stepped down in 2006, his son took over as king and the country adopted a democratic constitution.

Bolivia

Capital: La Paz (admin.); Sucre (legislative/judiciary)
Population: 9,947,418
Area: 424,164 sq mi (1,098,580 sq km)
Language: Spanish, Quechua, Aymara
Did You Know? Bolivia is named after Simón Bolívar, a military leader who freed much of South America from Spanish rule.

BRUSSELS, BELGIUM

Bosnia and Herzegovina

Capital: Sarajevo
Population: 4,621,598
Area: 19,772 sq mi (51,209 sq km)
Language: Bosnian, Croatian, Serbian
Did You Know? This country has three presidents, who serve consecutive eight-month terms.

Botswana

Capital: Gaborone
Population: 2,029,307
Area: 231,804 sq mi (600,370 sq km)
Language: Setswana, English
Did You Know? Chobe National Park is home to about 100,000 elephants, possibly the largest elephant population in the world.

OKAVANGO DELTA, BOTSWANA

Brazil

Capital: Brasília
Population: 201,103,330
Area: 3,286,488 sq mi (8,511,965 sq km)
Language: Portuguese, Spanish, English, French
Did You Know? Brazil was once a colony of Portugal. Today it has almost 20 times more people than Portugal. Most Brazilians speak Portuguese.

Brunei

Capital: Bandar Seri Begawan
Population: 395,027
Area: 2,228 sq mi (5,770 sq km)
Language: Malay, English, Chinese
Did You Know? The same royal family has ruled Brunei since the 1400s.

Bulgaria

Capital: Sofia
Population: 7,148,785
Area: 42,823 sq mi (110,910 sq km)
Language: Bulgarian, Turkish
Did You Know? The image of a man on horseback that appears on some Bulgarian coins is based on an 8th-century rock carving called the Madara Rider.

Burkina Faso

Capital: Ouagadougou
Population: 16,241,811
Area: 105,869 sq mi (274,200 sq km)
Language: French, indigenous languages
Did You Know? "Burkina Faso" means "land of honest people."

Burundi

Capital: Bujumbura
Population: 9,863,117
Area: 10,745 sq mi (27,830 sq km)
Language: Kirundi, French, Swahili
Did You Know? The Twa, a Pygmy group (adult males average about 5 feet tall), are thought to be Burundi's original inhabitants.

Cambodia

Capital: Phnom Penh
Population: 14,753,320
Area: 69,900 sq mi (181,040 sq km)
Language: Khmer, French, English
Did You Know? More than half of all Cambodians are under the age of 21.

COLOR KEY
- Africa
- Asia
- Australia
- Europe
- North America
- Pacific Islands
- South America

Cameroon

Capital: Yaoundé
Population: 19,294,149
Area: 183,568 sq mi (475,440 sq km)
Language: English, French, African languages
Did You Know? The Cameroon rain forest has the world's biggest frogs. With its back legs extended the Goliath frog can reach 2.5 feet in length.

Canada

Capital: Ottawa
Population: 33,759,742
Area: 3,855,103 sq mi (9,984,670 sq km)
Language: English, French
Did You Know? Canada is the world's second-biggest country in total area, after Russia. In land area alone it is the fourth biggest, after Russia, China, and the U.S.

Cape Verde

Capital: Praia
Population: 508,659
Area: 1,557 sq mi (4,033 sq km)
Language: Portuguese, Crioulo
Did You Know? More Cape Verdeans live abroad than live on the nation's islands. Severe droughts in the late 20th century forced many to leave.

Central African Republic

Capital: Bangui
Population: 4,844,927
Area: 240,535 sq mi (622,984 sq km)
Language: French, Sangho
Did You Know? In 1976, the country's ruler, Jean-Bedel Bokassa, proclaimed himself emperor, but he was overthrown a few years later.

Chad

Capital: N'Djamena
Population: 10,543,464
Area: 495,755 sq mi (1,284,000 sq km)
Language: French, Arabic, Sara
Did You Know? There are some 200 native ethnic groups living in Chad.

Chile

Capital: Santiago
Population: 16,746,491
Area: 292,260 sq mi (756,950 sq km)
Language: Spanish
Did You Know? The Atacama Desert in northern Chile is one of the earth's driest places. In some areas, rain has never been recorded.

China

Capital: Beijing
Population: 1,330,141,295
Area: 3,705,407 sq mi (9,596,960 sq km)
Language: Mandarin, and many dialects
Did You Know? The last emperor of China was a six-year old boy named Puyi. He was overthrown in 1912.

GREAT WALL OF CHINA

Colombia

Capital: Bogotá
Population: 44,205,293
Area: 439,736 sq mi (1,138,910 sq km)
Language: Spanish
Did You Know? The town of Lloro, on the slopes of the Andes Mountains, may be the world's rainiest place. It gets an average of more than 500 inches of rain each year.

COLOR KEY

- Africa
- Asia
- Australia
- Europe
- North America
- Pacific Islands
- South America

Comoros

Capital: Moroni
Population: 773,407
Area: 838 sq mi (2,170 sq km)
Language: Arabic, French, Shikomoro
Did You Know? The endangered Livingstone's flying fox, a fruit bat native to the islands of Comoros, has a wing span of more than 4 feet.

Congo, Democratic Republic of the

Capital: Kinshasa
Population: 70,916,439
Area: 905,568 sq mi (2,345,410 sq km)
Language: French, Lingala, Kingwana, Kikongo, Tshiluba
Did You Know? In 2006, the Democratic Republic of the Congo held its first free, democratic multi-party elections since 1960.

Congo, Republic of the

Capital: Brazzaville
Population: 4,125,916
Area: 132,047 sq mi (342,000 sq km)
Language: French, Lingala, Monokutuba, Kikongo
Did You Know? The Bantu people of the Congo have lived in the region since before A.D. 1000.

Costa Rica

Capital: San José
Population: 4,516,220
Area: 19,730 sq mi (51,100 sq km)
Language: Spanish, English
Did You Know? At its narrowest point, between the Pacific Ocean and Caribbean Sea, Costa Rica is only about 75 miles wide.

Côte d'Ivoire (Ivory Coast)

Capital: Yamoussoukro
Population: 21,058,798
Area: 124,503 sq mi (322,460 sq km)
Language: French, Dioula
Did You Know? The largest Christian church in the world is in Côte d'Ivoire's capital city of Yamoussoukro.

Croatia

Capital: Zagreb
Population: 4,486,881
Area: 21,831 sq mi (56,542 sq km)
Language: Croatian, Serbian
Did You Know? Croatia has more than 1,000 islands off its coast in the Adriatic Sea. Only about 50 are inhabited.

Cuba

Capital: Havana
Population: 11,477,459
Area: 42,803 sq mi (110,860 sq km)
Language: Spanish
Did You Know? One of the world's few remaining Communist countries, Cuba lies just 90 miles away from the tip of Florida.

Cyprus

Capital: Nicosia
Population: 1,102,677
Area: 3,571 sq mi (9,250 sq km)
Language: Greek, Turkish, English
Did You Know? Halloumi, a salty cheese made from a mixture of goat and sheep milk, is a traditional food in Cyprus.

SEA CAVES NEAR CAPE GRECO, CYPRUS

Czech Republic

Capital: Prague
Population: 10,201,707
Area: 30,450 sq mi (78,866 sq km)
Language: Czech, Slovak
Did You Know? The so-called "Velvet Revolution" brought about the end of communism in Czechoslovakia in 1989. The term "Velvet Divorce" was used to describe the 1993 division of the Czech Republic and Slovakia.

Denmark

Capital: Copenhagen
Population: 5,515,575
Area: 16,639 sq mi (43,094 sq km)
Language: Danish, Faroese
Did You Know? Legos (from the Danish *Leg Godt*—meaning "play well") were invented in Denmark.

Djibouti

Capital: Djibouti
Population: 740,528
Area: 8,880 sq mi (23,000 sq km)
Language: French, Arabic, Somali, Afar
Did You Know? Most of the country is barren. It receives little rainfall, and few plants survive in Djibouti's rocky deserts.

Dominica

Capital: Roseau
Population: 72,813
Area: 291 sq mi (754 sq km)
Language: English, French patois
Did You Know? Mary Eugenia Charles, who governed from 1980 to 1995, was the first female prime minister in the Caribbean.

Dominican Republic

Capital: Santo Domingo
Population: 9,794,487
Area: 18,815 sq mi (48,730 sq km)
Language: Spanish
Did You Know? Sancocho, a stew with vegetables and chunks of different meats, is a favorite dish in the Dominican Republic.

Ecuador

Capital: Quito
Population: 14,790,608
Area: 109,483 sq mi (283,560 sq km)
Language: Spanish, Quechua
Did You Know? Quito lies right near the equator but high in the mountains; the temperature tends to be comfortably cool year round.

Egypt

Capital: Cairo
Population: 80,471,869
Area: 386,662 sq mi (1,001,450 sq km)
Language: Arabic, English, French
Did You Know? The Great Pyramid of Giza, built around 2250 B.C., is made up of more than 2 million stone blocks.

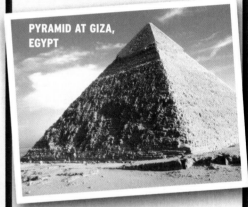

PYRAMID AT GIZA, EGYPT

El Salvador

Capital: San Salvador
Population: 6,052,064
Area: 8,124 sq mi (21,040 sq km)
Language: Spanish, Nahua
Did You Know? El Salvador is the most densely-populated country on the mainland of the Americas, with more than 900 people per square mile.

COLOR KEY
- Africa
- Asia
- Australia
- Europe
- North America
- Pacific Islands
- South America

MASKED BUTTERFLY
FISH, FIJI

Fiji

Capital: Suva
Population: 957,780
Area: 7,054 sq mi (18,270 sq km)
Language: English, Fijian, Hindustani
Did You Know? Wearing a hat is a sign of disrespect in Fijian culture.

Finland

Capital: Helsinki
Population: 5,255,068
Area: 130,559 sq mi (338,145 sq km)
Language: Finnish, Swedish
Did You Know? In Finland, fines for speeding are based on income. One of Finland's richest citizens was fined $216,900 for driving too fast.

France

Capital: Paris
Population: 64,768,389
Area: 248,429 sq mi (643,427 sq km)
Language: French
Did You Know? The longest-reigning monarch in Europe's history was France's Louis XIV. The "Sun King" ruled for 72 years, from 1643 to 1715.

Gabon

Capital: Libreville
Population: 1,545,255
Area: 103,347 sq mi (267,667 sq km)
Language: French, Fang, Myene, Nzebi
Did You Know? Oil and other natural resources have helped make Gabon one of Africa's more prosperous countries.

Equatorial Guinea

Capital: Malabo
Population: 650,702
Area: 10,831 sq mi (28,051 sq km)
Language: Spanish, French, Fang, Bubi
Did You Know? Equatorial Guinea is the only African country in which Spanish is an official language.

Eritrea

Capital: Asmara
Population: 5,792,984
Area: 46,842 sq mi (121,320 sq km)
Language: Afar, Arabic, Tigre, Kunama, Tigrinya
Did You Know? Eritrea was once a colony of Italy, then occupied by British forces, and finally annexed by Ethiopia before it achieved independence in 1993.

Estonia

Capital: Tallinn
Population: 1,291,170
Area: 17,462 sq mi (45,226 sq km)
Language: Estonian, Russian
Did You Know? The city of Talinn has streets and buildings that date back to medieval times, along with modern streets and high-rise buildings.

Ethiopia

Capital: Addis Ababa
Population: 88,013,491
Area: 435,186 sq mi (1,127,127 sq km)
Language: Amharic, Tigrinya, Oromigna, Guaragigna, Somali, Arabic
Did You Know? Ethiopia was taken over by Italy in 1936 but was freed by British forces five years later during World War II.

The Gambia

Capital: Banjul
Population: 1,824,158
Area: 4,363 sq mi (11,300 sq km)
Language: English, Mandinka, Wolof
Did You Know? The Gambia is the smallest country by area on the continent of Africa.

Georgia

Capital: T'bilisi
Population: 4,600,825
Area: 26,911 sq mi (69,700 sq km)
Language: Georgian, Russian, Armenian, Azeri, Abkhaz
Did You Know? The Georgian alphabet is one of only a few alphabets still in use today. It is believed to have been created in the 5th century.

Germany

Capital: Berlin
Population: 82,282,988
Area: 137,847 sq mi (357,021 sq km)
Language: German
Did You Know? Germany has the biggest economy of any country in Europe.

BRANDENBURG GATE, BERLIN, GERMANY

Ghana

Capital: Accra
Population: 24,339,838
Area: 92,456 sq mi (239,460 sq km)
Language: English, Akan, Moshi-Dagomba, Ewe, Ga
Did You Know? In 1957, the British colony known as the Gold Coast was merged with another territory to form Ghana.

Greece

Capital: Athens
Population: 10,749,943
Area: 50,942 sq mi (131,940 sq km)
Language: Greek, English, French
Did You Know? Mount Athos is a self-governing province of Greece, with about 20 Greek Orthodox monasteries. Women are not allowed there.

Grenada

Capital: Saint George's
Population: 107,818
Area: 133 sq mi (344 sq km)
Language: English, French patois
Did You Know? Grenada is sometimes referred to as the "Spice of the Caribbean" because its top export is nutmeg.

Guatemala

Capital: Guatemala City
Population: 13,550,440
Area: 42,043 sq mi (108,890 sq km)
Language: Spanish, Amerindian languages
Did You Know? Before the arrival of the Spanish, the Mayan Indian empire flourished for more than 1,000 years in what is today Guatemala.

Guinea

Capital: Conakry
Population: 10,324,025
Area: 94,926 sq mi (245,857 sq km)
Language: French, Susu, Pulaar, Malinke
Did You Know? In its first five decades as an independent country (1958-2008), Guinea had only 2 different rulers.

COLOR KEY
- Africa
- Asia
- Australia
- Europe
- North America
- Pacific Islands
- South America

Guinea-Bissau

Capital: Bissau
Population: 1,565,126
Area: 13,946 sq mi (36,120 sq km)
Language: Portuguese, Crioulo, African languages
Did You Know? Cashew nuts are the nation's biggest crop and largest export.

Guyana

Capital: Georgetown
Population: 748,486
Area: 83,000 sq mi (214,970 sq km)
Language: English, Amerindian dialects, Creole, Hindi
Did You Know? Christopher Columbus explored the coast of Guyana in 1498, and almost 100 years later, Sir Walter Raleigh searched for gold there.

Haiti

Capital: Port-au-Prince
Population: 9,203,083
Area: 10,714 sq mi (27,750 sq km)
Language: French, Creole
Did You Know? An earthquake in January 2010 killed more than 200,000 Haitians and left many more homeless. Haiti was already the poorest country in the Americas.

Honduras
Capital: Tegucigalpa
Population: 7,989,415
Area: 43,278 sq mi (112,090 sq km)
Language: Spanish, Amerindian dialects
Did You Know? Christopher Columbus was the first recorded European to reach Honduras, where he landed in 1502.

Hungary
Capital: Budapest
Population: 9,880,059
Area: 35,919 sq mi (93,030 sq km)
Language: Hungarian (Magyar)
Did You Know? Budapest was originally two separate cities, Buda and Pest. The two areas are separated by the Danube River.

Iceland
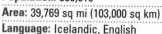
Capital: Reykjavik
Population: 308,910
Area: 39,769 sq mi (103,000 sq km)
Language: Icelandic, English
Did You Know? Iceland has no regular army, navy, or air force. It does have peacekeeping troops that it sends to different countries.

India

Capital: New Delhi
Population: 1,173,108,018
Area: 1,269,346 sq mi (3,287,590 sq km)
Language: Hindi, English, Bengali, Urdu
Did You Know? By around the year 2025, India is expected to have the largest population of any country in the world.

WATER TEMPLE BALI, INDONESIA

Indonesia
Capital: Jakarta
Population: 242,968,342
Area: 741,100 sq mi (1,919,440 sq km)
Language: Bahasa Indonesian, English, Dutch, Javanese
Did You Know? The country of Indonesia includes some 13,000 islands.

Iran

Capital: Tehran
Population: 67,037,517
Area: 636,296 sq mi (1,648,000 sq km)
Language: Farsi (Persian), Turkic, Kurdish
Did You Know? Iran has more known oil reserves than any other country except Saudi Arabia and Canada.

Iraq

Capital: Baghdad
Population: 29,671,605
Area: 168,754 sq mi (437,072 sq km)
Language: Arabic, Kurdish
Did You Know? The Sumer, one of the world's oldest known civilizations, lived in the Tigris-Euphrates Valley in the 4th millennium B.C.

Ireland

Capital: Dublin
Population: 4,250,163
Area: 27,135 sq mi (70,280 sq km)
Language: English, Irish
Did You Know? There is a legend that St. Patrick drove the snakes from Ireland, but Ireland has probably never had any wild snakes.

Israel

Capital: Jerusalem
Population: 7,353,985
Area: 8,019 sq mi (20,770 sq km)
Language: Hebrew, Arabic, English
Did You Know? The Dead Sea, on the Israel-Jordan border, is so salty that no fish can survive in its waters. But people can easily float on its surface.

COLOR KEY

- Africa
- Asia
- Australia
- Europe
- North America
- Pacific Islands
- South America

Italy

Capital: Rome
Population: 58,090,681
Area: 116,306 sq mi (301,230 sq km)
Language: Italian, German, French, Slovenian
Did You Know? In ancient times, Rome was the capital of a vast empire that covered most of Western Europe, North Africa, and the Middle East.

VENICE, ITALY

Jamaica

Capital: Kingston
Population: 2,847,232
Area: 4,244 sq mi (10,991 sq km)
Language: English, Jamaican Creole
Did You Know? Reggae, a mixture of native, rock, and soul music, was developed in Jamaica.

Japan

Capital: Tokyo
Population: 126,804,433
Area: 145,883 sq mi (377,835 sq km)
Language: Japanese
Did You Know? On special occasions many Japanese women, and some men, still wear the traditional robes known as kimonos. These robes come in many colors and styles.

Jordan

Capital: Amman
Population: 6,407,085
Area: 35,637 sq mi (92,300 sq km)
Language: Arabic, English
Did You Know? Philadelphia was the name in ancient times for the city that is now Amman.

Kazakhstan

Capital: Astana
Population: 15,460,484
Area: 1,049,155 sq mi (2,717,300 sq km)
Language: Kazakh, Russian
Did You Know? Like Russia, and unlike the other former Soviet republics, Kazakhstan has large oil reserves.

Kenya

Capital: Nairobi
Population: 40,046,566
Area: 224,962 sq mi (582,650 sq km)
Language: Kiswahili, English
Did You Know? Fossils of our human ancestors dating from more than 1 million years ago have been found in Kenya. Its National Museum is home to one of the world's best collections of human ancestral bones.

SAVANNA IN KENYA

Kiribati

Capital: Tarawa
Population: 99,482
Area: 313 sq mi (811 sq km)
Language: English, I-Kiribati
Did You Know? Kiribati's islands are spread across an area of the Pacific Ocean about the same size as the continental U.S.

Korea, North

Capital: Pyongyang
Population: 22,757,275
Area: 46,541 sq mi (120,540 sq km)
Language: Korean
Did You Know? North and South Korea have officially been at war for more than 50 years. A ceasefire has maintained the peace since 1953.

Korea, South

Capital: Seoul
Population: 48,636,068
Area: 38,023 sq mi (98,480 sq km)
Language: Korean
Did You Know? Ban Ki-moon, a former foreign minister of South Korea, became secretary-general of the UN in 2007.

Kosovo

Capital: Pristina
Population: 1,815,048
Area: 4,203 sq mi (10,887 sq km)
Language: Albanian, Serbian, Bosnian, Turkish, Roma
Did You Know? In 2008, the Kosovo Assembly declared its independence from Serbia, making it the world's newest country.

Kuwait

Capital: Kuwait City
Population: 2,789,132
Area: 6,880 sq mi (17,820 sq km)
Language: Arabic, English
Did You Know? In 2005, women were granted full political rights, including the right to vote and run in parliamentary elections.

Kyrgyzstan

Capital: Bishkek
Population: 5,508,626
Area: 76,641 sq mi (198,500 sq km)
Language: Kyrgyz, Russian
Did You Know? The region that is now Kyrgyzstan was conquered by the Mongol emperor Genghis Khan in the early 1200s.

VIENTIANE, LAOS

Laos

Capital: Vientiane
Population: 6,993,767
Area: 91,429 sq mi (236,800 sq km)
Language: Lao, French, English
Did You Know? The first kingdom in what is now Laos was called *Lan Xang*, or "Kingdom of the Million Elephants."

Latvia

Capital: Riga
Population: 2,217,969
Area: 24,938 sq mi (64,589 sq km)
Language: Latvian, Russian, Lithuanian
Did You Know? Latvia calls itself the "Land that Sings." Choirs and dance groups compete each year for a place in the Nationwide Latvian Song and Dance Celebration, which attracts more than 30,000 dancers, singers, and musicians.

Lebanon

Capital: Beirut
Population: 4,125,247
Area: 4,015 sq mi (10,400 sq km)
Language: Arabic, French, English, Armenian
Did You Know? The cedar of Lebanon is one of four cedar species in the world. The tree is mentioned in myths and even appears on the country's flag.

Lesotho

Capital: Maseru
Population: 1,919,552
Area: 11,720 sq mi (30,355 sq km)
Language: English, Sesotho, Zulu, Xhosa
Did You Know? The Kingdom of Lesotho is completely surrounded by South Africa.

Liberia

Capital: Monrovia
Population: 3,685,076
Area: 43,000 sq mi (111,370 sq km)
Language: English, ethnic languages
Did You Know? Liberia was founded in 1822 by freed African slaves from the U.S. It became an independent republic in 1847.

Libya

Capital: Tripoli
Population: 6,461,454
Area: 679,362 sq mi (1,759,540 sq km)
Language: Arabic, Italian, English
Did You Know? In 1969, Muammar al-Qaddafi led a military coup that overthrew the Libyan king. More than 40 years later, Qaddafi was still in power.

Liechtenstein

Capital: Vaduz
Population: 35,002
Area: 62 sq mi (160 sq km)
Language: German, Alemannic dialect
Did You Know? Liechtenstein and Qatar are the two richest countries in the world, as measured by economic output per person.

Lithuania

Capital: Vilnius
Population: 3,545,319
Area: 25,213 sq mi (65,300 sq km)
Language: Lithuanian, Russian, Polish
Did You Know? Lithuanians have many traditions relating to food and meals. For example, it was once considered a serious offense to place a loaf of bread upside down on the table.

COLOR KEY

- Africa
- Asia
- Australia
- Europe
- North America
- Pacific Islands
- South America

Luxembourg

Capital: Luxembourg
Population: 497,538
Area: 998 sq mi (2,586 sq km)
Language: French, German, Luxembourgish
Did You Know? Tiny Luxembourg has been ruled by Burgundy, Spain, Austria, and France, and it was overrun by Germany in two world wars.

Macedonia

Capital: Skopje
Population: 2,072,086
Area: 9,781 sq mi (25,333 sq km)
Language: Macedonian, Albanian, Turkish
Did You Know? Macedonia's Albanian and Turkish minorities are legacies of the Ottoman Empire, which ended its rule of Macedonia in 1913 after 500 years in power.

Madagascar

Capital: Antananarivo
Population: 21,281,844
Area: 226,657 sq mi (587,040 sq km)
Language: Malagasy, French
Did You Know? Madagascar is the world's fourth largest island after Greenland, New Guinea, and Borneo. Because of its isolation from mainland Africa, most of its wildlife and plants exist nowhere else on Earth.

Malawi

Capital: Lilongwe
Population: 15,447,500
Area: 45,745 sq mi (118,480 sq km)
Language: English, Chichewa
Did You Know? Malawi means "flaming waters" and is named for the sun setting on Lake Malawi, Africa's third largest lake.

Malaysia

Capital: Kuala Lumpur
Population: 26,160,256
Area: 127,317 sq mi (329,750 sq km)
Language: Malay, English, Chinese, Tamil
Did You Know? During the late 20th century, Malaysia grew into a major industrial power.

Maldives

Capital: Male
Population: 395,650
Area: 116 sq mi (300 sq km)
Language: Maldivian Divehi, English
Did You Know? The capital island of this 1,190-island nation is so overcrowded that Hulhumale, an artificial island, was created nearby.

Mali

Capital: Bamako
Population: 13,796,354
Area: 478,767 sq mi (1,240,000 sq km)
Language: French, Bambara
Did You Know? Until the 15th century, this area was part of the great Mali Empire in Africa.

Malta

Capital: Valletta
Population: 406,771
Area: 122 sq mi (316 sq km)
Language: Maltese, English
Did You Know? This island nation is located midway between Europe and Africa, but it considers itself part of Europe and joined the European Union in 2004.

TEA PLANTATION IN MALAYSIA

Marshall Islands

Capital: Majuro
Population: 65,859
Area: 70 sq mi (181 sq km)
Language: English, Marshallese
Did You Know? The United States occupied this island nation for several decades after World War II and the country still uses the U.S. dollar as its currency.

Mauritania

Capital: Nouakchott
Population: 3,205,080
Area: 397,955 sq mi (1,030,700 sq km)
Language: Arabic, Wolof, Pulaar
Did You Know? Since 80% of the country is covered by desert, most farming takes place on the banks of the Senegal River.

Mauritius

Capital: Port Louis
Population: 1,294,104
Area: 788 sq mi (2,040 sq km)
Language: Creole, Bhojpuri, French, English
Did You Know? About 70% of the people are descended from immigrants who came from India to work on Mauritius's sugar plantations.

Mexico

Capital: Mexico City
Population: 112,468,855
Area: 761,606 sq mi (1,972,550 sq km)
Language: Spanish, Mayan languages
Did You Know? Near Mexico City lie the ruins of an ancient city. It was abandoned in the eighth century A.D., and even its name was lost. The Aztecs later called it Teotihuacán, or "City of the Gods."

Micronesia

Capital: Palikir
Population: 107,154
Area: 271 sq mi (702 sq km)
Language: English, Trukese, Pohnpeian, Yapese
Did You Know? There are no formal political parties in Micronesia.

Moldova

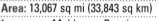

Capital: Chisinau
Population: 4,317,483
Area: 13,067 sq mi (33,843 sq km)
Language: Moldovan, Russian
Did You Know? On March 1, Moldovans celebrate the beginning of spring by wearing a pin with braided threads of red (symbolizing blood) and white (symbolizing life).

COASTLINE OF MONACO

Monaco

Capital: Monaco
Population: 30,586
Area: 0.76 sq mi (1.96 sq km)
Language: French, English, Italian, Monegasque
Did You Know? Except for a period of time when France annexed Monaco, the House of Grimaldi has been in power since 1297.

Mongolia

Capital: Ulaanbaatar
Population: 3,086,918
Area: 603,909 sq mi (1,564,116 sq km)
Language: Khalkha Mongolian
Did You Know? There is plenty of space in Mongolia, the most thinly populated country in the world.

Montenegro

Capital: Cetinje; Podgorica (admin.)
Population: 666,730
Area: 5,415 sq mi (14,026 sq km)
Language: Serbian, Bosnian, Albanian, Croatian
Did You Know? Montenegro adopted its first constitution in 2007, a little more than a year after it declared its independence from Serbia. Both countries had been a part of Yugoslavia.

Morocco

Capital: Rabat
Population: 31,627,428
Area: 172,414 sq mi (446,550 sq km)
Language: Arabic, Berber dialects, French
Did You Know? One of the world's most grueling foot races is the Marathon des Sables ("Marathon of Sands"), a 7-day, 143-mile trek across the Sahara Desert in Morocco.

Mozambique

Capital: Maputo
Population: 22,061,451
Area: 309,496 sq mi (801,590 sq km)
Language: Portuguese, Bantu languages
Did You Know? Mozambique has been hurt by colonial rule, civil war and famine. But after a peace deal in 1992 ended 16 years of civil conflict, the country has enjoyed a period of rapid economic growth.

Myanmar (Burma)

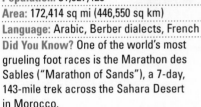

Capital: Nay Pyi Taw
Population: 53,414,374
Area: 261,970 sq mi (678,500 sq km)
Language: Burmese
Did You Know? The Mogok Stone Tract in northern Myanmar is known for producing some of the world's most brilliant rubies.

Namibia

Capital: Windhoek
Population: 2,128,471
Area: 318,696 sq mi (825,418 sq km)
Language: Afrikaans, English, German
Did You Know? The gap between rich and poor families in Namibia is one of the biggest in the world.

Nauru

Capital: Yaren district
Population: 14,264
Area: 8 sq mi (21 sq km)
Language: Nauruan, English
Did You Know? Named "Pleasant Island" by its first European visitors, Nauru is the world's smallest island nation in area.

Nepal

Capital: Kathmandu
Population: 28,951,852
Area: 56,827 sq mi (147,181 sq km)
Language: Nepali, Maithali, Bhojpuri, English
Did You Know? In Nepali, Mt. Everest is called Sagarmatha, which translates as "Goddess of the Sky."

Netherlands

Capital: Amsterdam; The Hague (admin.)
Population: 16,783,092
Area: 16,033 sq mi (41,526 sq km)
Language: Dutch, Frisian
Did You Know? There are twice as many bikes as cars in this country.

WINDMILLS IN THE NETHERLANDS

New Zealand

Capital: Wellington
Population: 4,252,277
Area: 103,738 sq mi (268,680 sq km)
Language: English, Maori
Did You Know? The first European to see the New Zealand coast was the 17th-century Dutch navigator Abel Tasman. The Maori natives did not let him land.

Nicaragua

Capital: Managua
Population: 5,995,928
Area: 49,998 sq mi (129,494 sq km)
Language: Spanish, Miskito, indigenous languages
Did You Know? The islands of the Miskito Cays, once an area for pirate hideouts, are now a protected area for coral reefs and wildlife.

Niger

Capital: Niamey
Population: 15,878,271
Area: 489,192 sq mi (1,267,000 sq km)
Language: French, Hausa, Djerma
Did You Know? Niger was a crossroads of ancient trade in Africa. Caravans would stop here on their way to Timbuktu, Mali.

Nigeria

Capital: Abuja
Population: 152,217,341
Area: 356,669 sq mi (923,768 sq km)
Language: English, Hausa, Yoruba, Ibo
Did You Know? Nigeria has more people than any other country in Africa.

Norway

Capital: Oslo
Population: 4,676,305
Area: 125,021 sq mi (323,802 sq km)
Language: Norwegian, Sami
Did You Know? The UN ranks Norway as the nation with the highest "quality of life."

BERGEN, NORWAY

Oman

Capital: Muscat
Population: 2,967,717
Area: 82,031 sq mi (212,460 sq km)
Language: Arabic, English, Indian dialects
Did You Know? As part of their traditional clothing, Omani men carry an ornate dagger called a khanjar tucked in the front of a special belt.

Pakistan

Capital: Islamabad
Population: 177,276,594
Area: 310,403 sq mi (803,940 sq km)
Language: Urdu, English, Punjabi, Sindhi
Did You Know? Pakistan and Syria both have close to 2 million refugees living within their borders, more than any other countries in the world.

COLOR KEY

- Africa
- Asia
- Australia
- Europe
- North America
- Pacific Islands
- South America

Palau

Capital: Melekeok
Population: 20,879
Area: 177 sq mi (458 sq km)
Language: English, Palauan, Sonsoral, Tobi, Angaur
Did You Know? Palau's marine life is among the world's most diverse—more than 1,400 species of fish and 500 species of coral can be found here.

Panama

Capital: Panama City
Population: 3,410,676
Area: 30,193 sq mi (78,200 sq km)
Language: Spanish, English
Did You Know? Panama is the shortest link between the Atlantic and Pacific Oceans in the Americas, making its 50-mile-long (80-km) canal of great strategic importance.

Papua New Guinea

Capital: Port Moresby
Population: 6,064,515
Area: 178,704 sq mi (462,840 sq km)
Language: English, Motu, Melanesian pidgin
Did You Know? There are only six species of poisonous birds in the world, and they all live in Papua New Guinea.

Paraguay

Capital: Asunción
Population: 6,375,830
Area: 157,047 sq mi (406,750 sq km)
Language: Spanish, Guarani
Did You Know? Paraguay and Bolivia are the only landlocked countries in the Americas.

Peru

Capital: Lima
Population: 29,907,003
Area: 496,226 sq mi (1,285,220 sq km)
Language: Spanish, Quechua, Aymara
Did You Know? Ceviche, made of raw seafood soaked in lemon or lime juice, is a favorite dish in Peru.

Philippines

Capital: Manila
Population: 99,900,177
Area: 115,831 sq mi (300,000 sq km)
Language: Filipino, English
Did You Know? The Battle of Leyte Gulf, fought in 1944 off the Philippines, was the biggest naval battle in history. It involved 282 Allied and Japanese ships and about 2,000 planes.

Poland

Capital: Warsaw
Population: 38,463,689
Area: 120,726 sq mi (312,679 sq km)
Language: Polish, Ukrainian, German
Did You Know? The first and only queen of Poland, Queen Jadwiga, married the grand duke of Lithuania in 1386, uniting the two kingdoms into one.

Portugal

Capital: Lisbon
Population: 10,735,765
Area: 35,672 sq mi (92,391 sq km)
Language: Portuguese
Did You Know? The national style of music, called *fado*, originated in Lisbon. It has a sad and longing sound.

PENA PALACA, SINTRA, PORTUGAL

Qatar

Capital: Doha
Population: 840,926
Area: 4,416 sq mi (11,437 sq km)
Language: Arabic, English
Did You Know? Qatar has one of the world's lowest unemployment rates. Out of every 200 people in the work force, only 1 is jobless.

Romania

Capital: Bucharest
Population: 22,181,287
Area: 91,699 sq mi (237,500 sq km)
Language: Romanian, Hungarian, German
Did You Know? Prince Vlad Tepes ("the Impaler"), who once ruled part of Romania, was the inspiration for the fictional Dracula.

Russia

Capital: Moscow
Population: 139,390,205
Area: 6,592,772 sq mi (17,075,200 sq km)
Language: Russian, many minority languages
Did You Know? The world's biggest country, Russia spans two continents (Europe and Asia) and borders 14 other nations.

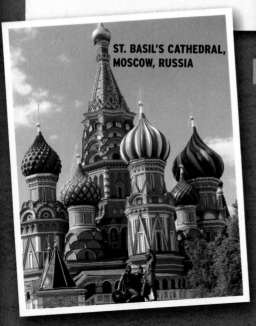

ST. BASIL'S CATHEDRAL, MOSCOW, RUSSIA

GORILLA IN VOLCANOES NATIONAL PARK, RWANDA

Rwanda

Capital: Kigali
Population: 11,055,976
Area: 10,169 sq mi (26,338 sq km)
Language: French, English, Kinyarwanda, Kiswahili
Did You Know? Volcanoes National Park is home to one of only two remaining mountain gorilla populations in the world.

Saint Kitts and Nevis

Capital: Basseterre
Population: 49,898
Area: 101 sq mi (261 sq km)
Language: English
Did You Know? This two-island state is the smallest independent nation in the Caribbean, in both size and population.

Saint Lucia

Capital: Castries
Population: 160,922
Area: 238 sq mi (616 sq km)
Language: English, French patois
Did You Know? The Caribbean island is a popular spot to visit because of its beautiful beaches, unusual plants, and the Qualibou volcano with its boiling sulphur springs.

COLOR KEY

- Africa
- Asia
- Australia
- Europe
- North America
- Pacific Islands
- South America

Saint Vincent and the Grenadines

Capital: Kingstown
Population: 104,217
Area: 150 sq mi (389 sq km)
Language: English, French patois
Did You Know? Christopher Columbus landed on the island of St. Vincent in January 1498.

Samoa (formerly Western Samoa)

Capital: Apia
Population: 192,001
Area: 1,137 sq mi (2,944 sq km)
Language: English, Samoan
Did You Know? This Pacific island nation has temperatures in the 70s and 80s (Fahrenheit) all year round.

San Marino

Capital: San Marino
Population: 31,477
Area: 24 sq mi (61 sq km)
Language: Italian
Did You Know? According to legend, San Marino was founded in 301 A.D. by a Christian stonemason, Marinus, for whom the country was named.

São Tomé and Príncipe

Capital: São Tomé
Population: 175,808
Area: 386 sq mi (1,001 sq km)
Language: Portuguese, Creole
Did You Know? Cocoa is the country's chief export, but output has declined in recent years, putting strains on the already weak economy.

Saudi Arabia

Capital: Riyadh
Population: 29,207,277
Area: 830,000 sq mi (2,149,960 sq km)
Language: Arabic
Did You Know? Saudi Arabia is the birthplace of Islam, and just about all Saudis today are Muslims. Only Muslim religious services are permitted in public.

MECCA, SAUDI ARABIA

Senegal

Capital: Dakar
Population: 14,086,103
Area: 75,749 sq mi (196,190 sq km)
Language: French, Wolof, Pulaar
Did You Know? Dakar is the westernmost point on the continent of Africa.

Serbia

Capital: Belgrade
Population: 7,344,847
Area: 29,913 sq mi (77,474 sq km)
Language: Serbian, Albanian, Romanian
Did You Know? The Roma (Gypsies), one of Serbia's largest minority groups, have helped to maintain the country's folk music tradition.

Seychelles

Capital: Victoria
Population: 88,340
Area: 176 sq mi (455 sq km)
Language: Creole, English, French
Did You Know? The colors of Seychelles' flag represent the sky and sea (blue), the sun (yellow), the people and their work (red), social justice and harmony (white), and the environment (green).

Sierra Leone

Capital: Freetown
Population: 5,245,695
Area: 27,699 sq mi (71,740 sq km)
Language: English, Mende, Temne, Krio
Did You Know? Diamonds are one of this country's major exports.

Singapore

Capital: Singapore
Population: 4,701,069
Area: 269 sq mi (697 sq km)
Language: Chinese, Malay, Tamil, English
Did You Know? Girls born in Singapore today can be expected, on average, to live to age 85.

SKYLINE OF SINGAPORE

Slovakia

Capital: Bratislava
Population: 5,470,306
Area: 18,859 sq mi (48,845 sq km)
Language: Slovak, Hungarian
Did You Know? Slovakia and the Czech Republic were joined together after World War I (as the country of Czechoslovakia), but they broke up into separate nations in 1993.

Slovenia

Capital: Ljubljana
Population: 2,003,136
Area: 7,827 sq mi (20,273 sq km)
Language: Slovenian, Serbo-Croatian
Did You Know? Slovenia was part of Yugoslavia from 1918 to 1991, when it declared independence. It later became a member of the European Union and the UN.

Solomon Islands

Capital: Honiara
Population: 609,794
Area: 10,985 sq mi (28,450 sq km)
Language: English, Melanesian pidgin
Did You Know? Because so many different languages are spoken in the Solomon Islands, many people communicate using a simplified English called Melanesian pidgin.

Somalia

Capital: Mogadishu
Population: 10,112,453
Area: 246,201 sq mi (637,657 sq km)
Language: Somali, Arabic, Italian, English
Did You Know? Pirates operating off the coast of Somalia captured 47 ships and close to 900 people during 2009, earning a great deal of ransom money.

South Africa

Capital: Pretoria (admin.); Cape Town (legis.); Bloemfontein (judicial)
Population: 49,109,107
Area: 471,011 sq mi (1,219,912 sq km)
Language: Afrikaans, English, Ndebele, Sotho, Zulu, Xhosa
Did You Know? South Africa is a leading source of valuable minerals, such as gold, diamonds, and platinum.

Spain

Capital: Madrid
Population: 40,548,753
Area: 194,897 sq mi (504,782 sq km)
Language: Castilian Spanish, Catalan, Galician
Did You Know? Every year in August, people crowd into the town of Buñol for a huge tomato fight. By the time it's over, everyone is wading in rivers of tomato juice.

KIO TOWERS, MADRID, SPAIN

Sri Lanka

Capital: Colombo
Population: 21,513,990
Area: 25,332 sq mi (65,610 sq km)
Language: Sinhala, Tamil, English
Did You Know? Ceylon tea takes its name from this country, which used to be called Ceylon while under European rule.

Sudan

Capital: Khartoum
Population: 41,980,182
Area: 967,499 sq mi (2,505,810 sq km)
Language: Arabic, Nubian, Ta Bedawie
Did You Know? Sudan is Africa's biggest country in total area. But if you only count land area, Algeria is a little bigger..

Suriname

Capital: Paramaribo
Population: 486,618
Area: 63,039 sq mi (163,270 sq km)
Language: Dutch, English, Sranang Tongo
Did You Know? Many Surinamers are descended from escaped West African slaves, who were brought to Suriname when it was still a Dutch colony.

Swaziland

Capital: Mbabane
Population: 1,354,051
Area: 6,704 sq mi (17,363 sq km)
Language: English, siSwati
Did You Know? Swaziland is ruled by a king, who has important powers.

Sweden

Capital: Stockholm
Population: 9,074,055
Area: 173,732 sq mi (449,964 sq km)
Language: Swedish, Sami, Finnish
Did You Know? Recent data show that Sweden has a smaller gap between rich and poor families than any other country in the world.

COLOR KEY

- Africa
- Asia
- Australia
- Europe
- North America
- Pacific Islands
- South America

THE ALPS, SWITZERLAND

Switzerland

Capital: Bern (admin.); Lausanne (judicial)
Population: 7,623,438
Area: 15,942 sq mi (41,290 sq km)
Language: German, French, Italian, Romansch
Did You Know? Switzerland has not fought in a war since 1515. It serves as headquarters for UN and other international organizations, but did not join the UN until 2002.

Syria

Capital: Damascus
Population: 22,198,110
Area: 71,498 sq mi (185,180 sq km)
Language: Arabic, Kurdish, Armenian
Did You Know? Tablets found in the ancient city of Ugarit contain one of the world's oldest alphabets, dating back to around 1400 B.C.

Taiwan

Capital: Taipei
Population: 23,024,956
Area: 13,892 sq mi (35,980 sq km)
Language: Mandarin Chinese, Taiwanese
Did You Know? Although Taiwan set up its own government in 1949, China considers Taiwan to be one of its provinces and still under its control.

Tajikistan

Capital: Dushanbe
Population: 7,487,489
Area: 55,251 sq mi (143,100 sq km)
Language: Tajik, Russian
Did You Know? Tajikistan's main source of energy is hydroelectricity. Its Nurek Dam is the highest dam in the world.

Tanzania

Capital: Dar es Salaam Dodoma (legislative)
Population: 41,892,895
Area: 364,900 sq mi (945,087 sq km)
Language: Kiswahili (Swahili), English, Arabic
Did You Know? Lake Victoria, the world's second biggest freshwater lake (after Lake Superior), is shared by Tanzania, Kenya, and Uganda.

Thailand

Capital: Bangkok
Population: 66,404,688
Area: 198,457 sq mi (514,000 sq km)
Language: Thai, English
Did You Know? Kitti's hog-nosed bat, the world's smallest mammal, is found only in Thailand. It is about an inch long.

BANGKOK, THAILAND

Timor-Leste (East Timor)

Capital: Dili
Population: 1,154,625
Area: 5,743 sq mi (14,874 sq km)
Language: Tetum, Portuguese, Indonesian, English
Did You Know? This country occupies the eastern half of Timor island; the island's western half (except for an area on the coast) belongs to Indonesia.

Togo

Capital: Lomé
Population: 6,199,841
Area: 21,925 sq mi (56,785 sq km)
Language: French, Ewe, Mina, Kabye, Dagomba
Did You Know? Togo is one of the world's leading producers of phosphates.

Tonga

Capital: Nuku'alofa
Population: 122,580
Area: 289 sq mi (748 sq km)
Language: Tongan, English
Did You Know? Tonga is ruled by the only surviving monarchy in Polynesia, though it does have a parliament in which most of the members are elected.

Trinidad and Tobago

Capital: Port-of-Spain
Population: 1,228,691
Area: 1,980 sq mi (5,128 sq km)
Language: English, Hindi, French, Spanish
Did You Know? Many people from India came to Trinidad in the 1800s to work on sugar cane plantations. Today, about 40 percent of Trinidad's population is of Indian descent.

PARLATUVIER BAY, TOBAGO

Tunisia

Capital: Tunis
Population: 10,589,025
Area: 63,170 sq mi (163,610 sq km)
Language: Arabic, French
Did You Know? The ancient city of Carthage was located in what is now Tunisia.

Turkey

Capital: Ankara
Population: 77,804,122
Area: 301,384 sq mi (780,580 sq km)
Language: Turkish, Kurdish, Arabic
Did You Know? The Bosporus Bridge, in Istanbul, spans two continents, linking Asia with Europe. About 3% of Turkey is in Europe, and the rest in Asia.

Turkmenistan

Capital: Ashgabat
Population: 4,940,916
Area: 188,456 sq mi (488,100 sq km)
Language: Turkmen, Russian, Uzbek
Did You Know? Turkmenistan has the world's fourth-largest reserves of natural gas, after Russia, Iran, and Qatar.

Tuvalu

Capital: Funafuti
Population: 10,472
Area: 10 sq mi (26 sq km)
Language: Tuvaluan, English
Did You Know? Tuvalu, with its 9 small islands, has the second-smallest population of any country in the world.

COLOR KEY

- Africa
- Asia
- Australia
- Europe
- North America
- Pacific Islands
- South America

LONDON EYE FERRIS WHEEL, UNITED KINDGOM

Uganda

Capital: Kampala
Population: 33,398,682
Area: 91,136 sq mi (236,040 sq km)
Language: English, Ganda, Swahili
Did You Know? The crested crane is a national symbol and appears on Uganda's flag.

Ukraine

Capital: Kiev (Kyiv)
Population: 45,415,596
Area: 233,090 sq mi (603,700 sq km)
Language: Ukrainian, Russian
Did You Know? Ukraine has the biggest area of any country in Europe, except Russia. Both Ukraine and Russia were once part of the Soviet Union.

United Arab Emirates

Capital: Abu Dhabi
Population: 4,975,593
Area: 32,278 sq mi (83,600 sq km)
Language: Arabic, Persian, English, Hindi, Urdu
Did You Know? In 2010, the skyscraper now called the Burj Khalifa (Khalifa Tower) opened in Dubai, becoming the world's tallest building.

United Kingdom (Great Britain)

Capital: London
Population: 61,284,806
Area: 94,526 sq mi (244,820 sq km)
Language: English, Welsh, Scottish Gaelic
Did You Know? Queen Elizabeth I, Sir Isaac Newton, Charles Darwin, and Charles Dickens are among many famous people buried in London's Westminster Abbey.

United States

Capital: Washington, DC
Population: 308,885,492*
Area: 3,795,951 sq mi (9,831,513 sq km)
Language: English, Spanish
Did You Know? The U.S. is the world's leading economic and military power. It is also a major source of entertainment: American TV, films, and music are all popular around the globe.

March 2010

Uruguay

Capital: Montevideo
Population: 3,510,386
Area: 68,039 sq mi (176,220 sq km)
Language: Spanish, Portunol
Did You Know? The leaves of the *yerba maté* shrub are used to brew a popular drink in Uruguay. The tea is often drunk from a gourd using a metal straw.

PAGODA IN VIETNAM

Uzbekistan

Capital: Tashkent
Population: 27,865,738
Area: 172,742 sq mi (447,400 sq km)
Language: Uzbek, Russian, Tajik
Did You Know? The city of Samarkand contains the tomb of Tamerlane (1336–1405), a conqueror who once ruled over much of Asia.

Vanuatu

Capital: Port-Vila
Population: 221,552
Area: 4,710 sq mi (12,200 sq km)
Language: French, English, Bislama, local languages
Did You Know? More than 100 local languages and dialects are spoken on the 80-plus islands that make up this Pacific nation.

Vatican City

Population: 845 (2009 estimate)
Area: 0.17 sq mi (0.44 sq km)
Language: Italian, Latin, French
Did You Know? Vatican City, the seat of the Roman Catholic Church, is the world's smallest nation in both size and population.

Venezuela

Capital: Caracas
Population: 27,223,228
Area: 352,144 sq mi (912,050 sq km)
Language: Spanish, indigenous dialects
Did You Know? Venezuela has more oil reserves by far than any other country in the Americas except Canada.

Vietnam

Capital: Hanoi
Population: 89,571,130
Area: 127,244 sq mi (329,560 sq km)
Language: Vietnamese, English, French, Chinese
Did You Know? Vietnam exports more goods to the U.S. than to any other country.

Yemen

Capital: Sana'a
Population: 23,495,361
Area: 203,850 sq mi (527,970 sq km)
Language: Arabic
Did You Know? One of Yemen's chief crops is coffee. "Mocha" coffee beans take their name from the Yemeni port city of Mocha.

Zambia

Capital: Lusaka
Population: 12,056,923
Area: 290,586 sq mi (752,614 sq km)
Language: English, indigenous languages
Did You Know? Victoria Falls, one of the world's largest waterfalls, provides Zambia with a source of hydroelectric power.

Zimbabwe

Capital: Harare
Population: 11,651,858
Area: 150,804 sq mi (390,580 sq km)
Language: English, Shona, Sindebele
Did You Know? The nation takes its name from the famous stone ruins of Great Zimbabwe, a city built by wealthy Shona-speaking cattlemen between the 13th and 14th centuries.

COLOR KEY

- Africa
- Asia
- Australia
- Europe
- North America
- Pacific Islands
- South America

Native Americans

Which state has the largest Native American population? → page 181

Native Americans are thought to have arrived in the Americas 18,000 years ago, most likely from northeast Asia. Although their population decreased significantly through the 17th, 18th, and 19th centuries from disease and war, there are still hundreds of tribes, or nations, each with unique languages and traditions.

WHAT CAME FROM NATIVE AMERICANS

FIRST NATIVE AMERICAN WRITING SYSTEM

Sequoyah was a Cherokee scholar born in Tennessee in about 1766. After observing white people writing and reading letters, or "talking leaves," Sequoyah began creating a writing system for the Cherokee language, which he completed probably in 1821. His system of about 85 symbols represented all the sounds used in the language. Thousands of Cherokee quickly became literate as a result of Sequoyah's work. By 1828, the nation's first bilingual newspaper (in Cherokee and English), the *Cherokee Phoenix*, was in print. Sequoyah's achievement emphasized the importance of literacy in passing on knowledge. He died in 1843. The sequoia, California's giant evergreen tree, is named in his honor.

NAVAJO (DINE) WAR CODE

The Navajo Nation spans 27,000 square miles across Arizona, New Mexico, and Utah and is America's most populated reservation, with about 175,000 residents. The Dine (dee-NAY), as they call themselves, belong to clans in which members trace descent through the mother. Many Dine still speak a highly descriptive and unique language called Athapaskan. Used as a code in World War II, it was never cracked. Code talkers from at least 16 tribes served during the war. Local radio still broadcasts sports, including New Mexico State University's football games, in Athapaskan.

World War II "code talkers" ▲

GAMES AND SPORTS

Many of today's games and sports came from early Native American ways of life. Lacrosse, for example, began as an ancient Indian event called baggataway. Many people today canoe, toboggan, or hike through the snow just for fun. Algonquian Indians in the northeastern U.S. first used birchbark canoes for fishing and travel. The toboggan started out as a Native American bark-and-skin runnerless sled to move game or other heavy objects over snow or ice. In the far north, the Inuit wore snowshoes strung with caribou skin to walk on deep, soft snow.

TIME LINE NORTH AMERICAN INDIANS

c. 10,000 B.C. Native Americans occupied much of North America.

c. 200 B.C.– A.D. 500 Hopewell Indians built earthen mounds for ceremonial purposes in today's Illinois and Ohio river valleys.

c. 1100 The Ancestral Puebloan Indians began building multistory cliff dwellings in the southwestern U.S.

1492 Christopher Columbus made contact with Taino tribes on the island he named Hispaniola.

c. 1600 Five tribes—the Mohawk, Oneida, Onondaga, Cayuga, and Seneca—formed the Iroquois Confederacy in the Northeast.

1637 Settlers in Connecticut defeated Pequot Indians in the Pequot War.

1754–63 Many Native Americans fought as allies of either French or British troops in the French and Indian War.

1804–06 Sacagawea served as an interpreter and guide for Lewis and Clark.

1827 Cherokee tribes in what is now Georgia formed the Cherokee Nation with a constitution and elected governing officials.

1830 Congress passed the Indian Removal Act, the first law that forced tribes to move so that U.S. citizens could settle certain areas of land.

1834 Congress created the Indian Territory for tribes removed from their lands. It covered present-day Oklahoma, Kansas, and Nebraska.

1835–42 Seminoles battled U.S. troops in the Second Seminole War. They lost the conflict and their homeland in Florida.

1838–39 The U.S. government forced Cherokees to move to Indian Territory. Thousands died during the so-called Trail of Tears.

1876 Sioux and Cheyenne Indians defeated troops led by U.S. colonel George Armstrong Custer in the Battle of the Little Bighorn.

1877 After the U.S. government tried to remove his people to Idaho, Chief Joseph led a Nez Percé retreat to Canada but surrendered before reaching the border.

1890 U.S. soldiers massacred more than 200 Sioux, including unarmed women and children, in the Battle of Wounded Knee, the last major conflict between U.S. troops and Native Americans.

1912 Jim Thorpe, a Native American, won the decathalon and the pentathalon in the 1912 Olympic Games.

1924 Congress granted all Native Americans U.S. citizenship.

1929 Charles Curtis, a member of the Kaw Nation, became the first American of Indian ancestry elected vice president of the U.S.

1934 Congress passed the Indian Reorganization Act to increase tribal self-government.

1968 The American Indian Movement, a civil rights organization, was founded.

2004 The National Museum of the American Indian opened in Washington, D.C.

2010 Wilma Mankiller, who in 1985 became the first female chief of the Cherokee Nation, died.

MAJOR CULTURAL AREAS OF NATIVE NORTH AMERICANS

Climate and geography influenced the culture of the people who lived in these regions. On the plains, for example, people depended on the great herds of buffalo for food. For Aleuts and Inuit in the far north, seals and whales were an important food source. There are more than 560 tribes officially recognized by the U.S. government today and more than 56 million acres of tribal lands. Below are some of the major Native North American cultural areas.

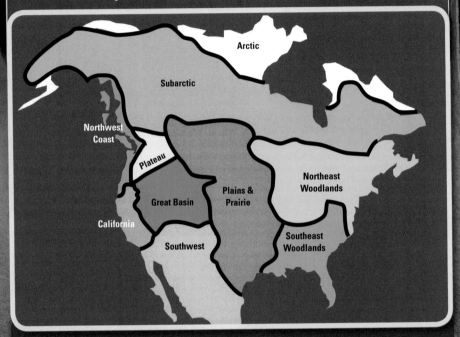

NORTHEAST WOODLANDS
The Illinois, Iroquois (Mohawk, Onondaga, Cayuga, Oneida, Seneca, and Tuscarora), Lenape, Menominee, Micmac, Narragansett, Potawatomi, Shawnee

SOUTHEAST WOODLANDS
The Cherokee, Chickasaw, Choctaw, Creek, Seminole

PLAINS & PRAIRIE The Arapaho, Blackfoot, Cheyenne, Comanche, Hidatsa, Kaw, Mandan, Sioux

SOUTHWEST The Apache, Navajo, Havasupai, Mojave, Pima, Pueblo (Hopi, Isleta, Laguna, Zuñi)

GREAT BASIN The Paiute, Shoshoni, Ute

CALIFORNIA The Klamath, Maidu, Miwok, Modoc, Patwin, Pomo, Wintun, Yurok

PLATEAU The Cayuse, Nez Percé, Okanagon, Salish, Spokan, Umatilla, Walla Walla, Yakima

NORTHWEST COAST The Chinook, Haida, Kwakiutl, Makah, Nootka, Salish, Tillamook, Tlingit, Tsimshian

SUBARCTIC The Beaver, Chipewyan, Chippewa, Cree, Ingalik, Kaska, Kutchin, Montagnais, Naskapi, Tanana

ARCTIC The Aleut, Inuit, and Yuit

NATIVE AMERICAN NUMBERS*

Here are some facts from the U.S. Census Bureau about the Native American population of the U.S. today, compared to statistics for the U.S. population as a whole:

	Native Americans	Total U.S. Population
Median age	30.9 years	36.9 years
Average number of people in a family	3.7	3.2
Percentage of people 5 years and older who speak only English at home	72%	80%
Percentage of households owning their own home	55%	67%

*2008 U.S. Census Bureau estimates (American Community Survey). Figures refer to the Native American population who reported only one race.

Native American and Alaska Native Populations by State*

State	Population	State	Population
Alabama	24,825	Nebraska	18,949
Alaska	104,990	Nevada	39,039
Arizona	315,727	New Hampshire	3,642
Arkansas	24,302	New Jersey	30,132
California	443,719	New Mexico	192,235
Colorado	60,375	New York	111,337
Connecticut	13,387	North Carolina	115,635
Delaware	3,691	North Dakota	35,666
Florida	91,412	Ohio	29,443
Georgia	35,528	Oklahoma	291,390
Hawaii	7,569	Oregon	54,405
Idaho	23,209	Pennsylvania	27,181
Illinois	45,128	Rhode Island	6,591
Indiana	20,390	South Carolina	19,091
Iowa	12,644	South Dakota	68,000
Kansas	28,895	Tennessee	20,709
Kentucky	11,006	Texas	184,649
Louisiana	28,230	Utah	38,102
Maine	7,889	Vermont	2,437
Maryland	20,321	Virginia	28,595
Massachusetts	20,361	Washington	112,965
Michigan	62,094	West Virginia	4,203
Minnesota	64,503	Wisconsin	55,844
Mississippi	14,740	Wyoming	13,555
Missouri	30,034	Wash., DC	2,367
Montana	62,303	U.S. total	3,083,434

*2008 U.S. Census Bureau estimates. Figures do not include people who reported belonging to additional ethnic groups.

TOTEM POLES

Northwest Coast Indians carve totem poles with painted images of animals and human faces. The carvings represent animals and spirits and may also tell stories about specific people or events. The poles, often carved from tree trunks, serve as memorials, gravemarkers, and welcome signs in front of homes. The tallest totem pole, erected in 1994 and dismantled in 1997, was located in Victoria, British Columbia, Canada. It was 180 feet, 3 inches tall.

Numbers

Where did the search engine Google get its name? → page 183

To Infinity...and Beyond

The set of numbers includes all different types—positive and negative numbers, fractions and decimals, and even irrational numbers that cannot be expressed as a fraction. In math, numbers are thought of as infinite because you can always imagine a larger number. For example, what's the biggest number you know? Add 1 to that number and you have a bigger number! Both positive and negative numbers go on to infinity.

The symbol for infinity looks like an eight lying on its side.

Prime Time

All numbers—except 0 and 1—are either prime numbers or composite numbers. A prime number is a number that can be divided only by itself and the number 1. So, prime numbers include 2, 3, 5, 7, 11, 13, 17, and so on. All other positive numbers (other than 1) are called composite numbers, because they have at least two factors (numbers they can be divided by evenly) other than 1. For example, 6 is a composite number. Its factors are 1, 2, 3, and 6.

Integers

Integers are whole numbers, both positive and negative. Zero is an integer. Fractions, decimals, and percentages are not.

The Prefix Tells the Number

After each number shown below, there are one or more prefixes, which are used to form words that include that number. Knowing what the prefix stands for can help you understand the meaning of the word. For example, a **bi**cycle has two wheels. The pieces in the video game *Tetris* have four squares.

1	uni-, mono-	unicorn, monorail		8	oct-	octopus
2	bi-	binoculars		9	non-	nonagon
3	tri-	triangle		10	dec-	decade
4	quadr-, tetr-	quadrangle, tetrahedron		100	cent-	century
5	pent-, quint-	pentagon, quintuplet		1,000	kilo-	kilometer
6	hex-, sext-	hexagon, sextuplet		million	mega-	megabyte
7	hept-, sept-	heptathlon, septuplet		billion	giga-	gigabyte

ROMAN NUMERALS

People have been counting since the earliest of times. The counting system used by the ancient Romans is still in use today. Roman numerals are built from different letters. The chart below shows some common Roman numerals.

1	I	16	XVI
2	II	17	XVII
3	III	18	XVIII
4	IV	19	XIX
5	V	20	XX
6	VI	30	XXX
7	VII	40	XL
8	VIII	50	L
9	IX	60	LX
10	X	70	LXX
11	XI	80	LXXX
12	XII	90	XC
13	XIII	100	C
14	XIV	500	D
15	XV	1,000	M

If one Roman numeral is followed by one with a greater value, the first is subtracted from the second. For example, IX means 10 – 1 = 9. Think of it as "one less than ten." On the other hand, if a Roman numeral is followed by one or more others that are equal or of lesser value, add them together. Thus, LXI means 50 + 10 + 1 = 61.

A Roman numeral can be repeated only three times to express a number. For example, XXX equals 30. You would have to write XL (50 minus 10) to show the number 40.

One place you might see Roman numerals used is in the Super Bowl. In 2010, the New Orleans Saints won Super Bowl XLIV. What number Super Bowl was that? How would you write 2010 in Roman numerals?

Super Bowl I was played in 1967. What was the Roman numeral used for the Super Bowl played in 1985?

ANSWERS ON PAGES 334–336.

Zero

Do you know the Roman numeral for 0? Probably not, because there isn't one! The Babylonians in Asia, Hindus in India, and Mayans in the Americas were among the first peoples to use the idea of zero as a "placeholder." In our number system "10" means 1 "ten" and 0 "ones." The 0 in 10 is a placeholder in the ones column.

Zero has some interesting properties. Any number multiplied by 0 equals 0. Any number added to 0 equals the original number.

Super Bowl XLIV

did you **Know?**

The popular search engine Google based its name on the word googol, which is a number represented by the numeral 1 followed by 100 zeros. The company name is meant to symbolize Google's mission to organize the huge amount of information on the Internet.

Fractions, Decimals, and Percents

FRACTIONS

A fraction is part of a whole. It helps to think of a fraction as a slice of a circle, with the circle being the whole (represented by the number 1). Check out the common fractions at right.

1/2	2/3	7/8

1/2 is missing   *1/3 is missing*   *1/8 is missing*

HOMEWORK TIP

To reduce a fraction to its lowest terms, divide both the numerator (top number) and the denominator (bottom number) by the largest number by which both can be divided evenly. For example, to reduce 8/16 to its lowest terms, divide the numerator and denominator by 8. You end up with 1/2.

PERCENTS

Percents also represent part of a whole. The word *percent* means "per hundred." So, a percent is like a fraction with a denominator of 100. You see percents every day. If you scored 80 percent on a test at school, you received 80 points out of a possible 100. Changing percents to fractions is not hard. Here are two examples:

80% = 80/100; reduced to its lowest terms, 80/100 becomes 4/5
23% = 23/100, which cannot be reduced

DECIMALS

Decimals are also part of a whole. They are represented with numerals placed to the right of a decimal point. Each position—or place—in a decimal has its own name.

7.75
↑ ones place   ↑ tenths place   ↑ hundredths place

HOMEWORK TIP

To convert a decimal to a fraction or a percent, you have to pay attention to the placement after the decimal point. For example, 0.2 means 2 tenths, or 2/10, which can be reduced to 1/5. And think of 0.25 as 25 hundredths, or 25/100, which can be reduced to 1/4. To convert a decimal to a percent, just move the decimal point to the right of the hundredths place:
0.25 = 25% and 0.025 = 2.5%

Can you change these decimals to fractions that are reduced to lowest terms?
0.4   0.75   0.9

ANSWERS ON PAGES 334–336.

By the Numbers

Grab your thinking cap—and a calculator! It's time to put your numbers knowledge to the test. Solve the math problem or puzzle in each clue. Then fill in the correct answer in the puzzle. (Write out the word or words. Don't use numerals.) We've filled in one of them for you. Ready? 1-2-3 go!

ACROSS

1. XV x VI

5. infinity, sideways?

6. 1, 1, 2, 3, 5, 8, ___

8. LX – XXVIII

10. Heather's grandmother has been alive for 1 century, minus 3 decades, plus 2 years. That means she is ___ years old.

12. one of two numbers that go into 17 evenly

13. 2, ___, 16, 256, 65,536

14. The book you want usually costs $10, but today it is 30 percent off. How much (in dollars) will it cost with the discount?

15. hexagon + pentagon = ___ sides

DOWN

2. 540 minutes = ___ hours

3. Joey bought 60 jelly beans. He ate 1/3 of them on Monday, and 1/2 of the remaining ones on Tuesday. How many jelly beans did he have left?

4. In a new video game, cars steer around the track at 120 miles per hour. How many minutes would it take to complete a lap around a 30-mile track?

6. 2, ___, 5, 7, 11, 13

7. 31, 28, 31, 30, ___, 30, 31, 31

9. 3/4 + 1/2 + 3/4

10. Your friend wants to meet you at the mall in 240 minutes and 7,200 seconds. In how many hours should you get there?

11. number of wheels on four tricycles

13. Raquel has $1.64. She has four pennies, three dimes, and a nickel. How many quarters does she have?

Population

What U.S. state has the fewest people? ➡ page 188

WHERE DO PEOPLE LIVE?

In 1959, there were 3 billion people in the world. By 1999, there were 6 billion. According to United Nations (UN) estimates, the world population reached almost 7 billion by 2010 and will pass 9 billion by 2050.

It's a big world out there! Our planet has about 200 million square miles of surface area, but about 70% of that is water. The total land area, 57.5 million square miles, is about 16 times the land area of the U.S.

Russia is the largest nation, with over 6.5 million square miles of land. China is a distant second, with 3.6 million square miles. The smallest countries in land area are Vatican City and Monaco.

Populations

Largest (2010)

1 **China*** 1,330,141,295

2 **India** 1,173,108,018

5 Brazil 201,103,330

4 Indonesia 242,968,842

3 United States 308,885,492**

Smallest (2010)

	COUNTRY	POPULATION
1.	Vatican City	845
2.	Tuvalu	10,472
3.	Nauru	14,264
4.	Palau	20,879
5.	San Marino	31,477

* Excluding Taiwan, pop. 23,024,956; Hong Kong, pop. 7,090,000; and Macau, pop. 568,000.

**March 2010 estimate

Source: U.S. Census Bureau

MOST SPARSELY POPULATED

	COUNTRY	PERSONS PER SQ MI
1.	Mongolia	5.1
2.	Namibia	6.7
3.	Australia	7.3
4.	Suriname	7.8
5.	Iceland	8.0

To get the population density, divide the population by the area. Density is calculated here according to land area and is based on 2010 population.

MOST DENSELY POPULATED

	COUNTRY	PERSONS PER SQ MI*
1.	Monaco	40,245
2.	Singapore	17,740
3.	Vatican City	4,970
4.	Maldives	3,410
5.	Malta	3,330

* For comparison, New Jersey is the most densely populated U.S. state, with about 1,180 people per square mile in 2009.

All About ››› POPULATION GROWTH

There are more people in the world now than ever before. About four in every ten people on Earth live in China or India. Historically, population growth rates were low but started to increase in the 17th and 18th centuries. The world grew very fast in the 20th century. While growth is expected to slow down, the United Nations estimates the world population will still increase by more than 2 billion people between now and 2050.

Almost all this growth will be in poorer countries. In developed countries more people are older, and families also have fewer children. In some of these countries, the population is falling. Japan's population is projected to decline about 20% between 2010 and 2050. People aged 65 or older will then make up almost 40% of the population.

India is expected to overtake China to become the world's most populous country by around 2025. Its population is projected to climb by about 30% between 2010 and 2050, to over 1.6 billion. About two-thirds of the people will be between 15 and 64 years old.

What does all that mean? For Japan, there will be fewer workers and fewer people to take care of the older population. Having more workers may help India develop its economy. But high population growth puts a strain on land and resources, especially in developing countries, where many people are poor.

YOUNGEST AND AGING POPULATIONS

Here are the countries that have the highest and lowest percentages of people who are under 15 years of age. (In the United States, 20.1% of the population is under 15 years old.)

YOUNGEST:	% under 15 years old	OLDEST:	% under 15 years old
Uganda	50.0%	Monaco	12.6%
Niger	49.7%	Japan	13.3%
Mali	47.5%	Italy	13.4%
Congo, Dem. Rep. of the	46.7%	Latvia	13.4%

Source: *CIA World Factbook;* estimates for 2010.

THE WORLD'S BIGGEST MEGA-CITIES

Many people live in and around cities, in a large area sometimes called a "mega-city" or an "urban agglomeration." The area may include more than one city when the cities are close together. These are the biggest mega-cities according to United Nations estimates for 2009. (See page 188 for the 10 biggest U.S. cities.)

Tokyo, Japan

CITY, COUNTRY	POPULATION	CITY, COUNTRY	POPULATION
1. Tokyo, Japan	36,500,000	4. Mumbai, India	19,700,000
2. Delhi, India	21,700,000	5. Mexico City, Mexico	19,300,000
3. Sao Paulo, Brazil	20,000,000	6. New York/Newark, U.S.	19,300,000

Source: *World Urbanization Prospects,* 2009 revision

POPULATION OF THE UNITED STATES, 2009

as of July 1, 2009

RANK & STATE NAME	POPULATION	RANK & STATE NAME	POPULATION
1. California (CA)	36,961,664	27. Oregon (OR)	3,825,657
2. Texas (TX)	24,782,302	28. Oklahoma (OK)	3,687,050
3. New York (NY)	19,541,453	29. Connecticut (CT)	3,518,288
4. Florida (FL)	18,537,969	30. Iowa (IA)	3,007,856
5. Illinois (IL)	12,910,409	31. Mississippi (MS)	2,951,996
6. Pennsylvania (PA)	12,604,767	32. Arkansas (AR)	2,889,450
7. Ohio (OH)	11,542,645	33. Kansas (KS)	2,818,747
8. Michigan (MI)	9,969,727	34. Utah (UT)	2,784,572
9. Georgia (GA)	9,829,211	35. Nevada (NV)	2,643,085
10. North Carolina (NC)	9,380,884	36. New Mexico (NM)	2,009,671
11. New Jersey (NJ)	8,707,739	37. West Virginia (WV)	1,819,777
12. Virginia (VA)	7,882,590	38. Nebraska (NE)	1,796,619
13. Washington (WA)	6,664,195	39. Idaho (ID)	1,545,801
14. Arizona (AZ)	6,595,778	40. Maine (ME)	1,318,301
15. Massachusetts (MA)	6,593,587	41. New Hampshire (NH)	1,324,575
16. Indiana (IN)	6,423,113	42. Hawaii (HI)	1,295,178
17. Tennessee (TN)	6,296,254	43. Rhode Island (RI)	1,053,209
18. Missouri (MO)	5,987,580	44. Montana (MT)	974,989
19. Maryland (MD)	5,699,478	45. Delaware (DE)	885,122
20. Wisconsin (WI)	5,654,774	46. South Dakota (SD)	812,383
21. Minnesota (MN)	5,266,214	47. Alaska (AK)	698,473
22. Colorado (CO)	5,024,748	48. North Dakota (ND)	646,844
23. Alabama (AL)	4,708,708	49. Vermont (VT)	621,760
24. South Carolina (SC)	4,561,242	50. District of Columbia (DC)	599,657
25. Louisiana (LA)	4,492,076	51. Wyoming (WY)	544,270
26. Kentucky (KY)	4,314,113		
		TOTAL U.S. POPULATION	**307,006,550**

Largest Cities in the United States

Cities grow and shrink in population. Below is a list of the largest U.S. cities in 2008. Their 1950 populations are shown for comparison. Populations are for people living within the city limits only.

RANK & CITY	2008	1950
1. New York, NY	8,363,710	7,891,957
2. Los Angeles, CA	3,833,995	1,970,358
3. Chicago, IL	2,853,114	3,620,962
4. Houston, TX	2,242,193	596,163
5. Phoenix, AZ	1,567,924	106,818
6. Philadelphia, PA	1,447,395	2,071,605
7. San Antonio, TX	1,353,105	408,442
8. Dallas, TX	1,279,910	334,387
9. San Diego, CA	1,279,329	434,462
10. San Jose, CA	948,279	95,280

2008 Population Estimates, U.S. Census Bureau

THE GROWING U.S. POPULATION

1790: 3,929,214	1970: 203,211,926
1850: 23,191,876	1980: 226,545,805
1900: 76,212,168	1990: 248,709,873
1930: 123,202,660	2000: 281,421,906
1950: 151,325,798	2010: 308,885,492*
	*March 2010 estimate

300,000,000
250,000,000
200,000,000
150,000,000
100,000,000
50,000,000

1790 1820 1850 1880 1910 1940 1970 2000 2010

THE 2010 CENSUS: COUNTING THE AMERICAN PEOPLE

As required by the Constitution, every ten years the U.S. government carries out a census—a count of all the people living in the United States. In March 2010, the Census Bureau mailed out forms for the latest census. The aim was to count everybody as of Census Day, April 1, 2010. People were asked to fill in the form and mail it back. Census workers tried to visit every household that did not send back a form.

What did the 2010 census form ask?

If you saw the census form yourself, you may remember! There were four questions that asked about the number of people living in each household and the ownership of the house. Then there were six questions for each person. These asked mainly about the person's name, age, gender, and race and whether the person is Hispanic or not.

What is this information used for?

The population of each state determines how many of the 435 seats it gets in the U.S. House of Representatives. These census figures are released by the end of 2010. Census population figures are also used to divide up seats in state legislatures. And the census information about people and where they live is used to help the government decide where to spend money for different services and try to make sure it is not being unfair to particular groups of people.

How was the 2010 census different from the one before?

In each census, the Census Bureau has tried to make greater use of new technology. In 2010, for example, special computer technology was used to make more detailed and accurate maps. These maps helped census workers find people.

Another difference is that every household in 2010 got the same census form. In previous censuses, one in six households received a "long form," with many added questions. Instead, the Census Bureau now collects certain information year by year, by sending sample surveys to some households.

Does everybody really get counted?

No census can be perfect. But census takers try to reach all the people, whether they are citizens or not, and wherever they may live. For example, the census counts people in hospitals and prisons, and census workers seek out homeless people. Census workers take an oath not to share any data about individuals.

The Many Faces of America:
IMMIGRATION

The number of Americans who were born in another country (foreign-born) has risen in recent decades. It reached 38 million in 2007, or almost 13% of the population. That was the highest percentage since 1930, and a big change from 1970, when only 4.7% of Americans were foreign-born. There has been some falloff in immigration since 2007, mostly because of the U.S. economic recession, but immigration levels remain high. In contrast to the early 1900s, when most immigrants came from Europe, most now come from other parts of the world. In 2008, 53% of foreign-born Americans could trace their origins to Latin America, and 27% to Asia. Only 13% were born in Europe.

Immigrants come for various reasons, such as to escape poverty or oppression and to make better lives for themselves and their children. The figures below, from the Department of Homeland Security, cover legal immigrants only. Each year hundreds of thousands of people come across the border illegally or overstay a temporary visa. (Visas are official government documents that grant permission for a person to visit, work, or attend school in another country.) Many of these people are workers who come by themselves to earn money for their families back home. The U.S. government estimated there were about 11 million unauthorized immigrants in the country in 2009, including about 7 million from Mexico.

What Countries Do Immigrants Come From?

A total of 743,715 immigrants were naturalized—that is, were sworn in—as U.S. citizens in the 12-month period ending September 30, 2009. The table below shows the countries where the largest numbers of these immigrants came from.

COUNTRY	Number	Percent of total
Mexico	111,630	15.0
India	52,889	7.1
Philippines	38,934	5.2
China*	37,130	5.9
Vietnam	31,168	4.2
Cuba	24,891	3.3
Dominican Republic	20,778	2.8
El Salvador	18,927	2.5
South Korea	17,576	2.4
Colombia	16,593	2.2
Jamaica	15,098	2.0
Haiti	13,290	1.8
Pakistan	12,528	1.7
Iran	12,069	1.6

*Excluding Taiwan, Hong Kong, and Macau

Where Do Immigrants Settle?

In the 12 months ending September 30, 2009, 1,130,818 people from foreign countries became "legal permanent residents" of the U.S. One out of five of these immigrants, including large numbers from Vietnam, Mexico, and the Philippines, settled in California. Around half of those born in the Dominican Republic settled in New York. Florida was the destination for most of the immigrants from Haiti and the vast majority of those from Cuba.

California
227,876

New York
150,722

Florida
127,006

Texas
95,384

New Jersey
58,879

Illinois
41,889

Massachusetts
32,607

The states shown here were home to two out of three immigrants who became legal permanent residents of the U.S. in 2009.

◀ Immigrants entering the U.S. at Ellis Island in New York, early 1900s

All About >> Hispanic Americans

Hispanics, or Latinos, are people of any race who trace their heritage back to Spain itself or to Mexico, Puerto Rico, Cuba, the Dominican Republic, or any Central American, South American, or other Spanish-speaking culture. In 2008, there were an estimated 47 million Hispanics in the U.S., making up about 15% of the population. Six out of ten were born in the U.S.

Hispanics are already the largest minority group in the U.S., and their numbers are growing rapidly. By 2050, they are expected to make up close to 30% of the population.

As of mid-2008, there were an estimated 13.4 million Hispanics living in California, more than in any other state. Texas ranked second, with a Hispanic population of 8.8 million. Florida followed, with about 3.8 million Hispanics, and then New York, with 3.2 million.

New Mexico had the highest percentage of Hispanics in its population. In 2008, about 45% of New Mexico's residents were Hispanic. California and Texas had the second- and third-highest percentage of Hispanics in their populations, with about 37% each.

U.S. Hispanic Population by Place of Origin, 2008

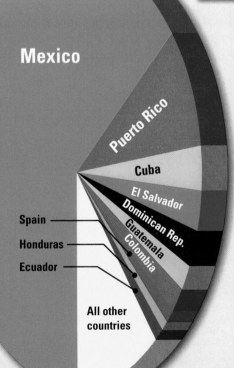

Place	Number	Percent of All Hispanics
Mexico	30,746,270	65.7%
Puerto Rico	4,150,802	8.9
Cuba	1,631,001	3.5
El Salvador	1,560,416	3.3
Dominican Rep.	1,334,228	2.8
Guatemala	985,601	2.1
Colombia	881,609	1.9
Spain	629,758	1.3
Honduras	607,970	1.3
Ecuador	590,602	1.3
All other countries	3,904,219	7.9
Total U.S. Hispanic Population (2008)	46,822,476	100.0

Source: Pew Hispanic Center; American Community Survey, U.S. Census Bureau

Prizes & Contests

Is it possible to make an outfit for the prom out of duct tape? → page 195

NOBEL PRIZES

The Nobel Prizes are named after Alfred B. Nobel (1833–1896), a Swedish scientist who invented dynamite and who left money for most of the prizes. They are given every year for promoting peace, as well as for achievements in physics, chemistry, physiology or medicine, literature, and economics.

In 2009, U.S. President **Barack Obama** was awarded the Nobel Peace Prize "for his extraordinary efforts to strengthen international diplomacy and cooperation between peoples.... Obama [has] captured the world's attention and given its people hope for a better future."

Past winners of the Nobel Peace Prize include:

2007 Al Gore Jr. (former U.S. vice president) and the **International Panel on Climate Change**, for their efforts in educating the world about global warming

2004 Wangari Maathai, Kenyan environmentalist and social reformer ▼

2002 Jimmy Carter, former U.S. president and peace negotiator

1997 Jody Williams and the International Campaign to Ban Landmines

1993 Nelson Mandela, leader of South African blacks; **F. W. de Klerk**, president of South Africa

1991 Aung San Suu Kyi, activist for democracy in Myanmar (Burma)

1989 Dalai Lama, Tibetan Buddhist leader, forced into exile in 1959

1986 Elie Wiesel, Holocaust survivor and author

1979 Mother Teresa, leader of the order of the Missionaries of Charity, who cared for the sick and dying in India

1964 Martin Luther King Jr., civil rights leader

1954 Albert Schweitzer, missionary, surgeon

1919 Woodrow Wilson, U.S. president who played a key role in founding the League of Nations

1905 Baroness Bertha von Suttner, advocate of peace through international cooperation; first woman to win the prize

1906 Theodore Roosevelt, U.S. president who helped negotiate a peace treaty between Japan and Russia

ENTERTAINMENT *Awards*

2010 KIDS' CHOICE AWARDS

The 2010 Kids' Choice Awards were held Saturday, March 27, 2010, and hosted by ◀Kevin James. For more information, go to: *www.nick.com*

KIDS' CHOICE AWARDS

More than 118 million votes were cast by kids in the 2010 Nickelodeon's Kids' Choice Awards. Winners included:

- Music Group . . . . The Black Eyed Peas
- Movie . . . . *Alvin and the Chipmunks: The Squeakquel*
- Book . . . . *Diary of a Wimpy Kid* series
- Video Game . . . . *Mario Kart*
- Cutest Couple . . . . Jacob & Bella
- Reality TV Show . . . . . . *American Idol*
- TV Show . . . . *iCarly*
- Cartoon . . . . *SpongeBob SquarePants*
- TV Actor . . . . Dylan Sprouse
- TV Actress . . . . Selena Gomez
- Movie Actor . . . . Taylor Lautner ▶
- Movie Actress . . . . Miley Cyrus
- Animated Movie . . . . *Up*
- Voice from an Animated Movie . . . . Jim Carrey *(A Christmas Carol)*
- Male Singer . . . . Jay-Z
- Female Singer . . . . Taylor Swift
- Song . . . . "You Belong with Me," Taylor Swift
- Male Athlete . . . . Ryan Sheckler
- Female Athlete . . . . Misty May Treanor
- The Big Help Award . . . . Michelle Obama

193

BEE INVOLVED

If you have a knack for spelling or an interest in world geography, then these two national contests may be for you.

National Spelling Bee

The **National Spelling Bee** was started in Louisville, Kentucky, by the *Courier-Journal* in 1925. Today, newspapers across the U.S. run spelling bees for kids 15 and under. Winners may qualify for the Scripps National Spelling Bee held in Washington, D.C., in late May or early June. If interested, ask your school principal to contact your local newspaper. (For a behind-the-scenes look at the National Spelling Bee, try the 2002 film *Spellbound*.)

Anamika Veeramani, 14, from North Royalton, Ohio, won the 83rd annual Scripps National Spelling Bee contest on June 4th, 2010. She won the bee by correctly spelling the word "stromuhr," an instrument that measures the amount and speed of blood flow through an artery. Veeramani broke a losing streak for Ohio, becoming the first National Spelling Bee winner from the state since 1964.

For more information, visit: *www.spellingbee.com*

Here are some of the words used in the 2010 spelling bee. Some of them are just a little bit difficult!

ochidore
terribilita
paravane
apogalacteum
fustanella
consuetude

paparazzo
phillumenist
alation
juvia
sarsaparilla
prabhu

National Geographic Bee

The 2010 winner is...

Aadith Moorthy, a 13-year-old from Palm Harbor, Florida. Moorthy won the 22nd National Geographic Bee by answering this question: "The largest city in northern Haiti was renamed following Haiti's independence from France. What is the present-day name of this city?" (The answer: Cap-Haïtien.) Moorthy won a $25,000 scholarship for college, a trip to the Galapagos Islands, and a lifetime membership in the National Geographic Society. He thanked his parents for taking him on trips around the world and giving him geography books. "I thought the questions would be harder," he said. A straight-A student, Moorthy is interested in astronomy and hopes to go into space one day. "He has this thirst for knowledge that I have never seen in anyone before," said the principal of Moorthy's school. "I know for a fact he is gong to make a huge difference in the world."

The National Geographic Bee draws 5 million contestants from nearly 15,000 schools in all parts of the United States. To enter, you must be in grades 4-8. School-level bees are followed by state-level bees and then the nationals (which are moderated by *Jeopardy!* host Alex Trebek).

For more information, visit: *www.nationalgeographic.com/geobee*

ODD CONTESTS

It just seems to be part of human nature to find out who is the best at something, no matter what it is! There are state, national, and international competitions in a wide variety of events. Most of them are normal ones such as foot races, trivia contests, and such. But then there are others that are just plain weird. Here are a few contests that are not very ordinary.

ROTTEN SNEAKER CONTEST

The National Odor-Eaters Rotten Sneaker Contest is held annually in Montpelier, Vermont. In 2010, the panel of judges included NASA "Master Sniffer" George Aldrich, Chemical Specialist for space missions. Each year, the winner's sneakers are added to the Odor-Eaters "Hall of Fumes." Other prizes for the 2010 winner included $2,500, the Golden Sneaker Award trophy, a supply of Odor-Eaters® products, and a trip to see the play *The Lion King* on Broadway in New York City.

For more information, visit: *www.odoreaters.com*

DUCT TAPE PROM OUTFITS

Couples entering the Duck® Brand Duct Tape Stuck on Prom Contest must attend a high school prom wearing complete outfits and accessories made from duct tape. The winning couple is chosen based on originality, workmanship, quantity of Duck Tape used, use of colors, and creative use of accessories. The first place couple each receives a $3,000 scholarship and a $3,000 cash prize is awarded to the school that hosted the prom.

For more information, visit: *www.stuckatprom.com*

DUCK CALLING FOR COLLEGE

High school seniors can compete for an unusual college scholarship in Stuttgart, Arkansas. Every November, students gather in the town for a duck calling contest. Contestants have 90 seconds to use four different types of duck calls. The winner is awarded $2,000 to help pay for college. The contest is open to any U.S. high school senior, but contestants must be in Arkansas for the contest.

For more information, visit: *www.stuttgartarkansas.org*

Religion

What is the Koran? → page 197

How did the universe begin? Why are we here on Earth? What happens to us after we die? For most people, religion provides answers to questions like these. Believing in a God or gods, or in a higher power, is one way people make sense of the world around them. Religion can also help guide people's lives.

Different religions have different beliefs. For example, Christians, Jews, and Muslims are monotheists, meaning they believe in only one God. Hindus are polytheists, meaning they believe in many gods. On this page and the next are some facts about the world's major religions.

Christianity

WHO STARTED CHRISTIANITY? Christianity is based on the teachings of Jesus Christ. He was born in Bethlehem between 8 B.C. and 4 B.C. and died about A.D. 29.

WHAT WRITINGS ARE THERE? The **Bible**, consisting of the Old Testament and New Testament, is the main spiritual text in Christianity.

WHAT DO CHRISTIANS BELIEVE? There is only one God. God sent his Son, Jesus Christ, to Earth. Jesus died to save humankind but later rose from the dead.

HOW MANY ARE THERE? Christianity is the world's biggest religion. In 2007, there were about 2.2 billion Christians worldwide.

WHAT KINDS ARE THERE? More than one billion Christians are **Roman Catholics**, who follow the Pope's leadership. **Orthodox Christians** accept similar teachings but follow different leadership. **Protestants** disagree with many Catholic teachings. They believe in the Bible's authority.

Buddhism

WHO STARTED BUDDHISM? Siddhartha Gautama (the Buddha), around 525 B.C.

WHAT WRITINGS ARE THERE? The **Tripitaka**, or "Three Baskets," contains three collections of teachings, rules, and commentaries. There are also other texts, many of which are called **sutras**.

WHAT DO BUDDHISTS BELIEVE? Buddha taught that life is filled with suffering. Through meditation and deeds, one can end the cycle of endless birth and rebirth and achieve a state of perfect peace known as **nirvana**.

HOW MANY ARE THERE? In 2007, there were about 385 million Buddhists in the world, 98% of them in Asia.

WHAT KINDS ARE THERE? There are two main kinds: **Theravada** ("Way of the Elders") Buddhism, the older kind, is more common in countries such as Sri Lanka, Myanmar, and Thailand. **Mahayana** ("Great Vehicle") Buddhism is more common in China, Korea, Japan, and Tibet.

Hinduism

WHO STARTED HINDUISM? The beliefs of Aryans, who migrated to India around 1500 B.C., intermixed with the beliefs of the people who already lived there.

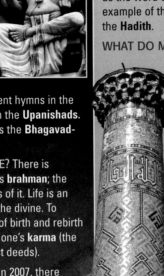

WHAT WRITINGS ARE THERE? The **Vedas** ("Knowledge") collect the most important writings in Hinduism, including the ancient hymns in the **Samhita** and the teachings in the **Upanishads**. Also important are the stories the **Bhagavad-Gita** and the **Ramayana**.

WHAT DO HINDUS BELIEVE? There is one divine principle, known as **brahman**; the various gods are only aspects of it. Life is an aspect of, yet separate from the divine. To escape a meaningless cycle of birth and rebirth (**samsara**), one must improve one's **karma** (the purity or impurity of one's past deeds).

HOW MANY ARE THERE? In 2007, there were about 875 million Hindus, mainly in India and in places that people from India have immigrated to.

WHAT KINDS ARE THERE? Most Hindus are primarily devoted to a single deity, the most common being the gods **Vishnu** and **Shiva** and the goddess **Shakti**.

Islam

WHO STARTED ISLAM? Muhammad, the Prophet, about A.D. 622.

WHAT WRITINGS ARE THERE? The **Koran** (*al-Qur'an* in Arabic), is regarded as the word of God. The **Sunna**, or example of the Prophet, is recorded in the **Hadith**.

WHAT DO MUSLIMS BELIEVE? People who practice Islam are known as Muslims. There is only one God. God revealed the Koran to Muhammad so he could teach humankind truth and justice. Those who "submit" (literal meaning of "Islam") to God will attain salvation.

HOW MANY ARE THERE? In 2007, there were almost 1.4 billion Muslims, mostly in parts of Africa and Asia.

WHAT KINDS ARE THERE? There are two major groups: the Sunnis, who make up about 83% of the world's Muslims, and the Shiites, who broke away in a dispute over leadership after Muhammad died in 632.

Judaism

WHO STARTED JUDAISM? Abraham is thought to be the founder of Judaism, one of the first monotheistic religions. He probably lived between 2000 B.C. and 1500 B.C.

WHAT WRITINGS ARE THERE? The most important is the **Torah** ("Law"), comprising the five books of Moses. The **Nevi'im** ("Prophets") and **Ketuvim** ("Writings") are also part of the Hebrew Bible.

WHAT DO JEWS BELIEVE? There is one God who created and rules the universe. One should be faithful to God and observe God's laws.

HOW MANY ARE THERE? In 2007, there were close to 15 million Jews around the world. Many live in Israel and the United States.

WHAT KINDS ARE THERE? In the U.S. there are three main forms: **Orthodox**, **Conservative**, and **Reform**. Orthodox Jews are the most traditional, following strict laws about dress and diet. Reform Jews are the least traditional. Conservative Jews are somewhere in-between.

Major Holy Days

FOR CHRISTIANS, JEWS, MUSLIMS, BUDDHISTS, AND HINDUS

CHRISTIAN HOLY DAYS

	2011	2012	2013
Ash Wednesday	March 9	February 22	February 13
Good Friday	April 22	April 6	March 29
Easter Sunday	April 24	April 8	March 31
Easter for Orthodox Churches	April 24	April 15	May 5
Christmas*	December 25	December 25	December 25

*Russian and some other Orthodox churches celebrate Christmas in January.

JEWISH HOLY DAYS

The Jewish holy days begin at sundown the night before the first full day of the observance. The dates of first full days are listed below.

	2011–2012 (5772)	2012–2013 (5773)	2013–2014 (5774)
Rosh Hashanah (New Year)	September 29, 2011	September 17, 2012	September 5, 2013
Yom Kippur (Day of Atonement)	October 8, 2011	September 26, 2012	September 14, 2013
Hanukkah (Festival of Lights)	December 21, 2011	December 9, 2012	November 28, 2013
Passover	April 7, 2012	March 26, 2013	April 15, 2014

ISLAMIC (MUSLIM) HOLY DAYS

The Islamic holy days begin at sundown the night before the first full day of the observance. The dates of first full days are listed below.

	2010–2011 (1432)	2011–2012 (1433)	2012–2013 (1434)
Muharram 1 (New Year)	December 7, 2010	November 26, 2011	November 15, 2012
Mawlid (Birthday of Muhammad)	February 15, 2011	February 4, 2012	January 24, 2013
Ramadan (Month of Fasting)	August 1, 2011	July 20, 2012	July 9, 2013
Eid al-Fitr (End of Ramadan)	August 30, 2011	August 19, 2012	August 8, 2013
Eid al-Adha	November 6, 2011	October 26, 2012	October 15, 2013

BUDDHIST HOLY DAYS

Not all Buddhists use the same calendar to determine holidays and festivals. A few well-known Buddhist observances and the months in which they may fall are listed below.

NIRVANA DAY, **February:** Marks the death of Siddhartha Gautama (the Buddha).

VESAK OR VISAKAH PUJA (BUDDHA DAY), **April/May:** Celebrates the birth, enlightenment, and death of the Buddha.

ASALHA PUJA (DHARMA DAY), **July:** Commemorates the Buddha's first teaching

MAGHA PUJA OR SANGHA DAY, **February:** Commemorates the day when 1,250 of Buddha's followers (**sangha**) visited him without his calling them.

VASSA (RAINS RETREAT), **July-October:** A three-month period during Asia's rainy season when monks travel little and spend more time on meditation and study. Sometimes called Buddhist Lent

HINDU HOLY DAYS

Different Hindu groups use different calendars. A few of the many Hindu festivals and the months in which they may fall are listed below.

MAHA SHIVARATRI, **February/March:** Festival dedicated to Shiva, creator and destroyer.

HOLI, **February/March:** Festival of spring

RAMANAVAMI, **March/April:** Celebrates the birth of Rama, the seventh incarnation of Vishnu.

DIWALI, **October/November:** Festival of Lights

All About >> The Dalai Lama

Dalai Lama is a title given to the leader of an order of Tibetan Buddhist monks. Whoever holds the position of Dalai Lama is, in effect, the spiritual and political leader of the Tibetan people. The current Dalai Lama was born in 1935. In the early 1950s, when China seized control of Tibet, he was essentially forced to recognize Chinese authority. In 1959, when a Tibetan uprising against Chinese rule failed, he fled into exile in India. Since that time, he has been a symbol of the desire of many Tibetan people for self-rule. The Dalai Lama has traveled to many different countries, promoting three basic commitments: to humane values such as tolerance, forgiveness, and understanding; to harmony and understanding between the world's different religions; and to Tibetan autonomy. The Dalai Lama has received many awards and honorary degrees, including the Nobel Peace Prize (1989).

▲ The Dalai Lama, Tibetan leader

Science

What is DNA? → page 206

THE WORLD OF Science

The Latin root of the word "science" is *scire,* meaning "to know." There are many kinds of knowledge, but when people use the word *science* they usually mean a kind of knowledge that can be discovered and backed up by observation or experiments.

The branches of scientific study can be loosely grouped into four main branches: Physical Science, Life Science (Biology), Earth Science, and Social Science. Each branch has more specific areas of study. For example, zoology includes entomology (study of insects), which in turn includes lepidopterology (the study of butterflies and moths).

In answering questions about our lives, our world, and our universe, scientists must often draw from more than one discipline. Biochemists, for example, deal with the chemistry that happens inside living things. Paleontologists study fossil remains of ancient plants and animals. Astrophysicists study matter and energy in outer space. And mathematics, considered by many to be both an art and a science, is used by all scientists.

Physical Science

ASTRONOMY: stars, planets, outer space

CHEMISTRY: properties and behavior of substances

PHYSICS: matter and energy

Life Science (Biology)

ANATOMY: structure of the human body

BOTANY: plants

ECOLOGY: living things in relation to their environment

GENETICS: heredity

PATHOLOGY: diseases and their effects on the human body

PHYSIOLOGY: the body's biological processes

ZOOLOGY: animals

Earth Science

GEOGRAPHY: Earth's surface and its relationship to humans

GEOLOGY: Earth's structure

HYDROLOGY: water

METEOROLOGY: Earth's atmosphere and weather

MINERALOGY: minerals

OCEANOGRAPHY: the sea, including currents and tides

PETROLOGY: rocks

SEISMOLOGY: earthquakes

VOLCANOLOGY: volcanoes

Social Science

ANTHROPOLOGY: human cultures and physical characteristics

ECONOMICS: production and distribution of goods and services

POLITICAL SCIENCE: governments

PSYCHOLOGY: mental processes and behavior

SOCIOLOGY: human society and community life

HOW DO
SCIENTISTS
MAKE DISCOVERIES? *THE SCIENTIFIC METHOD*

The scientific method was developed over many centuries. You can think of it as having five steps:

1. Ask a question.
2. Gather information through observation.
3. Based on that information, make an educated guess (hypothesis) about the answer to your question.
4. Design an experiment to test that hypothesis.
5. Evaluate the results.

If the experiment shows that your hypothesis is wrong, make up a new hypothesis. If the experiment supports your hypothesis, then your hypothesis may be correct! However, it is usually necessary to test a hypothesis with many different experiments before it can be accepted as a scientific law—something that is generally accepted as true.

You can apply the **scientific method** to problems in everyday life. For example, suppose you plant some seeds and they fail to sprout. You would probably **ask** yourself, "Why didn't they sprout?"—and that would be step one of the scientific method. The next step would be to make **observations**; for example, you might take note of how deep the seeds were planted, how often they were watered, and what kind of soil was used. Then, you would make an **educated guess** about what went wrong—for example, you might hypothesize that the seeds didn't sprout because you didn't water them enough. After that, you would **test** your hypothesis—perhaps by trying to grow the seeds again, under the exact same conditions as before, except that this time you would water them more frequently.

Finally, you would wait and **evaluate** the results of your experiment. If the seeds sprouted, then you could conclude that your hypothesis may be correct. If they didn't sprout, you'd continue to use the method to find a scientific answer to your original question.

did you know?

Some dinosaurs had feathers. But what colors were they? Paleontologists are starting to get answers. The fossilized remains of dinosaur feathers may still contain traces of tiny structures called melanosomes, which are largely responsible for feathers' color. One research team studied melanosomes from a well-preserved fossil of a small dinosaur called Anchiornis huxleyi. In order to get an idea of what the animal's coloration was like, the scientists looked at melanosome patterns in dinosaurs' closest living relatives—birds. They reported in early 2010 that Anchiornis very likely was mainly black or dark gray and had white patches on its limbs and a reddish-brown headdress with similarly colored spots on its face. Once researchers find ways to study other fossililzed parts of feathers that may affect color, they should be able to sharpen their portrait of Anchiornis.

Anchiornis huxleyi

WHAT EVERYTHING *IS* MADE OF

Everything we see and use is made of basic ingredients called elements. There are more than 100 elements. They are found in nature or made by scientists.

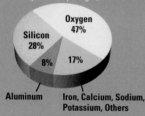

Elements in Earth's Crust
(percent by weight)

Oxygen 47%
Silicon 28%
8%
17%
Aluminum
Iron, Calcium, Sodium, Potassium, Others

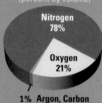

Elements in the Atmosphere
(percent by volume)

Nitrogen 78%
Oxygen 21%
1% Argon, Carbon Dioxide, Others

How Elements Are Named

Elements are named after places, scientists, figures in mythology, or properties of the element. But no element gets a name until the International Union of Pure and Applied Chemistry (IUPAC) accepts it. In 2009, the IUPAC officially accepted the 112th element. It approved the element's name—copernicium (honoring the 16th-century astronomer Copernicus)—in February 2010. Copernicium, with symbol Cn, was first produced by German scientists in 1996. As of 2010, claims for other new elements were being studied.

NAME	SYMBOL	WHAT IT IS	WHEN FOUND	NAMED FOR
Argon	Ar	gas	1894	the Greek word *argos,* which means inactive or lazy; it is one of the least reactive of all elements
Californium	Cf	radioactive metal	1950	state of California, and the University of California
Hydrogen	H	non-metal	1766	the Greek words *hydro* and *genes,* which mean water and forming
Iodine	I	nonmetallic solid	1811	the Greek word *iodes,* meaning violet
Iridium	Ir	transitional metal	1804	the Latin word *iridis,* meaning rainbow
Nickel	Ni	transitional metal	1774	the German word *kupfernickel,* meaning devil's copper
Tungsten	W	transitional metal	1783	the Swedish words *tung sten,* meaning heavy stone.
Vanadium	V	metal	1801	Vanadis, the Scandinavian Goddess of Beauty; its salts have beautiful colors

ALL ABOUT...
Compounds

Carbon, hydrogen, nitrogen, and oxygen are the most common chemical elements in the human body. Many other elements may be found in small amounts. These include calcium, iron, phosphorus, potassium, and sodium.

When elements join together, they form compounds. Water is a compound made up of hydrogen and oxygen. Salt is a compound made up of sodium and chlorine.

Common Name	Contains the Compound	Contains the Elements
Chalk	calcium carbonate	calcium, carbon, oxygen
Fool's Gold	iron disulfide	iron, sulfur
Marble	calcium carbonate	calcium, carbon, oxygen
Rust	iron oxide	iron, oxygen
Sugar	sucrose	carbon, hydrogen, oxygen
Toothpaste	sodium fluoride	sodium, fluorine
Vinegar	acetic acid	carbon, hydrogen, oxygen

CHEMICAL SYMBOLS ARE SCIENTIFIC SHORTHAND

When scientists write the names of elements, they often use a symbol instead of spelling out the full name. The symbol for each element is one or two letters. Scientists write O for oxygen and He for helium. The symbols usually come from the English name for the element (C for carbon). The symbols for some of the elements come from the element's Latin name. For example, the symbol for gold is Au, which is short for *aurum*, the Latin word for gold.

TURNING BASE METALS INTO GOLD?

Hundreds of years ago, during the Middle Ages, some people believed that they could change base metals like lead into gold. These people, called alchemists, believed that something called a philosopher's stone and intense faith could combine to cause the change. This belief persisted for centuries; even Isaac Newton, the great scientist, believed in alchemy!

Medieval physician and alchemist Philippus Aureolus Paracelsus

Physical Science
SOUND and LIGHT

What Is Sound?

Sound is a form of energy that is made up of waves traveling through matter. When you "hear" a sound, it is actually your ear detecting the vibrations of molecules as the sound wave passes through. To understand sound, you first have to understand waves. Take a bowl full of water and drop a penny into the middle of it. You'll see little circular waves move away from the area where the penny hit, spread out toward the bowl's edges, and bounce back. Sound moves in the same way. The waves must travel through a gas, liquid, or a solid. In the vacuum of space, there is no sound because there are no molecules to vibrate. When you talk, your vocal cords vibrate to produce sound waves.

What Is Light?

Light is a little tricky. It is a form of energy known as electromagnetic radiation that is emitted from a source. It travels as waves in straight lines and spreads out over a larger area the farther it goes. Scientists also think it goes along as particles known as photons. Light is produced in many ways. They generally involve changes in the energy levels of electrons inside atoms.

Regular white light is made up of all the colors of the spectrum from red to violet. Each color has its own frequency and wavelength. When you see a color on something, such as a red apple, that means that the apple absorbed all other colors of the spectrum and reflected the red light. Things that are white reflect almost all the light that hits them. Things that are black, on the other hand, absorb all the light that hits them.

Light vs. Sound

Sound travels fast but light travels a whole lot faster. You've probably noticed that when you see lightning, you don't hear thunder until several seconds later. That's because the light reaches you before the sound. The speed of sound in air varies depending mainly on temperature (sound also travels faster through liquids and many solids). A jet traveling at about 761 miles per hour is considered to be flying at the "speed of sound." But this is nothing compared to light. It goes 186,000 miles per *second*! It goes the same speed no matter what. Scientists don't think anything in the universe can travel faster.

How Simple Machines Work

Simple machines are devices that make our lives easier. Cars could not run, skyscrapers couldn't be built, and elevators couldn't carry people up—if it weren't for simple machines.

Inclined Plane When trying to get a refrigerator onto the back of a truck, a worker will use a ramp, or inclined plane. Instead of lifting something heavy a short distance, we can more easily push it over a longer distance, but to the same height.
Examples: escalators, staircases, slides

Lever Any kind of arm, bar, or plank that can pivot on something (known as a fulcrum), is a lever. Depending on where the fulcrum is located on the lever, it can be used for different things.
Examples: shovel, bottle opener, "claw" part of a hammer used for prying out nails, seesaw

Wedge These machines are two inclined planes fastened onto each other to make a point. Wedges are used to pull things apart and even cut.
Examples: axes, knives

Wheel and Axle This is another kind of lever, but instead of going up and down, it goes around. The wheel is the lever and the axle on which it turns is the fulcrum.
Examples: cars, bicycles, wagons

Pulley A pulley is similar to a wheel and axle, except that there's no axle. It can be used to change both the direction and level of force needed to move an object. The best example is a crane. An object is tied to a cable, which goes up and around the pulley, and down to the crane engine which is pulling it.
Examples: a block and tackle, a flag pole, tow trucks

Screw A screw is an inclined plane wrapped around a cylinder. In the case of a wood screw, as it is turned it travels deeper into the piece of wood. Another use of a screw is to hold things in place such as the lid on a jar.
Examples: drills, corkscrews

Biological Science

WHAT ARE LIVING THINGS MADE OF?

Plant cell

Cells are sometimes called the "building blocks" of living things. Complex life forms have many cells. There are trillions of them in the human body.

There are two main kinds of cells: **eukaryotic** and **prokaryotic**. All the cells in your body—along with the cells of other animals, plants, and fungi—are eukaryotic. These contain several different structures called **organelles**. Like tools in a toolbox, each kind of organelle has its own function. The **nucleus**, for example, contains most of the cell's DNA, while the **mitochondria** provide energy for the cell. The **ribosomes** are involved in making proteins.

Plant and animal cells differ in a few ways. Animal cells rely on mitochondria for energy, but plant cells also have an organelle called a **chloroplast**. This contains chlorophyll, a green chemical plants use to get oxygen and energy from sunlight and water, a process called **photosynthesis**. Unlike animal cells, plant cells have a rigid cell wall made largely of **cellulose**.

Prokaryotes (living things, or organisms, with prokaryotic instead of eukaryotic cells) are all around you—and even inside of you. For example, bacteria are prokaryotes. Most prokaryotes are single-celled. They don't have the variety of organelles that eukaryotic cells do.

WHAT IS DNA?

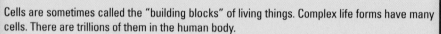

Every cell has **DNA**, a molecule that holds all the information about the organism containing the cell. The structure of DNA was discovered in 1953 by the British scientist Francis Crick and the American scientist James Watson.

Lengths of connected bits of a DNA molecule, called **genes**, are tiny pieces of code. They determine what each organism is like. Almost all the DNA and genes come packaged in thread-like structures called **chromosomes**. Humans have 46. There are 22 almost identical pairs, plus the X and Y chromosomes, which determine whether a human is male (one X chromosome and one Y chromosome) or female (two X chromosomes).

Genes are passed on from parents to children, and no two organisms (except clones or identical twins) have the same DNA.

Many things—the color of our eyes or hair, whether we're tall or short, our chances of getting certain diseases—depend on our genes.

What Is the Human Genome?

A genome is all the DNA in an organism, including its genes. The human genome contains 20,000 to 25,000 genes. That's fewer than the 50,000-plus genes of a rice plant! Human genes can produce more than one kind of protein. Proteins perform most life functions and make up a large part of cellular structures.

Tiny Creatures

Microbes Anton van Leeuwenhoek (pronounced Lay-wen-ook) made the first practical microscope in 1674. When he looked through it, he saw tiny bacteria, plant cells, and fungi, among other things. When he wrote about his findings, Leeuwenhoek called the creatures "wee beasties." We call them **microorganisms** ("micro" means *little*), or microbes. Before the microscope, people had no idea that there were millions of tiny living things crawling all over them.

Amoebas Amoebas (uh-ME-buhz) are eukaryotic jelly-like blobs of protoplasm that ooze through their microscopic world. They eat by engulfing their food and slowly digesting it. To move around, the cell extends a part of its goo to create something called a **pseudopod** (SOO-doh-pod), which means "false foot." The amoeba uses this to pull the rest of its "body" along. Amoebas normally live in water or on moist surfaces. In humans, most kinds of amoebas are harmless, but some cause diseases.

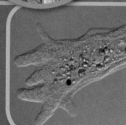

Diatoms Diatoms are one-celled algae that make glass shells to protect themselves. When they die, their shells collect at the bottom of the ocean in great numbers and form something called **diatomaceous earth**. It's gritty like sandpaper. Diatomaceous earth was once used in toothpaste to help scrape plaque off teeth. Nowadays, among other things, it is used as a pesticide—when sprayed in the air, it gets caught in the lungs of insects and slowly suffocates them.

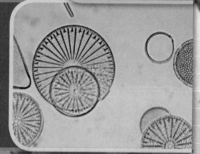

WHAT ABOUT VIRUSES?

Viruses are often thought of as not really alive. But it depends on how you define life. Tiny in size and lacking cells, viruses consist of genetic material—either DNA or the similar RNA—and a protein coat. They don't grow. They don't appear to react to the environment. They don't do anything—unless they are located inside a living thing, in which case they can reproduce, by borrowing the living thing's genetic machinery. In recent years super-sized viruses, dubbed the mimivirus and mamavirus, have been discovered in amoebas. They are as big as small bacteria. Scientists have also found a very tiny virus that appears to use the mamavirus's genetic machinery to reproduce.

Mimivirus

SCIENCE Q&A

HOW STRONG IS GRAVITY? Compared to other forces, gravity is weak. It may feel powerful on Earth, where it takes lots of energy for airplanes and rockets to leave the ground. But this is only because the planet is so massive that it pulls everything toward its center. Magnets use a force stronger than gravity when they stick on metal. Static electricity defies gravity when it makes your hair stand on end.

WHY CAN'T SCUBA DIVERS GO TO THE BOTTOM OF THE OCEAN? Pressure, that's why. On dry land at sea level, there is about 14.7 pounds per square inch (psi) of atmospheric pressure pressing down on you. That's like having a 14.7-pound weight on every square inch of the surface of your body. We don't feel it because we've adapted to it. In water, the pressure increases the deeper you go. For every 33 feet a person dives, it goes up by 14.7 psi. The pressure can get to be so great that it literally crushes people. Scuba divers don't normally go deeper than 100 feet without special equipment. Even then, it's hard to go lower than 300 feet because of the pressure. Instead, people use special submarines to reach the deepest parts of the oceans.

HOW LONG CAN YOU SURVIVE IN FREEZING WATER? It depends. If you fall into really cold water, the shock of the sudden cold can make you start hyperventilating—breathing very fast and deep. If you are underwater when this happens, you will drown right away. If you survive the cold shock, the next worry is that your body temperature may get too low. This condition, called hypothermia, can be fatal. In 41°F water, you might last 10 to 20 minutes before starting to feel weak. A heavier person may last longer than a thin one, since body fat serves as insulation. Also, the less of your body that is in the water, the longer you'll tend to survive, since water carries heat away faster than air.

WHAT MAKES SPIDER SILK SO STRONG? Dragline silk—the silk a spider uses to hang from a ceiling—is only about one-tenth as thick as a human hair, but it is several times stronger than steel. Other strong materials, such as ceramics, tend to be stiff or breakable. Spider silk can stretch and bend without breaking. Its secret is its structure. It contains proteins that help make the silk stretchable. It also has proteins that form stacks of thin flat crystals connected by the normally weak type of chemical link called a hydrogen bond. As long as the crystals are small enough, the bonds work together, taking on great strength and letting the silk stretch and bend rather than break.

SOME FAMOUS SCIENTISTS

NICOLAUS COPERNICUS (1473–1543), Polish scientist who is known as the founder of modern astronomy. He came up with the theory that Earth and other planets revolve around the Sun. But most thinkers continued to believe that Earth was the center of the universe.

JOHANNES KEPLER (1571–1630), German astronomer who developed three laws of planetary motion. He was the first to propose a force (later named gravity) that governs planets' orbits around the Sun.

JOSEPH HENRY (1797–1878), American physicist who made key discoveries about electromagnetism. The henry, a commonly used unit of measure for the property of an electric circuit known as inductance, was named in his honor. In 1846 he became the first secretary, or head, of the Smithsonian Institution in Washington, D.C.

CHARLES DARWIN (1809–1882), British scientist who is best known for his theory of **evolution by natural selection**. According to this theory, living creatures, by gradually changing so as to have the best chances of survival, slowly developed over millions of years into the forms they have today.

GEORGE WASHINGTON CARVER (1864–1943), African-American scientist and inventor best known for his work with plants and soils. He came up with hundreds of products from peanuts, pecans, sweet potatoes, and soybeans and developed a hardy new hybrid cotton.

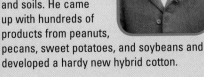

MARIE CURIE (1867–1934), Polish-born French physicist who discovered the radioactive elements polonium and radium with her husband, Pierre, and later carried out important research on radium. Marie and Pierre Curie shared the Nobel Prize for Physics in 1903, and Marie by herself won the Nobel Prize for Chemistry in 1911.

Marie and Pierre Curie

ALBERT EINSTEIN (1879–1955), German-American physicist who developed revolutionary theories about the relationships between time, space, matter, and energy. Probably the most famous and influential scientist of the 20th century, he won a Nobel Prize in 1921.

NIELS BOHR (1885–1962), Danish physicist who studied the structure of properties of atoms. His work led to the development of quantum mechanics. In 1922, he won the Nobel Prize for Physics for his work on atomic structure.

RACHEL CARSON (1907–1964), U.S. biologist and leading environmentalist whose 1962 book *Silent Spring* warned that chemicals used to kill pests were killing harmless wildlife. Eventually, DDT and certain other pesticides were banned in the U.S.

STEPHEN HAWKING (1942–), British physicist and leading authority on **black holes**—dense objects in space whose gravity is so strong that not even light can escape them. Hawking has also written best-selling books, including *A Brief History of Time* (1988) and *The Universe in a Nutshell* (2001).

Space

How many galaxies are there? page 219

The Solar System

Mercury Venus Earth Mars Jupiter Saturn Uranus Neptune

— Planets

Dwarf Planets

Ceres Pluto Haumea Makemake Eris

The SUN Is a STAR

Did you know that the Sun is a star, like the other stars you see at night? It is a typical, medium-size star. But because the Sun is much closer to our planet than any other star, we can study it in great detail. The diameter of the Sun is 865,000 miles—more than 100 times Earth's diameter. The gravity of the Sun at its surface is nearly 28 times the gravity of Earth.

How hot is the Sun? The surface temperature of the Sun is close to 10,000° F, and it is believed that the Sun's inner core may reach temperatures around 28 million degrees! The Sun provides enough light and heat energy to support life on our planet.

HOMEWORK TIP

Here's a useful way to remember the names of planets in order of their distance from the Sun. Think of this sentence: My Very Excellent Mother Just Sent Us Nachos.

M = Mercury, **V** = Venus, **E** = Earth, **M** = Mars, **J** = Jupiter, **S** = Saturn, **U** = Uranus, **N** = Neptune

The Planets Are in Motion

The planets in the solar system move around the Sun in oval-shaped paths called **orbits**. One complete trip around the Sun is called a **revolution**. Earth takes one year, or 365¼ days, to make one revolution. Planets farther away from the Sun take longer. Most planets have one or more moons. A moon orbits a planet in much the same way that the planets orbit the Sun. Each planet also spins, or rotates, on its axis. An axis is an imaginary line running through the center of a planet. The time it takes Earth to rotate on its axis equals one day.

Saturn

Largest planet:
Jupiter (88,846 miles diameter)

Smallest planet:
Mercury (3,032 miles diameter)

Shortest orbit:
Mercury (88 days)

Longest orbit:
Neptune (164.8 years)

Tallest mountain:
Mars (Olympus Mons, 16.8 miles high)

Hottest planet:
Venus (867° F)

Coldest planet:
Neptune (–330° F)

Shortest day:
Jupiter (9 hours, 55 minutes, 33 seconds)

Longest day:
Mercury (175.94 days)

No moons:
Mercury, Venus

Most moons:
Jupiter (63 known satellites)

WHAT IS AN ECLIPSE?

During a solar eclipse, the Moon casts a shadow on Earth. A total solar eclipse is when the Sun is completely blocked out. When this happens, the halo of gas around the Sun, called the **corona**, can be seen.

The most recent total solar eclipse took place on July 11, 2010. It was seen in the South Pacific Ocean and in southern Chile and Argentina. Four partial solar eclipses—in which the Sun is only partly blocked out—are predicted for 2011.

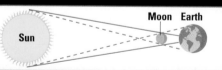

Sometimes Earth casts a shadow on the Moon. During a total lunar eclipse, the Moon remains visible, but it looks dark.

In 2010 a total lunar eclipse was expected on December 21, visible mainly in North America. In 2011, total lunar eclipses will occur on June 15 and December 10. Only the second one will be seen in North America.

Earth

Sun

THE PLANETS

1 MERCURY

Average distance from the Sun: 36 million miles
Diameter: 3,032 miles
Average temp.: 333° F
Surface: silicate rock
Time to revolve around the Sun: 88 days
Day (synodic—midday to midday): 175.94 days
Number of moons: 0

did you Know? *In 2009, scientists made a nearly complete map of Mercury. It was based on photos taken by the Messenger probe when it flew by the planet in 2008 and 2009 and by the Mariner 10 probe during flybys in the 1970s.*

2 VENUS

Average distance from the Sun: 67 million miles
Diameter: 7,521 miles
Average temp.: 867° F
Surface: silicate rock
Time to revolve around the Sun: 224.7 days
Day (synodic): 116.75 days
Number of moons: 0

did you Know? *From Earth, Venus usually appears brighter than any other planet or star. At certain times, Venus can even be seen in daylight.*

3 EARTH

Average distance from the Sun: 93 million miles
Diameter: 7,926 miles
Average temp.: 59° F
Surface: water, basalt, and granite rock
Time to revolve around the Sun: 365 ¼ days
Day (synodic): 24 h
Number of moons: 1

did you Know? *Earth is a "water planet" with about 71 percent of its surface covered by water. However, most of the water is in oceans—too salty for drinking. Only about 3 percent of Earth's water is fresh and suitable for drinking.*

4 MARS

Average distance from the Sun: 142 million miles
Diameter: 4,222 miles
Average temp.: −81° F
Surface: iron-rich basaltic rock
Time to revolve around the Sun: 687 days
Day (synodic): 24 h 39 min 35 s
Number of moons: 2

did you Know? *Was there ever life on Mars? Life as we know it depends on water. Scientists have found clues suggesting that lakes, seas, and rivers once existed on the surface of the Red Planet.*

5 JUPITER

Average distance from the Sun: 484 million miles
Diameter: 88,846 miles
Average temp.: −162° F
Surface: liquid hydrogen
Time to revolve around the Sun: 11.9 years
Day (synodic): 9 h 55 min 33 s
Number of moons: 63

did you Know? *A comet or asteroid slammed into Jupiter in mid-2009, producing an area 5,000 miles long that appears black.*

6 SATURN

Average distance from the Sun: 887 million miles
Diameter: 74,898 miles
Average temp.: −218° F
Surface: liquid hydrogen
Time to revolve around the Sun: 29.5 years
Day (synodic): 10 h 34 min 13 s
Number of moons: 62

did you Know? *Saturn's rings are the most famous in the solar system. Jupiter, Uranus, and Neptune have less dramatic rings. Scientists say even Saturn's moon Rhea may have rings.*

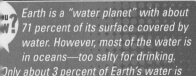

❼ URANUS

Average distance from the Sun: 1.8 billion miles
Diameter: 31,763 miles
Average temp.: −323° F
Surface: liquid hydrogen and helium
Time to revolve around the Sun: 84 years
Day (synodic): 17 h 14 min 23 s
Number of moons: 27

did you Know? *William Herschel, who discovered Uranus in 1781, worked as a music teacher and organist until a stipend from King George III allowed him to study astronomy full-time in 1782. He went on to make several other important discoveries.*

❽ NEPTUNE

Average distance from the Sun: 2.8 billion miles
Diameter: 30,775 miles
Average temp.: −330° F
Surface: liquid hydrogen and helium
Time to revolve around the Sun: 164.8 years
Day (synodic): 16 h 6 min 36 s
Number of moons: 13

did you Know? *Neptune, Jupiter, Saturn, and Uranus are often called gas-giant planets because they consist largely of gas (and liquid). But they all also are thought to have rocky cores.*

Dwarf Planets and Plutoids

In 2006 the International Astronomical Union (IAU) officially changed the definition of "planet." It decided that a planet must "clear the neighborhood" around its orbit. In other words, a planet has to have strong enough gravity that nearby bodies either merge with it or orbit around it. As a result, Pluto, an object that travels around the Sun in an orbit lying mostly past Neptune's, lost planet status. Pluto is rather small—smaller even than Earth's Moon—and it does not clear its neighborhood, which happens to be part of a collection of objects called the Kuiper Belt. The IAU put Pluto in a new category called dwarf planet.

Like a planet, a dwarf planet orbits the Sun. It doesn't have enough gravity to clear its neighborhood, but the gravity must be strong enough to give the dwarf a rounded shape. The first objects to be officially classified as dwarf planets were Pluto, Ceres, and Eris in 2006 and Haumea and Makemake in 2008. Ceres orbits the Sun in the asteroid belt between Mars and Jupiter. Dwarf planets with orbits beyond Neptune's are called plutoids by the IAU. Pluto, Eris, Haumea, and Makemake are all plutoids.

CERES

Average distance from the Sun: 257 million miles
Diameter: 592 miles
Number of moons: 0

PLUTO

Average distance from the Sun: 3.67 billion miles
Diameter: 1,430 miles
Number of moons: 3

HAUMEA

Average distance from the Sun: 4 billion miles
Diameter: roughly 900 miles
Number of moons: 2

MAKEMAKE

Average distance from the Sun: 4.2 billion miles
Diameter: 930 miles
Number of moons: 0

ERIS

Average distance from the Sun: 6.3 billion miles
Diameter: 1,600 miles
Number of moons: 1

PLANET EARTH
SEASONS

Axis

23.5°

The Earth spins on its axis of rotation. That's
how we get day and night. But the Earth's axis
isn't straight up and down. It is tilted about 23½
degrees. Because of this tilt, different parts of the
globe get different amounts of sunlight during the
year as the Earth orbits the Sun. This is why
we have seasons.

WINTER Winter begins at the
winter solstice (around December
21) in the Northern Hemisphere
(north of the equator, where we
live). Our hemisphere is tilted away
from the Sun, so the Sun's rays
reach us less directly. While days
get longer during winter, they are
still shorter than in spring and
summer, so it's cold. Everything
is reversed in the Southern
Hemisphere, where it's summer!

SPRING At the vernal equinox
(around March 21), daylight is 12
hours long throughout the world
because Earth is not tilted toward
or away from the Sun. Days continue
to get longer and the sunlight
gets more direct in the Northern
Hemisphere during spring.

Vernal Equinox

**Summer
Solstice**

**Winter
Solstice**

Autumnal Equinox

SUMMER The summer
solstice (around June 21)
marks the longest day of year
in the Northern Hemisphere
and the beginning of summer.
The build-up of heat caused
by more-direct sunlight during
the long late spring and early
summer days in the Northern
Hemisphere makes summer
our warmest season.

FALL After the autumnal
equinox (around September
21) the Northern Hemisphere
tilts away from the Sun;
sunlight is less direct and
lasts less than 12 hours.
The hemisphere cools off as
winter approaches.

THE MOON

The Moon is about 238,900 miles from Earth. It is 2,160 miles in diameter and has almost no atmosphere. The dusty surface is covered with deep craters. It takes the same time for the Moon to rotate on its axis as it does to orbit Earth (27 days, 7 hours, 43 minutes). This is why one side of the Moon is always facing Earth. The Moon has no light of its own but reflects light from the Sun. The lighted part of the Moon that we see changes in a regular cycle, waxing (growing) and waning (shrinking). It takes the Moon about 29½ days to go through all the "phases" in this cycle. This is called a lunar month.

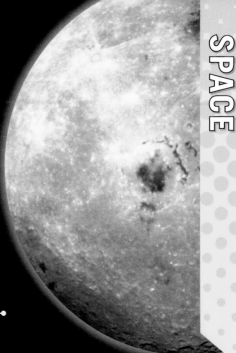

PHASES OF THE MOON

| New Moon | Waxing Crescent | First Quarter | Waxing Gibbous | Full Moon | Waning Gibbous | Last Quarter | Waning Crescent | New Moon |

MOON Q&A

Why are there dark spots on the face of the Moon?

The dark spots you see on the face of the Moon are called *maria*. They were once thought to be seas. ("Maria" means "seas" in Latin.) Maria actually are low plains made out of basalt, a fine, dark volcanic rock. The paler areas on the Moon's surface are mountains and highlands.

Does the Moon really cause the ocean tides?

Yes. Because the Moon is so big, its gravity causes the water in our seas and oceans to rise and fall as the Moon revolves around Earth. The Sun's gravitational pull also has an effect on ocean tides, but it is much weaker than the Moon's. That's because the Moon is so much closer to Earth than the Sun.

Are there any plans to go back to the Moon?

Countries such as the U.S., China, Russia, and India plan to use unmanned spacecraft to explore the Moon in coming years. Most recently, in mid-2009, the U.S. put the *Lunar Reconnaissance Orbiter* into orbit around the Moon to carry out a thorough mapping job. The U.S. and some other countries have talked about sending humans to the Moon in the future. Manned missions are very costly, however, and it's hard to say exactly when the next one to the Moon will take place.

SOME UNMANNED MISSIONS
in the Solar System

LAUNCH DATE	Mission
1959	**Luna 2** First spacecraft to hit the surface of the Moon
1962	**Mariner 2** First successful flyby of Venus
1964	**Mariner 4** First probe to reach Mars, 1965
1972	**Pioneer 10** First probe to reach Jupiter, 1973
1973	**Mariner 10** Only U.S. probe to reach Mercury, 1974
1975	**Viking 1 and 2** Landed on Mars in 1976
1977	**Voyager 1** Reached Jupiter in 1979 and Saturn in 1980
1977	**Voyager 2** Reached Jupiter in 1979, Saturn in 1981, Uranus in 1986, Neptune in 1989
1989	**Magellan** Orbited Venus and mapped its surface
1989	**Galileo** Reached Jupiter in 1995
1996	**Mars Global Surveyor** Began mapping surface in 1999
1996	**Mars Pathfinder** Landed on Mars. Carried a roving vehicle (Sojourner)
1997	**Cassini** Reached Saturn in June 2004
2001	**Mars Odyssey** Began mapping and studying Mars in early 2002
2003	**Mars rovers Spirit and Opportunity** Landed on Mars in early 2004
2004	**Messenger** Flew past Mercury in 2008 and 2009. Sent back first up-close data since 1975
2005	**Deep Impact** Reached comet Tempel 1 July 4, 2005
2006	**New Horizons** Due to reach Pluto in 2015
2007	**Phoenix** Landed in 2008 to search for signs that Mars once held life
2007	**Dawn** Due to reach asteroid Vesta in 2011 and Ceres in 2015
2009	**LCROSS** Slammed into the Moon, kicking up debris for study. Scientists detected signs of water

Phoenix Mars Lander

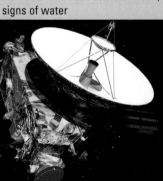

Artist's concept of the New Horizons spacecraft as it approaches Pluto and its three moons

Milestones
in Human Spaceflight

The U.S. formed NASA in 1958. It was in response to the Soviet Union's launching of the first artificial satellite *Sputnik I* on October 4, 1957. Since then, more than 500 astronauts have made trips into space to conduct research, visit orbiting space stations, and explore the Moon. Below are some of the biggest moments in human spaceflight.

1961	On April 12, Soviet cosmonaut Yuri Gagarin, in *Vostok 1*, became the first person to orbit Earth. On May 5, U.S. astronaut Alan B. Shepard Jr. during the *Mercury 3* mission became the first American in space.
1962	On February 20, U.S. astronaut John H. Glenn Jr. during the *Mercury 6* mission became the first American to orbit Earth.
1963	From June 16 to 19, the Soviet spacecraft *Vostok 6* carried the first woman into space, Valentina V. Tereshkova.
1965	On March 18, Soviet cosmonaut Aleksei A. Leonov became the first person to "walk" in space.
1966	On March 16, U.S. *Gemini 8* became the first craft to dock with (become attached to) another vehicle (an unmanned Agena rocket).
1969	On July 20, U.S. *Apollo 11's* lunar module *Eagle* landed on the Moon's surface in the area known as the Sea of Tranquility. Neil Armstrong was the first person ever to walk on the Moon.
1970	In April, *Apollo 13* astronauts returned safely to Earth after an explosion damaged their spacecraft and prevented them from landing on the Moon.
1973	On May 14, the U.S. put its first space station, *Skylab*, into orbit. The last *Skylab* crew left in February 1974.
1975	American and Soviet spacecraft docked in July, and for several days their crews worked and spent time together in space.
1981	*Columbia* was launched on April 12 and became the first space shuttle to reach space.
1986	On January 28, space shuttle *Challenger* exploded 73 seconds after takeoff. All seven astronauts, including teacher Christa McAuliffe, died. In February, the Soviet space station *Mir* was launched into orbit, where it remained for 15 years.
1998	In December, space shuttle *Endeavour* carried into orbit *Unity*, a U.S.-built part of the International Space Station (ISS). *Unity* was linked up to the Russian-built *Zarya* control module, which had been carried into orbit the preceding month. The first ISS crew arrived in November 2000.
2001	In April, U.S. businessman Dennis Tito rode a Russian Soyuz rocket to the ISS, becoming the first paying space tourist.
2003	On February 1, space shuttle *Columbia* disintegrated during its reentry into the Earth's atmosphere, killing the seven-member crew. China launched its first manned spacecraft on October 15.
2004	On June 21, Mike Melvill piloted *SpaceShipOne*, the first privately funded spacecraft, into space.
2009	A May mission by space shuttle *Atlantis* repaired and enhanced the aging Hubble Space Telescope, which was launched in 1990.
2010	Last flights scheduled for space shuttles *Atlantis*, *Endeavour*, and *Discovery*, to carry into orbit nearly all the final major components for completion of the ISS.

SPACE NEWS 2011

Shuttle Farewell!

The U.S. space shuttle program was scheduled to end in 2010, and there was much debate as to what might replace it. Some members of Congress wanted to keep it going a bit longer. But even if they succeeded in squeezing a few more flights out of the aging shuttles, an entire era in U.S. manned spaceflight was coming to an end.

Launches for Hire

In February 2010, President Barack Obama called for major changes in NASA's spaceflight operations. He wanted to stop programs set in motion six years before by then-President George W. Bush. Bush's plans included sending a manned mission to the Moon by the year 2020, with more ambitious manned missions—to Mars and beyond—to follow later. NASA accordingly began developing new rockets and spacecraft, including a replacement for the space shuttle. The projects made slow progress, however. They were very expensive—too expensive for some critics. Funding the projects became harder as the U.S. fell into a deep economic recession.

Obama's proposals might not all be accepted by Congress, but the ideas behind them seemed likely to guide NASA's future. Obama wanted more cooperation with other countries on space projects, as well as more U.S. spending on new fuels and engines for spaceflight. He also wanted NASA to get out of the business of flying astronauts into orbit. Instead, it would hire others, such as commercial companies or foreign space agencies, to do the job.

Destinations on Tap

NASA plans three launches for the second half of 2011 to explore other worlds. It expects to send *Juno* on a five-year trip to Jupiter. On arrival, *Juno* will go into orbit around the giant planet in order to study its atmosphere, gravity, and magnetic field. A mission called *GRAIL* (for "Gravity Recovery and Interior Laboratory") involves two spacecraft. They are to go into orbit around the Moon in order to study the lunar interior. A NASA rover called the *Mars Science Laboratory* is expected to reach the Red Planet in 2012. It will study the ability of Mars to support life today and in the past.

Juno

ISS Goes Online

In early 2010, astronauts aboard the International Space Station finally got a live Internet connection. "Hello Twitterverse!" typed NASA astronaut Timothy ("T. J.") Creamer (a.k.a. @Astro_TJ). "We r now LIVE tweeting from the International Space Station—the 1st live tweet from Space! :) More soon, send your ?s." Previously, ISS astronauts had to go through Mission Control to use the Internet. Now they had direct access and could even surf the Web.

Timothy Creamer

WHAT'S OUT THERE?

Spiral galaxy M100

What else is in space besides planets?

A GALAXY is a group of billions of stars held close together by gravity. The universe may have more than 100 billion galaxies! The one we live in is called the Milky Way. Our Sun and planets are only a small part of it. Scientists think there are as many as 200 billion stars in the Milky Way!

NEBULA is the name astronomers give to any fuzzy patch in the sky, even galaxies and star clusters. Planetary nebulas come from the late stages of some stars, while star clusters and galaxies are groups of stars. Emission nebulas, reflection nebulas, and dark dust clouds are regions of gas and dust that may be hundreds of light-years wide and are often birthplaces of stars. Emission nebulas often give off a reddish glow, caused when their hydrogen gas is heated by hot, newly formed stars nearby. Dust particles in some areas reflect hot blue starlight and appear as reflection nebulas. Dark dust clouds, though still mainly gas, contain enough dust to absorb starlight and appear as dark nebulas.

BLACK HOLE is the name given to a region in space with gravity so strong that nothing can get out—not even light. Many black holes are probably formed when giant stars at least 20 times as massive as our Sun burn up their fuel and collapse, creating very dense cores. Scientists think bigger, "supermassive" black holes may form from the collapse of many stars, or from the merging of smaller black holes, in the centers of galaxies. Black holes can't be seen, because they do not give off light. Astronomers watch for signs, such as effects on the orbits of nearby stars, X-ray bursts from matter being sucked into the black hole, or long jets of particles.

SATELLITES are objects that move in an orbit around a planet. Moons are natural satellites. Artificial satellites, launched into orbit by humans, are used as space stations and observatories. They are also used to take pictures of Earth's surface and to transmit communications signals.

ASTEROIDS are solid chunks of rock or metal that range in size from small boulders to hundreds of miles across. Some asteroids orbit other asteroids. Hundreds of thousands of asteroids orbit the Sun in the main asteroid belt between Mars and Jupiter.

COMETS are moving chunks of ice, dust, and rock that form huge gaseous heads and tails as they move nearer to the Sun. One of the most well-known is Halley's Comet. It can be seen about every 76 years and will appear again in the year 2061.

Comet McNaught, discovered in 2006

METEOROIDS are small pieces of stone or metal traveling in space. Most meteoroids are fragments from comets or asteroids that broke off from crashes in space with other objects. A few are actually chunks that blew off the Moon or Mars after an asteroid hit. When a meteoroid enters the Earth's atmosphere, it usually burns up completely. This streak of light is called a **meteor**, or **shooting star**. If a piece of a meteoroid survives its trip through our atmosphere and lands on Earth, it is called a **meteorite**.

Sports

Who were the M&M Boys?   page 230

You don't have to serve like Serena or shoot like Kobe to love playing sports. Indoors or out, in a league or your backyard, with friends or on your own—there are plenty of great ways to have fun and stay fit.

FAVORITE SPORTS

Here are the most popular sports and activities among kids in the United States in 2008.

Boys (ages 6–17)			Girls (ages 6–17)		
1.	Bicycling	8.2 million	1.	Bowling	5.3 million
2.	Bowling	7.7 million	2.	Bicycling	5.2 million
3.	Basketball	7.4 million	3.	Walking	5.1 million
4.	Freshwater Fishing	6.6 million	4.	Running/Jogging	3.9 million
5.	Baseball	6.6 million	5.	Outdoor Soccer	3.3 million
6.	Running/Jogging	5.5 million	6.	Freshwater Fishing	3.3 million
7.	Outdoor Soccer	5.0 million	7.	Basketball	3.2 million
8.	Walking	4.3 million	8.	Inline Skating	2.6 million
9.	Skateboarding	4.3 million	9.	Slow-Pitch Softball	1.4 million
10.	Billiards/Pool	3.9 million	10.	Skateboarding	1.2 million

Source: Sporting Goods Manufacturers Association's Sports & Participation Report, 2009

LITTLE League

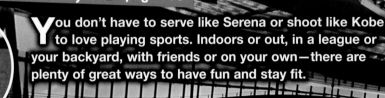

Little League Baseball is the largest youth sports program in the world. It began in 1939 in Williamsport, Pennsylvania, with 30 boys playing on three teams. Today, more than 2.5 million boys and girls ages 5 to 18 play on nearly 169,000 Little League baseball and softball teams in more than 75 countries.

Find out more at *www.littleleague.org*

Global GAMES

Football, baseball, and auto racing are among the most popular professional sports in the United States. But around the world, soccer (called football in other countries) rules. What other sports do kids in other countries love to watch and play? Here are a few of them.

Cricket

Cricket started in England in the 16th century. Today it is most popular in Great Britain and in former British colonies, such as India, Pakistan, and Australia. In some ways, cricket is like baseball. A pitcher, called a bowler, throws a ball (on a bounce) toward a target, called a wicket. A batsman guards the wicket by hitting the ball in any direction. The batting team scores runs and makes outs, and the matches are divided into innings. Major international matches are four innings, but they can take up to five days to complete.

Rugby

Rugby is similar to football but with a bigger ball and much less protective equipment. Teams score a try (much like a touchdown) by crossing the goal line with the ball. They also score by kicking the ball through goalposts. Players cannot pass the ball forward—only backward or sideways. They advance the ball mainly by running with it while trying to avoid being tackled by defenders. There are two popular types of the sport—rugby union has 15 players per team, and rugby league has 13.

Cricket match

Field Hockey

In the United States, field hockey is mainly popular among girls in high school. But across the globe, the sport—officially called "hockey"—is a hit with male and female players of all ages. Australia defeated Germany to win the 2010 Men's Hockey World Cup in India. The Netherlands was set to defend its title at the Women's Hockey World Cup in Argentina in September 2010.

Badminton

To many Americans, badminton is a fun pastime for backyard barbecues. Yet it is serious business in Asian countries such as China, South Korea, and Indonesia. In 2005, Chinese player Fu Haifeng clocked a record return shot of 206 miles per hour.

WHO AM I?

I've been around pro football for most of my life. My father is a well-known sportswriter in Minnesota. In high school, I was a ball boy for the Minnesota Vikings. I later played for the University of Pittsburgh before being selected by the Arizona Cardinals as the third pick of the 2004 National Football League (NFL) Draft. In 2009, I caught a record seven touchdowns in the postseason, including two in the Super Bowl. In 2010, I played in the Pro Bowl for the fourth time. But one of my biggest honors was being asked to appear on the cover of the *Madden NFL 10* video game.

Answer: Larry Fitzgerald

THE OLYMPIC GAMES

The first Olympics were held in Greece more than 2,500 years ago. In 776 B.C. they featured one event—a footrace. For more than 1,000 years, the Olympic Games were held every four years. In 393 A.D. the Roman emperor Theodosius put an end to the Olympics. The first modern Games were held in Athens in 1896. Since then, the Summer Olympics have taken place every four years at a different location. (The Games were canceled due to world wars in 1916, 1940, and 1944.)

The first Winter Olympics were held in Chamonix, France, in 1924. The competition was originally called the Winter Sports Week. The event wasn't officially recognized as the first Winter Olympics until after the Games were completed. Sixteen countries were represented by 258 athletes—only 11 were women.

2010 WINTER OLYMPICS

Vancouver, Canada, hosted the 21st Winter Games from February 12 to 28, 2010. More than 2,500 athletes from a record 82 countries competed for 86 gold medals in the sports listed below. The United States sent the most athletes, 212. Seven countries sent athletes to the Winter Games for the first time in 2010—the Cayman Islands, Colombia, Ghana, Montenegro, Pakistan, Peru, and Serbia.

2010 Winter Olympic Sports

Alpine Skiing	Luge
Biathlon	Nordic Combined
Bobsleigh (bobsled)	Short Track Speed Skating
Cross-Country Skiing	Skeleton
Curling	Ski Jumping
Figure Skating	Snowboarding
Freestyle Skiing	Speed Skating
Ice Hockey	

TORCH RELAY AND OPENING CEREMONIES

The 2010 Olympic torch relay began in British Columbia, Canada, on October 30, 2009. Over the next 106 days, about 12,000 torchbearers carried the torch more than 27,000 miles to every corner of Canada. It was the longest torch relay through one country in Olympic history.

The Opening Ceremonies were held on February 12 at BC Place Stadium in Vancouver—the first time they were held indoors. The festivities honored Canada's diverse regions and people, including its First Nations, or native peoples. The ceremony was dedicated to luge athlete Nodar Kumaritashvili from the country Georgia. He had died in a training accident earlier that day.

Four Canadian athletes were picked to light the indoor Olympic cauldron: hockey legend Wayne Gretzky, skier Nancy Greene, speed skater Catriona Le May Doan, and basketball star Steve Nash. A mechanical error prevented one of the cauldron's four huge legs from moving into place, however, so Doan was unable to participate. Gretzky then left the arena with a torch, which he used to light a giant outdoor cauldron.

2010 Medal Count

A total of 26 countries won at least one medal in Vancouver. The 37 medals won by the United States were the most by any country in Winter Olympic history. Canada's 14 gold medals were also a Winter Olympic record. Here are the top 10 medal-winning nations.

COUNTRY	Gold	Silver	Bronze	TOTAL
UNITED STATES	9	15	13	37
GERMANY	10	13	7	30
CANADA	14	7	5	26
NORWAY	9	8	6	23
AUSTRIA	4	6	6	16
RUSSIA	3	5	7	15
SOUTH KOREA	6	6	2	14
CHINA	5	2	4	11
SWEDEN	5	2	4	11
FRANCE	2	3	6	11

did you know? Skicross, or skiercross, made its Olympic debut in Vancouver. In the event, skiers race against a clock—and each other—over a course that has jumps, twisting turns, and other obstacles. Ashleigh McIvor of Canada brought home the first-ever Olympic gold medal in the women's event. Switzerland's Michael Schmid was the men's champ.

THE WAIT IS OVER

The United States has been competing in the Winter Olympics since 1924, yet it had never won a gold medal in any of the Nordic skiing events: cross-country skiing, biathlon, ski jumping, and Nordic combined (which includes cross-country skiing and ski jumping). That drought ended when 29-year-old Bill Demong finished first in the individual large hill/10-kilometer Nordic combined event in Vancouver. U.S. teammate Johnny Spillane took home the silver.

Olympic Hockey: OH, CANADA!

Both Olympic ice hockey finals featured talented teams from the United States and Canada. The U.S. and Canadian men's teams were made up completely of National Hockey League (NHL) players. Canada was the gold-medal favorite before the Games, but it was Team USA that went undefeated in the early rounds—including a 5–3 win over Canada. In the gold-medal game, Canada jumped out to a 2–0 lead. The U.S. scored in the second period and again with less than a minute to play to force sudden-death overtime. Almost eight minutes into the tense extra period, Sidney Crosby flipped a wrist shot past U.S. goaltender Ryan Miller to give Canada the gold medal. Despite the loss, Miller, who plays for the Buffalo Sabres, was named the most valuable player (MVP) of the tournament.

On the women's side, both teams had dominated the competition. The U.S. and Canadian teams combined to outscore opponents 86 to 4 on their way to the gold-medal game. However, the final was mostly a defensive battle. Marie-Philip Poulin put Canada ahead with two goals in the first period, and goaltender Shannon Szabados made 28 saves to preserve a 2–0 victory. The win gave the Canadian women's team its third straight Olympic gold medal.

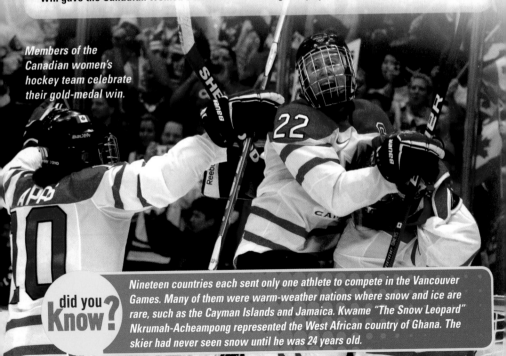

Members of the Canadian women's hockey team celebrate their gold-medal win.

did you Know? Nineteen countries each sent only one athlete to compete in the Vancouver Games. Many of them were warm-weather nations where snow and ice are rare, such as the Cayman Islands and Jamaica. Kwame "The Snow Leopard" Nkrumah-Acheampong represented the West African country of Ghana. The skier had never seen snow until he was 24 years old.

Olympic
ALL-STARS

Some of the best-known U.S. athletes from past Olympics were back in action in Vancouver.

Snowboarder **Shaun White** wowed the crowds at the 2006 Winter Olympics in Turin, Italy, and took home the gold medal in the halfpipe. In Vancouver, the 23-year-old redhead was assured of a second straight gold after scoring 46.8 out of 50.0 on his first run. White could have taken it easy on his second run, but instead he made history. He ended the run with his new signature move, the Double McTwist 1260—which includes two flips and three-and-a-half spins.

Shaun White

Before the Olympics, skier **Bode Miller** was largely a forgotten man. After winning two silver medals at the 2002 Olympics, Miller was one of the top American hopefuls in 2006. Yet he failed to win a single medal in five events. Many people criticized his work ethic and wild lifestyle. In Vancouver, Miller silenced his critics by winning three medals—including a gold in the super combined event.

Apolo Ohno entered the Vancouver Games as the most successful short track speed skater in Olympic history. The 27-year-old added three medals to his total: a silver in the 1,500 meters and bronzes in the 1,000 meters and 5,000-meter relay. He now has more Winter Olympic medals than any other U.S. athlete.

Apolo Ohno

Top U.S. Olympic Winter Games Medal Winners

Athlete	Sport	Years*	G	S	B	Total
Apolo Ohno	short track speed skating	2002, 2006, 2010	2	2	4	8
Bonnie Blair	speed skating	1988, 1992, 1994	5	0	1	6
Eric Heiden	speed skating	1980	5	0	0	5
Bode Miller	alpine skiing	2002, 2010	1	3	1	5
Cathy Turner	short track speed skating	1992, 1994	2	1	1	4

*Only years in which the athlete won medals are listed.

The Spirit of the Games

By overcoming difficult challenges, these athletes displayed the true Olympic spirit.

Joannie Rochette

A few years ago, **Steve Holcomb's** dreams of Olympic gold seemed dim. The U.S. bobsled pilot had a rare eye disorder that was causing him to slowly go blind. He feared his poor vision would put his teammates in danger. In 2008, Holcomb had experimental surgery. Doctors placed permanent contact lenses in his eyes. With his vision restored, Holcomb led his team to the 2009 World Cup championship. In Vancouver, he piloted his four-man sled, nicknamed Night Train, to the gold. It was the first U.S. gold medal in bobsled since 1948.

In women's figure skating, Yu-Na Kim of South Korea posted record scores in winning the gold medal. Yet the performance that won the hearts of most fans was by Canadian skater **Joannie Rochette**. Only two days before the skating competition began, Rochette's mother died suddenly from a heart attack. Rather than withdrawing from the event, Rochette decided to compete in honor of her mother. The 23-year-old skated beautifully and won the bronze medal.

SOME MODERN OLYMPIC FIRSTS

1896 — The first modern Olympic Games were held in Athens, Greece. Athletes from about a dozen nations participated in nine sports.

1900 — Women competed in the Olympic Games for the first time.

1904 — For the first time, medals were awarded to the top three competitors in each event—a gold for first, a silver for second, and a bronze for third.

1920 — The Olympic flag was raised for the first time, and the Olympic oath was introduced. The five interlaced rings of the flag represent Africa, America (North and South), Europe, Asia, and Australia.

1924 — The first Winter Olympic events, featuring skiing and skating, were held.

1936 — The torch relay was introduced at the Olympic Games. A relay of runners carries a lit torch from Olympia, Greece, to the site of each Olympics.

1994 — Starting with the 1994 Winter Olympics, the winter and summer Games have alternated every two years, instead of being held in the same year, every fourth year.

The Youth Olympic Games

The first-ever Youth Olympic Games were set to take place in Singapore, in Southeast Asia, from August 14 to 26, 2010. More than 3,000 athletes ages 14 to 18 from around the world were set to compete in the summer sports listed below. The International Olympic Committee (IOC) plans to hold the Youth Olympic Games every two years, alternating between summer and winter events. The first Winter Youth Olympic Games are scheduled be held in Innsbruck, Austria, in 2012.

2010 Youth Olympic Games Sports

Archery	Fencing	Sailing	Track and Field
Badminton	Field Hockey	Shooting	Triathlon
Basketball	Gymnastics	Soccer	Volleyball
Boxing	Handball	Swimming/Diving	Weightlifting
Canoe/Kayak	Judo	Table Tennis	Wrestling
Cycling	Modern Pentathlon	Tae Kwon Do	
Equestrian	Rowing	Tennis	

Looking AHEAD

2012 Summer Olympics | London, England | July 27 to August 12, 2012

In 2012, London will become the first city to host three separate Olympics. It previously hosted the 1908 and 1948 Summer Games. The London Olympics will feature the 26 sports listed above. The 2008 Olympics in Beijing, China, included 28 sports, but the IOC voted to discontinue baseball and softball for 2012.

2014 Winter Olympics | Sochi, Russia | February 7 to February 23, 2014

Sochi, a city on the coast of the Black Sea in southern Russia, will host the 22nd Winter Olympics. The 2014 Games will be the first Winter Olympics held in Russia. (Russia used to be part of the Soviet Union, which hosted the 1980 Summer Olympics.) The IOC voted not to add any new sports for the Sochi Olympics.

2016 Summer Olympics | Rio de Janeiro, Brazil | August 5 to August 21, 2016

On October 2, 2009, people flooded the streets of Rio de Janeiro (below) after the IOC announced that the city had been awarded the 2016 Summer Games. The Rio Olympics will be the first ever held in South America. The Games will include two new sports: golf and rugby sevens (a seven-man version of rugby union).

PARALYMPICS

The Paralympic Games are the official Olympic Games for athletes with physical, mental, or sensory disabilities. The Games got their start in 1948, when Sir Ludwig Guttman organized a competition in England for World War II veterans with spinal-cord injuries. When athletes from the Netherlands joined in 1952, the movement went international.

Olympic-style competition began in Rome in 1960, and the first Winter Paralympics were held in Sweden in 1976. Since 1988, the Paralympics have been held just after the Winter and Summer Olympic competitions. Following the 2010 Winter Olympics in Vancouver, about 500 athletes from 44 countries took part in the Paralympic Games at the Vancouver Olympic venues. Athletes from around the world will compete in the 2012 Summer Paralympic Games in London.

OFFICIAL PARALYMPIC SPORTS

Six Competitive Levels: wheelchair, intellectual disabilities, amputees, visual disabilities, cerebral palsy, and other mobility disabilities

Winter: alpine skiing, biathlon, cross-country skiing, ice sledge hockey, wheelchair curling

Summer: archery, boccia, cycling, equestrian, goalball, judo, powerlifting, rowing, sailing, shooting, soccer, swimming, table tennis, track and field, volleyball, wheelchair basketball, wheelchair fencing, wheelchair rugby, wheelchair tennis

Find out more at *www.paralympic.org*

Sledge hockey players compete at the 2010 Winter Paralympics.

SPECIAL OLYMPICS

The Special Olympics is the world's largest program of sports training and athletic competition for children and adults with intellectual disabilities. Founded in 1968, Special Olympics has offices in all 50 states, Washington, D.C., and throughout the world. The organization offers training and competition to more than 3 million athletes in about 175 countries.

Special Olympics holds World Games every two years. These alternate between summer and winter sports. The last Special Olympics Winter Games were held in Boise, Idaho, in February 2009. The next World Summer Games are scheduled to take place June 25 to July 4, 2011, in Athens, Greece.

To volunteer or find out more, visit: *www.specialolympics.org*

AUTO RACING

NASCAR®

Bill France founded the National Association for Stock Car Auto Racing (NASCAR) in 1947. Stock cars look a lot like the cars that are "in stock" at a car dealership. In 1949, Red Byron won the first NASCAR championship as the top driver of the season. Since 2008, the championship has been known as the Sprint Cup. Races in the Sprint Cup series include the Daytona 500 and the Brickyard 400.

PAST NASCAR CHAMPIONS

1983	Bobby Allison	1992	Alan Kulwicki	2001	Jeff Gordon
1984	Terry Labonte	1993	Dale Earnhardt	2002	Tony Stewart
1985	Darrell Waltrip	1994	Dale Earnhardt	2003	Matt Kenseth
1986	Dale Earnhardt	1995	Jeff Gordon	2004	Kurt Busch
1987	Dale Earnhardt	1996	Terry Labonte	2005	Tony Stewart
1988	Bill Elliott	1997	Jeff Gordon	2006	Jimmie Johnson
1989	Rusty Wallace	1998	Jeff Gordon	2007	Jimmie Johnson
1990	Dale Earnhardt	1999	Dale Jarrett	2008	Jimmie Johnson
1991	Dale Earnhardt	2000	Bobby Labonte	2009	Jimmie Johnson

Jimmie Johnson

INDIANAPOLIS 500

The Indianapolis 500 is the biggest event in open-wheel racing. Open-wheel cars have narrow bodies and big uncovered tires. The first Indianapolis 500 was held at the world-famous Indianapolis Motor Speedway in 1911. Ray Harroun won the first Indy 500 with an average speed of only 74.602 mph.

PAST INDY WINNERS

1911	Ray Harroun	74.602 mph	
1920	Gaston Chevrolet	88.618 mph	
1930	Billy Arnold	100.448 mph	
1940	Wilbur Shaw	114.277 mph	
1950	Johnnie Parsons	124.002 mph	
1960	Jim Rathmann	138.767 mph	
1970	Al Unser	155.749 mph	
1980	Johnny Rutherford	142.862 mph	
1990	Arie Luyendyk	185.981 mph*	
2000	Juan Montoya	167.607 mph	
2001	Helio Castroneves	131.294 mph	
2002	Helio Castroneves	166.499 mph	
2003	Gil de Ferran	156.291 mph	
2004	Buddy Rice	138.518 mph	
2005	Dan Wheldon	157.603 mph	

2006	Sam Hornish Jr.	157.085 mph
2007	Dario Franchitti	151.774 mph
2008	Scott Dixon	143.567 mph
2009	Helio Castroneves	150.318 mph
2010	Dario Franchitti	161.623 mph

Dario Franchitti

*Race record for average lap speed.

BASEBALL

The first known game of baseball with rules similar to those of the modern game was played at Elysian Fields in Hoboken, New Jersey, on June 19, 1846. The current National League (NL) was formed in 1876. The American League (AL) was established in 1901. Since the early 1900s, the champions of the NL and AL have met in the World Series.

NEW YORK, NEW YORK

The 2010 baseball season got underway on April 4, with the 2009 World Series champion New York Yankees losing to the Boston Red Sox. In 2009, the Yankees had won their 27th World Series title by defeating the Philadelphia Phillies four games to two. For only the second time ever, the series didn't end until November. (The first was in 2001, when the season was interrupted by the terrorist attacks on September 11.) World Series MVP Hideki Matsui batted .615 (8 for 13) with three home runs and eight runs batted in for the Yankees. The championship was the fifth for New York's "core four" players: shortstop Derek Jeter, catcher Jorge Posada, and pitchers Andy Pettitte and Mariano Rivera.

2009 AWARD WINNERS

MVP	CY YOUNG (top pitcher)	ROOKIE OF THE YEAR
AL: Joe Mauer, Minnesota Twins	AL: Zack Greinke, Kansas City Royals	AL: Andrew Bailey, Oakland Athletics
NL: Albert Pujols, St. Louis Cardinals	NL: Tim Lincecum, San Francisco Giants	NL: Chris Coghlan, Florida Marlins

61 in '61

The 2011 season will mark the 50th anniversary of the greatest home run chase in baseball history. In 1961, the Yankees had two great sluggers, Mickey Mantle (far left) and Roger Maris (left). By midseason, it was clear that "the M&M Boys" both had a shot at breaking baseball's most famous record: Babe Ruth's 60 home runs in 1927. A hip infection in late September forced Mantle out of the race with 54 homers. The pressure on Maris was so great that his hair started to fall out, but he kept piling up home runs. On October 1, the final day of the season, Maris hit number 61 and forever etched his name in baseball history.

SOME MAJOR LEAGUE RECORDS*

BATTERS

Most Home Runs

Career: 762, Barry Bonds (1986–2007)
Season: 73, Barry Bonds (2001)
Game: 4, by 12 different players

Most Hits

Career: 4,256, Pete Rose (1963–86)
Season: 262, **Ichiro Suzuki** (2004)
Game: 7, Rennie Stennett (1975)

Most Stolen Bases

Career: 1,406, Rickey Henderson (1979–2003)
Season: 130, Rickey Henderson (1982)
Game: 6, by four different players

PITCHERS

Most Strikeouts

Career: 5,714, Nolan Ryan (1966–93)
Season: 383, Nolan Ryan (1973)
Game: 20, Roger Clemens (1986, 1996);
Kerry Wood (1998)

Most Wins

Career: 511, Cy Young (1890–1911)
Season: 41, Jack Chesbro (1904)

Most Saves

Career: 591, **Trevor Hoffman** (1993–2009)
Season: 62, **Francisco Rodriguez** (2008)

*Through the 2009 season. Players in bold played in 2009. Game stats are for nine-inning games only.

Honoring a Pioneer

On April 15, 2010, all major league players wore uniform number 42. They were honoring the anniversary of the date in 1947 that Jackie Robinson broke baseball's color barrier. Wearing number 42 for the Brooklyn Dodgers, Robinson became the first African-American player in Major League Baseball.

Before then, African Americans could play only on all-black teams in the Negro Leagues. Dodgers president Branch Rickey wanted to end the unwritten ban on African-American players, but he knew he needed a special player to do it. That player had to have the courage to tolerate insults and threats from fans and other players without fighting back. Rickey chose Jackie Robinson, who had starred in four sports at the University of California, Los Angeles (UCLA).

Jackie Robinson steals home in the 1955 World Series.

On April 15, 1947, Robinson was in the Brooklyn lineup, batting second and playing first base. He led the Dodgers to the World Series that season and was named Rookie of the Year. More important, he paved the way for African Americans to break barriers that existed in other areas of society.

BASEBALL Hall of Fame

In 2011, baseball will celebrate the 75th anniversary of its first Hall of Fame class. The 1936 inductees were five baseball legends: Babe Ruth, Ty Cobb, Honus Wagner, Christy Mathewson, and Walter Johnson. In 1939, the current home of the National Baseball Hall of Fame and Museum officially opened in Cooperstown, New York. Three new members were inducted in 2010: Eight-time All-Star outfielder Andre Dawson, manager Whitey Herzog, and umpire Doug Harvey. That brought the total number of members to 292.

Find out more about baseball's legends at www.baseballhall.org

BASKETBALL

Dr. James Naismith invented basketball in Springfield, Massachusetts, in 1891. He used peach baskets as hoops. At first, each team had nine players instead of five. Big-time pro basketball started in the late 1940s, when the National Basketball Association (NBA) was formed. The Women's National Basketball Association (WNBA) began play in 1997.

Like Old Times

Kobe Bryant (24)

The 2010 NBA Finals featured the league's two most successful franchises, the Boston Celtics and the Los Angeles Lakers. The longtime rivals met in the finals for the 12th time. Boston had won nine of the previous series, including the 2008 championship. But the 2009–2010 Lakers got their revenge during a hard-fought seven-game series. Kobe Bryant and Pau Gasol led the way, as L.A. won its second straight NBA title. The Lakers have now won 16 championships— one less than the rival Celtics.

The Cleveland Cavaliers finished with the best regular-season record but fell to Boston in the playoffs. Cleveland's LeBron James was named regular-season MVP for the second straight year. One of the NBA's breakout stars was Kevin Durant of the Oklahoma City Thunder, who led the league in scoring. He helped the Thunder improve by 27 wins from 2008–2009 and make the playoffs for the first time.

Hall of Fame

The Naismith Memorial Hall of Fame in Springfield, Massachusetts, honors great players, coaches, and others who have had a big impact on the game. The 2010 class included Karl Malone and Scottie Pippen, who were also inducted as members of the 1992 Olympic "Dream Team." The 1960 men's Olympic team was inducted as well. Other new members included guard Dennis Johnson, forward Gus Johnson, international star Maciel "Ubiratan" Pereira, WNBA star Cynthia Cooper, Los Angeles Lakers owner Jerry Buss, and high school coach Bob Hurley Sr.

Find out more about the legends of basketball at
www.hoophall.com

Some **All-Time** NBA Records*

POINTS	ASSISTS	REBOUNDS	3-POINTERS
Career: 38,387, Kareem Abdul-Jabbar (1969–89)	**Career:** 15,806, John Stockton (1984–2003)	**Career:** 23,924, Wilt Chamberlain (1959–73)	**Career:** 2,560, Reggie Miller (1987–2005)
Season: 4,029, Wilt Chamberlain (1961–62)	**Season:** 1,164, John Stockton (1990–91)	**Season:** 2,149, Wilt Chamberlain (1960–61)	**Season:** 269, **Ray Allen** (2005–2006)
Game: 100, Wilt Chamberlain (1962)	**Game:** 30, Scott Skiles (1990)	**Game:** 55, Wilt Chamberlain (1960)	**Game:** 12, **Kobe Bryant** (2003); Donyell Marshall (2005)

*Through the 2009–2010 season. Players in bold played in 2009–2010.

The WNBA

Diana Taurasi

High-scoring guard Diana Taurasi led the Phoenix Mercury to the 2009 WNBA championship. Phoenix defeated the Indiana Fever three games to two to win its second league crown in three years. Taurasi was named MVP of both the regular season and the Finals.

The 2010 season brought about big changes. The Detroit Shock moved to Tulsa, Oklahoma. The Sacramento Monarchs folded after the 2009 season, leaving the league with 12 teams. The Connecticut Sun selected college player of the year Tina Charles as the first pick in the 2010 WNBA Draft. Charles had led the nearby University of Connecticut to back-to-back national championships.

COLLEGE BASKETBALL

The men's National Collegiate Athletic Association (NCAA) Tournament began in 1939. Today, it is a spectacular 65-team extravaganza that is part of March Madness. Games on the Final Four weekend, when the semifinals and finals are played, are watched by millions of viewers. The Women's NCAA Tournament began in 1982 and has soared in popularity.

THE 2010 NCAA TOURNAMENT RESULTS

MEN'S FINAL FOUR
Semifinals:
Butler 52, Michigan State 50
Duke 78, West Virginia 57
Final:
Duke 61,
Butler 59
Most Outstanding Player:
Kyle Singler, Duke

WOMEN'S FINAL FOUR
Semifinals:
Stanford 73, Oklahoma 66
Connecticut 70, Baylor 50
Final:
Connecticut 53,
Stanford 47
Most Outstanding Player:
Maya Moore, Connecticut

FOOTBALL

Football began as a college sport in the 1800s. The professional league that became the modern National Football League (NFL) started in 1920. The rival American Football League began in 1960. The two leagues played the first Super Bowl in 1967. In 1970, the leagues merged to become the NFL as we know it today, with an American Football Conference (AFC) and a National Football Conference (NFC).

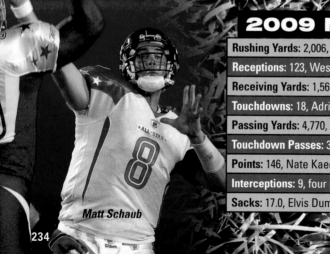

Tracy Porter

SUPER SAINTS

On February 7, 2010, the New Orleans Saints defeated the Indianapolis Colts to win their first Super Bowl. The win was extra special for the people of New Orleans, whose city had been devastated by Hurricane Katrina in August 2005. The game was the most-watched TV program in U.S. history, drawing an average of 106.5 million viewers. The record audience for Super Bowl XLIV saw a back-and-forth battle. A touchdown pass by Drew Brees and a two-point conversion put New Orleans ahead 24–17 late in the fourth quarter. On the Colts' next possession, Saints safety Tracy Porter intercepted a Peyton Manning pass and returned it 74 yards for a touchdown to seal a 31–17 win.

2010 PRO BOWL

In 2010, for the first time ever, the Pro Bowl was played the week before the Super Bowl. In past years, the NFL all-star game was played the week after the championship game. Because of the switch, the seven Saints and seven Colts players selected to the Pro Bowl were unable to play. In a high-scoring contest, the AFC beat the NFC, 41–34. Matt Schaub of the Houston Texans, who threw for two long touchdowns in the first quarter, was named MVP.

2009 NFL Leaders

Rushing Yards: 2,006, Chris Johnson, Tennessee Titans
Receptions: 123, Wes Welker, New England Patriots
Receiving Yards: 1,569, Andre Johnson, Houston Texans
Touchdowns: 18, Adrian Peterson, Minnesota Vikings
Passing Yards: 4,770, Matt Schaub, Houston Texans
Touchdown Passes: 34, Drew Brees, New Orleans Saints
Points: 146, Nate Kaeding, San Diego Chargers
Interceptions: 9, four players tied
Sacks: 17.0, Elvis Dumervil, Denver Broncos

Matt Schaub

234

NFL All-Time Record Holders*

RUSHING YARDS
- Career: 18,355, Emmitt Smith (1990–2004)
- Season: 2,105, Eric Dickerson (1984)
- Game: 296, **Adrian Peterson** (2007)

RECEIVING YARDS
- Career: 22,895, Jerry Rice (1985–2004)
- Season: 1,848, Jerry Rice (1995)
- Game: 336, Willie Anderson (1989)

PASSING YARDS
- Career: 69,329, **Brett Favre** (1991–2009)
- Season: 5,084, Dan Marino (1984)
- Game: 554, Norm Van Brocklin (1951)

POINTS SCORED
- Career: 2,544, Morten Andersen (1982–2004, 2006–2007)
- Season: 186, **LaDainian Tomlinson** (2006)
- Game: 40, Ernie Nevers (1929)

*Through the 2009 season.
Players in bold played in 2009.

NFL DRAFT

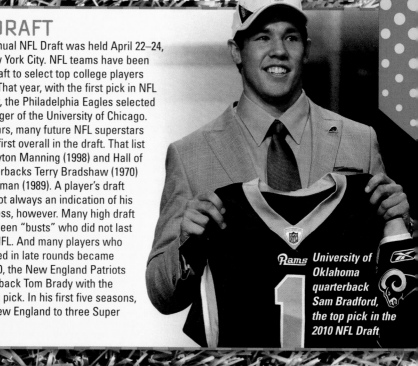

The 75th annual NFL Draft was held April 22–24, 2010, in New York City. NFL teams have been holding a draft to select top college players since 1936. That year, with the first pick in NFL Draft history, the Philadelphia Eagles selected Jay Berwanger of the University of Chicago. Over the years, many future NFL superstars were taken first overall in the draft. That list includes Peyton Manning (1998) and Hall of Fame quarterbacks Terry Bradshaw (1970) and Troy Aikman (1989). A player's draft position is not always an indication of his future success, however. Many high draft picks have been "busts" who did not last long in the NFL. And many players who were selected in late rounds became stars. In 2000, the New England Patriots took quarterback Tom Brady with the 199th overall pick. In his first five seasons, Brady led New England to three Super Bowl wins.

University of Oklahoma quarterback Sam Bradford, the top pick in the 2010 NFL Draft

Pro Football *Hall of Fame*

The Pro Football Hall of Fame in Canton, Ohio, was founded in 1963 to honor outstanding players, coaches, and contributors to the NFL. Running back Emmitt Smith and receiver Jerry Rice topped the list of seven members who were scheduled to be inducted on August 7, 2010. Smith holds career records for rushing yards and rushing touchdowns. Rice scored a record 208 touchdowns and owns most major receiving records. They were joined by guard Russ Grimm, linebacker Rickey Jackson, cornerback Dick LeBeau, running back Floyd Little, and defensive tackle John Randle.

Learn more about football's biggest names at *www.profootballhof.com*

COLLEGE FOOTBALL

Mark Ingram

On January 7, 2010, the Alabama Crimson Tide met the Texas Longhorns in the Bowl Championship Series (BCS) National Championship Game in Pasadena, California. Both teams entered the game undefeated. The game's biggest play came early in the first quarter, when 'Bama defensive lineman Marcell Dareus knocked Texas star quarterback Colt McCoy out of the game. Alabama took a 24–6 lead into halftime and held off a late Texas comeback for a 37–21 win. Crimson Tide running back Mark Ingram was named the game's MVP after rushing for 116 yards and two touchdowns. With the win, Alabama joined Notre Dame as the only schools with eight national championships.

Bowled Over!

Here are the results of other major bowl games played in January 2010.

Rose Bowl	Pasadena, CA	Ohio State 26, Oregon 17
Sugar Bowl	New Orleans, LA	Florida 51, Cincinnati 24
Fiesta Bowl	Glendale, AZ	Boise State 17, Texas Christian (TCU) 10
Orange Bowl	Miami, FL	Iowa 24, Georgia Tech 14

HEISMAN TROPHY

Alabama running back Mark Ingram was awarded the 2009 Heisman Trophy as the top college player in the nation. Ingram narrowly beat running back Toby Gerhart of Stanford in the closest voting in the 75-year history of the award. Ingram was only the third sophomore to win the Heisman—all three have come in the past three years. Tim Tebow of Florida (2007) and Sam Bradford of Oklahoma (2008) were the previous winners. Ingram rushed for 15 touchdowns and a school record 1,542 yards in leading Alabama to the BCS National Championship Game.

ALL-TIME DIVISION I NCAA LEADERS*

RUSHING

YARDS
Career: 6,397, Ron Dayne, Wisconsin (1996–99)
Season: 2,628, Barry Sanders, Okla. St. (1988)
Game: 406, LaDainian Tomlinson, TCU (1999)

TOUCHDOWNS
Career: 73, Travis Prentice, Miami of Ohio (1996–99)
Season: 37, Barry Sanders, Okla. St. (1988)

PASSING

YARDS
Career: 17,072, Timmy Chang, Hawaii (2000–04)
Season: 5,833, B.J. Symons, Texas Tech (2003)
Game: 716, David Klingler, Houston (1990)

TOUCHDOWNS
Career: 134, Graham Harrell, Texas Tech (2005–08)
Season: 58, Colt Brennan, Hawaii (2006)

*Through the 2009 season

GOLF

Golf began in Scotland as early as the 1400s. The first golf course in the United States opened in 1888 in Yonkers, New York. The sport has grown to include both men's and women's professional tours. And millions of other golfers play just for fun.

The men's tour in the U.S. is run by the Professional Golf Association (PGA). The four major championships (with the year first played) are:
- British Open (1860)
- United States Open (1895)
- PGA Championship (1916)
- Masters Tournament (1934)

The women's tour in the U.S. is guided by the Ladies Professional Golf Association (LPGA). The four major championships are:
- United States Women's Open (1946)
- McDonald's LPGA Championship (1955)
- Kraft Nabisco Championship (1972)
- Women's British Open (1976)

The All-Time "Major" Players

These pro golfers have won the most major championships through 2009.

MEN	WOMEN
1. Jack Nicklaus, 18	1. Patty Berg, 15
2. Tiger Woods, 14	2. Mickey Wright, 13
3. Walter Hagen, 11	3. Louise Suggs, 11
4. Ben Hogan, 9	4. Babe Didrikson Zaharias, 10
Gary Player, 9	Annika Sorenstam, 10

Phil Mickelson won his third Masters in 2010.

GYMNASTICS

Bridget Sloan

Although the sport dates back to ancient Egypt, modern-day gymnastics began in Europe in the early 1800s. It has been part of the Olympics since 1896. The first World Gymnastic Championships were held in the city of Antwerp, Belgium, in 1903.

Artistic gymnastics is the most popular form of gymnastics. Men compete in the high bar, parallel bars, rings, vault, pommel horse, floor exercise, individual all-around, and team events. The women's events are the uneven parallel bars, vault, balance beam, floor exercise, individual all-around, and team competition. Only women compete in rhythmic gymnastics, which includes the rope, hoop, ball, clubs, ribbon, and all-around events.

The two biggest stars of the 2008 Olympics, Shawn Johnson and Nastia Liukin, took time off from gymnastics in 2009. That gave other U.S. artistic gymnasts a chance to shine. In October 2009, 17-year-old Bridget Sloan won the all-around competition at the World Championships. U.S. teammate Rebecca Bross finished second.

ICE HOCKEY

Ice hockey began in Canada in the mid-1800s. The National Hockey League (NHL) was formed in 1917. Today the NHL has 30 teams—24 in the U.S. and six in Canada.

2009–2010 HIGHLIGHTS

The Chicago Blackhawks defeated the Philadelphia Flyers in six games to win their first Stanley Cup since 1961. Patrick Kane scored the game-winner in overtime of Game 6 to give Chicago the championship. Blackhawks captain Jonathan Toews won the Conn Smythe Trophy as the playoff MVP. The loss ended a remarkable playoff run for the Flyers, who had clinched a playoff spot with a shootout win on the last day of the regular season.

SEASON	WINNER	RUNNER-UP
1999–2000	New Jersey Devils	Dallas Stars
2000–01	Colorado Avalanche	New Jersey Devils
2001–02	Detroit Red Wings	Carolina Hurricanes
2002–03	New Jersey Devils	Anaheim Mighty Ducks
2003–04	Tampa Bay Lightning	Calgary Flames
2004–05	Season canceled	
2005–06	Carolina Hurricanes	Edmonton Oilers
2006–07	Anaheim Ducks	Ottawa Senators
2007–08	Detroit Red Wings	Pittsburgh Penguins
2008–09	Pittsburgh Penguins	Detroit Red Wings
2009–10	Chicago Blackhawks	Philadelphia Flyers

2009–2010 NHL League Leaders

Points: 112, Henrik Sedin, Vancouver Canucks

Goals: 51, Sidney Crosby, Pittsburgh Penguins; Steve Stamkos, Tampa Bay Lightning

Assists: 83, Henrik Sedin, Vancouver Canucks

Save Percentage: .931, Tuukka Rask, Boston Bruins

Wins: 45, Martin Brodeur, New Jersey Devils

Martin Brodeur

Hall of Fame

Located in Toronto, Ontario, Canada, the Hockey Hall of Fame honors contributors to the sport both on and off the ice. The 2010 inductees were former NHL star Dino Ciccarelli, women's hockey stars Cammi Granato and Angela James, Detroit Red Wings executive Jim Devellano, and Calgary Flames founder Daryl "Doc" Seaman.
Learn more at *www.hhof.com*

Some All-Time NHL Records*

GOALS SCORED
Career: 894, Wayne Gretzky (1979–99)
Season: 92, Wayne Gretzky (1981–82)
Game: 7, Joe Malone (1920)

GOALIE WINS
Career: 602, **Martin Brodeur** (1992–2010)
Season: 48, **Martin Brodeur** (2006–07)

POINTS
Career: 2,857, Wayne Gretzky (1979–99)
Season: 215, Wayne Gretzky (1985–86)
Game: 10, Darryl Sittler (1976)

GOALIE SHUTOUTS
Career: 110, **Martin Brodeur** (1992–2010)
Season: 22, George Hainsworth (1928–29)

* Through the 2009–2010 season. Player in bold played in 2009–2010.

SOCCER

World Cup

The 2010 Men's FIFA World Cup kicked off on June 11, 2010, in South Africa. Held every four years, this month-long tournament is one of the most popular sporting events in the world. Thirty-two teams from across the globe competed in ten stadiums around South Africa, leading up to a July 11 final match in Johannesburg.

The women's World Cup is also held every four years. The next one is scheduled to begin in June 2011 in Germany.

World Cup Champions

	Year	Winner	Year	Winner	Year	Winner
MEN	1930	Uruguay	1958	Brazil	1986	Argentina
	1934	Italy	1962	Brazil	1990	West Germany
	1938	Italy	1966	England	1994	Brazil
	1942	not held	1970	Brazil	1998	France
	1946	not held	1974	West Germany	2002	Brazil
	1950	Uruguay	1978	Argentina	2006	Italy
	1954	West Germany	1982	Italy		

	Year	Winner
WOMEN	1991	United States
	1995	Norway
	1999	United States
	2003	Germany
	2007	Germany

Kristine Lilly of the Boston Breakers of WPS has played more international matches than any other player in the world—male or female.

Major League Soccer

In 2009, Major League Soccer (MLS) expanded to 15 teams with the addition of the Seattle Sounders FC. The new club sold out all its home games and set a league attendance record. The season ended with Real Salt Lake beating the Los Angeles Galaxy in a penalty shootout for the 2009 MLS Cup. Real Salt Lake goalkeeper Nick Rimando was named MVP of the MLS Cup. The Galaxy's Landon Donovan was named regular-season MVP.

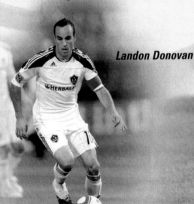

Landon Donovan

Women's Professional Soccer

Women's Professional Soccer (WPS) added two new teams, the Atlanta Beat and Philadelphia Independence, for the 2010 season. But two of the seven original teams, the Los Angeles Sol and Saint Louis Athletica, folded. WPS is the first top pro women's league in the United States since the Women's United Soccer Association (WUSA) folded after the 2003 season.

TENNIS

Modern tennis began in 1873. The first championships were held in Wimbledon, near London, four years later. In 1881, the first official U.S. men's championships were held at Newport, Rhode Island. Six years later, the first U.S. women's championships took place in Philadelphia. Today, the four most important tournaments, or Grand Slams, are the Australian Open, the French Open, the All-England (Wimbledon) Championships, and the U.S. Open.

ALL-TIME GRAND SLAM SINGLES WINS

MEN	Australian	French	Wimbledon	U.S.	Total
Roger Federer (b. 1981)**	4	1	6	5	16
Pete Sampras (b. 1971)	2	0	7	5	14
Roy Emerson (b. 1936)	6	2	2	2	12
Bjorn Borg (b. 1956)	0	6	5	0	11
Rod Laver (b. 1938)	3	2	4	2	11
Bill Tilden (1893–1953)	*	0	3	7	10
WOMEN					
Margaret Smith Court (b. 1942)	11	5	3	5	24
Steffi Graf (b. 1969)	4	6	7	5	22
Helen Wills Moody (1905–1998)	*	4	8	7	19
Chris Evert (b. 1954)	2	7	3	6	18
Martina Navratilova (b. 1956)	3	2	9	4	18

*Never played in tournament. **Player active in 2010. Wins through May 2010.*

SLAM SUCCESS

Roger Federer

The world's top-ranked men's and women's players were at the top of their game at the 2010 Australian Open. In the men's final, Roger Federer defeated Andy Murray in straight sets to win the Open for the fourth time. The victory was Federer's 16th Grand Slam title—the most of any men's player.

In the women's final, Serena Williams beat Justine Henin to win the tournament for the fifth time. It was her 12th career Grand Slam singles title.

Federer and Williams both lost in the quarterfinals of the French Open, however. Francesca Schiavone won the women's singles title—the first Italian woman ever to win a Grand Slam event. Rafael Nadal won the men's singles crown for the fifth time in six years. In doing so, he regained the world number 1 ranking from his rival Federer.

X GAMES

ESPN held the first X Games (originally called the Extreme Games) in Rhode Island and Vermont in 1995. The first Winter X Games followed two years later, in Big Bear Lake, California. Considered the Olympics of extreme sports, the X Games showcase fearless athletes who are always looking for new ways to go higher and faster and invent more outrageous tricks.

Winter X Games

The 14th Winter X Games took place in Aspen, Colorado, January 28–31, 2010—only two weeks before the start of the Vancouver Olympics. Many of the top performances belonged to repeat champions. Shaun White took home his third consecutive snowboard superpipe gold medal. Tyler Walker won his third gold medal in mono-skier X (a race for disabled sit-skiers). Ophelie David (right, in yellow) from France won her fourth straight women's skier X (skicross) gold medal. Not to be outdone, Nate Holland recorded a "five-peat," winning the men's snowboard X for the fifth straight year.

Summer X Games

The 16th Summer X Games were set to be held in Los Angeles in late July 2010. The X Games feature events in Moto X (motocross), BMX, skateboarding, surfing, and rallying (car racing).

Learn more about extreme sports at
http://espn.go.com/action

WORD Whirl

Use the clues to figure out which athletes' last names spiral around the red rule. Each name after number 1 begins with the last letter of the previous name. The names wind up, down, forward, and backward. Hint: Each athlete in the puzzle is featured in the Sports section.

1. One of the M&M Boys

2. Canadian goalie with the golden touch

3. Texas gunslinger and Pro Bowl MVP

4. OK passer who was tops on Draft Day

5. NBA shooter who brings the thunder

6. Phoenix star who's on the rise

7. Rusher who had the Longhorns seeing red

8. Lefty who's a three-time Master

ANSWERS ON PAGES 334–336.

Technology & Computers

What is a URL? → page 243

COMPUTER HIGHLIGHTS TIME LINE

100 B.C. The Antikythera Mechanism, which used gears to predict the positions of astronomical bodies, was built by the ancient Greeks. It was the first known mechanical computer.

1623 Wilhelm Schickard built the first machine that could automatically add, subtract, multiply, and divide. He called it a "calculating clock."

1946 The first electronic, programmable, general-purpose computer was invented. It was called ENIAC, for "Electronic Numerical Integrator and Computer."

1967 The Advanced Research Projects Agency (ARPA) allotted money toward creating a computer network. It became ARPAnet, which evolved into the Internet.

1968 The first hypertext system was built by Douglas Engelbart of Stanford Research Institute. Called NLS (oN Line System), the system's design allowed users to move text and data with a mouse (which Engelbart invented in 1963).

1971 The "floppy disk" was introduced by IBM as a means of affordable portable storage.

1975 The Altair 8800 entered the market. It was the first widely sold personal microcomputer.

1975 Bill Gates and Paul Allen founded Microsoft. Later came the first version of Windows.

1990 The World Wide Web was first launched with one server by British physicist Tim Berners-Lee. He also created Uniform Resource Locators (URLs), the Hypertext Transfer Protocol (HTTP), and Hypertext Markup Language (HTML).

1996 Google, the Internet's most popular search engine, began as a graduate student project at Stanford University called BackRub.

2003 MySpace, a popular online community that allows Internet users to connect and share interests and pictures, was founded. Facebook, another popular social networking site, got its start the following year. Membership in it was at first limited to college students.

2005 YouTube, a popular video sharing service, was founded.

2006 Twitter, a Web service letting people send or post short messages, was founded. The messages, called tweets, cannot be longer than 140 characters and are searchable.

2010 Apple introduced the iPad, a tablet computer using a version of the same operating system as Apple's iPhone.

did you Know?

Top Secret

The top-secret Colossus, built in England during World War II, was the first programmable digital electronic computer. It was designed specifically for breaking German codes. Several were built, with the first going into operation in 1944.

COMPUTER TALK

BIT   The smallest unit of data

BYTE   An amount of data equal to 8 bits

COOKIE   Some websites store information like your password on your computer's hard drive. When you go back to that site later, your browser sends the information (the "cookie") to the website.

ENCRYPTION   The process of changing information into a code to keep others from reading it

HTTP   Hypertext Transfer Protocol is the method of file exchange used on the World Wide Web.

MEGABYTE (MB)   An amount of information equal to 1,048,516 bytes, or (in some situations) 1 million bytes

RAM OR RANDOM ACCESS MEMORY   Memory your computer uses to open programs and store your work until you save it to a hard drive or disk. Information in RAM disappears when the computer is turned off.

ROM OR READ ONLY MEMORY   Memory that contains permanent instructions for the computer and cannot be changed. The information in ROM stays after the computer is turned off.

SPYWARE   Software that observes computer activity without the user's knowledge. May record key strokes or fill the screen with ads.

TABLET   A portable computer with a touch-sensitive screen

URL OR UNIFORM RESOURCE LOCATOR   The technical name for a website address

VIRUS   A program that damages other programs and data. It gets into a computer through the Internet or shared disks.

WI-FI OR WIRELESS FIDELITY   Technology that allows people to link to other computers and the Internet from their computers without wires

PLAYING IT SAFE
ONLINE

Social networking websites such as Facebook, Kidzworld, and MySpace can be a lot of fun. But if you're not careful, they can also be a source of problems. To be on the safe side, you should always keep an eye out for risks.

Be careful about what personal information you make public. Carefully guard your password, birthday, bank account number, credit card number, social security number, address, and phone number. Watch out for "phishing" scams: fake emails and posts that look as if they came from an official source and are meant to trick you into revealing your private details. Keeping your personal information private will reduce the risk that someone will be able to use your online accounts. Guarding personal information will also help protect against potential online bullies.

Don't forget to take advantage of the website's security features. Pick a unique, hard-to-guess password. Keep your profile viewable only by friends. If the website allows your username to be different from your real name, make sure yours is different—and does not include personal information, such as your age or town. If someone sends you an offensive message, report it to the website.

Beware of viruses. Antivirus software may not recognize new viruses. For this reason it is important to think twice before downloading an app or any other file from a source that you don't know or don't have reason to trust.

Limit the Keyword Search

Before you start researching a topic with a search engine, decide exactly what you need. Being as specific as possible makes it easier to find sites that have information about your topic. It can also help you evaluate the source.

As you search the Internet, keep the following tips in mind:

> Be as specific as possible with the terms you use in your search. Suppose you have an assignment that asks you to describe three famous inventions of Thomas Edison. Search for: famous inventions Thomas Edison.

> Put words in quotes when you are searching for a specific phrase. To find out which president said, "I cannot live without books," type the exact phrase in quotation marks (as shown) to search. Some search engines have an "Advanced Search" tool that allows you to search for particular combinations of terms.

> Try using a synonym if you are having trouble with your search. Suppose you are searching for the different ways in which moisture, or water, reaches the ground. Try searching for "forms of precipitation."

> Try different search engines if one isn't producing results. The three most popular general search engines—Google (www.google.com), Yahoo (www.yahoo.com), and Bing (www.bing.com)— usually come up with slightly different sets of results.

Identify the Website

Huge amounts of information are on the Internet. While this makes the Internet great for research, not all sources are reliable. Recognize that a wide variety of information is available, from facts and data to stories and opinions.

The ending of the main part of a web page's address may offer clues to the type of page. Government sites in the U.S. generally end in **.gov** or **.us**. These sites are reliable sources for data and objective reports. Nonprofit organizations often end in **.org**. Educational institutions end in **.edu**. Business sites usually end in **.com** or **.net**. Many international organizations end in **.int**.

THE WORLD ALMANAC FOR KIDS

ON THE JOB:
COMPUTER CAREERS

THE COMPUTER INDUSTRY is a pretty busy place right now. Internet use keeps expanding. More and more companies and government agencies do more and more of their work online. Software and hardware makers constantly upgrade old products and come up with new ones.

There are many different types of jobs in the industry. Simpler, less technical work, such as selling and data entry (typing data into a computer), may not demand much more than basic computer skills, at least to get started. The better-paying jobs, such as software or hardware engineer, usually call for a good technical education, including courses in computer science. Most of these jobs require at least a bachelor's degree, although in some cases an associate degree or special certification may be acceptable. Some systems management positions may require a master's in business administration.

Here are some of the kinds of jobs the computer industry offers:

SUPPORT SPECIALIST When a computer doesn't work right, or just plain doesn't work, a technical support specialist is the first person you call for help in fixing the problem. Often he or she works at a "help desk." Many support specialists are computer technicians who install programs and equipment or handle maintenance and repair. Also sometimes considered support specialists are people who write instruction manuals and people who teach how to use computers and computer programs.

WEBMASTER Webmasters create and maintain websites. On more complex sites, a webmaster may work with artists, designers, and writers who contribute the art and words to be used.

DATABASE ADMINISTRATOR These days, nearly every company and government agency has special collections of electronic data—databases—for keeping track of important information. A database might deal with anything from customer accounts, to stock or supplies on hand, to new projects. Database administrator jobs typically involve finding out what users of the data might need, setting up and organizing the databases, and making sure the databases work as they should.

HARDWARE ENGINEER Hardware includes things such as computer chips, circuit boards, systems, keyboards, and printers. Hardware engineers design, develop, and test such equipment, and they manage its installation.

SOFTWARE ENGINEER Software engineers develop and test programs. People who specialize in writing programs are called programmers.

SYSTEMS ANALYST When a business or organization wants to upgrade or expand its computer capabilities, or simply use its current systems more efficiently, it turns to a systems analyst for help. The systems analyst studies the situation, figures out what hardware and software should be obtained, and guides the process of getting the machines and programs to work together well.

Transportation

When did San Francisco's cable cars begin service? → page 248

Getting from There to Here:
A SHORT HISTORY OF TRANSPORTATION

5000 B.C.
People harness animal-muscle power. Oxen and donkeys carry heavy loads.

3500 B.C.
Egyptians create the first **sailboat**. Before this, people made rafts or canoes and paddled them with poles or their hands.

983
First **locks** to raise water level are built on China's Grand Canal. By 1400, a 1,500-mile water highway system was developed.

1450s
Portuguese build fast ships with three masts. These plus the compass usher in an age of exploration.

1681
France's 150-mile Canal du Midi connects the Atlantic Ocean with the Mediterranean Sea.

5000 B.C.

3500 B.C.
In Mesopotamia (modern-day Iraq), vehicles with wheels are invented. But the first wheels are made of heavy wood, and the roads are terrible.

A.D. 800
Fast, shallow-draft longships make Vikings a powerful force in Europe from 800 to 1100.

Around 1000
Using magnetic compasses, Chinese are able to sail long distances in flat-bottomed ships called junks.

1660s
Horse-drawn stagecoaches begin running in France. They stop at "stages" to switch horses and passengers—the first mass transit system.

1730s Stagecoach service begins in the U.S.

1783 In Paris, the Montgolfier brothers fly the first hot air balloon.

1825 The 363-mile Erie Canal connects the Hudson River with Lake Erie, opening up the U.S. frontier and making New York City the nation's top port.

1832 The first U.S. horse-drawn streetcar is driven up and down the Bowery in New York City.

1769 James Watt patents the first successful steam engine.

1807 Robert Fulton patents a highly efficient steamboat.

1830 Inter-city passenger rail service begins in England with a steam engine built by George Stephenson. It goes about 24 miles per hour.

1839 Kirkpatrick Macmillan of Scotland invents the first pedaled bicycle.

1862
Etienne Lenoir of Belgium builds the first car with an internal-combustion engine.

1869
Transcontinental railroad is completed at Promontory Point, Utah. The Suez Canal in Egypt opens, saving ships a long trip around Africa.

1887
First practical electric street railway system opens in the U.S. in Richmond, Virginia. Suburbs soon grow around cities as trolley systems let people live farther away from the workplace.

1908
Henry Ford builds the first Model T, a practical car for the general public.

1860s
Paddle-wheel steamboats dominate U.S. river travel.

1863
Using steam locomotives, the London subway (known as the "tube") opens.

1873
San Francisco's cable car system begins service.

1897
The first U.S. subway service begins in Boston. New York City follows in 1904.

1903
At Kitty Hawk, North Carolina, the Wright brothers fly the first powered heavier-than-air machine.

1939

The first practical helicopter and first jet plane are invented. The jet flies up to 434 mph. Jet passenger service began in 1952.

1969

U.S. astronauts aboard *Apollo 11* land on the Moon.

1994

Trains cross under the English Channel in the new Channel Tunnel or "Chunnel."

2007

Hybrid cars, which run on gasoline and batteries, are widely available.

Now

1914

The 50-mile Panama Canal opens, saving ships a nearly 6,000-mile trip around South America.

1964

Shinkansen "bullet train" service (124 mph) begins in Japan.

1981

The first space shuttle is launched on April 12, 1981.

2009

2010

Toyota recalls more than 8 million cars worldwide after driver complaints about sudden speed-ups and braking problems.

General Motors says its hybrid-electric Chevy Volt, to be released in late 2010, will get more than 300 miles per gallon of gasoline.

Travel

At what national park can you see alligators roaming free? → page 255

In the late 13th century, famed Italian adventurer Marco Polo took a winding 5,600-mile journey overland from Venice, Italy, to Beijing, China. When he returned to Venice, Polo published a chronicle of his travels. The stories were so fantastic that many people didn't believe his tales.

You may not be taking a journey of thousands of miles on your next trip, but the excitement of traveling is the same. People travel for all kinds of reasons—business, fun, or to see distant friends and relatives. But whatever the reason, people have always had the desire to stretch their legs, explore new places, and have adventures that others may—or may not—believe.

► The World's 10 Most-Visited Countries*	► The 10 Most-Visited U.S. Tourist Sites*
1. France	1. Times Square, NY
2. United States	2. Las Vegas Strip, Las Vegas
3. Spain	3. National Mall and Memorials, Washington, D.C. ►
4. China	4. Faneuil Hall, Boston
5. Italy	5. Magic Kingdom, Lake Buena Vista, FL
6. United Kingdom	6. Disneyland, Anaheim, CA
7. Ukraine	7. Fisherman's Wharf, San Francisco, CA
8. Turkey	8. Niagara Falls, NY
9. Germany	9. Great Smoky Mountains National Park, NC and TN
10. Mexico	10. Navy Pier, Chicago, IL
*2008	*2008

World's Five Most-Visited Amusement Parks*
1. Magic Kingdom (Lake Buena Vista, Florida), 17.0 million
2. Disneyland (Anaheim, California), 14.7 million
3. Tokyo Disneyland (Japan), 14.3 million
4. Disneyland Paris (Marne-La-Vallee, France), 12.7 million
5. Universal Studios (Osaka, Japan), 8.3 million
*2008

The first amusement parks appeared in Europe more than 400 years ago. Attractions included flower gardens, bowling, music, and a few simple rides.

Today's amusement parks are much more impressive. With super-fast roller coasters, parades, shows, and other attractions, amusement parks now have something to amuse just about anyone. Here's a look at some of the most popular amusement parks in the U.S.

FABULOUS FACTS

Biggest Park: Walt Disney World, Lake Buena Vista, Florida, 28,000 acres

Most Rides: 74, Cedar Point, Sandusky, Ohio

Most Roller Coasters: 17, Cedar Point, Sandusky, Ohio

Fastest Roller Coaster: 128 mph, Kingda Ka, Six Flags Great Adventure, Jackson, New Jersey ▶

Tallest Roller Coaster: 456 feet, Kingda Ka, Six Flags Great Adventure, Jackson, New Jersey

▶ **Cedar Point (Sandusky, Ohio)** One of the oldest amusement parks in the U.S., Cedar Point (on Lake Erie) opened in 1870. Its first roller coaster, the Switchback Railway, opened in 1892. It had a then-dizzying 25-foot-high hill, on which riders traveled at about 10 mph. Today at Cedar Point, the Top Thrill Dragster roller coaster reaches a height of 420 feet, and the cars zip along at a top speed of 120 mph! There are also plenty of other attractions, including Soak City, which features water rides and a wave pool.

▶ **Water World (Denver, Colorado)** One of the largest water parks in the United States, Water World opened in 1982. There are 46 rides on its 64 acres. Among a wide variety of attractions are more family tube rides than any other water park in the U.S. and Wally World for young children. Voyage to the Center of the Earth is an enclosed tube ride that spans more than a quarter of a mile. The park also includes some of the highest water slides in the world (Flatline, Redline, and Pipeline), where riders can reach speeds of up to 40 miles per hour.

▶ **Universal Studios Florida/Islands of Adventure (Orlando, Florida)** Universal Studios opened in 1990 and visitors have been "riding the movies" there ever since. Rides, shows, and other attractions feature favorite movie and TV characters, like Shrek, and take visitors behind the scenes. Islands of Adventure has been open since 1999. The rides and attractions there pay tribute to favorite characters from books and comic books, like Spiderman, the Incredible Hulk, and Dr. Doom.

SOME MUST-SEE MUSEUMS

As you travel to new places, you can learn a lot—and have a lot of fun—by visiting local museums. Some museums have exhibits about space, the history of life on Earth, and other areas of science. Some display great art. Some focus on American history. And there are museums about almost any subject you can imagine. Here is a small sampling of some of the leading museums in the United States.

✓ The **Smithsonian Institution**, in Washington, D.C., is actually 18 separate museums, most of them along the National Mall. Among the most popular are the Air and Space Museum, the National Museum of American History, and the National Zoo. The Smithsonian displays an unbelievable range of exhibits, from the Inaugural Ball gowns of the First Ladies to the *Apollo 11* command module and a moon rock.

For more information, see: ***www.si.edu***

▲ The *Apollo 11* command module

✓ The **Metropolitan Museum of Art**, in New York City, is among the largest museums of fine art in the world. Its collection covers art from all parts of the world and includes works by the most important artists in history. The Met also has collections of furniture from past centuries, medieval arms and armor, and a beautiful, peaceful Chinese garden.

For more information, see: ***www.metmuseum.org***

✓ The **Field Museum**, in Chicago, Illinois, is an amazing museum that focuses on the history of plant and animal life on Earth. Among its most famous exhibits is Lucy, a cast of the fossil of a woman who lived some 3.2 million years ago in Africa and who is one of the earliest human ancestors yet discovered. The Field also displays a dinosaur nicknamed "Sue," the largest and the most complete *Tyrannosaurus rex* skeleton ever found.

For more information, see: ***www.fieldmuseum.org***

◀ The huge *T. rex* nicknamed "Sue"

THE 7 WONDERS
OF THE WORLD

These 7 Wonders of the World were chosen in 2007 through an online poll in which over 100 million people from 200 countries cast votes. The 7 Wonders, all equal in rank, are:

The Great Wall of China
(220 B.C. and A.D. 1368–1644), China

The Pyramid at Chichén Itzá
(before A.D. 800), Yucatan Peninsula, Mexico

Petra
(9 B.C.–A.D. 40), Jordan

The Roman Colosseum
(A.D. 70–82), Rome, Italy

Machu Picchu
(A.D. 1460–1470), Peru

Christ the Redeemer
(A.D. 1931), Rio de Janiero, Brazil

The Taj Mahal
(A.D. 1630), Agra, India

SOME UNUSUAL MUSEUMS

Here are a few museums that show exhibits you won't find elsewhere.

The Newseum, in Washington, D.C., shows how news has been gathered and told to people over five centuries, from the earliest newspapers to today's high-tech methods. Among its displays are a piece of the Berlin Wall and two television studios.

The International UFO Museum and Research Center, in Roswell, New Mexico, is dedicated to the study of UFOs, or "unidentified flying objects." Some people believe a UFO crashed in the desert near Roswell in 1947.

NATIONAL PARKS

The world's first national park was Yellowstone, established in 1872. Today in the U.S., there are 58 national parks, including parks in the Virgin Islands, Guam, Puerto Rico, and American Samoa. The National Park Service manages 391 units in all, including national monuments, memorials, battlefields, military parks, historic parks, historic sites, lakeshores, seashores, recreation areas, scenic rivers and trails, wilderness areas, and the White House—almost 85 million acres in all! For more information, you can write to the National Park Service, Department of the Interior, 1849 C Street NW, Washington, D.C. 20240; or go to: *www.nps.gov/parks.html*

YOSEMITE NATIONAL PARK

This park, established in 1890, covers 761,266 acres in east-central California. It has the world's largest concentration of granite domes—mountain-like rocks that were created by glaciers millions of years ago. You can see many of them rising thousands of feet above the valley floor. Two of the most famous are Half Dome, which looks smooth and rounded, and El Capitan, which is the biggest single granite rock on Earth. Skilled climbers come from all over the world to scale this 3,000-foot-high wall of rock. Yosemite Falls, which drops 2,425 feet, is the highest waterfall in North America. It is actually two waterfalls, called the upper and lower falls, connected by a series of smaller waterfalls. Yosemite also features lakes, meadows, and giant sequoia trees, and is home to bighorn sheep and bears.

GRAND CANYON NATIONAL PARK

This national park, established in 1919, has one of the world's most spectacular landscapes, covering more than a million acres in northwestern Arizona. The canyon is 6,000 feet deep at its deepest point and 15 miles wide at its widest. Most of the 40 identified rock layers that form the canyon's 277-mile-long wall are exposed, offering a detailed look at the Earth's geologic history. The walls display a cross section of the Earth's crust from as far back as two billion years ago. The Colorado River—which carved out the giant canyon—still runs through the park, which is a valuable wildlife preserve with many rare, endangered animals. The pine and fir forests, painted deserts, plateaus, caves, and sandstone canyons offer a wide range of habitats.

DENALI NATIONAL PARK

Located in the southern part of the Alaska Mountain Range in the south central part of Alaska, Denali is home to North America's highest mountain, 20,320-foot Mt. McKinley. The park was originally established in 1917 as Mount McKinley National Park, but it was expanded in 1980 and renamed Denali National Park and Preserve. Denali covers more than 6 million acres and is almost as big as the state of Massachusetts. The park is also teeming with wildlife. Among many other animals, it's possible to see what are known in Denali as the "Denali Big Five": caribou, Dall sheep, grizzly bears, moose, and wolves. Denali is the only national park that is patrolled mostly by staff riding on dog sleds.

EVERGLADES NATIONAL PARK

Located in southern Florida, the Everglades is the largest subtropical wilderness in the U.S. Almost 1.4 million acres of this wilderness are now protected in Everglades National Park. More than 360 species of birds, 40 species of mammals, and 50 kinds of reptiles live in the park's varied ecosystems, which include swamps, saw grass prairies, and mangrove forests. The park's different habitats allow a huge variety of life forms to thrive. As you move from place to place, you may see all kinds of animals, from tiny frogs to free-roaming alligators and crocodiles, graceful herons, several varieties of geckos, and lots of snakes, including boa constrictors. You can visit a mahogany forest and pine forests, and you can walk along raised boardwalks to get beautiful views of miles of swaying saw grass marshes full of wildlife. The park has a visitor's center near the entrance, and there is another visitor's center, called Flamingo, at the southern tip. From the marina at Flamingo, visitors can take boat tours.

YELLOWSTONE NATIONAL PARK

Located mostly in northwestern Wyoming and partly in eastern Idaho and southwestern Montana, Yellowstone is known for its 10,000 hot springs and geysers—more than anyplace else in the world. Old Faithful, the most famous geyser, erupts for about four minutes every one to two hours, shooting 3,700-8,400 gallons of hot water as high as 185 feet. Other geysers include the Giant, which shoots a column of hot water 200 feet high, and the Giantess, which erupts for over four hours at a time, but only about two times per year. There are grizzly bears, wolves, elk, moose, buffalo, deer, beavers, coyotes, antelopes, and 300 species of birds. The use of snowmobiles in the park has been a big controversy. Some people want to ban them because of noise and air pollution; others disagree. They are allowed now, but their use is somewhat limited.

United States

What part of the Constitution creates the U.S. Senate? page 258

& FACTS FIGURES

AREA	50 states and Washington, D.C.
LAND	3,531,822 square miles
WATER	264,129 square miles
TOTAL	3,795,951 square miles

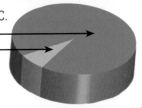

POPULATION (March 2010 est.): 308,885,492

CAPITAL: WASHINGTON, D.C.

LARGEST, HIGHEST, and OTHER STATISTICS

Largest state:	Alaska (663,267 square miles)
Smallest state:	Rhode Island (1,545 square miles)
Northernmost city:	Barrow, Alaska (71°17' north latitude)
Southernmost city:	Hilo, Hawaii (19°44' north latitude)
Easternmost city:	Eastport, Maine (66°59' west longitude)
Westernmost city:	Atka, Alaska (174°12' west longitude)
Highest settlement:	Climax, Colorado (11,360 feet)
Lowest settlement:	Calipatria, California (184 feet below sea level)
Oldest national park:	Yellowstone National Park (Idaho, Montana, Wyoming), 2,219,791 acres, established 1872
Largest national park:	Wrangell-St. Elias, Alaska (8,323,148 acres)
Longest river system:	Mississippi-Missouri-Red Rock (3,710 miles)
Deepest lake:	Crater Lake, Oregon (1,932 feet)
Highest mountain:	Mount McKinley, Alaska (20,320 feet)
Lowest point:	Death Valley, California (282 feet below sea level)
Tallest building:	Willis Tower, Chicago, Illinois (1,450 feet)
Tallest structure:	TV tower, Blanchard, North Dakota (2,063 feet)
Longest bridge span:	Verrazano-Narrows Bridge, New York (4,260 feet)
Highest bridge:	Royal Gorge, Colorado (1,053 feet above water)

did you Know?

The "largest" city in the United States—the one that covers the largest amount of land—is Juneau, Alaska, which covers nearly 3,000 square miles. Juneau is larger than either Rhode Island or Delaware.

SYMBOLS OF THE UNITED STATES

The Great Seal

The Great Seal of the United States shows an American bald eagle with a ribbon in its mouth bearing the Latin words *e pluribus unum* (out of many, one). In its talons are the arrows of war and an olive branch of peace. On the back of the Great Seal is an unfinished pyramid with an eye (the eye of Providence) above it. The seal was approved by Congress on June 20, 1782.

The Flag

The flag of the United States has 50 stars (one for each state) and 13 stripes (one for each of the original 13 states). It is unofficially called the "Stars and Stripes."

1777

The first U.S. flag was commissioned by the Second Continental Congress in 1777 but did not exist until 1783, after the American Revolution. Historians are not certain who designed the Stars and Stripes. Many different flags are believed to have been used during the American Revolution.

1795

The flag of 1777 was used until 1795. In that year, Congress passed an act ordering that a new flag have 15 stripes, alternate red and white, and 15 stars on a blue field. In 1818, Congress directed that the flag have 13 stripes and that a new star be added for each new state of the Union. The last star was added in 1960 for the state of Hawaii.

1818

There are many customs for flying the flag and treating it with respect. For example, it should not touch the floor and no other flag should be flown above it, except for the UN flag at UN headquarters. When the flag is raised or lowered, or passes in a parade, or during the Pledge of Allegiance, people should face it and stand at attention. Those in military uniform should salute. Others should put their right hand over their heart. The flag is flown at half-staff as a sign of mourning.

Pledge of Allegiance to the Flag

"I pledge allegiance to the flag of the United States of America and to the republic for which it stands, one nation under God, indivisible, with liberty and justice for all."

The National Anthem

"The Star-Spangled Banner" was a poem written in 1814 by Francis Scott Key after he watched British ships bombard Fort McHenry, Maryland, during the War of 1812. It became the National Anthem by an act of Congress in 1931. The music to "The Star-Spangled Banner" was originally a tune called "Anacreon in Heaven."

THE U.S. CONSTITUTION

The Foundation of American Government

The Constitution is the document that created the present government of the United States. It was written in 1787 and went into effect in 1789. It establishes the three branches of the U.S. government—the executive (headed by the president), the legislative (Congress), and the judicial (the Supreme Court and other federal courts). The first 10 amendments to the Constitution (the **Bill of Rights**) explain the basic rights of all American citizens.

You can find the Constitution online at: *www.archives.gov/exhibits/charters/constitution.html.*

THE PREAMBLE TO THE CONSTITUTION

The Constitution begins with a short statement called the Preamble. The Preamble states that the government of the United States was established by the people.

"We the people of the United States, in order to form a more perfect union, establish justice, insure domestic tranquility, provide for the common defense, promote the general welfare, and secure the blessings of liberty to ourselves and our posterity, do ordain and establish this Constitution for the United States of America."

THE ARTICLES

The original Constitution contained seven articles. The first three articles of the Constitution establish the three branches of the U.S. government.

Article 1, Legislative Branch Creates the Senate and House of Representatives and describes their functions and powers.

Article 2, Executive Branch Creates the office of the President and the Electoral College and lists their powers and responsibilities.

Article 3, Judicial Branch Creates the Supreme Court and gives Congress the power to create lower courts. The powers of the courts and certain crimes are defined.

Article 4, The States Discusses the relationship of the states to one another and to the citizens. Defines the states' powers.

Article 5, Amending the Constitution Describes how the Constitution can be amended (changed).

Article 6, Federal Law Makes the Constitution the supreme law of the land over state laws and constitutions.

Article 7, Ratifying the Constitution Establishes how to ratify (approve) the Constitution.

Amendments to the Constitution

The writers of the Constitution understood that it might need to be amended, or changed, in the future, but they wanted to be careful and made it hard to change. Article 5 describes how the Constitution can be amended.

In order to take effect, an amendment must be approved by a two-thirds majority in both the House of Representatives and the Senate. It must then be approved (ratified) by three-fourths of the states (38 states). So far, there have been 27 amendments. One of them (the 18th, ratified in 1919) banned the manufacture or sale of liquor. It was canceled by the 21st Amendment, in 1933.

The Bill of Rights: The First Ten Amendments

The first ten amendments were adopted in 1791 and contain the basic freedoms Americans enjoy as a people. These amendments are known as the Bill of Rights.

1. Guarantees freedom of religion, speech, and the press.
2. Guarantees the right to have firearms.
3. Guarantees that soldiers cannot be lodged in private homes unless the owner agrees.
4. Protects people from being searched or having property searched or taken away by the government without reason.
5. Protects rights of people on trial for crimes.
6. Guarantees people accused of crimes the right to a speedy public trial by jury.
7. Guarantees the right to a trial by jury for other kinds of cases.
8. Prohibits "cruel and unusual punishments."
9. Says specific rights listed in the Constitution do not take away rights that may not be listed.
10. Establishes that any powers not given specifically to the federal government belong to states or the people.

Other Important Amendments

13 (1865): Ends slavery in the United States.

14 (1868): Bars states from denying rights to citizens; guarantees equal protection under the law for all citizens.

15 (1870): Guarantees that a person cannot be denied the right to vote because of race or color.

19 (1920): Gives women the right to vote.

22 (1951): Limits the president to two four-year terms of office.

24 (1964): Outlaws the poll tax (a tax people had to pay before they could vote) in federal elections. (The poll tax had been used to keep African Americans in the South from voting.)

25 (1967): Specifies presidential succession; also gives the president the power to appoint a new vice president, if one dies or leaves office in the middle of a term.

26 (1971): Lowers the voting age to 18 from 21.

THE EXECUTIVE BRANCH

The **executive branch** of the federal government is headed by the president, who enforces the laws passed by Congress and is commander in chief of the U.S. armed forces. It also includes the vice president, people who work for the president or vice president, the major departments of the government, and special agencies. The **cabinet** is made up of the vice president, heads of major departments, and other officials. It meets when the president chooses. The chart at right shows cabinet departments in the order in which they were created.

PRESIDENT

VICE PRESIDENT

CABINET DEPARTMENTS

1. State
2. Treasury
3. Defense
4. Justice
5. Interior
6. Agriculture
7. Commerce
8. Labor
9. Housing and Urban Development
10. Transportation
11. Energy
12. Education
13. Health and Human Services
14. Veterans Affairs
15. Homeland Security

Who Can Be President?

To be eligible to serve as president, a person must be a native-born U.S. citizen, must be at least 35 years old, and must have been a resident of the United States for at least 14 years.

How Long Does the President Serve?

The president serves a four-year term, starting on January 20. No president can be elected more than twice, or more than once if he or she had served two years as president filling out the term of a president who left office.

What Happens If the President Dies?

If the president dies in office or cannot complete the term, the vice president becomes president. If the president is temporarily unable to perform his or her duties, the vice president can become acting president.

The White House has a web site. It is:

www.whitehouse.gov

You can send e-mail to the president at:

president@whitehouse.gov

The White House, home of the U.S. president

Voter Turnout in Presidential Elections, 1968–2008

(Percent of voting age population: 18 and over in 1972 and afterward, 21 and over in 1968.)	Year	Turnout	Year	Turnout
	1968	60.7%	1992	55.2%
	1972	55.1%	1996	49.0%
	1976	53.6%	2000	50.3%
	1980	52.8%	2004	55.5%
	1984	53.3%	2008	58.2%
	1988	50.3%		

Source: U.S. Census Bureau

THE LEGISLATIVE BRANCH

CONGRESS

Congress is the legislative branch of the federal government. Congress's major responsibility is to pass the laws that govern the country and determine how money collected in taxes is spent. Congress consists of two parts—the Senate and the House of Representatives. ▶

THE SENATE

The Senate has 100 members, two from each state. The Constitution says that the Senate will have equal representation (the same number of representatives) from each state. Thus, small states have the same number of senators as large states. Senators are elected for six-year terms. There is no limit on the number of terms a senator can serve.

The Senate also has the responsibility of approving people the president appoints for certain jobs: for example, cabinet members and Supreme Court justices. The Senate must approve all treaties by at least a two-thirds vote. It also has the responsibility under the Constitution of putting on trial high-ranking federal officials who have been impeached by the House of Representatives.

For more information, see: *www.senate.gov*

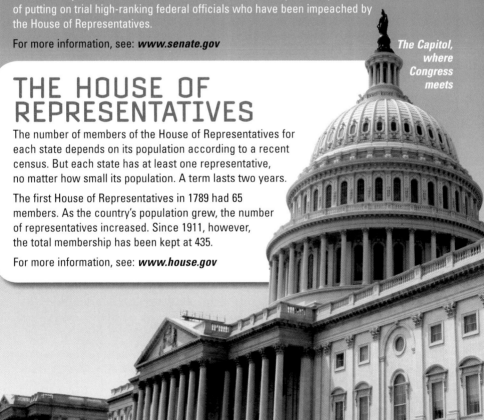

The Capitol, where Congress meets

THE HOUSE OF REPRESENTATIVES

The number of members of the House of Representatives for each state depends on its population according to a recent census. But each state has at least one representative, no matter how small its population. A term lasts two years.

The first House of Representatives in 1789 had 65 members. As the country's population grew, the number of representatives increased. Since 1911, however, the total membership has been kept at 435.

For more information, see: *www.house.gov*

The House of Representatives, by State

Here are the numbers of representatives each state had in 2010, compared with earlier times:

	2010	1995	1975		2010	1995	1975
Alabama	7	7	7	Montana	1	1	2
Alaska	1	1	1	Nebraska	3	3	3
Arizona	8	6	4	Nevada	3	2	1
Arkansas	4	4	4	New Hampshire	2	2	2
California	53	52	43	New Jersey	13	13	15
Colorado	7	6	5	New Mexico	3	3	2
Connecticut	5	6	6	New York	29	31	39
Delaware	1	1	1	North Carolina	13	12	11
Florida	25	23	15	North Dakota	1	1	1
Georgia	13	11	10	Ohio	18	19	23
Hawaii	2	2	2	Oklahoma	5	6	6
Idaho	2	2	2	Oregon	5	5	4
Illinois	19	20	24	Pennsylvania	19	21	25
Indiana	9	10	11	Rhode Island	2	2	2
Iowa	5	5	6	South Carolina	6	6	6
Kansas	4	4	5	South Dakota	1	1	2
Kentucky	6	6	7	Tennessee	9	9	9
Louisiana	7	7	8	Texas	32	30	24
Maine	2	2	2	Utah	3	3	2
Maryland	8	8	8	Vermont	1	1	1
Massachusetts	10	10	12	Virginia	11	11	10
Michigan	15	16	19	Washington	9	9	7
Minnesota	8	8	8	West Virginia	3	3	4
Mississippi	4	5	5	Wisconsin	8	9	9
Missouri	9	9	10	Wyoming	1	1	1

Washington, D.C., Puerto Rico, American Samoa, Guam, and the Virgin Islands each has one nonvoting member of the House of Representatives.

HOW A BILL BECOMES LAW

A proposed law is called a bill. To become a law, a bill must first be approved by both houses, or chambers, of Congress. Most kinds of bills can start in either the House of Representatives or the Senate. One or more members of the chamber can introduce the bill.

Let's assume that a bill starts in the House of Representatives. It is then assigned to one of the many House committees, where it is studied and possibly changed. The committee may get advice from outside experts and hold public hearings, or meetings, on the proposal. Then the committee votes on the bill. If a majority of the committee members support the bill, it goes to the full House. The House will then debate the bill, perhaps make changes to it, and then vote on the bill. If a majority of the full House votes for the bill, it is approved. It then goes to the Senate, where the process is repeated.

If the two chambers approve different versions of the same bill, a committee made up of members from the House and the Senate must work out the disagreements and come up with one revised bill. If both chambers of Congress pass this new version, the bill goes to the president. The president can either sign the bill, making it a law, or veto it (turn it down). If the president vetoes the bill, it can still become law if it is passed again by a two-thirds

THE JUDICIAL BRANCH

The Supreme Court

The highest court in the United States is the Supreme Court. It has nine justices who are appointed for life by the president with the approval of the Senate. Eight of the nine members are called associate justices. The ninth is the Chief Justice, who presides over the Court's meetings.

What Does the Supreme Court Do?

The Supreme Court's major responsibilities are to judge cases that involve reviewing federal laws, actions of the president, treaties of the United States, and laws passed by state governments to be sure they do not conflict with the U.S. Constitution. If the Supreme Court finds that a law or action violates the Constitution, the law is struck down or the action is reversed.

The Supreme Court's Decision Is Final.

Most cases must go through other state courts or federal courts before they reach the Supreme Court. The Supreme Court is the final court for a case, and the justices generally can decide which cases they will review. After the Supreme Court hears a case, it may agree or disagree with the decision by a lower court. Each justice has one vote, and the majority rules. When the Supreme Court makes a ruling, its decision is final, so each of the justices has a very important job.

Below are the nine justices who were on the Supreme Court in the 2009–2010 term (October 2009 to June 2010). The justices are (standing from left to right) Samuel Alito, Ruth Bader Ginsburg, Stephen Breyer, and Sonia Sotomayor; (seated from left to right) Anthony Kennedy, John Paul Stevens, Chief Justice John Roberts, Antonin Scalia, and Clarence Thomas. Justice Stevens resigned as of the end of the 2009–2010 term.

Election

What two major duties does the vice president have?　page 265

The Obama-Biden Team

In a long and often suspenseful primary season, Senator Barack Obama defeated Senator and former First Lady Hillary Clinton, among other rivals, to win the Democratic Party nomination for president in 2008. He went on to defeat the Republican nominee, Senator John McCain, in November. Obama and his running mate, Senator Joe Biden, took office as president and vice president on January 20, 2009.

President Barack Obama

Born in Honolulu, Hawaii, in 1961, Barack Obama graduated from Columbia University in 1983. He became a community organizer in Chicago, helping poor residents cope with a wave of unemployment. He then attended Harvard Law School, where he became the first African-American editor of the *Harvard Law Review*.

After graduating, Obama practiced civil-rights law, taught in law school, and served in the Illinois state senate. He gained national attention by giving a rousing keynote speech at the Democratic National Convention in 2004, and he was elected to the U.S. Senate later that year. In 2007, he began his campaign for president, promising to bring change to Washington.

He and his wife, Michelle, have two children, Malia and Sasha.

★ ★ ★ ★ ★

Vice President Joe Biden

Joe Biden was born in 1942, in Scranton, Pennsylvania. He is a lawyer by profession. In 1972, he was elected to the U.S. Senate, representing the state of Delaware. He served in the Senate for 35 years and became known as an expert on foreign policy. In the summer of 2008, Obama chose him to be his running mate.

What Does the President Do?

According to the U.S. Constitution, the president is the chief executive, or head, of the executive branch of the government. The president has a role in all parts of government. Following are some of the president's jobs:

★ Suggest laws to Congress;

★ Send Congress a budget, which recommends how the government should raise and spend money;

★ Approve or veto (reject) bills passed by Congress;

★ Act as commander-in-chief of the U.S. armed forces; ▶

★ Make treaties, or agreements, with other countries;

★ Appoint justices to the Supreme Court and judges to other federal courts.

President Obama greets troops on a 2010 visit to Afghanistan.

The president must share power with the other two branches of government. They are the legislative branch, or Congress, and the judicial branch, headed by the U.S. Supreme Court.

The U.S. Constitution tells how each of the three branches of government checks, or limits, the powers of the other two. This system of checks and balances is intended to prevent any branch from becoming too powerful.

★ ★ ★ ★ ★

What Does the Vice President Do?

John Adams, the first vice president, found the job very frustrating. He described it as "the most insignificant office that ever the invention of man contrived or his imagination conceived." But the vice president is just a heartbeat away from the presidency.

According to the U.S. Constitution, the vice president has two major duties. First, the vice president takes over as president if the president dies, resigns, or is removed from office. Second, the vice president presides over the Senate and can cast the deciding vote in case of a tie.

	John McCain		Barack Obama	
	Popular Votes	Electoral Votes	Popular Votes	Electoral Votes
Alabama	1,266,546	9	813,479	
Alaska	193,841	3	123,594	
Arizona	1,230,111	10	1,034,707	
Arkansas	638,017	6	422,310	
California	5,011,781		8,274,473	55
Colorado	1,073,589		1,288,576	9
Connecticut	629,428		997,772	7
Delaware	152,374		255,394	3
District of Columbia	17,367		245,200	3
Florida	4,045,624		4,282,074	27
Georgia	2,048,744	15	1,844,137	
Hawaii	120,566		325,871	4
Idaho	403,012	4	236,440	
Illinois	2,031,527		3,419,673	21
Indiana	1,345,648		1,374,039	11
Iowa	682,379		828,940	7
Kansas	699,655	6	514,765	
Kentucky	1,048,462	8	751,985	
Louisiana	1,148,275	9	782,989	
Maine	295,273		421,923	4
Maryland	959,862		1,629,467	10
Massachusetts	1,108,854		1,904,097	12
Michigan	2,048,639		2,872,579	17
Minnesota	1,275,409		1,573,354	10
Mississippi	724,597	6	554,662	
Missouri	1,445,814	11	1,441,991	

* Official results from the Federal Election Commission

	John McCain		Barack Obama	
	Popular Votes	Electoral Votes	Popular Votes	Electoral Votes
Montana	242,763	3	231,667	
Nebraska	452,979	4	333,319	1
Nevada	412,827		533,736	5
New Hampshire	316,534		384,826	4
New Jersey	1,613,207		2,215,422	15
New Mexico	346,832		472,422	5
New York	2,742,298		4,769,700	31
North Carolina	2,128,474		2,142,651	15
North Dakota	168,601	3	141,278	
Ohio	2,674,491		2,933,388	20
Oklahoma	960,165	7	502,496	
Oregon	738,475		1,037,291	7
Pennsylvania	2,655,885		3,276,363	21
Rhode Island	165,391		296,571	4
South Carolina	1,034,896	8	862,449	
South Dakota	203,054	3	170,924	
Tennessee	1,479,178	11	1,087,437	
Texas	4,479,328	34	3,528,633	
Utah	596,030	5	327,670	
Vermont	98,974		219,262	3
Virginia	1,725,005		1,959,532	13
Washington	1,229,216		1,750,848	11
West Virginia	397,466	5	303,857	
Wisconsin	1,262,393		1,677,211	10
Wyoming	164,958	3	82,868	
TOTALS	59,934,814	173	69,456,897	365

Who Can Vote?

Voting rules vary from state to state. However, rules in each state must agree with the Constitution, its amendments, and federal laws. States allow voters who must be away or who are serving in the military on Election Day to vote by mail using an absentee ballot. A growing number of states allow any qualified voter to vote before Election Day.

Some states require voters to have an I.D. that was issued by the state, such as a driver's license. In some states, people convicted of a felony lose the right to vote for the rest of their lives.

These are the qualifications for voting in the United States:

- ☑ U.S. citizenship
- ☑ At least 18 years old
- ☑ Registration: citizens must register, or sign up, before voting *(required except in North Dakota)*

Who Does Vote?

Everyone has heard the statement, "Every vote counts." Well, it's true. A remarkably small number of votes can be the margin between victory and defeat. In 2000, for example, George W. Bush defeated Al Gore in Florida by only 537 votes and became president!

The 2008 election stirred a lot of interest. Increased numbers of young people and members of minority groups went to the polls in November. But many people still did not vote, and in the end voter turnout was only slightly higher than four years earlier.

Electing a President

Who elects the president?

The president is actually elected by a group of "electors" known as the Electoral College. Members of this group from each state meet in December in their state capitals to cast their votes.

But I thought Election Day was in November!

It is, but on Election Day voters don't directly vote for president. Instead, they vote for a group of presidential electors who have pledged to support whichever candidate wins that state's popular vote.

What's the total number of electoral votes?

There are 538 total votes. A presidential candidate must win at least 270 of those.

How many electoral votes does each state get?

Each state gets one vote for each of its senators (2) and one for each of its members in the House of Representatives. Also Washington, D.C., has 3 electoral votes.

What if there's a tie in the end?

Then the election is in the hands of the U.S. House of Representatives. That's what happened in 1801, after Thomas Jefferson and Aaron Burr each received an equal number of electoral votes in the 1800 election. The House then voted to make Jefferson president.

Electoral College MAP

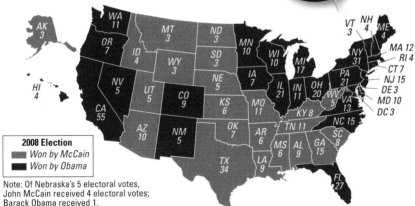

2008 Election
- Won by McCain
- Won by Obama

Note: Of Nebraska's 5 electoral votes, John McCain received 4 electoral votes; Barack Obama received 1.

On November 4, 2008, Barack Obama won about 53 percent of the popular vote. But what really counted was the electoral votes. He picked up 365 of them, from 29 states and the District of Columbia, more than enough for a majority.

Can a candidate who didn't win the most popular votes still win a majority of electoral votes? Yes. That's what happened in 1876, 1888, and again in 2000, when George W. Bush was elected to a first term.

THE PRESIDENTS
OF THE UNITED STATES

1 GEORGE WASHINGTON Federalist Party   1789–1797
Born: Feb. 22, 1732, at Wakefield, Westmoreland County, Virginia
Married: Martha Dandridge Custis (1731–1802); no children
Died: Dec. 14, 1799; buried at Mount Vernon, Fairfax County, Virginia
Vice President: John Adams (1789–1797)

2 JOHN ADAMS Federalist Party   1797–1801
Born: Oct. 30, 1735, in Braintree (now Quincy), Massachusetts
Married: Abigail Smith (1744–1818); 3 sons, 2 daughters
Died: July 4, 1826; buried in Quincy, Massachusetts
Vice President: Thomas Jefferson (1797–1801)

3 THOMAS JEFFERSON Democratic-Republican Party   1801–1809
Born: Apr. 13, 1743, at Shadwell, Albemarle County, Virginia
Married: Martha Wayles Skelton (1748–1782); 1 son, 5 daughters
Died: July 4, 1826; buried at Monticello, Albemarle County, Virginia
Vice President: Aaron Burr (1801–1805), George Clinton (1805–1809)

4 JAMES MADISON Democratic-Republican Party   1809–1817
Born: Mar. 16, 1751, at Port Conway, King George County, Virginia
Married: Dolley Payne Todd (1768–1849); no children
Died: June 28, 1836; buried at Montpelier Station, Virginia
Vice President: George Clinton (1809–1813), Elbridge Gerry (1813–1817)

5 JAMES MONROE Democratic-Republican Party   1817–1825
Born: Apr. 28, 1758, in Westmoreland County, Virginia
Married: Elizabeth Kortright (1768–1830); 1 son, 2 daughters
Died: July 4, 1831; buried in Richmond, Virginia
Vice President: Daniel D. Tompkins (1817–1825)

6 JOHN QUINCY ADAMS Democratic-Republican Party   1825–1829
Born: July 11, 1767, in Braintree (now Quincy), Massachusetts
Married: Louisa Catherine Johnson (1775–1852); 3 sons, 1 daughter
Died: Feb. 23, 1848; buried in Quincy, Massachusetts
Vice President: John C. Calhoun (1825–1829)

7 · ANDREW JACKSON — Democratic Party · 1829–1837
Born: Mar. 15, 1767, in Waxhaw, South Carolina
Married: Rachel Donelson Robards (1767–1828); 1 son (adopted)
Died: June 8, 1845; buried in Nashville, Tennessee
Vice President: John C. Calhoun (1829–1833),
　　　　　　　　Martin Van Buren (1833–1837)

8 · MARTIN VAN BUREN — Democratic Party · 1837–1841
Born: Dec. 5, 1782, at Kinderhook, New York
Married: Hannah Hoes (1783–1819); 4 sons
Died: July 24, 1862; buried at Kinderhook, New York
Vice President: Richard M. Johnson (1837–1841)

9 · WILLIAM HENRY HARRISON — Whig Party · 1841
Born: Feb. 9, 1773, at Berkeley, Charles City County, Virginia
Married: Anna Symmes (1775–1864); 6 sons, 4 daughters
Died: Apr. 4, 1841; buried in North Bend, Ohio
Vice President: John Tyler (1841–1845)

10 · JOHN TYLER — Whig Party · 1841–1845
Born: Mar. 29, 1790, in Greenway, Charles City County, Virginia
Married: Letitia Christian (1790–1842); 3 sons, 5 daughters
　　　　　Julia Gardiner (1820–1889); 5 sons, 2 daughters
Died: Jan. 18, 1862; buried in Richmond, Virginia
Vice President: none

11 · JAMES KNOX POLK — Democratic Party · 1845–1849
Born: Nov. 2, 1795, in Mecklenburg County, North Carolina
Married: Sarah Childress (1803–1891); no children
Died: June 15, 1849; buried in Nashville, Tennessee
Vice President: George M. Dallas (1845–1849)

12 · ZACHARY TAYLOR — Whig Party · 1849–1850
Born: Nov. 24, 1784, in Orange County, Virginia
Married: Margaret Smith (1788–1852); 1 son, 5 daughters
Died: July 9, 1850; buried in Louisville, Kentucky
Vice President: Millard Fillmore (1849–1850)

13 · MILLARD FILLMORE — Whig Party · 1850–1853
Born: Jan. 7, 1800, in Cayuga County, New York
Married: Abigail Powers (1798–1853); 1 son, 1 daughter
　　　　　Caroline Carmichael McIntosh (1813–1881); no children
Died: Mar. 8, 1874; buried in Buffalo, New York
Vice President: none

14 FRANKLIN PIERCE Democratic Party 1853–1857
Born: Nov. 23, 1804, in Hillsboro, New Hampshire
Married: Jane Means Appleton (1806–1863); 3 sons
Died: Oct. 8, 1869; buried in Concord, New Hampshire
Vice President: William R. King (1853–1857)

15 JAMES BUCHANAN Democratic Party 1857–1861
Born: Apr. 23, 1791, Cove Gap, near Mercersburg, Pennsylvania
Married: Never
Died: June 1, 1868, buried in Lancaster, Pennsylvania
Vice President: John C. Breckinridge (1857–1861)

16 ABRAHAM LINCOLN Republican Party 1861–1865
Born: Feb. 12, 1809, in Hardin County, Kentucky
Married: Mary Todd (1818–1882); 4 sons
Died: Apr. 15, 1865; buried in Springfield, Illinois
Vice President: Hannibal Hamlin (1861–1865),
                Andrew Johnson (1865)

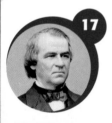

17 ANDREW JOHNSON Democratic Party 1865–1869
Born: Dec. 29, 1808, in Raleigh, North Carolina
Married: Eliza McCardle (1810–1876); 3 sons, 2 daughters
Died: July 31, 1875; buried in Greeneville, Tennessee
Vice President: none

18 ULYSSES S. GRANT Republican Party 1869–1877
Born: Apr. 27, 1822, in Point Pleasant, Ohio
Married: Julia Dent (1826–1902); 3 sons, 1 daughter
Died: July 23, 1885; buried in New York City
Vice President: Schuyler Colfax (1869–1873),
                Henry Wilson (1873–1877)

19 RUTHERFORD B. HAYES Republican Party 1877–1881
Born: Oct. 4, 1822, in Delaware, Ohio
Married: Lucy Ware Webb (1831–1889); 7 sons, 1 daughter
Died: Jan. 17, 1893; buried in Fremont, Ohio
Vice President: William A. Wheeler (1877–1881)

20   **JAMES A. GARFIELD**   Republican Party   **1881**
Born: Nov. 19, 1831, in Orange, Cuyahoga County, Ohio
Married: Lucretia Rudolph (1832–1918); 5 sons, 2 daughters
Died: Sept. 19, 1881; buried in Cleveland, Ohio
Vice President: Chester A. Arthur (1881)

21   **CHESTER A. ARTHUR**   Republican Party   **1881–1885**
Born: Oct. 5, 1829, in Fairfield, Vermont
Married: Ellen Lewis Herndon (1837–1880); 2 sons, 1 daughter
Died: Nov. 18, 1886; buried in Albany, New York
Vice President: none

22   **GROVER CLEVELAND**   Democratic Party   **1885–1889**
Born: Mar. 18, 1837, in Caldwell, New Jersey
Married: Frances Folsom (1864–1947); 2 sons, 3 daughters
Died: June 24, 1908; buried in Princeton, New Jersey
Vice President: Thomas A. Hendricks (1885–1889)

23   **BENJAMIN HARRISON**   Republican Party   **1889–1893**
Born: Aug. 20, 1833, in North Bend, Ohio
Married: Caroline Lavinia Scott (1832–1892); 1 son, 1 daughter
      Mary Scott Lord Dimmick (1858–1948); 1 daughter
Died: Mar. 13, 1901; buried in Indianapolis, Indiana
Vice President: Levi Morton (1889–1893)

24   **GROVER CLEVELAND**   **1893–1897**
See 22, above
Vice President: Adlai E. Stevenson (1893–1897)

25   **WILLIAM MCKINLEY**   Republican Party   **1897–1901**
Born: Jan. 29, 1843, in Niles, Ohio
Married: Ida Saxton (1847–1907); 2 daughters
Died: Sept. 14, 1901; buried in Canton, Ohio
Vice President: Garret A. Hobart (1897–1901),
      Theodore Roosevelt (1901)

26   **THEODORE ROOSEVELT**   Republican Party   **1901–1909**
Born: Oct. 27, 1858, in New York City
Married: Alice Hathaway Lee (1861–1884); 1 daughter
      Edith Kermit Carow (1861–1948); 4 sons, 1 daughter
Died: Jan. 6, 1919; buried in Oyster Bay, New York
Vice President: none 1901–1905, Charles W. Fairbanks (1905–1909)

27   WILLIAM HOWARD TAFT   Republican Party   1909–1913

Born: Sept. 15, 1857, in Cincinnati, Ohio
Married: Helen Herron (1861–1943); 2 sons, 1 daughter
Died: Mar. 8, 1930; buried in Arlington National Cemetery, Virginia
Vice President: James S. Sherman (1909–1913)

28   WOODROW WILSON   Democratic Party   1913–1921

Born: Dec. 28, 1856, in Staunton, Virginia
Married: Ellen Louise Axson (1860–1914); 3 daughters
     Edith Bolling Galt (1872–1961); no children
Died: Feb. 3, 1924; buried in Washington, D.C.
Vice President: Thomas R. Marshall (1913–1921)

29   WARREN G. HARDING   Republican Party   1921–1923

Born: Nov. 2, 1865, near Corsica (now Blooming Grove), Ohio
Married: Florence Kling De Wolfe (1860–1924; no children)
Died: Aug. 2, 1923; buried in Marion, Ohio
Vice President: Calvin Coolidge (1921–1923)

30   CALVIN COOLIDGE   Republican Party   1923–1929

Born: July 4, 1872, in Plymouth, Vermont
Married: Grace Anna Goodhue (1879–1957); 2 sons
Died: Jan. 5, 1933; buried in Plymouth, Vermont
Vice President: none 1923–1925, Charles G. Dawes (1925–1929)

31   HERBERT C. HOOVER   Republican Party   1929–1933

Born: Aug. 10, 1874, in West Branch, Iowa
Married: Lou Henry (1875–1944); 2 sons
Died: Oct. 20, 1964; buried in West Branch, Iowa
Vice President: Charles Curtis (1929–1933)

32   FRANKLIN DELANO ROOSEVELT   Democratic Party   1933–1945

Born: Jan. 30, 1882, in Hyde Park, New York
Married: Anna Eleanor Roosevelt (1884–1962); 4 sons, 1 daughter
Died: Apr. 12, 1945; buried in Hyde Park, New York
Vice President: John N. Garner (1933–1941),
                Henry A. Wallace (1941–1945),
                Harry S. Truman (1945)

33 HARRY S. TRUMAN Democratic Party 1945–1953
Born: May 8, 1884, in Lamar, Missouri
Married: Elizabeth Virginia "Bess" Wallace (1885–1982); 1 daughter
Died: Dec. 26, 1972; buried in Independence, Missouri
Vice President: none from 1945–1949, Alben W. Barkley (1949–1953)

34 DWIGHT D. EISENHOWER Republican Party 1953–1961
Born: Oct. 14, 1890, in Denison, Texas
Married: Mary "Mamie" Geneva Doud (1896–1979); 2 sons
Died: Mar. 28, 1969; buried in Abilene, Kansas
Vice President: Richard M. Nixon (1953–1961)

35 JOHN FITZGERALD KENNEDY Democratic Party 1961–1963
Born: May 29, 1917, in Brookline, Massachusetts
Married: Jacqueline Lee Bouvier (1929–1994); 2 sons, 1 daughter
Died: Nov. 22, 1963; buried in Arlington National Cemetery, Virginia
Vice President: Lyndon B. Johnson (1961–1963)

36 LYNDON BAINES JOHNSON Democratic Party 1963–1969
Born: Aug. 27, 1908, near Stonewall, Texas
Married: Claudia "Lady Bird" Alta Taylor (1912–2007); 2 daughters
Died: Jan. 22, 1973; buried in Johnson City, Texas
Vice President: none 1963–1965, Hubert H. Humphrey (1965–1969)

37 RICHARD MILHOUS NIXON Republican Party 1969–1974
Born: Jan. 9, 1913, in Yorba Linda, California
Married: Thelma "Pat" Ryan (1912–1993); 2 daughters
Died: Apr. 22, 1994; buried in Yorba Linda, California
Vice President: Spiro T. Agnew (1969–1973),
　　　　　　　 Gerald R. Ford (1973–1974)

38 GERALD R. FORD Republican Party 1974–1977
Born: July 14, 1913, in Omaha, Nebraska
Married: Elizabeth "Betty" Bloomer (b. 1918); 3 sons, 1 daughter
Died: Dec. 26, 2006; buried in Grand Rapids, Michigan
Vice President: Nelson A. Rockefeller (1974–1977)

39 JIMMY (JAMES EARL) CARTER Democratic Party 1977–1981
Born: Oct. 1, 1924, in Plains, Georgia
Married: Rosalynn Smith (b. 1927); 3 sons, 1 daughter
Vice President: Walter F. Mondale (1977–1981)

40 RONALD REAGAN Republican Party   1981–1989
Born: Feb. 6, 1911, in Tampico, Illinois
Married: Jane Wyman (1914–2007); 1 son, 1 daughter
    Nancy Davis (b. 1923); 1 son, 1 daughter
Died: June 5, 2004; buried in Simi Valley, California
Vice President: George H. W. Bush (1981–1989)

41 GEORGE H. W. BUSH Republican Party   1989–1993
Born: June 12, 1924, in Milton, Massachusetts
Married: Barbara Pierce (b. 1925); 4 sons, 2 daughters
Vice President: Dan Quayle (1989–1993)

42 BILL (WILLIAM JEFFERSON) CLINTON   1993–2001
Democratic Party
Born: Aug. 19, 1946, in Hope, Arkansas
Married: Hillary Rodham (b. 1947); 1 daughter
Vice President: Al Gore (1993–2001)

43 GEORGE W. BUSH Republican Party   2001–2009
Born: July 6, 1946, in New Haven, Connecticut
Married: Laura Welch (b. 1946); 2 daughters
Vice President: Dick Cheney (2001–2009)

44 BARACK OBAMA Democratic Party   2009–
Born: August 4, 1961, in Honolulu, Hawaii
Married: Michelle Robinson (b. 1964); 2 daughters
Vice President: Joe Biden (2009–)

Meet the *First Ladies*

For many years there was no title for the wife of the president. Early first ladies were sometimes addressed as "Lady," "Mrs. President," "Mrs. Presidentress," or even "Queen." The term "First Lady" did not become common until after 1849. That year, President Zachary Taylor called Dolley Madison "First Lady" in a eulogy at her funeral.

Here are a few of the best-known "First Ladies" of the United States.

ABIGAIL ADAMS, wife of John Adams, never went to school, but she learned to read at home. She was a close adviser to her husband. She is well-known for the many letters she wrote to him when they were separated. The Adamses became the first family to move into the White House.

DOLLEY MADISON, wife of James Madison, was famous as a hostess and for saving a portrait of George Washington during the War of 1812, when the British were about to burn the White House.

MARY TODD LINCOLN, wife of Abraham Lincoln, was a well-educated Southerner who strongly opposed slavery. She suffered many tragedies in her lifetime. Her husband was assassinated, and three of her four children died young.

FRANCES FOLSOM CLEVELAND, wife of Grover Cleveland, was the only First Lady to be married in the White House and the only one to give birth to a child there. At age 21, she was the youngest woman ever to become First Lady. She was very popular, and many women tried to dress and style their hair as she did.

EDITH WILSON, wife of Woodrow Wilson, was one of the most powerful First Ladies in U.S. history. After her husband suffered a stroke in 1919, she played a key role, in his last 18 months in office, in deciding whom he would meet with and what papers he would see. According to some, she made decisions that normally would have been made by a president.

LOU HENRY HOOVER, wife of Herbert Hoover, spoke several languages, including Chinese, and had a degree in geology. As First Lady, she worked to involve more children in sports.

Meet the First Ladies

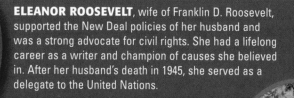

ELEANOR ROOSEVELT, wife of Franklin D. Roosevelt, supported the New Deal policies of her husband and was a strong advocate for civil rights. She had a lifelong career as a writer and champion of causes she believed in. After her husband's death in 1945, she served as a delegate to the United Nations.

JACQUELINE KENNEDY, wife of John F. Kennedy, met her husband while she was working as a photographer and reporter. As First Lady, she filled the White House with historic furnishings and artwork. Her elegant clothes and hairstyle were copied by millions of women.

CLAUDIA "LADY BIRD" JOHNSON, wife of Lyndon B. Johnson, was a successful business leader in the broadcasting industry in Texas. As First Lady, she took a special interest in preschool education and promoted efforts to plant millions of flowers in public spaces across the nation.

BETTY FORD, wife of Gerald Ford, studied modern dance as a young woman and was part of the Martha Graham dance company. As First Lady, she was an advocate for women's rights. After leaving the White House, she founded the Betty Ford Center for the treatment of drug and alcohol dependency.

NANCY REAGAN, wife of Ronald Reagan, met her husband when they both were Hollywood actors in the 1940s. As First Lady, she led a campaign to encourage young people to "just say no" if offered illegal drugs.

MICHELLE OBAMA, wife of Barack Obama, met her husband when they both were working as lawyers in Chicago. They were married in 1992 and have two daughters, Malia, born in 1998, and Sasha, born in 2001. One of her main projects as First Lady has been working to promote good eating habits for children.

United States History

14,000 B.C.– 11,000 B.C.
Paleo-Indians use stone points attached to spears to hunt big **mammoths** in northern parts of North America.

11,000 B.C.
Big mammoths disappear and Paleo-Indians begin to gather **plants** for food.

After A.D. 500
The Ancestral Puebloans in the Southwestern United States live in homes on cliffs, called **cliff dwellings**. These people's pottery and dishes are known for their beautiful patterns.

After A.D. 700
Mississippian Indian people in the Southeastern United States **develop farms** and build burial mounds.

30,000 B.C.– 11,000 B.C.
First people (called **Paleo-Indians**) cross from Siberia to Alaska and begin to move into North America.

9500 B.C.– 1000 B.C.
North American Indians begin using **stone** to grind food and to hunt bison and smaller animals.

1000 B.C.– A.D. 500
Woodland Indians, who lived east of the Mississippi River, bury their dead under large **mounds** of earth (which can still be seen today).

700–1492
Many **different Indian cultures** develop throughout North America.

279

Colonial America
and the American Revolution:
1492-1783

1492
Christopher **Columbus** sails across the Atlantic Ocean and reaches an island in the Bahamas in the Caribbean Sea.

1513
Juan **Ponce de León** explores the Florida coast.

1524
Giovanni da **Verrazano** explores the coast from Carolina north to Nova Scotia, enters New York harbor.

1540
Francisco Vásquez de **Coronado** explores the Southwest.

1565
St. Augustine, Florida, the *first town* established by Europeans in the United States, is founded by the Spanish. Later burned by the English in 1586.

BENJAMIN FRANKLIN (1706–1790)
was a great American leader, printer, scientist, and writer. In 1732, he began publishing a magazine called *Poor Richard's Almanack*. Poor Richard was a make-believe person who gave advice about common sense and honesty. Many of Poor Richard's sayings are still known today. Among the most famous are "God helps them that help themselves" and "Early to bed, early to rise, makes a man healthy, wealthy, and wise."

1634
Maryland is founded as a Catholic colony, with religious freedom for all granted in 1649.

1664
The English seize **New Amsterdam** from the Dutch. The city is renamed New York.

1699
French settlers move into Mississippi and Louisiana.

1732
Benjamin Franklin begins publishing *Poor Richard's Almanack*.

1754–1763
French and Indian War between England and France. The French are defeated and lose their lands in Canada and the American Midwest.

1764–1766
England places taxes on sugar that comes from their North American colonies. England also requires colonists to buy stamps to help pay for royal troops. Colonists protest, and the **Stamp Act** is repealed in 1766.

1607
Jamestown, Virginia, the first permanent English settlement in North America, is founded by Captain John Smith.

1609
Henry Hudson sails into **New York Harbor,** explores the Hudson River. Spaniards settle Santa Fe, New Mexico.

1619
The first African **slaves** are brought to Jamestown. (Slavery is made legal in 1650.)

1620
Pilgrims from England arrive at Plymouth, Massachusetts, on the *Mayflower*.

1626
Peter Minuit buys **Manhattan** island for the Dutch from Manahata Indians for goods worth $24. The island is renamed New Amsterdam.

1630
Boston is founded by Massachusetts colonists led by John Winthrop.

FAMOUS WORDS FROM THE DECLARATION OF INDEPENDENCE, JULY 4, 1776
"We hold these truths to be self-evident, that all men are created equal, that they are endowed by their Creator with certain unalienable rights, that among these are life, liberty, and the pursuit of happiness."

1770
Boston Massacre: During a demonstration against English taxes, protestors begin throwing rocks at English troops. The troops open fire, killing 7.

1773
Boston Tea Party: English tea is thrown into the harbor to protest a tax on tea.

1775
Fighting at **Lexington and Concord,** Massachusetts, marks the beginning of the American Revolution.

1776
The Declaration of Independence is approved July 4 by the Continental Congress (made up of representatives from the American colonies).

1781
British General **Charles Cornwallis** surrenders to the Americans at Yorktown, Virginia, ending the fighting in the Revolutionary War.

The New Nation
1784-1900

1784

The first successful daily **newspaper** in the U.S., the *Pennsylvania Packet & General Advertiser*, is published.

1787

The **Constitutional Convention** meets to write a Constitution for the U.S.

1789

The new **Constitution** is approved by the states. George Washington is chosen as the first president.

1800

The federal government moves from Philadelphia to a new capital, **Washington, D.C.**

1803

The U.S. makes the **Louisiana Purchase** from France. The Purchase doubles the area of the U.S.

WHO ATTENDED THE CONVENTION?

The **Constitutional Convention** met in Philadelphia in the hot summer of 1787. Most of the great founders of America attended. Among those present were George Washington, James Madison, and John Adams. They met to form a new government that would be strong and, at the same time, protect the liberties that were fought for in the American Revolution. The Constitution they created is still the law of the United States.

1836

Texans fighting for independence from Mexico are defeated at the **Alamo**.

1838

Cherokee Indians are forced to move to Oklahoma, along "The **Trail of Tears**." On the long march, thousands die because of disease and the cold weather.

1844

The **first telegraph** line connects Washington, D.C., and Baltimore.

1846– 1848

U.S. war with Mexico: Mexico is defeated, and the United States takes control of the Republic of Texas and of Mexican territories in the West.

1848

The discovery of **gold** in California leads to a "rush" of 80,000 people to the West in search of gold.

1852

Uncle Tom's Cabin Harriet Beecher Stowe's novel about the suffering of slaves, is published.

1804
Lewis and Clark, with their guide Sacagawea, explore what is now the northwestern United States.

1812–1814
War of 1812 with Great Britain: British forces burn the Capitol and White House. Francis Scott Key writes the words to "The Star-Spangled Banner."

1820
The **Missouri Compromise** bans slavery west of the Mississippi River and north of 36°30' latitude, except in Missouri.

1823
The **Monroe Doctrine** warns European countries not to interfere in the Americas.

1825
The **Erie Canal** opens, linking New York City with the Great Lakes.

1831
The Liberator, a newspaper opposing slavery, is published in Boston.

1869
The **first railroad** connecting the East and West coasts is completed.

1898
Spanish-American War: The U.S. defeats Spain, gains control of the Philippines, Puerto Rico, and Guam.

1858
Abraham Lincoln and Stephen Douglas **debate about slavery** during their Senate campaign in Illinois.

1860
Abraham **Lincoln** is elected president.

1861
The **Civil War** begins.

1863
President Lincoln issues the **Emancipation Proclamation**, freeing most slaves.

1865
The **Civil War** ends as the South surrenders. President Lincoln is assassinated.

1890
Battle of Wounded Knee is fought in South Dakota—the last major battle between Indians and U.S. troops.

CIVIL WAR DEAD AND WOUNDED
The U.S. **Civil War** between the North and South lasted four years (1861-1865) and resulted in the death or wounding of more than 600,000 people. Little was known at the time about the infections and spread of diseases. As a result, many soldiers died from illnesses such as influenza and measles. Many also died from infections from battle wounds.

United States Since 1900

1903

The United States begins digging the **Panama Canal**. The canal opens in 1914, connecting the Atlantic and Pacific oceans.

1908

Henry Ford introduces the **Model T** car, priced at $850.

1916

Jeannette Rankin of Montana becomes the first woman elected to Congress.

1917–1918

The United States joins **World War I** on the side of the Allies against Germany.

1927

Charles A. **Lindbergh** becomes the first person to fly alone nonstop across the Atlantic Ocean.

1929

A stock market crash marks the beginning of the **Great Depression**.

WORLD WAR I
In **World War I** the United States fought with Great Britain, France, and Russia (the Allies) against Germany and Austria-Hungary. The Allies won the war in 1918.

SCHOOL SEGREGATION
The U.S. Supreme Court ruled that **separate schools** for black students and white students were **not equal**. The Court said such schools were in violation of the U.S. Constitution.

1954

The U.S. Supreme Court **forbids racial segregration** in public schools.

1963

President John **Kennedy** is assassinated.

1964

Congress passes the **Civil Rights Act**, which outlaws discrimination in voting and jobs.

1965

The United States sends first soldiers to fight in the **Vietnam War**.

1968

Civil rights leader **Martin Luther King Jr.** is assassinated in Memphis. Senator **Robert F. Kennedy** is assassinated in Los Angeles.

1969

U.S. astronaut Neil Armstrong becomes the **first person** to walk **on the moon**.

1973

U.S. participation in the **Vietnam War** ends.

THE GREAT DEPRESSION

The stock market crash of October 1929 led to a period of severe hardship for the American people—the **Great Depression**. As many as 25 percent of all workers could not find jobs. The Depression lasted until the early 1940s. The Depression also led to a great change in politics. In 1932, Franklin D. Roosevelt, a Democrat, was elected president. He served as president for 12 years, longer than any other president.

1933
President Franklin D. Roosevelt's **New Deal** increases government help to people hurt by the Depression.

1941
Japan attacks **Pearl Harbor**, Hawaii. The United States enters World War II.

1945
Germany surrenders in May. The U.S. drops atomic bombs on **Hiroshima** and Nagasaki in August, leading to Japan's surrender and the end of **World War II**.

1947
Jackie Robinson becomes the **first black baseball player** in the major leagues when he joins the Brooklyn Dodgers.

1950–1953
U.S. armed forces fight in the **Korean War**.

WORLD WAR II

From 1941 to 1945 the United States, joining Britain, the Soviet Union, and other Allied powers, fought the Axis powers, led by Germany, Italy, and Japan, in the deadliest conflict in human history.

1991
The Persian Gulf War: The United States and its allies defeat Iraq.

2008
Barack Obama defeats **John McCain** to become the first African-American president.

2010
After a long battle in Congress, President Obama wins passage of—and signs into law—major **health care reform** legislation.

1974
President Richard **Nixon resigns** because of the **Watergate** scandal.

1979
U.S. **hostages** are taken **in Iran**, beginning a 444-day crisis that ends with their release in 1981.

1981
Sandra Day O'Connor becomes the **first woman** on the U.S. Supreme Court.

1985
U.S. President Ronald Reagan and Soviet leader Mikhail Gorbachev begin working together to **improve relations** between their countries.

1999
After an **impeachment** trial, the Senate finds President Bill Clinton not guilty.

2001
Hijacked jets crash into the **World Trade Center** and the **Pentagon**, September 11, killing about 3,000 people.

2003
U.S.-led forces invade Iraq and remove dictator **Saddam Hussein**.

African Americans:
A Time Line

From the era of slavery to the present, African Americans have struggled to obtain freedom and equal opportunity. The timeline below pinpoints many of the key events and personalities that helped shape this long struggle.

Thurgood Marshall ▶

1619	**First slaves** from Africa are brought to Virginia.
1831	Nat Turner starts a **slave revolt** in Virginia that is unsuccessful.
1856–57	**Dred Scott**, a slave, sues to be freed because he had left slave territory, but the Supreme Court denies his claim.
1861–65	The North defeats the South in the brutal Civil War; the **13th Amendment** ends nearly 250 years of slavery. The Ku Klux Klan is founded.
1865–77	Southern blacks play leadership roles in government under **Reconstruction**; the 15th Amendment (1870) gives black men the right to vote.
1896	Supreme Court rules in a case called *Plessy v. Ferguson* that racial segregation is legal when facilities are "**separate but equal.**" Discrimination and violence against blacks increase.
1910	W. E. B. Du Bois (1868–1963) founds National Association for the Advancement of Colored People (**NAACP**), fighting for equality for blacks.
1920s	African-American culture (jazz music, dance, literature) flourishes during the **Harlem Renaissance**.
1954	Supreme Court rules in a case called ***Brown v. Board of Education*** of Topeka that school segregation is unconstitutional.
1957	Black students, backed by federal troops, enter recently desegregated Central High School in **Little Rock**, Arkansas.
1955–65	**Malcolm X** (1925–1965) emerges as key spokesperson for black nationalism.
1963	**Rev. Dr. Martin Luther King, Jr.** (1929–1968) gives his "I Have a Dream" speech at a march that inspires more than 200,000 people in Washington, D.C.—and many others throughout the nation.
1964	Sweeping **civil rights bill** banning racial discrimination is signed by President Lyndon Johnson.
1965	Martin Luther King leads protest march in **Selma**, Alabama. Blacks riot in **Watts** section of Los Angeles.
1967	Gary, Indiana, and Cleveland, Ohio, are first major U.S. cities to elect black mayors. **Thurgood Marshall** (1908–1993) becomes first African American on the Supreme Court.
2001	**Colin Powell** becomes first African-American secretary of state.
2005	**Condoleezza Rice** becomes first African-American woman secretary of state.
2008	Barack Obama becomes the **first African-American elected president** of the United States.

People of many different backgrounds have played important roles in the history of the United States.

FREDERICK DOUGLASS (1818–1895) escaped from slavery at age 20. In the decades before the Civil War (1861–1865), he had a major influence on the anti-slavery movement through his lectures and writings. He became a friend and adviser to President Abraham Lincoln and encouraged him to issue the Emancipation Proclamation (1863), which declared free all slaves in Confederate-controlled territory in the South.

CRAZY HORSE (1840s–1877) led the Oglala Sioux Indians in battles with the U.S. Army over land, including in the Black Hills of what is now South Dakota. He helped defeat General George Armstrong Custer at the Battle of the Little Bighorn in Montana. He later surrendered to the Army and was killed in a scuffle with troops at a military outpost.

DALIP SINGH SAUND (1899–1973) was the first Asian-American member of Congress. Born in India, Saund immigrated to California, where he became a farmer, businessman, and judge. Elected to the House of Representatives in 1956, he worked hard to aid farmers and to uphold the rights of immigrants.

ROSA PARKS (1913–2005) refused to give up her bus seat to a white man one day in 1955. Spurred on by her brave action, blacks in Montgomery, Alabama, started a boycott of the bus system. It led to desegregation of the city's buses, a key event in the history of the civil rights movement.

MALCOLM X (1925–1965) was a Nation of Islam (Black Muslim) leader who spoke out against injustices toward African Americans and believed they should live and develop separately from white people. After leaving the Nation of Islam, he was assassinated by rivals. His life story, *The Autobiography of Malcolm X*, published after he died, became a best-seller and helped make him a hero to many.

CESAR CHAVEZ (1927–1993), a Mexican American who was raised in migrant worker camps, started the union known as the United Farm Workers of America in 1966. Along with UFW cofounder **DOLORES HUERTA** (born 1930), he organized boycotts that eventually made growers agree to better conditions for field workers.

REV. DR. MARTIN LUTHER KING, JR. (1929–1968) was the most influential leader of the civil rights movement from the mid-1950s to his assassination in 1968. A believer in peaceful protest, he received the Nobel Peace Prize in 1964. The federal government and all 50 states now have a holiday in his honor. His wife, **CORETTA SCOTT KING** (1927–2006), helped carry on his work.

STEVEN CHU (born 1948), a prominent Chinese-American scientist, won a 1997 Nobel Prize in physics for his nuclear research. More recently, his work focused on studying and promoting the use of alternative fuels. Chu became U.S. secretary of energy in 2009.

SONIA SOTOMAYOR (born 1954), who grew up in a public housing project in New York City, went on to graduate from Princeton University and Yale Law School. Experienced as a prosecutor and a judge, she was named to the U.S. Supreme Court in 2009, becoming the court's first Hispanic justice.

BARACK OBAMA (born 1961), is the son of an American mother and a Kenyan father. After serving in the Illinois Senate for eight years, he was elected to the U.S. Senate in 2004. From there he launched a successful campaign to become president of the U.S. Inaugurated in 2009, he worked to help resolve the nation's economic problems and to give more people access to health care.

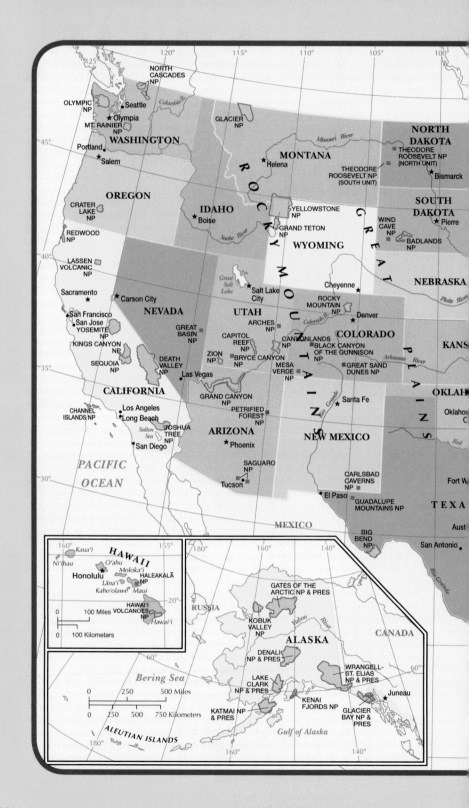

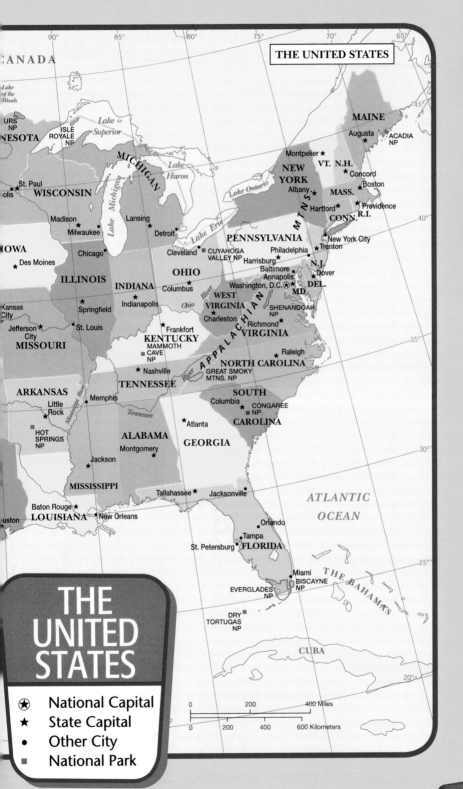

THE UNITED STATES

CANADA

MAINE

Augusta ★   ACADIA
            NP

Montpelier ★

VT. N.H.
     ★ Concord
NEW   Albany ★   MASS. Boston ★
YORK
          Hartford ★   ★ Providence
          CONN. R.I.

Lake Superior

ISLE
ROYALE
NP

URS
NP

NESOTA

MINNESOTA

Lake
of the
Woods

St. Paul ★
olis

WISCONSIN

Madison ●   Lansing ●

Milwaukee ●

MICHIGAN

Lake Michigan

Lake
Huron

Lake Ontario

Lake Erie

Detroit ●

Cleveland ■   CUYAHOGA
              VALLEY NP

PENNSYLVANIA

Philadelphia ★
Harrisburg ★   ★ Trenton
              New York City ★

N.J.
★ Dover

DEL.

Baltimore ●
Annapolis ★
Washington, D.C. ⊛
MD.

IOWA

OWA

Des Moines ★

Chicago ●

ILLINOIS

OHIO

Columbus ★

INDIANA

Indianapolis ●

Springfield ★

Kansas
City

Jefferson ★
City

St. Louis ●

MISSOURI

Frankfort ★

KENTUCKY
MAMMOTH
■ CAVE
  NP

Nashville ★

TENNESSEE

Ohio River

WEST
VIRGINIA

Charleston ●

APPALACHIAN MTNS.

SHENANDOAH
NP

Richmond ★
VIRGINIA

Raleigh ●

NORTH CAROLINA

GREAT SMOKY
MTNS. NP

ARKANSAS

Little
Rock ★

Memphis ●

Mississippi River

Tennessee River

HOT
SPRINGS
NP

ALABAMA

Montgomery ★

Jackson ★

MISSISSIPPI

SOUTH

Columbia ★
CONGAREE
■ NP

CAROLINA

Atlanta ★

GEORGIA

Tallahassee ★   Jacksonville ●

Baton Rouge ★
uston   LOUISIANA   ● New Orleans

ATLANTIC
OCEAN

Orlando ●

Tampa ●
St. Petersburg ●   FLORIDA

Miami ●
BISCAYNE
NP

THE BAHAMAS

EVERGLADES
NP

DRY ■
TORTUGAS
NP

CUBA

90°   85°   80°   75°   70°   65°

45°

40°

35°

30°

25°

20°

THE
UNITED
STATES

⊛   National Capital
★   State Capital
●   Other City
■   National Park

0   200   400 Miles

0   200   400   600 Kilometers

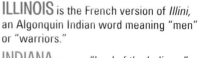

ALABAMA comes from an Indian word for "tribal town."

Arizona

ALASKA comes from *alakshak*, an Aleut word meaning "peninsula" or "land that is not an island."

ARIZONA comes from a Pima Indian word meaning "little spring place" or the Aztec word *arizuma*, meaning "silver-bearing."

ARKANSAS is a variation of Quapaw, the name of an Indian tribe. Quapaw means "south wind."

CALIFORNIA is the name of an imaginary island in a Spanish story. It was named by Spanish explorers of Baja California, a part of Mexico.

COLORADO comes from a Spanish word meaning "red." It was first given to the Colorado River because of its reddish color.

CONNECTICUT comes from an Algonquin Indian word meaning "long river place."

DELAWARE is named after Lord De La Warr, the English governor of Virginia in colonial times.

FLORIDA, which means "flowery" in Spanish, was named by the explorer Ponce de León, who landed there during Easter.

GEORGIA was named after King George II of England, who granted the right to create a colony there in 1732.

HAWAII probably comes from *Hawaiki*, or *Owhyhee*, the native Polynesian word for "homeland."

IDAHO's name is of uncertain origin, but it may come from a Kiowa Apache name for the Comanche Indians.

Idaho

ILLINOIS is the French version of *Illini*, an Algonquin Indian word meaning "men" or "warriors."

INDIANA means "land of the Indians."

IOWA comes from the name of an American Indian tribe that once lived in the region.

KANSAS comes from a Sioux Indian word that possibly meant "people of the south wind."

KENTUCKY comes from an Iroquois Indian word, possibly meaning "meadowland."

LOUISIANA, which was first settled by French explorers, was named after King Louis XIV of France.

MAINE means "the mainland." English explorers called it that to distinguish it from islands nearby.

Massachusetts

MARYLAND was named after Queen Henrietta Maria, wife of King Charles I of England, who granted the right to establish an English colony there.

MASSACHUSETTS comes from an Indian word meaning "large hill place."

MICHIGAN comes from the Chippewa Indian words *mici gama*, meaning "great water" (referring to Lake Michigan).

MINNESOTA got its name from a Dakota Sioux Indian word meaning "cloudy water" or "sky-tinted water."

MISSISSIPPI is probably from Chippewa Indian words meaning "great river" or "gathering of all the waters," or from an Algonquin word, *messipi*.

MISSOURI comes from an Algonquin Indian term meaning "river of the big canoes."

Got Their Names

MONTANA comes from a Latin or Spanish word meaning "mountainous."

NEBRASKA comes from "flat river" or "broad water," an Omaha or Otos Indian name for the Platte River.

NEVADA means "snow-clad" in Spanish. Spanish explorers gave the name to the Sierra Nevada Mountains.

NEW HAMPSHIRE was named by an early settler after his home county of Hampshire, in England.

NEW JERSEY was named for the English Channel island of Jersey.

North Carolina

NEW MEXICO was given its name by 16th-century Spaniards in Mexico.

NEW YORK, first called New Netherland, was renamed for the Duke of York after the English took it from Dutch settlers.

NORTH CAROLINA, the northern part of the English colony of Carolana, was named for King Charles I.

NORTH DAKOTA comes from a Sioux Indian word meaning "friend" or "ally."

OHIO is the Iroquois Indian word for "good river."

OKLAHOMA comes from a Choctaw Indian word meaning "red man."

OREGON may have come from *Ouaricon-sint*, a name on an old French map that was once given to what is now called the Columbia River. That river runs between Oregon and Washington.

PENNSYLVANIA meaning "Penn's woods," was the name given to the colony founded by William Penn.

RHODE ISLAND may have come from the Dutch *Roode Eylandt* ("red island") or may have been named after the Greek island of Rhodes.

SOUTH CAROLINA, the southern part of the English colony of Carolana, was named for King Charles I.

SOUTH DAKOTA comes from a Sioux Indian word meaning "friend" or "ally."

TENNESSEE comes from *Tanasi*, the name of Cherokee Indian villages on what is now the Little Tennessee River.

TEXAS comes from a word meaning "friends" or "allies," used by the Spanish to describe some of the American Indians living there.

Utah

UTAH comes from a Navajo word meaning "upper" or "higher up."

VERMONT comes from two French words, *vert* meaning "green" and *mont* meaning "mountain."

VIRGINIA was named in honor of Queen Elizabeth I of England, who was known as the Virgin Queen because she was never married.

WASHINGTON was named after George Washington, the first president of the United States. It is the only state named after a president.

WEST VIRGINIA got its name from the people of western Virginia, who formed their own government during the Civil War.

WISCONSIN comes from a Chippewa name that is believed to mean "grassy place." It was once spelled *Ouisconsin* and *Mesconsing*.

Wyoming

WYOMING comes from Algonquin Indian words that are said to mean "at the big plains," "large prairie place," or "on the great plain."

291

Facts
About the
States

After every state name is the postal abbreviation The Area includes both land and water; it is given in square miles (sq mi) and square kilometers (sq km). Numbers in parentheses after Population, Area, and Entered Union show the state's rank compared with other states. City populations are for mid-2008, unless otherwise noted.

ALABAMA

(AL) Heart of Dixie, Camellia State

Birmingham

Montgomery

POPULATION (2009): 4,708,708 (23rd) **AREA:** 52,420 sq mi (30th) (135,768 sq km) 🌸 Camellia 🐦Yellowhammer 🌲Southern longleaf pine 🎵"Alabama" **ENTERED UNION:** December 14, 1819 (22nd) ⭐Montgomery **LARGEST CITIES (WITH POP.):** Birmingham, 228,798; Montgomery, 202,696; Mobile, 191,022; Huntsville, 176,645

⚙ clothing and textiles, metal products, transportation equipment, paper, industrial machinery, food products, lumber, coal, oil, natural gas, livestock, peanuts, cotton

did you Know? *Helen Keller, one of history's most remarkable women, was born and raised at Ivy Green, an estate in Tuscumbia, AL, that is now a museum. It was there that she learned to understand words, despite being both blind and deaf.*

ALASKA

(AK) The Last Frontier State

Anchorage

Juneau ⭐

POPULATION (2009): 698,473 (47th) **AREA:** 664,988 sq mi (1st) (1,722,319 sq km) 🌸Forget-me-not 🐦Willow ptarmigan 🌲Sitka spruce 🎵"Alaska's Flag" **ENTERED UNION:** January 3, 1959 (49th) ⭐Juneau **LARGEST CITIES (WITH POP.):** Anchorage, 279,243; Fairbanks, 35,132; Juneau, 30,988; Wasilla, 10,256

⚙ oil, natural gas, fish, food products, lumber and wood products, fur

did you Know? *U.S. Secretary of State William Seward bought all of Alaska from Russia in 1867 for just $7.2 million. At the time, many Americans made fun of what they called "Seward's folly" or "Seward's icebox."*

ARIZONA

(AZ) Grand Canyon State

Phoenix ⭐

Tucson

POPULATION (2009): 6,595,778 (14th) **AREA:** 113,990 sq mi (6th) (295,235 sq km) 🌸Blossom of the Saguaro cactus 🐦Cactus wren 🌲Paloverde 🎵"Arizona" **ENTERED UNION:** February 14, 1912 (48th) ⭐Phoenix **LARGEST CITIES (WITH POP.):** Phoenix, 1,567,924; Tucson, 541,811; Mesa, 463,552; Glendale, 251,522; Chandler, 247,170; Scottsdale, 235,371

⚙ electronic equipment, transportation and industrial equipment, instruments, printing and publishing, copper and other metals

did you Know? *You can find London Bridge in Lake Havasu City, AZ. Built in London, England, in the 1830s, the bridge was taken down and sold to Robert P. McCulloch in 1968. He re-assembled it on Lake Havasu in 1971.*

ARKANSAS (AR) Natural State, Razorback State

Little Rock ⭐

POPULATION (2009): 2,889,450 (32nd) **AREA:** 53,178 sq mi (29th) (137,732 sq km) 🌼 Apple blossom 🐦 Mockingbird 🌲 Pine 🎵 "Arkansas" **ENTERED UNION:** June 15, 1836 (25th) ⭐ Little Rock **LARGEST CITIES (WITH POP.):** Little Rock, 189,515; Fort Smith, 84,716; Fayetteville, 73,372; Springdale, 68,180

⚙ food products, paper, electronic equipment, industrial machinery, metal products, lumber and wood products, livestock, soybeans, rice, cotton, natural gas

did you Know? *Wal-Mart, now the world's biggest retail company and the biggest private employer in the U.S., started from a single discount store that opened in Rogers, AR, in 1962.*

CALIFORNIA (CA) Golden State

Sacramento ⭐

San Francisco

Los Angeles

San Diego

POPULATION (2009): 36,961,664 (1st) **AREA:** 163,694 sq mi (3rd) (423,967 sq km) 🌼 Golden poppy 🐦 California valley quail 🌲 California redwood 🎵 "I Love You, California" **ENTERED UNION:** September 9, 1850 (31st) ⭐ Sacramento **LARGEST CITIES (WITH POP.):** Los Angeles, 3,833,995; San Diego, 1,279,329; San Jose, 948,279; San Francisco, 808,976; Fresno, 476,050; Sacramento, 463,794; Long Beach, 463,789; Oakland, 404,155

⚙ transportation and industrial equipment, electronic equipment, oil, natural gas, motion pictures, milk, cattle, fruit, vegetables

did you Know? *The redwood is California's state tree. One redwood, deep in the forest of California's Redwood National Park, is said to be the world's tallest tree, at 378 feet. Its exact location is kept secret so it can remain undisturbed.*

COLORADO (CO) Centennial State

Denver ⭐

● **Colorado Springs**

POPULATION (2009): 5,024,748 (22nd) **AREA:** 104,094 sq mi (8th) (269,604 sq km) 🌼 Rocky Mountain columbine 🐦 Lark bunting 🌲 Colorado blue spruce 🎵 "Where the Columbines Grow" **ENTERED UNION:** August 1, 1876 (38th) ⭐ Denver **LARGEST CITIES (WITH POP.):** Denver, 598,707; Colorado Springs, 380,307; Aurora, 319,057; Lakewood, 140,989; Fort Collins, 136,509

⚙ instruments and industrial machinery, food products, printing and publishing, metal products, electronic equipment, oil, coal, cattle

did you Know? *The Anasazi Indians built entire cities into cliffsides across the American southwest. The settlements built between 1100 and 1300 at Mesa Verde in southwestern Colorado are the largest and best preserved.*

Key: 🌼 Flower 🐦 Bird 🌲 Tree 🎵 Song ⭐ Capital ⚙ Important Products

CONNECTICUT (CT) Constitution State, Nutmeg State

Hartford ★

POPULATION (2009): 3,518,288 (29th) **AREA:** 5,544 sq mi (48th) (14,358 sq km) 🌼Mountain laurel 🐦American robin 🌳White oak 🎵"Yankee Doodle" **ENTERED UNION:** January 9, 1788 (5th) ★ Hartford **LARGEST CITIES (WITH POP.):** Bridgeport, 136,405; Hartford, 124,062; New Haven, 123,669; Stamford, 119,303; Waterbury, 107,037

⚙ aircraft parts, helicopters, industrial machinery, metals and metal products, electronic equipment, printing and publishing, medical instruments, chemicals, dairy products, stone

did you Know?

Mystic Seaport, on the Connecticut shore, contains a re-creation of a 19th-century seafaring village, along with many historic ships and other exhibits. The Mystic Aquarium nearby has a wide variety of sea creatures—and even a bat cave.

DELAWARE (DE) First State, Diamond State

Dover ★

POPULATION (2009): 885,122 (45th) **AREA:** 2,489 sq mi (49th) (6,445 sq km) 🌼Peach blossom 🐦Blue hen chicken 🌳American holly 🎵"Our Delaware" **ENTERED UNION:** December 7, 1787 (1st) ★Dover **LARGEST CITIES (WITH POP.):** Wilmington, 72,592; Dover, 36,107; Newark, 29,886

⚙ chemicals, transportation equipment, food products, chickens

did you Know?

People from Sweden first settled at Fort Christina (later Wilmington) in 1636. In 1787, Delaware became the first state to ratify the U.S. Constitution.

FLORIDA (FL) Sunshine State

Tallahassee ★
Jacksonville •

POPULATION (2009): 18,537,969 (4th) **AREA:** 65,758 sq mi (22nd) (170,312 sq km) 🌼Orange blossom 🐦Mockingbird 🌳Sabal palmetto palm 🎵"Old Folks at Home" **ENTERED UNION:** March 3, 1845 (27th) ★Tallahassee **LARGEST CITIES (WITH POP.):** Jacksonville, 807,815; Miami, 413,201; Tampa, 340,882; St. Petersburg, 245,314; Orlando, 230,519 Hialeah, 210,542; Ft. Lauderdale, 183,126

⚙ electronic and transportation equipment, industrial machinery, printing and publishing, food products, citrus fruits, vegetables, livestock, phosphates, fish

Miami •

did you Know?

Jacksonville is the biggest city in the lower 48 U.S. states—if you go by area. It's about the size of New York City and Los Angeles combined. The city is named after Andrew Jackson, who was military governor of Florida before it became a state.

GEORGIA

(GA) Empire State of the South, Peach State

★ **Atlanta**

POPULATION (2009): 9,829,211 (9th) **AREA:** 59,425 sq mi (24th) (153,911 sq km) ✿Cherokee rose 🐦Brown thrasher 🌲Live oak 🎵"Georgia on My Mind" **ENTERED UNION:** January 2, 1788 (4th) ★Atlanta **LARGEST CITIES (WITH POP.):** Atlanta, 537,958; Augusta, 199,486; Columbus, 186,984; Savannah, 132,410

⚙ clothing and textiles, transportation equipment, food products, paper, chickens, peanuts, peaches, clay

Hartsfield-Jackson Atlanta International Airport has ranked in recent years as the world's busiest airport. It serves nearly 100 million airline passengers each year. Chicago's O'Hare Airport ranks second.

HAWAII

(HI) Aloha State

POPULATION (2009): 1,295,178 (42nd) **AREA:** 10,926 sq mi (43rd) (28,300 sq km) ✿Yellow hibiscus 🐦Hawaiian goose 🌲Kukui 🎵"Hawaii Ponoi" **ENTERED UNION:** August 21, 1959 (50th) ★Honolulu **LARGEST CITIES (WITH POP.):** Honolulu, 374,676; (2000 census): Hilo, 40,759; Kailua, 36,513; Kaneohe, 34,970

★ **Honolulu**

⚙ food products, pineapples, sugar, printing and publishing, fish, flowers

Polynesians from about 2,000 miles to the south first settled in the Hawaiian Islands around A.D. 300 to 600. Kings and queens ruled Hawaii from 1810 until 1893, when Queen Liliuokalani was overthrown.

IDAHO

(ID) Gem State

POPULATION (2009): 1,545,801 (39th) **AREA:** 83,568 sq mi (14th) (216,442 sq km) ✿Syringa 🐦Mountain bluebird 🌲White pine 🎵"Here We Have Idaho" **ENTERED UNION:** July 3, 1890 (43rd) ★Boise **LARGEST CITIES (WITH POP.):** Boise, 205,314; Nampa, 80,362; Meridian, 66,916; Pocatello, 54,901; Idaho Falls, 54,334

⚙ potatoes, hay, wheat, cattle, milk, lumber and wood products, food products

★ **Boise**

Craters of the Moon National Monument, in southern Idaho, has an unusual, almost unearthly landscape, with its lava flows, craters, and cinder cones. They are left over from volcanic eruptions, the last of which came about 1,600 years ago.

Key: ✿Flower 🐦Bird 🌲Tree 🎵Song ★Capital ⚙Important Products

ILLINOIS (IL) Prairie State

Chicago

POPULATION (2009): 12,910,409 (5th) **AREA:** 57,916 sq mi (25th) (150,002 sq km) 🌼Native violet 🐦Cardinal 🌳White oak 🎵"Illinois" **ENTERED UNION:** December 3, 1818 (21st) ⭐Springfield **LARGEST CITIES (WITH POP.):** Chicago, 2,853,114; Aurora, 171,782; Rockford, 157,272; Joliet, 146,125; Naperville, 143,117; Springfield, 117,352; Peoria, 114,114

Springfield ⭐

⚙ industrial machinery, metals and metal products, printing and publishing, electronic equipment, food products, corn, soybeans, hogs

did you Know? *The world's first skyscraper was built in Chicago, in 1885, and the city's Willis Tower (formerly the Sears Tower) is the tallest U.S. building. Presidents Abraham Lincoln, Ulysses S. Grant, and Barack Obama lived in Illinois, and President Ronald Reagan was born there.*

INDIANA (IN) Hoosier State

POPULATION (2009): 6,423,113 (16th) **AREA:** 36,417 sq mi (38th) (94,321 sq km) 🌼Peony 🐦Cardinal 🌳Tulip poplar 🎵"On the Banks of the Wabash, Far Away" **ENTERED UNION:** December 11, 1816 (19th) ⭐Indianapolis **LARGEST CITIES (WITH POP.):** Indianapolis, 808,466; Fort Wayne, 251,591; Evansville, 116,309; South Bend, 103,807; Gary, 95,920

Indianapolis ⭐

⚙ transportation equipment, electronic equipment, industrial machinery, iron and steel, metal products, corn, soybeans, livestock, coal

did you Know? *Two main routes of the Underground Railroad, a movement that helped free black slaves, went through Indiana. From 1827 to 1847, the Coffin family ran a stop, in Newport (now Fountain City). They helped more than 2,000 runaway slaves escape.*

IOWA (IA) Hawkeye State

POPULATION (2009): 3,007,856 (30th) **AREA:** 56,273 sq mi (26th) (145,746 sq km) 🌼Wild rose 🐦Eastern goldfinch 🌳Oak 🎵"The Song of Iowa" **ENTERED UNION:** December 28, 1846 (29th) ⭐Des Moines **LARGEST CITIES (WITH POP.):** Des Moines, 197,052; Cedar Rapids, 128,056; Davenport, 100,827; Sioux City, 82,807

Des Moines ⭐

⚙ corn, soybeans, hogs, cattle, industrial machinery, food products

did you Know? *Famous people born in Iowa include "Buffalo Bill" Cody (1846), baseball player/manager "Cap" Anson (1851), President Herbert Hoover (1874), and actors John Wayne (1907) and Elijah Wood (1981).*

KANSAS

(KS) Sunflower State

POPULATION (2009): 2,818,747 (33rd) **AREA:** 82,278 sq mi (15th) (213,101 sq km) Native sunflower Western meadowlark Cottonwood "Home on the Range" **ENTERED UNION:** January 29, 1861 (34th) Topeka **LARGEST CITIES (WITH POP.):** Wichita, 366,046; Overland Park, 171,231; Kansas City, 142,562; Topeka, 123,446

cattle, aircraft and other transportation equipment, industrial machinery, food products, wheat, corn, hay, oil, natural gas

did you Know? *A tornado on a Kansas farm swept Dorothy away to the land of Oz in the classic children's novel that was made into the famous Wizard of Oz film. Today, one out of five Kansans still works on a farm or in a job related to farming or food processing.*

KENTUCKY

(KY) Bluegrass State

POPULATION (2009): 4,314,113 (26th) **AREA:** 40,411 sq mi (37th) (104,665 sq km) Goldenrod Cardinal Tulip poplar "My Old Kentucky Home" **ENTERED UNION:** June 1, 1792 (15th) Frankfort **LARGEST CITIES (WITH POP.):** Louisville, 713,877; Lexington-Fayette, 282,114; Owensboro, 55,516; Bowling Green, 55,097

coal, industrial machinery, electronic equipment, transportation equipment, metals, tobacco, cattle

did you Know? *More than 360 miles of natural caves and underground passageways have been mapped under Mammoth Cave National Park. It's the largest network of natural tunnels in the world and extends up to 1,000 miles.*

LOUISIANA

(LA) Pelican State

POPULATION (2009): 4,492,076 (25th) **AREA:** 51,988 sq mi (31st) (134,649 sq km) Magnolia Eastern brown pelican Cypress "Give Me Louisiana" **ENTERED UNION:** April 30, 1812 (18th) Baton Rouge **LARGEST CITIES (WITH POP.):** New Orleans, 311,853; Baton Rouge, 223,689; Shreveport, 199,729; Lafayette, 113,656

natural gas, oil, chemicals, transportation equipment, paper, food products, cotton, fish

did you Know? *Louisiana is the only state whose legal system comes from Napoleonic Code, the system put into place in France by Napoleon Bonaparte. This is because Louisiana used to belong to France. The law codes of the other 49 states are based on English common law, which was practiced in England. The differences are minor.*

Key: Flower Bird Tree Song Capital Important Products

MAINE

 (ME) Pine Tree State

Augusta

POPULATION (2009): 1,318,301 (40th) **AREA:** 35,384 sq mi (39th) (91,644 sq km) White pine cone and tassel Chickadee Eastern white pine "State of Maine Song" **ENTERED UNION:** March 15, 1820 (23rd) Augusta **LARGEST CITIES (WITH POP.):** Portland, 62,561; Lewiston, 35,131; Bangor, 31,756

paper, transportation equipment, wood and wood products, electronic equipment, footwear, clothing, potatoes, milk, eggs, fish, seafood

did you Know? *In 1948, Maine elected its first female U.S. senator, Margaret Chase Smith; she served for 24 years, a record for a woman senator. In the mid-1990s, Maine elected women to both of its Senate seats—Olympia Snowe and Susan Collins.*

MARYLAND

 (MD) Old Line State, Free State

Baltimore •

Annapolis

POPULATION (2009): 5,699,478 (19th) **AREA:** 12,406 sq mi (42nd) (32,131 sq km) Black-eyed susan Baltimore oriole White oak "Maryland, My Maryland" **ENTERED UNION:** April 28, 1788 (7th) Annapolis **LARGEST CITIES (WITH POP.):** Baltimore, 636,919; Rockville, 60,734; Frederick, 59,213; Gaithersburg, 58,744; Bowie, 52,544

printing and publishing, food products, transportation equipment, electronic equipment, chickens, soybeans, corn, stone

did you Know? *Maryland's official state sport is jousting. Competitors on horseback ride through a course and use their lances to collect rings. Competitors are called either "knights" or "maids."*

MASSACHUSETTS

 (MA) Bay State, Old Colony

Boston

POPULATION (2009): 6,593,587 (15th) **AREA:** 10,554 sq mi (44th) (27,336 sq km) Mayflower Chickadee American elm "All Hail to Massachusetts" **ENTERED UNION:** February 6, 1788 (6th) Boston **LARGEST CITIES (WITH POP.):** Boston, 609,023; Worcester, 175,011; Springfield, 150,640; Cambridge, 105,596; Lowell, 103,615

industrial machinery, electronic equipment, fish, instruments, printing, publishing, metal products, flowers, shrubs, cranberries

did you Know? *Pink flamingos, the plastic lawn ornaments, were first made by a young sculptor named Don Featherstone in 1957. Every "authentic" pink flamingo was made by Union Products, of Leominster, from 1957 until the factory closed in 2006.*

MICHIGAN (MI) Great Lakes State, Wolverine State

POPULATION (2009): 9,969,727 (8th) **AREA:** 96,713 sq mi (11th) (250,486 sq km) Apple blossom Robin 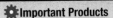White pine "Michigan, My Michigan"
ENTERED UNION: January 26, 1837 (26th)
Lansing **LARGEST CITIES (WITH POP.):** Detroit, 912,062; Grand Rapids, 193,396; Warren, 133,939; Sterling Heights, 127,160; Ann Arbor, 114,386; Lansing, 113,968; Flint, 112,900

 automobiles, industrial machinery, metal products, office furniture, plastic products, chemicals, food products, milk, corn, natural gas, iron ore, blueberries

 did you Know? *Battle Creek, the headquarters for Kellogg's, Ralston Foods, and the Post Cereal division of Kraft Foods, is known as the Cereal Capital of the World.*

Lansing
Detroit

MINNESOTA (MN) North Star State, Gopher State

POPULATION (2009): 5,266,214 (21st) **AREA:** 86,935 sq mi (12th) (225,163 sq km) Pink and white lady slipper Common loon Red pine "Hail! Minnesota" **ENTERED UNION:** May 11, 1858 (32nd) St. Paul **LARGEST CITIES (WITH POP.):** Minneapolis, 382,605; St. Paul, 279,590; Rochester, 100,413; Duluth, 84,284; Bloomington, 81,280

 industrial machinery, printing and publishing, computers, food products, scientific and medical instruments, milk, hogs, cattle, corn, soybeans, iron ore

did you Know? *Every summer, at the State Fair in St. Paul, the state dairy industry has a competition to pick its princess. Statues of all the women who are finalists are put on display, each one carved out of butter.*

Minneapolis
St. Paul

MISSISSIPPI (MS) Magnolia State

POPULATION (2009): 2,951,996 (31st) **AREA:** 48,432 sq mi (32nd) (125,438 sq km) Magnolia Mockingbird Magnolia "Go, Mississippi!" **ENTERED UNION:** December 10, 1817 (20th) Jackson **LARGEST CITIES (WITH POP.):** Jackson, 173,861; Gulfport, 70,055; Hattiesburg, 51,993; Biloxi, 45,670

 transportation equipment, furniture, electrical machinery, lumber and wood products, cotton, rice, chickens, cattle

did you Know? *In 1902, President Theodore "Teddy" Roosevelt went bear hunting in Mississippi. He refused to shoot a bear that had been tied to a tree by his companions. The story inspired some toy makers to create a stuffed toy bear, which they called "Teddy's Bear." That's how the teddy bear was born.*

Jackson

Key: Flower Bird Tree Song Capital Important Products

MISSOURI (MO) Show Me State

POPULATION (2009): 5,987,580 (18th) **AREA:** 69,702 sq mi (21st) (180,529 sq km) 🌼Hawthorn 🐦Bluebird 🌳Dogwood 🎵"Missouri Waltz" **ENTERED UNION:** August 10, 1821 (24th) ⭐Jefferson City **LARGEST CITIES (WITH POP.):** Kansas City, 451,572; St. Louis, 354,361; Springfield, 156,206; Independence, 110,440

⚙ transportation equipment, electrical and electronic equipment, printing and publishing, food products, cattle, hogs, milk, soybeans, corn, hay, lead

did you Know? *The stainless steel Gateway Arch (630 feet high), in St. Louis, is the state's most famous landmark. The state's most famous citizen is probably President Harry S. Truman, who was born and lived most of his life in Missouri.*

MONTANA (MT) Treasure State

POPULATION (2009): 974,989 (44th) **AREA:** 147,039 sq mi (4th) (380,831 sq km) 🌼Bitterroot 🐦Western meadowlark 🌳Ponderosa pine 🎵"Montana" **ENTERED UNION:** November 8, 1889 (41st) ⭐Helena **LARGEST CITIES (WITH POP.):** Billings, 103,994; Missoula, 68,202; Great Falls, 59,251; Bozeman, 39,442

⚙ cattle, copper, gold, wheat, barley, wood and paper products

did you Know? *The capital, Helena, was started by miners who found gold in a creek, or gulch, in 1864. It was first called Crabtown after one of the miners, John Crab. The city's main street, Last Chance Gulch, covers the length of the gulch.*

NEBRASKA (NE) Cornhusker State

POPULATION (2009): 1,796,619 (38th) **AREA:** 77,349 sq mi (16th) (200,334 sq km) 🌼Goldenrod 🐦Western meadowlark 🌳Cottonwood 🎵"Beautiful Nebraska" **ENTERED UNION:** March 1, 1867 (37th) ⭐Lincoln **LARGEST CITIES (WITH POP.):** Omaha, 438,646; Lincoln, 251,624; Bellevue, 49,699; Grand Island, 45,801

⚙ cattle, hogs, milk, corn, soybeans, hay, wheat, sorghum, food products, industrial machinery

did you Know? *Nebraska has the only unicameral (one-house) state legislature in the U.S. It is called the Nebraska Unicameral. The members are called senators, and they serve four-year terms. The leader of the legislature is called the Speaker.*

NEVADA (NV) Sagebrush State, Battle Born State, Silver State

POPULATION (2009): 2,643,085 (35th) **AREA:** 110,572 sq mi (7th) (286,382 sq km) 🌼Sagebrush 🐦Mountain bluebird 🌲Single-leaf piñon, bristlecone pine 🎵"Home Means Nevada" **ENTERED UNION:** October 31, 1864 (36th) ⭐Carson City **LARGEST CITIES (WITH POP.):** Las Vegas, 558,383; Henderson, 252,064; North Las Vegas, 217,253; Reno, 217,016

⚙ gold, silver, cattle, hay, food products, plastics, chemicals

Extending for about 110 miles, Lake Mead is the largest artificial lake in the U.S. It provides water for Nevada, Arizona, California, and northern Mexico. It was formed on the Colorado River when the Hoover Dam was built in 1936.

⭐ Carson City

Las Vegas

NEW HAMPSHIRE (NH) Granite State

POPULATION (2009): 1,324,575 (41st) **AREA:** 9,348 sq mi (46th) (24,210 sq km) 🌼Purple lilac 🐦Purple finch 🌲White birch 🎵"Old New Hampshire" **ENTERED UNION:** June 21, 1788 (9th) ⭐Concord **LARGEST CITIES (WITH POP.):** Manchester, 108,586; Nashua, 86,576; Concord, 42,255

⚙ industrial machinery, electric and electronic equipment, metal products, plastic products, dairy products, maple syrup and maple sugar

Tiny Dixville Notch (population, about 75) is famous for reporting early results in presidential elections. All the registered voters get together and cast ballots at midnight, so the votes can get counted right away.

Concord ⭐

NEW JERSEY (NJ) Garden State

POPULATION (2009): 8,707,739 (11th) **AREA:** 8,723 sq mi (47th) (22,592 sq km) 🌼Purple violet 🐦Eastern goldfinch 🌲Red oak 🎵none **ENTERED UNION:** December 18, 1787 (3rd) ⭐Trenton **LARGEST CITIES (WITH POP.):** Newark, 278,980; Jersey City, 241,114; Paterson, 145,643; Elizabeth, 124,755; Trenton, 82,883

⚙ chemicals, pharmaceuticals/drugs, electronic equipment, nursery and greenhouse products, food products, tomatoes, blueberries, peaches

Newark •

⭐

Trenton

One of the first dinosaur skeletons discovered in North America was unearthed at Haddonfield, New Jersey, in 1858. It was a duck-billed, plant-eating Hadrosaurus. The Hadrosaurus was later named as the official state dinosaur.

Key: 🌼Flower 🐦Bird 🌲Tree 🎵Song ⭐Capital ⚙Important Products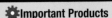

NEW MEXICO (NM) Land of Enchantment

Santa Fe ★

• Albuquerque

POPULATION (2009): 2,009,671 (36th) **AREA:** 121,590 sq mi (5th) (314,919 sq km) 🌼Yucca 🐦Roadrunner 🌲Piñon 🎵"O, Fair New Mexico" **ENTERED UNION:** January 6, 1912 (47th) ⭐Santa Fe **LARGEST CITIES (WITH POP.):** Albuquerque, 521,999; Las Cruces, 91,865; Rio Rancho, 79,655; Santa Fe, 71,831

⚙ electronic equipment, foods, machinery, clothing, lumber, transportation equipment, hay, onions, chiles

did you **Know?** *New Mexico has been inhabited for more than 10,000 years, by a series of different peoples. It is also the birthplace of the nuclear age; the world's first atom bomb was exploded at a test site near Alamogordo in 1945.*

NEW YORK (NY) Empire State

Albany ★

• Buffalo

New York City •

POPULATION (2009): 19,541,453 (3rd) **AREA:** 54,555 sq mi (27th) (141,298 sq km) 🌼Rose 🐦Bluebird 🌲Sugar maple 🎵"I Love New York" **ENTERED UNION:** July 26, 1788 (11th) ⭐Albany **LARGEST CITIES (WITH POP.):** New York, 8,363,710; Buffalo, 270,919; Rochester, 206,886; Yonkers, 201,588; Syracuse, 138,068

⚙ books and magazines, automobile and aircraft parts, toys and sporting goods, electronic equipment, machinery, clothing and textiles, metal products, milk, cattle, hay, apples

did you **Know?** *New York City is the largest city in the U.S. and was the nation's first capital. It was also the home of another major first in American history—the first pizza restaurant in the U.S. opened there in 1895.*

NORTH CAROLINA  (NC) Tar Heel State, Old North State

Raleigh ★

• Charlotte

POPULATION (2009): 9,380,884 (10th) **AREA:** 53,819 sq mi (28th) (139,391 sq km) 🌼Dogwood 🐦Cardinal 🌲Pine 🎵"The Old North State" **ENTERED UNION:** November 21, 1789 (12th) ⭐Raleigh **LARGEST CITIES (WITH POP.):** Charlotte, 687,456; Raleigh, 392,552; Greensboro, 250,642; Durham, 223,284; Winston-Salem, 217,600; Fayetteville 174,091

⚙clothing and textiles, tobacco and tobacco products, industrial machinery, electronic equipment, furniture, cotton, soybeans, peanuts

did you **Know?** *The Outer Banks, a line of offshore sandy islands, were full of pirates and smugglers in the early 1700s. The most notorious, Blackbeard, terrorized sailors along the coast before the crews of two British ships sent him to his watery grave there in 1718.*

NORTH DAKOTA (ND) Peace Garden State

★ Bismarck

POPULATION (2009): 646,844 (48th) **AREA:** 70,698 sq mi (19th) (183,109 sq km) 🌸Wild prairie rose 🐦Western meadowlark 🌲American elm 🎵"North Dakota Hymn" **ENTERED UNION:** November 2, 1889 (39th) ★Bismarck **LARGEST CITIES (WITH POP.):** Fargo, 93,531; Bismarck, 60,389; Grand Forks, 51,313; Minot, 35,419

⚙ wheat, barley, hay, sunflowers, sugar beets, cattle, sand and gravel, food products, farm equipment, high-tech electronics

 During their expedition, Lewis and Clark spent the winter of 1804–05 in North Dakota. They named their fort after the Mandan tribe that lived nearby. They met Sacagawea, who gave birth to her son at Fort Mandan.

OHIO (OH) Buckeye State

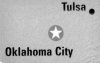
Cleveland
Columbus ★
Cincinnati

POPULATION (2009): 11,542,645 (7th) **AREA:** 44,825 sq mi (34th) (116,097 sq km) 🌸Scarlet carnation 🐦Cardinal 🌲Buckeye 🎵"Beautiful Ohio" **ENTERED UNION:** March 1, 1803 (17th) ★Columbus **LARGEST CITIES (WITH POP.):** Columbus, 754,885; Cleveland, 433,748; Cincinnati, 333,336; Toledo, 293,201; Akron, 207,510; Dayton, 154,200

⚙ metal and metal products, transportation equipment, industrial machinery, rubber and plastic products, electronic equipment, printing and publishing, chemicals, food products, corn, soybeans, livestock, milk

Seven presidents were born in Ohio, more than in any other state except Virginia. They are Ulysses S. Grant, Rutherford B. Hayes, James Garfield, Benjamin Harrison, William McKinley, William Howard Taft, and Warren Harding.

OKLAHOMA (OK) Sooner State

Tulsa
★
Oklahoma City

POPULATION (2009): 3,687,050 (28th) **AREA:** 69,899 sq mi (20th) (181,038 sq km) 🌸Mistletoe 🐦Scissor-tailed flycatcher 🌲Redbud 🎵"Oklahoma!" **ENTERED UNION:** November 16, 1907 (46th) ★Oklahoma City **LARGEST CITIES (WITH POP.):** Oklahoma City, 551,789; Tulsa, 385,635; Norman, 106,957; Broken Arrow, 92,931; Lawton, 90,091

⚙ natural gas, oil, cattle, nonelectrical machinery, transportation equipment, metal products, wheat, hay

The American Indian nations called the Five Civilized Tribes (Cherokee, Chickasaw, Choctaw, Creek, and Seminole) were resettled from the Southeast to Oklahoma by the federal government between 1817 and 1842.

Key: Flower Bird Tree Song Capital 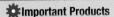Important Products

OREGON

 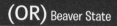

(OR) Beaver State

• Portland

⭐ Salem

POPULATION (2009): 3,825,657 (27th) **AREA:** 98,379 sq mi (9th) (254,801 sq km) 🌼Oregon grape 🐦Western meadowlark 🌲Douglas fir 🎵"Oregon, My Oregon" **ENTERED UNION:** February 14, 1859 (33rd) ⭐Salem **LARGEST CITIES (WITH POP.):** Portland, 557,706; Salem, 153,435; Eugene, 150,104; Gresham, 101,221

⚙ lumber and wood products, electronics and semiconductors, food products, paper, cattle, hay, vegetables, Christmas trees

did you Know?
Crater Lake, in southern Oregon, is almost 2,000 feet deep. It is the deepest lake in the United States and seventh deepest in the world. The lake occupies the crater of a huge volcano that erupted thousands of years ago.

PENNSYLVANIA

(PA) Keystone State

Harrisburg
⭐

• Pittsburgh

Philadelphia •

POPULATION (2009): 12,604,767 (6th) **AREA:** 46,055 sq mi (33rd) (119,281 sq km) 🌼Mountain laurel 🐦Ruffed grouse 🌲Hemlock 🎵"Pennsylvania" **ENTERED UNION:** December 12, 1787 (2nd) ⭐Harrisburg **LARGEST CITIES (WITH POP.):** Philadelphia, 1,447,395; Pittsburgh, 310,037; Allentown, 107,250; Erie, 103,817

⚙ iron and steel, coal, industrial machinery, printing and publishing, food products, electronic equipment, transportation equipment, stone, clay and glass products

did you Know?
Philadelphia was the capital of Pennsylvania for many years in the 1600s and 1700s and capital of the U.S. from 1790 to 1800. Independence Hall, perhaps the city's most famous building, is where the Declaration of Independence was approved in 1776 and the U.S. Constitution was written in 1787.

RHODE ISLAND

(RI) Little Rhody, Ocean State

Providence
⭐

POPULATION (2009): 1,053,209 (43rd) **AREA:** 1,545 sq mi (50th) (4,001 sq km) 🌼Violet 🐦Rhode Island red 🌲Red maple 🎵"Rhode Island" **ENTERED UNION:** May 29, 1790 (13th) ⭐Providence **LARGEST CITIES (WITH POP.):** Providence, 171,557; Warwick, 84,483; Cranston, 79,980; Pawtucket, 71,765

⚙ costume jewelry, toys, textiles, machinery, electronic equipment, fish

did you Know?
Newport is known for its huge mansions, many built during the "Gilded Age" of the late 19th century. Years before then, the city was a major whaling port—and even earlier, a haven for pirates.

SOUTH CAROLINA

(SC) Palmetto State

Columbia

POPULATION (2009): 4,561,242 (24th) **AREA:** 32,021 sq mi (40th) (82,934 sq km) 🌼Yellow jessamine 🐦Carolina wren 🌲Palmetto 🎵"Carolina" **ENTERED UNION:** May 23, 1788 (8th) ⭐Columbia **LARGEST CITIES (WITH POP.):** Columbia, 127,029; Charleston, 111,978; North Charleston, 94,407; Rock Hill, 67,339

⚙ clothing and textiles, chemicals, industrial machinery, metal products, livestock, tobacco, Portland cement

Gullahs are descendants of West African slaves who have chosen to live a traditional African life along the coast and islands of South Carolina, Georgia, and Florida. They have their own language, arts, crafts, religious beliefs, and foods that have been passed down for generations.

SOUTH DAKOTA

(SD) Mt. Rushmore State, Coyote State

POPULATION (2009): 812,383 (46th) **AREA:** 77,116 sq mi (17th) (199,730 sq km) 🌼Pasqueflower 🐦Chinese ring-necked pheasant 🌲Black Hills spruce 🎵"Hail, South Dakota" **ENTERED UNION:** November 2, 1889 (40th) ⭐Pierre **LARGEST CITIES (WITH POP.):** Sioux Falls, 154,997; Rapid City, 65,491; Aberdeen, 24,460

⭐ Pierre

⚙ food and food products, machinery, electric and electronic equipment, corn, soybeans

The four presidents whose faces are carved on South Dakota's famous Mount Rushmore are George Washington, Thomas Jefferson, Abraham Lincoln, and Theodore Roosevelt. Each sculpture is 50 to 70 feet high.

TENNESSEE

(TN) Volunteer State

POPULATION (2009): 6,296,254 (17th) **AREA:** 42,144 sq mi (36th) (109,154 sq km) 🌼Iris 🐦Mockingbird 🌲Tulip poplar 🎵"My Homeland, Tennessee"; "When It's Iris Time in Tennessee"; "My Tennessee"; "Tennessee Waltz"; "Rocky Top" **ENTERED UNION:** June 1, 1796 (16th) ⭐Nashville **LARGEST CITIES (WITH POP.):** Memphis, 669,651; Nashville-Davidson, 626,144; Knoxville, 184,802; Chattanooga, 170,880

⭐ Nashville
● Memphis

⚙ chemicals, machinery, vehicles, food products, metal products, publishing, electronic equipment, paper products, rubber and plastic products, tobacco

The Grand Ole Opry, the world's longest-running live radio program, was first broadcast from Nashville in 1925. It was originally called the WSM Barn Dance, but the name changed to the Grand Ole Opry in 1927.

Key: 🌼Flower 🐦Bird 🌲Tree 🎵Song ⭐Capital ⚙Important Products

TEXAS

(TX) Lone Star State

Dallas •

• El Paso

Austin Houston •

San Antonio

POPULATION (2009): 24,782,302 (2nd) **AREA:** 268,597 sq mi (2nd) (695,666 sq km) 🌼Bluebonnet 🐦Mockingbird 🌳Pecan 🎵"Texas, Our Texas" **ENTERED UNION:** December 29, 1845 (28th) ⭐Austin **LARGEST CITIES (WITH POP.):** Houston, 2,242,193; San Antonio, 1,351,305; Dallas, 1,279,910; Austin, 757,688; Fort Worth, 703,073; El Paso, 613,190; Arlington, 374,417; Corpus Christi, 286,462; Plano, 267,480

⚙ oil, natural gas, cattle, milk, eggs, transportation equipment, chemicals, clothing, industrial machinery, electrical and electronic equipment, cotton, grains

did you Know? *Texas has more farmland than any other state and produces more oil (excluding offshore oil) and natural gas than any other state. It leads the nation in wind-powered energy, too. Texas also uses more energy than any other state.*

UTAH

(UT) Beehive State

⭐

Salt Lake City

POPULATION (2009): 2,784,572 (34th) **AREA:** 84,897 sq mi (13th) (219,883 sq km) 🌼Sego lily 🐦Seagull 🌳Blue spruce 🎵"Utah, This is the Place" **ENTERED UNION:** January 4, 1896 (45th) ⭐Salt Lake City **LARGEST CITIES (WITH POP.):** Salt Lake City, 181,698; West Valley City, 123,447; Provo, 118,581; West Jordan, 104,447

⚙ transportation equipment, medical instruments, electronic parts, food products, steel, copper, cattle, corn, hay, wheat, barley

did you Know? *The Great Salt Lake, in northwest Utah, is the biggest lake in the U.S. outside of the Great Lakes, and is the world's saltiest lake except for the Dead Sea. It holds 6 billion tons of dissolved salts, mostly common table salt.*

VERMONT

(VT) Green Mountain State

Montpelier

⭐

POPULATION (2009): 621,760 (49th) **AREA:** 9,616 sq mi (45th) (24,906 sq km) 🌼Red clover 🐦Hermit thrush 🌳Sugar maple 🎵"These Green Mountains" **ENTERED UNION:** March 4, 1791 (14th) ⭐Montpelier **LARGEST CITIES (WITH POP.):** Burlington, 38,897; South Burlington, 17,574; Rutland, 16,742

⚙ machine tools, furniture, scales, books, computer parts, foods, dairy products, apples, maple syrup

did you Know? *The Green Mountain Boys, who famously fought against the British during the American Revolution, were originally formed in 1770 to fight off New York settlers. When the revolution broke out, Vermonters and New Yorkers set aside their differences and united against the British.*

VIRGINIA

(VA) Old Dominion

POPULATION (2009): 7,882,590 (12th) **AREA:** 42,775 sq mi (35th) (110,787 sq km) Dogwood Cardinal Dogwood "Carry Me Back to Old Virginia" **ENTERED UNION:** June 25, 1788 (10th) Richmond **LARGEST CITIES (WITH POP.):** Virginia Beach, 433,746; Norfolk, 234,220; Chesapeake, 220,110; Richmond, 202,002; Newport News, 179,614

Alexandria

Richmond ☆
Virginia Beach

transportation equipment, textiles, chemicals, printing, machinery, electronic equipment, food products, coal, livestock, tobacco, wood products, furniture

did you Know? *Eight presidents were born in Virginia, more than in any other state. They are George Washington, Thomas Jefferson, James Madison, James Monroe, William Henry Harrison, John Tyler, Zachary Taylor, and Woodrow Wilson.*

WASHINGTON

(WA) Evergreen State

POPULATION (2009): 6,664,195 (13th)
AREA: 71,298 sq mi (18th) (184,661 sq km) Western rhododendron Willow goldfinch Western hemlock "Washington, My Home" **ENTERED UNION:** November 11, 1889 (42nd) Olympia **LARGEST CITIES (WITH POP.):** Seattle, 598,541; Spokane, 202,319; Tacoma, 197,181; Vancouver, 163,186; Bellevue, 123,771

Seattle
☆ **Olympia**

aircraft, lumber, pulp and paper, machinery, electronics, computer software, aluminum, processed fruits and vegetables

did you Know? *The Seattle suburb of Redmond is the home of the computer software giant Microsoft, founded in the 1970s by Seattle native Bill Gates. Seattle also helped give birth to grunge music, Starbucks coffee, and Amazon.com.*

WEST VIRGINIA

(WV) Mountain State

POPULATION (2009): 1,819,777 (37th) **AREA:** 24,230 sq mi (41st) (62,755 sq km) Big rhododendron Cardinal Sugar maple "The West Virginia Hills"; "This Is My West Virginia"; "West Virginia, My Home Sweet Home" **ENTERED UNION:** June 20, 1863 (35th) Charleston **LARGEST CITIES (WITH POP.):** Charleston, 50,302; Huntington, 49,185; Parkersburg, 31,611; Morgantown, 29,642; Wheeling, 28,913

☆ **Charleston**

coal, natural gas, fabricated metal products, chemicals, automobile parts, aluminum, steel, machinery, cattle, hay, apples, peaches, tobacco

did you Know? *When Virginia seceded from the Union in 1861 and joined the Confederacy, people in the northwestern counties got together and agreed to split off from the rest of Virginia. "West Virginia" was admitted to the Union in June 1863.*

Key: Flower Bird Tree Song Capital Important Products

WISCONSIN (WI) Badger State

POPULATION (2009): 5,654,774 (20th) **AREA:** 65,496 sq mi (23rd) (169,636 sq km) ✿Wood violet ♪Robin ♣Sugar maple ♫ "On, Wisconsin!" **ENTERED UNION:** May 29, 1848 (30th) ✪Madison
LARGEST CITIES (WITH POP.): Milwaukee, 604,477; Madison, 231,916; Green Bay, 101,025; Kenosha, 96,950; Racine, 82,196

✿ paper products, printing, milk, butter, cheese, foods, food products, motor vehicles and equipment, medical instruments and supplies, plastics, corn, hay, vegetables

Madison ✪
Milwaukee •

 Besides producing lots of milk and butter, Wisconsin leads the nation in the production of cheese. The nation's first kindergarten opened in Wisconsin in 1856.

WYOMING (WY) Cowboy State

POPULATION (2009): 544,270 (50th) **AREA:** 97,812 sq mi (10th) (253,334 sq km) ✿Indian paintbrush ♪Western meadowlark ♣Plains cottonwood ♫"Wyoming" **ENTERED UNION:** July 10, 1890 (44th) ✪Cheyenne **LARGEST CITIES (WITH POP.):** Cheyenne, 56,915; Casper, 54,047; Laramie, 27,664

✿ oil, natural gas, petroleum (oil) products, cattle, wheat, beans

Cheyenne
✪

 The burrowing Wyoming toad is found only in the Laramie Basin of southeast Wyoming, where it is nearly extinct, partly because of a fungus. Some Wyoming toads are reared in captivity and released into the wild.

COMMONWEALTH OF PUERTO RICO (PR)

San Juan ✪

HISTORY: Christopher Columbus landed in Puerto Rico in 1493. Puerto Rico was a Spanish colony for centuries, then was ceded (given) to the United States in 1898 after the Spanish-American War. In 1952, still associated with the United States, Puerto Rico became a commonwealth with its own constitution.
POPULATION (2009): 3,967,288 **AREA:** 5,325 sq mi (13,791 sq km) ✿Maga ♪Reinita ♣Ceiba **NATIONAL ANTHEM:** "La Borinqueña" ✪San Juan **LARGEST CITIES (WITH POP.; 2000 census):** San Juan, 421,958; Carolina, 168,164; Ponce, 155,038; Caguas, 88,680

✿ chemicals, food products, electronic equipment, clothing and textiles, industrial machinery, coffee, sugarcane, fruit, hogs

 The El Yunque National Forest, in the east, is the only tropical rain forest in the U.S. National Forest system. Only 44 square miles in area, it is home to many exotic plants and animals, including Puerto Rico's tiny coquí frogs and the rare Puerto Rican parrot.

Washington, D.C.

The Capital of the UNITED STATES

AREA: 68 sq mi (177 sq km) **POPULATION (2009):** 599,657
FLOWER: American beauty rose **BIRD:** Wood thrush
For more information, see: *www.dc.gov • www.washington.org*

HISTORY The District of Columbia, or Washington, D.C., became the capital of the United States in 1800, when the federal government moved there from Philadelphia. The city of Washington was designed and built to be the capital. It was named after George Washington. Many of its major sights are on the Mall, an open grassy area that runs from the Capitol to the Potomac River.

CAPITOL, which houses the U.S. Congress, is at the east end of the Mall on Capitol Hill. Its dome can be seen from far away.

JEFFERSON MEMORIAL, a circular marble building located near the Potomac River, is partly based on a design by Thomas Jefferson for the University of Virginia.

LIBRARY OF CONGRESS, research library for Congress and the largest library in the world, is on Independence Avenue across the street from the Capitol.

LINCOLN MEMORIAL, at the west end of the Mall, is built of white marble and styled like a Greek temple. Inside is a large, seated statue of Abraham Lincoln. His Gettysburg Address is carved on a nearby wall.

NATIONAL ARCHIVES, on Constitution Avenue, holds the Declaration of Independence, Constitution, and Bill of Rights.

NATIONAL WORLD WAR II MEMORIAL, located between the Lincoln Memorial and the Washington Monument at the Mall, honors the 16 million Americans who served during the war. ▼

SMITHSONIAN INSTITUTION has 18 museums (2 of them are in New York City), including the new National Museum of the American Indian, the National Air and Space Museum and the Museum of Natural History. The National Zoo is part of the Smithsonian.

U.S. HOLOCAUST MEMORIAL MUSEUM presents the history of the Nazis' murder of more than six million Jews and millions of other people from 1933 to 1945. The exhibit *Daniel's Story* tells the story of the Holocaust from a child's point of view.

VIETNAM VETERANS MEMORIAL, located near the Lincoln Memorial, includes a wall with all the names of those killed or missing in action during the conflict.

WASHINGTON MONUMENT is a white marble pillar, or obelisk, standing on the Mall and rising to more than 555 feet. From the top there are wonderful views of the city.

WHITE HOUSE, at 1600 Pennsylvania Avenue, has been the home of every U.S. president except George Washington.

WOMEN IN MILITARY SERVICE FOR AMERICA MEMORIAL, stands near the entrance to Arlington National Cemetery in Virginia. It honors the 2 million women who have served in the U.S. armed forces.

Volunteering

What is the Fishin' Mission? ⟫ page 311

Threats to the environment, poverty, natural disasters...sometimes the problems of the world seem so large that it's hard to imagine how we can help. But just one person really can make a difference. And people who help others also help themselves! Studies have shown that kids who volunteer perform better in school, feel happier, and feel better about themselves. Does this win-win situation have you ready to take action? Here's how to get started.

RESEARCH ▶ Pick an area that interests you, and research different ways you can help. The web site ***www.dosomething.org*** features a great search tool to get you started. First pick a cause—such as the environment, animal welfare, or disaster relief. Then decide whom you want to work with (alone? with your family? with friends?), where you want to help, and how much time you have to volunteer. The search generates a list of action guides that fit your needs.

ASK AROUND ▶ There's a good chance that different groups in your community already have projects underway—and would welcome another helping hand. Many people volunteer through their **religious community**. Churches often organize soup kitchens, even homeless shelters. Many **schools** also offer opportunities for their students to volunteer. Schools may sponsor plant sales to raise money for a good cause or ask students to visit elderly people in a nursing home. The Boy Scouts, Girl Scouts, and other **community groups** participate in volunteering projects such as cleaning up a local park or organizing a car wash to raise money for a cause.

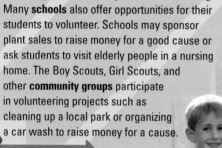

MAKE A CHOICE ▶ Do you want to provide direct services for your cause or raise money? For example, you can plan a park cleanup day or you can hold a bake sale to raise money to buy an acre of rain forest. You can collect books and read to kids in a children's hospital or hold a fund-raising walk to buy netting to protect children in Africa from malaria.

Volunteering All-Stars

Step by Step

More than 1 million Americans under the age of 18 are homeless, according to the National Law Center on Homelessness and Poverty. Zach Bonner from Valrico, Florida, is trying to help them—one step at a time. In 2005, at age 7, he started the Little Red Wagon Foundation to help underprivileged kids. At age 11, Zach finished a long-term walking project he called My House to the White House. His goal was to raise awareness about homelessness and to raise money for his cause. After walking a total of about 1,200 miles, he arrived in Washington, D.C., in July 2009. Zach didn't rest for long. He began March Across America on December 25, 2009. He plans to walk from Tampa, Florida, to Los Angeles to help homeless kids.

Bear Facts

Faith Killian-Fassnacht of Lafayette, Indiana, is sending "bear hugs" to soldiers and children in Iraq and Afghanistan. She began sending teddy bears to troops overseas in fall 2007. Faith also set up "bear drop" sites around her community to collect donated bears, and she started raising money for shipping. She gets other kids involved by holding "milk and cookie nights" where young people get together to write thank-you cards to troops. "This is a very dangerous job for our soldiers, and I want them to know they're not forgotten," Faith says.

Fishin' Mission

Michael Lipinski is getting kids at Children's Hospital of Michigan hooked on his favorite sport, fishing. In 2007, he held a one-day seminar at the hospital to teach children with brain injuries how to fish. The following year, he asked guests at his 10th birthday party to bring fishing gear instead of gifts. Fishing vendors and clubs also donated equipment. Michael wanted to expand the program, called Fishin' Mission, to let the patients test their skills at a local pond and feel the joy of actually catching a fish. "The joy and excitement on the kids' faces when they caught a fish was priceless!" he says.

AND THE WINNER IS...

Are you or is someone you know a volunteer all-star? The Prudential Spirit of Community Awards honor young people for outstanding volunteer community service. To find out more, visit *http://spirit.prudential.com*

Weather

What is a moonbow? → page 312

How to Read a Weather Map

Meteorologists around the world basically use the same set of symbols to show weather conditions. This allows them to quickly and easily communicate with one another. The symbols in a newspaper or TV weather map might vary somewhat from the ones shown below.

By examining this map, meteorologists can predict what the weather might be like in the future. They are able to do this because they know how the weather usually changes. For example, dry, calm weather typically occurs in high-pressure areas while precipitation is seen in low-pressure areas. Storms usually come before a cold front. As a cold front passes through an area, its temperature drops. Light rain might herald a warm front. As a warm front moves through an area, it gets warmer.

Because so many things—big and small—can influence the weather, only forecasts of up to five days tend to be accurate.

Selected Weather Symbols		
Sky Cover	**Fronts**	**Weather**
◯ Clear	▲▲▲ Cold front	▪ Rain = Fog
◐ Scattered	●●● Warm front	✳ Snow ∞ Haze
● Overcast	▲●▲● Stationary front	◸ Thunderstorm
Wind: ◎ Calm	—— 1-2 knots (1-2 mph)	↖ 3-7 knots (3-8 mph)
L Low Pressure Center		**H** High Pressure Center

WILD WEATHER FACTS

• A lightning bolt can be as hot as 55,000 degrees Fahrenheit. That's about five times hotter than the surface of the sun!

• The largest hailstone known to have fallen in the United States was found in Aurora, Nebraska, on June 22, 2003. The chunk of ice was about seven inches wide, almost as big as a soccer ball.

• When is a snowstorm considered a blizzard? It must have fierce winds of 35 miles per hour or higher and enough falling or blowing snow to reduce visibility below a quarter-mile for at least three hours.

did you know? *A **moonbow** is a rainbow that appears at night. Though rare, it occurs when falling raindrops are lit by moonlight rather than sunlight. Moonbows are typically faint because there is a smaller amount of light in moonlight than in sunlight.*

RECORD TEMPERATURES BY STATE
(Through May 2010)

STATE	Lowest °F	Latest date	Highest °F	Latest date
Alabama	−27	Jan. 30, 1966	112	Sept. 5, 1925
Alaska	−80	Jan. 23, 1971	100	June 27, 1915
Arizona	−40	Jan. 7, 1971	128	July 5, 2007
Arkansas	−29	Feb. 13, 1905	120	Aug. 10, 1936
California	−45	Jan. 20, 1937	134	July 10, 1913
Colorado	−61	Feb. 1, 1985	118	July 11, 1888
Connecticut	−32	Jan. 22, 1961	106	July 15, 1995
Delaware	−17	Jan. 17, 1893	110	July 21, 1930
Florida	−2	Feb. 13, 1899	109	June 29, 1931
Georgia	−17	Jan. 27, 1940	112	Aug. 20, 1983
Hawaii	12	May 17, 1979	100	Apr. 27, 1931
Idaho	−60	Jan. 18, 1943	118	July 28, 1934
Illinois	−36	Jan. 5, 1999	117	July 14, 1954
Indiana	−36	Jan. 19, 1994	116	July 14, 1936
Iowa	−47	Feb. 3, 1996	118	July 20, 1934
Kansas	−40	Feb. 13, 1905	121	July 24, 1936
Kentucky	−37	Jan. 19, 1994	114	July 28, 1930
Louisiana	−16	Feb. 13, 1899	114	Aug. 10, 1936
Maine	−50	Jan. 16, 2009	105	July 10, 1911
Maryland	−40	Jan. 13, 1912	109	July 10, 1936
Massachusetts	−35	Jan. 12, 1981	107	Aug. 2, 1975
Michigan	−51	Feb. 9, 1934	112	July 13, 1936
Minnesota	−60	Feb. 2, 1996	114	July 6, 1936
Mississippi	−19	Jan. 30, 1966	115	July 29, 1930
Missouri	−40	Feb. 13, 1905	118	July 14, 1954
Montana	−70	Jan. 20, 1954	117	July 5, 1937
Nebraska	−47	Dec. 22, 1989	118	July 24, 1936
Nevada	−50	Jan. 8, 1937	125	June 29, 1994
New Hampshire	−47	Jan. 29, 1934	106	July 4, 1911
New Jersey	−34	Jan. 5, 1904	110	July 10, 1936
New Mexico	−50	Feb. 1, 1951	122	June 27, 1994
New York	−52	Feb. 18, 1979	108	July 22, 1926
North Carolina	−34	Jan. 21, 1985	110	Aug. 21, 1983
North Dakota	−60	Feb. 15, 1936	121	July 6, 1936
Ohio	−39	Feb. 10, 1899	113	July 21, 1934
Oklahoma	−27	Jan. 18, 1930	120	June 27, 1994
Oregon	−54	Feb. 10, 1933	119	Aug. 10, 1898
Pennsylvania	−42	Jan. 5, 1904	111	July 10, 1936
Rhode Island	−25	Feb. 5, 1996	104	Aug. 2, 1975
South Carolina	−19	Jan. 21, 1985	111	June 28, 1954
South Dakota	−58	Feb. 17, 1936	120	July 15, 2006
Tennessee	−32	Dec. 30, 1917	113	Aug. 9, 1930
Texas	−23	Feb. 8, 1933	120	June 28, 1994
Utah	−69	Feb. 1, 1985	117	July 5, 1985
Vermont	−50	Dec. 30, 1933	105	July 4, 1911
Virginia	−30	Jan. 22, 1985	110	July 15, 1954
Washington	−48	Dec. 30, 1968	118	Aug. 5, 1961
West Virginia	−37	Dec. 30, 1917	112	July 10, 1936
Wisconsin	−55	Feb. 4, 1996	114	July 13, 1936
Wyoming	−66	Feb. 9, 1933	115	Aug. 8, 1983

Record temperatures may have occurred on earlier dates. Dates listed here are for most recent occurrence of a record temperature.

Weights & Measures

What was the first definition of an inch? → page 314

Metrology isn't the study of weather. (That's meteorology.) It is the science of measurement. Almost everything you use (or eat or drink) is measured—either when it is made or when it's sold. Materials for buildings and parts for machines must be measured carefully so they will fit together. Clothes have sizes so you'll know which to wear. Many items sold in a supermarket are priced by weight or by volume.

EARLIEST MEASUREMENTS

The human body was the first "ruler." An "inch" was the width of a thumb; a "hand" was five fingers wide; a "foot" was—you guessed it—the length of a foot! A "cubit" ran from the elbow to the tip of the middle finger (about 20 inches), and a "yard" was roughly the length of a whole arm.

Later, measurements came from daily activities, like plowing a field. A "furlong" was the distance a pair of oxen could plow before stopping to rest (now we say it is about 220 yards). The trouble with these units is that they vary from person to person, place to place, and ox to ox.

MEASUREMENTS WE USE TODAY

The official system in the U.S. is the customary system (sometimes called the imperial or English system). Scientists and most other countries use the International System of Units (SI, or the metric system). The Weights and Measures Division of the U.S. National Institute of Standards and Technology (NIST) makes sure that a gallon of milk in California is the same as one in New York. When the NIST was founded in 1901, there were as many as eight different "standard" gallons in the U.S. and four different legal measures of a "foot" in Brooklyn, New York, alone.

ANCIENT MEASURE

1 foot =
length of a person's foot

1 yard =
from nose to fingertip

1 acre =
land a pair of oxen could plow in a day

MODERN MEASURE

| 12 inches | 3 feet or 36 inches | 4,840 square yards |

TAKING TEMPERATURES

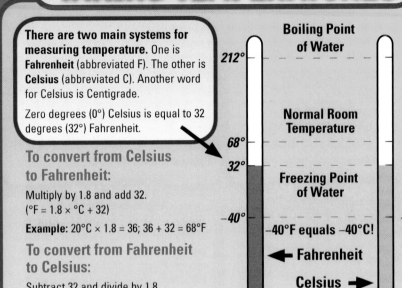

There are two main systems for measuring temperature. One is Fahrenheit (abbreviated F). The other is Celsius (abbreviated C). Another word for Celsius is Centigrade.

Zero degrees (0°) Celsius is equal to 32 degrees (32°) Fahrenheit.

To convert from Celsius to Fahrenheit:

Multiply by 1.8 and add 32. (°F = 1.8 × °C + 32)

Example: 20°C × 1.8 = 36; 36 + 32 = 68°F

To convert from Fahrenheit to Celsius:

Subtract 32 and divide by 1.8.

Example: 68°F − 32 = 36; 36 ÷ 1.8 = 20°C

Boiling Point of Water
212°   100°

Normal Room Temperature
68°   20°
32°   0°

Freezing Point of Water

−40°   −40°
−40°F equals −40°C!

← Fahrenheit

Celsius →

F   C

HOTTEST and COLDEST Places in the World

Continent	Highest Temperature	Lowest Temperature
AFRICA	El Azizia, Libya, 136°F (58°C)	Ifrane, Morocco, −11°F (−24°C)
ANTARCTICA	Vanda Station, 59°F (15°C)	Vostok, −129°F (−89°C)
ASIA	Tirat Tsvi, Israel, 129°F (54°C)	Verkhoyansk, Russia, and Oimekon, Russia, −90°F (−68°C)
AUSTRALIA	Cloncurry, Queensland, 128°F (53°C)	Charlotte Pass, New South Wales, −9°F (−23°C)
EUROPE	Seville, Spain, 122°F (50°C)	Ust'Shchugor, Russia, −67°F (−55°C)
NORTH AMERICA	Death Valley, California, 134°F (57°C)	Snag, Yukon Territory, Canada, −81°F (−63°C)
SOUTH AMERICA	Rivadavia, Argentina, 120°F (49°C)	Sarmiento, Argentina, −27°F (−33°C)

did you Know?

The place with the world's lowest average rainfall is Arica, Chile, which gets 0.03 inches (0.76 millimeters) of rain a year. The wettest spot on Earth is also in South America. On average, 524 inches (13 meters) of rain fall a year in Lloro, Colombia.

LENGTH

The basic unit of **length** in the U.S. system is the **inch**. Length, width, and thickness all use the inch or larger related units.

1 foot (ft) = 12 inches (in)

1 yard (yd) = 3 feet = 36 inches

1 rod (rd) = 5½ yards

1 furlong (fur) = 40 rods = 220 yards
= 660 feet

1 mile (mi) (also called statute mile) =
8 furlongs = 1,760 yards = 5,280 feet

1 nautical mile = 6,076 feet = 1.15 statute miles

1 league = 3 miles

AREA

Area measures a section of a two-dimensional surface like a floor or a piece of paper. Most area measurements are given in **square units**. Land is measured in **acres**.

1 square foot (sq ft) = 144 square inches
(sq in)

1 square yard (sq yd) = 9 square feet =
1,296 square inches

1 square rod (sq rd) = 30¼ square yards

1 acre = 160 square rods = 4,840 square yards
= 43,560 square feet

1 square mile (sq mi) = 640 acres

CAPACITY

Units of **capacity** measure how much of something will fit into a container. **Liquid measure** is used to measure liquids such as water or gasoline. **Dry measure** is used with large amounts of solid materials such as grain or fruit. Although both liquid and dry measures use the terms "pint" and "quart," they mean different amounts and should not be confused.

Dry Measure

1 quart (qt) = 2 pints (pt)
1 peck (pk) = 8 quarts
1 bushel (bu) = 4 pecks

Liquid Measure

1 gill = 4 fluid ounces (fl oz)
1 pint (pt) = 4 gills = 16 ounces (oz)
1 quart (qt) = 2 pints = 32 ounces
1 gallon (gal) = 4 quarts = 128 ounces

For measuring most U.S. liquids,
1 barrel (bbl) = 31½ gallons

For measuring oil, 1 barrel = 42 gallons

Cooking Measurements

The measurements in cooking are based on the **fluid ounce**.

1 teaspoon (tsp) = ⅙ fluid ounce (fl oz)
1 tablespoon (tbsp) = 3 teaspoons
= ½ fluid ounce
1 cup = 16 tablespoons = 8 fluid ounces
1 pint = 2 cups
1 quart (qt) = 2 pints (pt)
1 gallon (gal)= 4 quarts

VOLUME

The amount of space taken up by a three-dimensional object (or the amount of space available within an object) is measured in **volume**. Volume is usually expressed in **cubic units**. If you wanted to buy a room air conditioner, you would have to measure the room in cubic feet.

1 cubic foot (cu ft) = 12 inches x 12 inches
x 12 inches
= 1,728 cubic inches
(cu in)
1 cubic yard (cu yd) = 27 cubic feet

DEPTH

Some measurements of length measure ocean depth and distance.

1 fathom = 6 feet (ft)
1 cable = 120 fathoms = 720 feet

WEIGHT

Although 1 cubic foot of popcorn and 1 cubic foot of rock take up the same amount of space, lifting them isn't the same. We measure heaviness as **weight**. Most objects are measured in **avoirdupois weight** (pronounced a-ver-de-POIZ):

1 dram (dr) = 27.344 grains (gr)
1 ounce (oz) = 16 drams
= 437.5 grains
1 pound (lb) = 16 ounces
1 hundredweight (cwt) = 100 pounds
1 (short) ton = 2,000 pounds

THE **METRIC** SYSTEM

The metric system was created in France in 1795. Standardized in 1960 and given the name International System of Units, it is now used in most countries and in scientific works. The system is based on 10, like the decimal counting system. The basic unit for length is the **meter**. The **liter** is a basic unit of volume or capacity, and the **gram** is a basic unit of mass. Related units are made by adding a prefix to the basic unit. The prefixes and their meanings are:

milli-	=	$\frac{1}{1,000}$
centi-	=	$\frac{1}{100}$
deci-	=	$\frac{1}{10}$
deka-	=	**10**
hecto-	=	**100**
kilo-	=	**1,000**

For Example

millimeter (mm) = $\frac{1}{1,000}$ of a meter

kilometer (km) = 1,000 meters

milligram (mg) = $\frac{1}{1,000}$ of a gram

kilogram (kg) = 1,000 grams

To get a rough idea of measurements in the metric system, it helps to know that a **liter** is a little more than a quart. A **meter** is a little more than a yard. A **kilogram** is a little more than 2 pounds. And a **kilometer** is just over half a mile.

HOMEWORK TIP

Converting Measurements

If you have:	Multiply by:	To get:	If you have:	Multiply by:	To get:
inches	2.54	centimeters	centimeters	0.3937	inches
inches	0.0254	meters	centimeters	0.0328	feet
feet	30.48	centimeters	meters	39.3701	inches
feet	0.3048	meters	meters	3.2808	feet
yards	0.9144	meters	meters	1.0936	yards
miles	1.6093	kilometers	kilometers	0.621	miles
square inches	6.4516	square centimeters	square centimeters	0.155	square inches
square feet	0.0929	square meters	square meters	10.7639	square feet
square yards	0.8361	square meters	square meters	1.196	square yards
acres	0.4047	hectares	hectares	2.471	acres
cubic inches	16.3871	cubic centimeters	cubic centimeters	0.061	cubic inches
cubic feet	0.0283	cubic meters	cubic meters	35.3147	cubic feet
cubic yards	0.7646	cubic meters	cubic meters	1.308	cubic yards
quarts (liquid)	0.9464	liters	liters	1.0567	quarts (liquid)
ounces	28.3495	grams	grams	0.0353	ounces
pounds	0.4536	kilograms	kilograms	2.2046	pounds

World History

When was apartheid abolished in South Africa? → page 321

Each of the five sections in this chapter tells the history of a major region of the world: the Middle East, Africa, Asia, Europe, or the Americas. Major events from ancient times to the present are described under the headings for each region.

THE ANCIENT MIDDLE EAST

◄ *hieroglyphics*

▲ *The pyramids at Giza*

4000–3000 B.C. The world's first cities are built by the Sumerian peoples in Mesopotamia, now southern Iraq. Sumerians develop a kind of writing called **cuneiform**. Egyptians develop a kind of writing called **hieroglyphics**.

2700 B.C. Egyptians begin building the great pyramids in the desert.

1792 B.C. Some of the first written laws are created in Babylonia. They are called the **Code of Hammurabi**.

1200 B.C. Hebrew people settle in Canaan in Palestine after escaping from slavery in Egypt. They are led by the prophet Moses.

1000 B.C. King David unites the Hebrews.

ANCIENT PALESTINE Palestine is invaded by many different peoples after 1000 B.C., including the Babylonians, Egyptians, Persians, and Romans.

336 B.C. Alexander the Great, King of Macedonia, builds an empire from Egypt to India. ▶

ISLAM: A RELIGION GROWS IN THE MIDDLE EAST
A.D. 610–632 Around 610, the prophet Muhammad starts to proclaim and teach Islam. This religion spreads from Arabia to all the neighboring regions in the Middle East and North Africa. Its followers are called Muslims.

THE KORAN
The holy book of Islam is the Koran. It was related by Muhammad beginning in 611.

The Koran

THE SPREAD OF ISLAM
The Arab armies that move across North Africa bring great change:
- The people who live there are converted to Islam.
- The Arabic language replaces many local languages as an official language. North Africa is still an Arabic-speaking region today, and Islam is the major faith.

63 B.C. Romans conquer Palestine and make it part of their empire.

Around 4 B.C. Jesus Christ, the founder of the Christian religion, is born in Bethlehem. He is crucified about A.D. 29.

A.D. 632 Muhammad dies. By now, Islam is accepted in Arabia as a religion.

641 Arab Muslims conquer the Persians.

Late 600s Islam begins to spread to the west into Africa and Spain.

THE MIDDLE EAST

THE UMAYYAD AND ABBASID DYNASTIES The Umayyads (661–750) and the Abbasids (750–1256) are the first two Muslim-led dynasties. Both empires stretch across northern Africa and the Middle East into Asia.

711–732 Umayyads invade Europe but are defeated by Frankish leader Charles Martel in France. This defeat halts the spread of Islam into Western Europe.

1071 Muslim Turks conquer Jerusalem.

1095–1291 Europeans try to take back Jerusalem and other parts of the Middle East for Christians during the Crusades.

1300–1900s The Ottoman Turks, who are Muslims, create a huge empire, covering the Middle East, North Africa, and part of Eastern Europe. European countries take over portions of it beginning in the 1800s.

1914–1918 World War I begins in 1914. Most of the Middle East falls under British or French control.

1921 Two new Arab kingdoms are created: Transjordan and Iraq. The French take control of Syria and Lebanon.

1922 Egypt becomes independent from Great Britain.

JEWS MIGRATE TO PALESTINE Jews begin migrating to Palestine in the 1880s. In 1945, after World War II, many Jews who survived the Holocaust migrate to Palestine.

1948 The state of Israel is created.

THE ARAB-ISRAELI WARS Arab countries near Israel (Egypt, Iraq, Jordan, Lebanon, and Syria) attack the new country in 1948 but fail to destroy it. Israel and its neighbors fight wars again in 1956, 1967, and 1973. Israel wins each war. In the 1967 war, Israel captures the Sinai Peninsula and Gaza from Egypt, the Golan Heights from Syria, and the West Bank from Jordan.

▲ *Anwar al-Sadat, Jimmy Carter, Menachem Begin celebrate signing of peace treaty.*

1979 Egypt and Israel sign a peace treaty. Israel returns the Sinai to Egypt.

THE MIDDLE EAST AND OIL About 30% of the oil the world uses to power cars, heat homes, make electricity, and run machines comes from the Middle East. Many countries rely on oil imports from the region, which has more than half the world's crude oil reserves.

The 1990s and 2000s

• In 1991, the U.S. and its allies go to war with Iraq after Iraq invades Kuwait. Iraq is defeated but is accused of violating the peace treaty. In 2003, the U.S. and its allies invade Iraq and remove the regime of dictator Saddam Hussein. Iraqis hold elections in 2005 and again in March 2010. U.S. troop withdrawal begins in 2009.

• The Palestinian Authority is created in the mid-1990s to provide some self-rule for Palestinians in the West Bank and Gaza. In 2005, Israel pulls out from Gaza. Palestinian legislative elections in 2006 in the West Bank and Gaza are won by Hamas, an organization that has historically been dedicated to eliminating the state of Israel. In 2007, Hamas takes full control of Gaza.

Dome of the Rock and the Western Wall, Jerusalem ▶

ANCIENT AFRICA

▲ Camel train moving across the Sahara

ANCIENT AFRICA In ancient times, northern Africa was dominated by the Egyptians, Greeks, and Romans. However, we know very little about the lives of ancient Africans south of the Sahara Desert. They did not have written languages. What we learn about them comes from weapons, tools, and other items from their civilization.

2000 B.C. The Nubian Kingdom of Kush, rich with gold, ivory, and jewels, arises south of Egypt. It is a major center of art, learning, and trade until around A.D. 350.

1000 B.C. Bantu-speaking people around Cameroon begin an 1,800-year expansion into much of eastern and southern Africa.

500 B.C. Carthage, an empire centered in Tunisia, becomes rich and powerful through trading. Its ports span the African coast of the Mediterranean. Rome defeats Carthage and ▼Hannibal, its most famous leader, during the second Punic War (218–201 B.C.).

• The Nok in Nigeria are the earliest users of iron for tools and weapons south of the Sahara Desert. They are also known for their terracotta sculptures.

• The Christian Kingdom of Aksum in northern Ethiopia becomes a wealthy trading center on the Red Sea for treasures like ivory. It makes its own coins and monuments, many of which survive today.

By A.D. 700 Ghana, the first known empire south of the Sahara Desert, takes power through trade around the upper Senegal and Niger Rivers. Its Mande people control the trade in gold from nearby mines to Arabs in the north.

By 900 Arab Muslim merchants bring Islam to the Bantu speakers along the east coast of Africa, creating the Swahili language and culture. Traders in Kenya and Tanzania export ivory, slaves, perfumes, and gold to Asia.

1054–1145 Islamic Berbers unite into the Almoravid Kingdom centered at Marrakech, Morocco. They spread into Ghana and southern Spain.

1230–1400s A Mande prince named Sundiata (the "Lion King") forms the Mali Kingdom where Ghana once stood. Timbuktu becomes its main city.

TIMBUKTU Located on the trade routes between North Africa and West Africa, Timbuktu was one of the wealthiest cities in Africa in the 1300s, as well as a center for scholarship. Gold, ivory, cloth, salt, and slaves were all traded in Timbuktu.

1250–1400s Great Zimbabwe becomes the largest settlement (12,000–20,000 Bantu-speaking people) in southern Africa.

1464–1591 As Mali loses power, Songhai rises to become the third and final great empire of western Africa.

1481 Portugal sets up the first permanent European trading post south of the Sahara Desert at Elmina, Ghana. Slaves, in addition to gold and ivory, are soon exported.

1483–1665 Kongo, the most powerful kingdom on central Africa's west coast, provides thousands of slaves each year for Portugal. Portugal's colony Angola overtakes the Kongo in 1665.

AFRICA

1650–1810 Slave trading peaks across the "Slave Coast" from eastern Ghana to western Nigeria as competing African states sell tens of thousands of captured foes each year to competing European traders.

THE AFRICAN SLAVE TRADE

African slaves are taken to the Caribbean to harvest sugar on European plantations. Later, slaves are taken to South America and the United States. The ships from Africa are overcrowded and diseased. About 20% of the slaves die during the long journey.

1652 The Dutch East India Company sets up a supply camp in southern Africa at the Cape of Good Hope (later Cape Town). Dutch settlers and French Protestants called Huguenots establish Cape Colony. Their descendants are known as the Boers or Afrikaners and develop a distinct language and culture.

1792 Freed slaves, mostly from Britain and the Americas, found Freetown in Sierra Leone.

1803 Denmark is the first European country to ban slave trading. Britain follows in 1807, the U.S. in 1808. Most European nations ban the trade by 1820, but illegal trading continues for decades.

1814 Britain purchases the Dutch South African colony at Cape Town. British colonists arrive after 1820.

1835–43 The "Great Trek" (march) of the Boers away from British Cape Town takes place.

1884–85 European nations meet in Berlin and agree to divide control of Africa. No African states are invited to the agreements. The "Scramble for Africa" lasts until World War I.

1899–1902 Great Britain and the Boers fight in South Africa in the Boer War. The Boers accept British rule but are allowed a role in government.

1948 The white Afrikaner-dominated South African government creates the policy of apartheid ("apartness"), the total separation of races. Blacks are banned from many public places. Apartheid sparks protests, many of which end in bloodshed.

1957 Ghana gains independence from Britain, becoming the first territory in Africa below the Sahara to regain freedom from European rule. Over the next 20 years, the rest of Africa gains independence.

1990–94 South Africa abolishes its policy of apartheid. In 1994, Nelson Mandela becomes South Africa's first black president. ▶

1994 Militias made up of members of Rwanda's Hutu majority launch a genocide against the country's Tutsi minority, killing an estimated 800,000 people in only 100 days. The killing stops when Tutsi from other countries invade Rwanda and bring the massacre to a halt.

1998–2004 Fighting in the Democratic Republic of the Congo involves 9 nations. About 4 million die, mostly from starvation and disease. While the war is officially over by 2003, fighting continues.

▼ **2006** Ellen Johnson-Sirleaf becomes president of Liberia, and Africa's first elected female leader.

2009 Conflict that began in 2003 continues in the Darfur region of Sudan, although there is some evidence that a truce is holding.

A savanna in Kenya

ANCIENT ASIA

▲ *The Great Wall*

3500 B.C. People settle in the Indus River Valley of India and Pakistan and the Yellow River Valley of China.

2500 B.C. Cities of Mohenjo-Daro and Harappa in Pakistan become centers of trade and farming.

Around 1523 B.C. Shang peoples in China build walled towns and use a kind of writing based on pictures. This writing develops into the writing Chinese people use today.

Around 1050 B.C. Chou peoples in China overthrow the Shang and control large territories.

563 B.C. Siddhartha Gautama is born in India. He becomes known as the Buddha—the "Enlightened One"— and is the founder of the Buddhist religion (Buddhism). ▶

551 B.C. The Chinese philosopher Confucius is born. His teachings—especially rules about how people should treat each other—spread throughout China and are still followed today. ▼

320–232 B.C.
• Northern India is united under the emperor Chandragupta Maurya.
• Asoka, emperor of India, sends Buddhist missionaries throughout southern Asia to spread the Buddhist religion.

221 B.C. The Chinese begin building the Great Wall. Its main section is more than 2,000 miles long and is meant to keep invading peoples out.

202 B.C. The Han people of China win control of all of China.

A.D. 320 The Gupta Empire controls northern India. The Guptas, who are Hindus, drive the Buddhist religion out of India. They are well known for their many advances in mathematics and medicine.

618 The Tang dynasty begins in China. The Tang dynasty is well known for music, poetry, and painting. They export silk and porcelains as far away as Africa.

THE SILK ROAD Around 100 B.C., only the Chinese know how to make silk. To get this light, comfortable material, Europeans send fortunes in glass, gold, jade, and other items to China. The exchanges between Europeans and Chinese create one of the greatest trading routes in history—the Silk Road. Chinese inventions such as paper and gunpowder are also spread via the Silk Road. Europeans find out how to make silk around A.D. 500, but trade continues until about 1400.

960 The Northern Sung dynasty in China makes advances in banking and paper money. China's population of 50 million doubles over 200 years, thanks to improved ways of farming that lead to greater food production.

ASIA

1000 The Samurai, a warrior people, become powerful in Japan. They live by a code of honor known as *Bushido*.

1180 The Khmer Empire in Cambodia becomes widely known for its beautiful temples.

1206 The Mongol leader Genghis Khan creates an empire that stretches from China to India, Russia, and Eastern Europe. ▶

1264 Kublai Khan, grandson of Genghis Khan, rules China as emperor from his new capital at Beijing.

1368 The Ming dynasty comes to power in China. The Ming drive the Mongols out of the country.

1526 The Mughal Empire in India begins under Babur. The Mughals are Muslims who invade and conquer India.

1644 The Ming dynasty in China is overthrown by the Manchu peoples.

1839 The Opium War takes place in China between the Chinese and the British. The British and other Western powers want to control trade in Asia. The Chinese want the British to stop selling opium to the Chinese. Britain wins the war in 1842.

1858 The French begin to take control of Indochina (Southeast Asia).

1868 In Japan, Emperor Meiji comes to power. Western ideas begin to influence the Japanese.

THE JAPANESE IN ASIA Japan becomes a powerful country during the early 20th century. In the 1930s, Japan begins to invade some of its neighbors. In 1941, the United States and Japan go to war after Japan attacks the U.S. Navy base at Pearl Harbor, Hawaii.

◀ *Statues from Angkor Wat temple, Cambodia*

1945 Japan is defeated in World War II after the U.S. drops atomic bombs on the Japanese cities of Hiroshima and Nagasaki.

1947 India and Pakistan become independent from Great Britain.

1949 China comes under the rule of the Communists led by Mao Zedong. The Communist government abolishes private property and takes over all businesses. ▶

1950–1953 **THE KOREAN WAR** North Korea, a Communist country, invades South Korea. The U.S. and other nations join to fight the invasion. China joins North Korea. The fighting ends in 1953. Neither side wins.

1954–1975 **THE VIETNAM WAR** The French are defeated in Indochina in 1954 by Vietnamese nationalists. The U.S. sends troops in 1965 to fight on the side of South Vietnam against the Communists in the North. The U.S. withdraws in 1973. In 1975, South Vietnam is taken over by North Vietnam.

1989 Chinese students protest for democracy, but the protests are crushed by the army in Beijing's Tiananmen Square.

The 2000s Britain returns Hong Kong to China. China builds its economy into one of the strongest in the world but does not allow democracy.

North Korea admits it has been developing nuclear weapons, and Iran is believed to be developing them.

A powerful earthquake in the Indian Ocean in December 2004 sets off huge waves (tsunamis) that kill more than 225,000 people in Indonesia, Sri Lanka, and other countries.

In August 2008, for the first time, China hosts the Summer Olympic Games in Beijing.

U.S.-led military action overthrows the Taliban regime in Afghanistan (2001) and seeks to root out terrorists there. In 2009, the United States sends additional troops to Afghanistan to fight the Taliban, which had regained strength. After a December 2009 presidential election marred by charges of fraud, President Hamid Karzai is declared the winner.

ANCIENT EUROPE

▲ Stonehenge

4000 B.C. People in Europe start building monuments out of large stones called megaliths, such as Stonehenge in England.

2500 B.C. –1200 B.C.
The Minoans and the Mycenaeans
- People on the island of Crete (Minoans) in the Mediterranean Sea build great palaces and become sailors and traders.
- People from Mycenae invade Crete and destroy the power of the Minoans.

THE TROJAN WAR
The Trojan War is a conflict between invading Greeks and the people of Troas (Troy) in Southwestern Turkey around 1200 B.C. Although little is known today about the real war, it has become a part of Greek mythology (pages 136–137). According to legend, a group of Greek soldiers hides inside a huge wooden horse. The horse is pulled into the city of Troy. Then the soldiers jump out of the horse and conquer Troy.

900–600 B.C. Celtic peoples in Northern Europe settle on farms and in villages and learn to mine for iron ore.

600 B.C. Etruscan peoples take over most of Italy. They build many cities and become traders.

SOME ACHIEVEMENTS OF THE GREEKS
The early Greeks are responsible for:
- the first governments that were elected by the people,
- great poets such as Homer, who composed the *Iliad* and the *Odyssey*,
- great thinkers such as Socrates, Plato, and Aristotle,
- great architecture, like the Parthenon and the Temple of Athena Nike on the Acropolis in Athens.

▲ Aristotle

431 B.C. The Peloponnesian Wars begin between the Greek cities of Athens and Sparta. The wars end in 404 B.C. when Sparta wins.

338 B.C. King Philip II of Macedonia in northern Greece conquers all of Greece.

336 B.C. Philip's son Alexander the Great becomes king. He makes an empire from the Mediterranean Sea to India. For the next 300 years, Greek culture dominates this vast area.

264 B.C. – A.D. 476 THE ROMAN EMPIRE

The city of Rome in Italy begins to expand and capture surrounding lands. The Romans gradually build a great empire and control all of the Mediterranean region. At its height, the Roman Empire includes Western Europe, Greece, Egypt, and much of the Middle East. It lasts until A.D. 476.

ROMAN ACHIEVEMENTS

- Roman law; many of our laws are based on Roman law.
- Great roads to connect their huge empire; the Appian Way, south of Rome, is a Roman road that is still in use today.
- Aqueducts to bring water to the people in large cities.
- Great sculpture; Roman statues can still be seen in Europe.
- Great architecture; the Colosseum, which still stands in Rome today, is an example.
- Great writers, such as the poet Virgil, who wrote the *Aeneid*.

49 B.C. A civil war breaks out that destroys Rome's republican form of government.

45 B.C. Julius Caesar becomes the sole ruler of Rome but is murdered one year later by rivals.

27 B.C. Octavian becomes the first emperor of Rome. He takes the name Augustus.

▲ *Julius Caesar*

THE CHRISTIAN FAITH Christians believe that Jesus Christ is the Son of God. The history and beliefs of Christianity are found in the New Testament of the Bible. Christianity spreads slowly throughout the Roman Empire. The Romans try to stop the new religion, and they persecute Christians, who are forced to hold their services in hiding. Some are crucified. Eventually, more and more Romans become Christian.

▼ *The Colosseum, Rome*

THE BYZANTINE EMPIRE, centered in modern-day Turkey, is the eastern half of the old Roman Empire. Byzantine rulers extend their power into western Europe; the Byzantine Emperor Justinian rules parts of Spain, North Africa, and Italy. Constantinople (now Istanbul, Turkey) becomes the capital of the Byzantine Empire in A.D. 330.

A.D. 313 The Roman Emperor Constantine gives full rights to Christians. He eventually becomes a Christian himself.

▲ *Constantine*

410 The Visigoths and other barbarian tribes from northern Europe invade the Roman Empire and begin to take over its lands.

476 The last Roman emperor, Romulus Augustus, is overthrown.

768 Charlemagne becomes king of the Franks in northern Europe. He rules a kingdom that includes parts of France, Germany, and northern Italy.

800 Feudalism becomes important in Europe. Feudalism means that poor farmers are allowed to farm a lord's land in return for certain services to the lord.

896 Magyar peoples found Hungary.

800s–900s Viking warriors and traders from Scandinavia begin to move into the British Isles, France, and parts of the Mediterranean.

989 The Russian state of Kiev becomes Christian.

EUROPE

◀ *Arc de Triomphe, Paris*

1066 William of Normandy, a Frenchman, successfully invades England and makes himself king. He is known as William the Conqueror.

1096–1291 THE CRUSADES Beginning in 1096, Christian leaders send a series of armies to try to capture Jerusalem from the Muslims. In the end, the Christians do not succeed. However, trade increases greatly between the Middle East and Europe.

1215 The Magna Carta is a document agreed to by King John of England and the English nobility. The English king agrees that he does not have absolute power and has to obey the laws of the land. The Magna Carta is an important step toward democracy.

1290 The Ottoman Empire begins. It is controlled by Turkish Muslims who conquer lands in the eastern Mediterranean and the Middle East.

▲ *King John*

1337 The Hundred Years' War begins in Europe between France and England. The war lasts until 1453 when France wins.

1348 The bubonic plague (Black Death) begins in Europe. As much as one-third of the whole population of Europe dies from this disease, caused by the bite of infected fleas.

1453 The Ottoman Turks capture the city of Constantinople and rename it Istanbul.

1517 THE REFORMATION The Protestant Reformation splits European Christians apart. It starts when German priest Martin Luther breaks away from the Roman Catholic pope.

▲ *Martin Luther*

1534 King Henry VIII of England breaks away from the Roman Catholic church. He names himself head of the English (Anglican) church.

1558 The reign of King Henry's daughter Elizabeth I begins in England.

1588 The Spanish Armada (fleet of warships) is defeated by the English Navy as Spain tries to invade England.

1600s The Ottoman Turks expand their empire through most of eastern and central Europe.

1618 Much of Europe is destroyed in the Thirty Years' War, which ends in 1648.

1642 The English Civil War begins. King Charles I fights against the forces of the Parliament. The king is defeated, and executed in 1649. His son, Charles II, returns as king in 1660.

1789 THE FRENCH REVOLUTION The French Revolution ends the rule of kings in France and leads to democracy there. At first, however, there are wars and times when dictators take control. Many people are executed. King Louis XVI and Queen Marie Antoinette are overthrown in the Revolution, and both are executed in 1793.

1762 Catherine the Great becomes Empress of Russia. She extends the Russian Empire.

1799 Napoleon Bonaparte, an army officer, becomes dictator of France. Under his rule, France conquers most of Europe by 1812.

1815 Napoleon's forces are defeated by the British and German armies at Waterloo (in Belgium). Napoleon is exiled to a remote island and dies there in 1821.

1848 Revolutions break out in countries of Europe. People force their rulers to make more democratic changes.

1914–1918 WORLD WAR I IN EUROPE
At the start of World War I in Europe, Germany, Austria-Hungary, and the Ottoman Empire oppose Britain, France, Russia—later joined by the U.S. (the Allies). The Allies win in 1918.

▼ *Tsar Nicholas II*

1917 The Tsar is overthrown in the Russian Revolution. The Bolsheviks (Communists) under Vladimir Lenin take control. Millions are starved, sent to labor camps, or executed under Joseph Stalin (1929–1953).

THE RISE OF HITLER
Adolf Hitler becomes dictator of Germany in 1933. He joins forces with rulers in Italy and Japan to form the Axis powers. In World War II (1939–1945), the Axis powers are defeated by the Allies—Great Britain, the Soviet Union, the U.S., and others. During his rule, Hitler's Nazis kill millions of Jews and other people in the Holocaust.

▲ *Italian leader Benito Mussolini with Adolf Hitler*

The 1990s Communist governments in Eastern Europe are replaced by democratic ones. Divided Germany becomes one nation, and the Soviet Union breaks up. The European Union (EU) forms. The North Atlantic Treaty Organization (NATO) bombs Yugoslavia in an effort to protect Albanians driven out of the Kosovo region.

2009 Europe suffers through major economic recession, and unemployment surges.

2010 As some countries' economies begin to improve, those of Greece and Spain worsen.

All About >> AUSTRALIA

Australian aborigines (native peoples) have lived there for more than 60,000 years. In the 17th century, Portuguese, Dutch, and Spanish expeditions explored Australian coasts. In the 1770s, Capt. James Cook of Britain made three voyages to the continent, cementing Britain's claims of ownership. On May 13, 1787, Capt. Arthur Phillip brought 11 ships from Britain, carrying convicts and guards. Although the first communities were prison colonies, other immigrants settled around the continent over the 19th century. Wool and mining were major industries. Australia was established as a commonwealth of Great Britain on January 1, 1901. Today, it is a country of more than 21 million people. It is famous for such animals as kangaroos and koalas. The Sydney Opera House is a world-famous landmark.

Sydney Opera House ▶

THE AMERICAS

Chac Mool, Mayan Figure ▶

10,000–8000 B.C. People in North and South America gather plants for food and hunt animals using stone-pointed spears.

Around 3000 B.C. People in Central America begin farming, growing corn and beans for food.

1500 B.C. Mayan people in Central America begin to live in small villages.

500 B.C. People in North America begin to hunt buffalo to use for meat and for clothing.

100 B.C. The city of Teotihuacán is founded in Mexico. It becomes the center of a huge empire extending from central Mexico to Guatemala. Teotihuacán contains many large pyramids and temples.

A.D. 150 Mayan people in Guatemala build many centers for religious ceremonies. They create a calendar and learn mathematics and astronomy.

900 Toltec warriors in Mexico begin to invade lands of Mayan people. Mayans leave their old cities and move to the Yucatan Peninsula of Mexico.

1000 Native Americans in the southwestern United States begin to live in settlements called pueblos. They learn to farm.

1325 Mexican Indians known as Aztecs create the huge city of Tenochtitlán and rule a large empire in Mexico. They are warriors who practice human sacrifice.

1492 Christopher Columbus sails from Europe across the Atlantic Ocean and lands in the Bahamas, in the Caribbean Sea. This marks the first step toward the founding of European settlements in the Americas.

Christopher Columbus ▶

1500 Portuguese explorers reach Brazil and claim it for Portugal.

1519 Spanish conqueror Hernán Cortés travels into the Aztec Empire in search of gold. The Aztecs are defeated in 1521 by Cortés. The Spanish take control of Mexico. ▶

WHY DID THE SPANISH WIN? How did the Spanish defeat the powerful Aztec Empire? One reason is that the Spanish had better weapons. Another is that many Aztecs died from diseases brought to the New World by the Spanish. The Aztecs had never had these illnesses before and so did not have immunity to them. Also, many neighboring Indians hated the Aztecs as conquerors and helped the Spanish.

1534 Jacques Cartier of France explores Canada.

1583 The first English colony in Canada is set up in Newfoundland.

1607 English colonists led by Captain John Smith settle in Jamestown, Virginia. Virginia becomes the oldest of the thirteen colonies that will form the United States.

1619 First African slaves arrive in English-controlled America.

1682 The French explorer René Robert Cavelier, sieur de La Salle, sails down the Mississippi River. The area is named Louisiana after the French King Louis XIV.

THE AMERICAS

EUROPEAN COLONIES By 1700, most of the Americas are under the control of Europeans.

Spain: Florida, southwestern United States, Mexico, Central America, western South America

Portugal: eastern South America

France: central United States, parts of Canada

England: eastern U.S., parts of Canada

Holland: West Indies, eastern South America

1700s European colonies in North and South America grow in population and wealth.

1775–1783 AMERICAN REVOLUTION The American Revolution begins in 1775 when the first shot is fired in Lexington, Massachusetts. The thirteen British colonies that become the United States officially gain independence under the Treaty of Paris, signed in 1783.

SIMÓN BOLÍVAR: LIBERATOR OF SOUTH AMERICA

In 1810, Simón Bolívar begins a revolt against Spain. He fights against the Spanish and in 1824 becomes president of the independent country of Greater Colombia. As a result of his leadership, nine South American countries gain their independence from Spain by 1830.

1846–1848 MEXICAN-AMERICAN WAR In 1846, Mexico and the United States go to war. Mexico loses parts of the Southwest and California to the U.S.

1911 A revolution in Mexico that began in 1910 overthrows Porfirio Díaz. ▼

Becoming Independent

Most countries of Latin America gained independence from Spain in the early 1800s. Others weren't liberated until much later.

COUNTRY	YEAR OF INDEPENDENCE
Argentina	1816
Bolivia	1825
Brazil	1822[1]
Chile	1818
Colombia	1819
Ecuador	1822
Guyana	1966[2]
Mexico	1821
Paraguay	1811
Peru	1824
Suriname	1975[3]
Uruguay	1825
Venezuela	1821

(1) From Portugal (2) From Britain (3) From the Netherlands

1867 The Canadian provinces are united as the Dominion of Canada.

1898 SPANISH-AMERICAN WAR Spain and the U.S. fight a brief war in 1898. Spain loses its colonies Cuba, Puerto Rico, and the Philippines.

U.S. POWER IN THE 1900s During the 1900s, the U.S. sent troops to various countries, including Mexico (1914; 1916–1917), Nicaragua (1912–1933), Haiti (1915–1934; 1994–1995), and Panama (1989). In 1962, the U.S. went on alert when the Soviet Union put missiles in Cuba.

1994 The North American Free Trade Agreement (NAFTA) increases trade between the U.S., Canada, and Mexico.

2001 Radical Muslim terrorists crash planes into U.S. targets, killing about 3,000 people; the U.S. launches a "war on terrorism."

2009 Barack Obama is sworn in as president of the United States. He is the country's first African American president.

2010 About 230,000 people are killed in a devastating earthquake in Haiti. Chile is also hit by a major quake.

THEN & NOW

FROM 2011

10 Years Ago–2001

Then: Four U.S. airliners are hijacked on September 11. Two are flown into the World Trade Center in New York City, one hits the Pentagon in Arlington, Virginia, and one crashes in Pennsylvania. About 3,000 people are killed.

Now: Work on permanent memorials in New York City and in Pennsylvania has begun. The Pentagon Memorial opened in 2008.

Then: Apple introduces the first iPod music player and iTunes, which allows buyers to download music online.

Now: Apple releases the iPad, a large touch-screen tablet for reading ebooks, watching videos, and surfing the Internet. In 2010, *Fortune* magazine names Apple the most admired company in the world.

▲ Pentagon Memorial

50 Years Ago–1961

Then: U.S. president John F. Kennedy Jr. establishes the Peace Corps, a government program that sends volunteers to assist developing nations.

Now: Almost 200,000 Peace Corps volunteers have served in 139 host nations since the program's founding. Most volunteers work in education. The largest portion serves in Africa.

Then: The Communist government of East Germany erects the Berlin Wall to keep its citizens from fleeing to the West.

Now: Berlin is now the capital of a reunified Germany, with Angela Merkel as its first woman chancellor.

100 Years Ago–1911

Machu Picchu

Then: U.S. explorer Hiram Bingham rediscovers Machu Picchu, an ancient fortress city of the Incas in the Peruvian Andes.

Now: Tourists are evacuated from Machu Picchu in 2010 after heavy rains and mud slides.

Then: Workers break ground for Fenway Park in Boston, Massachusetts.

Now: Fenway Park remains the oldest Major League Baseball stadium in use.

500 Years Ago–1511

The city of Malacca, in today's Malaysia, falls to the Portuguese. A Malay prince from Sumatra, now part of Indonesia, founded the important port in about 1400.

Today, the historical city, now called Melaka, is listed as a UNESCO World Heritage site for its cultural and architectural significance.

THEN & NOW

FROM 2012

10 Years Ago–2002

Then: The 2002 Winter Olympics are held in Salt Lake City, Utah.

Now: A record 82 nations compete in the 2010 Winter Olympics in Vancouver, British Columbia.

Then: Euro notes and coins replace all other currency in 12 European Union countries.

Now: The euro is used by 16 European Union and 6 other countries.

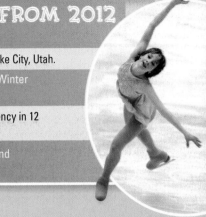

U.S. figure skater ▲ Sarah Hughes at the 2002 Winter Olympics

50 Years Ago–1962

Then: During the Cold War, the Cuban missile crisis takes place after the U.S. discovers that the Soviet Union has installed missiles in Cuba. Experts say it was the closest the world ever came to nuclear war.

Now: After the collapse of Communism in Eastern Europe, the Soviet Union officially dissolves in 1991. Cuba remains one of the world's few Communist nations.

Then: Nelson Mandela, leader of the opposition to white-minority rule in South Africa, is jailed by the South African government.

Now: Mandela was a winner of the 1993 Nobel Peace Prize and served as South Africa's first black president from 1994 to 1999. He continues to speak out for human rights.

500 Years Ago–1512

The Italian sculptor and painter Michelangelo completes work on the Sistine Chapel ceiling in Rome's Vatican Palace. These religious paintings are considered among the greatest in the world. Today, millions of tourists visit the site every year.

100 Years Ago–1912

Then: New Mexico and Arizona are admitted as the 47th and 48th U.S. states.

Now: Arizona is one of the country's fastest-growing states. New Mexico's population has more than doubled in the past 50 years.

Then: The British ocean liner RMS *Titanic* strikes an iceberg and sinks. More than 1,500 people lose their lives.

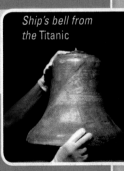

Ship's bell from the Titanic

Now: In 1985, underwater explorers find the wreck of the *Titanic*. An exhibition of artifacts from the ship travels the world in 2010.

Then: The Girl Scouts of America is founded. The group teaches good citizenship and life skills to girls of all backgrounds.

Now: With more than 3 million members, the Girl Scouts is one of the world's largest voluntary organizations for girls.

WOMEN IN HISTORY

The following women played important roles in shaping history and made major contributions to human knowledge and culture.

CLEOPATRA (69–30 B.C.), queen of Egypt famous for her association with Roman leaders Julius Caesar and Mark Antony. After her father's death, Cleopatra, at the age of about 17, and her 12-year-old brother Ptolemy jointly ruled. By custom, they were forced to marry each other. A few years later, she was sent away, but came back to rule when Caesar defeated her enemies. For a time, she lived with Caesar in Rome until his assassination in 44 B.C. She later went back to Egypt, where she met and married Antony.

SOJOURNER TRUTH (c. 1797–1883), abolitionist and women's rights activist (born Isabella Baumfree). She was raised as a slave on an estate in upstate New York. She escaped in 1826. In 1843, she became a traveling preacher and took the name Sojourner Truth. She traveled widely, speaking out against slavery and for women's rights. Her famous speech, "Ain't I a Woman?" was about how women were as smart and strong as men.

JOAN OF ARC (1412–1431), heroine and patron saint of France, known as the Maid of Orléans. She led French troops to a big victory over the English in the Battle of Orléans (1429), a turning point in the Hundred Years' War. Joan believed she was guided by voices from God, and she dressed like a male soldier. In 1431, she was burned at the stake as a heretic. The Catholic Church later declared her innocent, and she was made a saint in 1920. She is the subject of many monuments, paintings, and works of literature.

HARRIET TUBMAN (1820?–1913), born Arminta Ross, escaped slave and abolitionist. Before the Civil War, she repeatedly risked her life to lead hundreds of slaves to freedom by way of a network of homes and churches that was called the "Underground Railroad." During her nineteen trips back into the South, none of the fugitive slaves she guided was ever captured. During the Civil War, Tubman acted as a scout, spy, and nurse for Union troops in South Carolina.

ELIZABETH BLACKWELL (1821–1910), first woman to receive a degree from a medical school in the United States. She became interested in medicine as a child. At first she couldn't find a medical school that would accept her, but finally she did—and she graduated first in her class. She later trained nurses during the Civil War and founded the New York Infirmary for Women and Children. She also started a medical school for women. Blackwell eventually moved back to England, where she was born, and continued to practice medicine.

CATHERINE THE GREAT (1729–1796), empress of Russia (1762–1796). Catherine made Russia a European power and greatly expanded the territory of the Russian Empire. She raised the status of the nobles by granting them privileges such as freedom from military service and legal control over their serfs. She promoted culture, as well as the education of women and religious tolerance.

ANNE FRANK

(1929–1945), young German-born Jewish girl whose diary of her family's two years in hiding—in the back rooms of an Amsterdam office building—during the German occupation of the Netherlands became a worldwide classic in literature. The Gestapo arrested the occupants of the secret annex after acting on a tip. Frank died in the Bergen-Belsen concentration camp in 1945. Her diary was saved by office worker Miep Gies and presented to Frank's father, Otto, who was the only family member to return from the camps. Published in 1947 as *Het Achterhuis* (The House Behind), it appearred in the U.S. in 1952 as *Anne Frank: The Diary of a Young Girl*.

TONI MORRISON (born 1931),

distinguished writer, editor, teacher, and critic. Born in Ohio, she is a graduate of Howard University and Cornell University. She has won the National Book Critics Award, the Pulitzer Prize for fiction, the American Book Award, and, in 1993, the Nobel Prize for literature. Morrison's most famous book, *Beloved*, for which she won the Pulitzer Prize, was made into a movie. Her books focus on the brutality of African-American slavery, the lives of black women, and the emotional ties that bind families together.

VALENTINA TERESHKOVA

(born 1937), Russian cosmonaut and the first woman in space. During her 3-day spaceflight in June 1963 aboard the *Vostok 6,* she orbited Earth 48 times. Five months later, she married cosmonaut Andrian Nikolayev. In 1964, she gave birth to a daughter, the first child born to parents who had both flown in space.

BILLIE JEAN KING

(born 1943), American tennis player who became a symbol for women's equality. King won 12 Grand Slam singles titles. But her most famous victory may have been in the 1973 "Battle of the Sexes" match, when she beat male player Bobby Riggs in three straight sets. King helped start the first women's pro tennis tour in 1970. In 1971, she became the first woman athlete to win more than $100,000 in one season.

JODY WILLIAMS

(born 1950), activist who helped found the International Campaign to Ban Landmines. A landmine is a weapon that is placed in the ground and explodes when triggered by a vehicle or person. Landmines stay in place long after a war is over, and thousands of people, mostly civilians, are injured or killed by landmines each year. Williams has traveled the world, speaking about how landmines kill and injure innocent civilians and working with governments to create a worldwide ban. Williams and her organization won the 1997 Nobel Peace Prize for their work.

ANGELA MERKEL (born 1954),

political leader who became chancellor of Germany in 2005. She is the first woman to hold that office. The chancellor is the head of the German government. Merkel, who has a Ph.D. in physics, previously held various lower-level positions in the German government and was the leader of Germany's Christian Democratic Union, a conservative party. As chancellor, she has favored close ties with the United States and has supported policies to help boost employment in Germany.

Answers

Buildings Word Scramble, p. 54

LSILWI ETWRO	WILLIS TOWER
ATJ HALMA	TAJ MAJAL
HEMGIGUGNE SUMEMU	GUGGENHEIM MUSEUM
IDFEOBRDN YICT	FORBIDDEN CITY

Energy Quiz, p. 75

1 C. United States
2 A. Saudi Arabia
3 B. natural gas
4 D. two-thirds
5 B. Iceland
6 B. uranium

Movies & TV Scramble, p. 131

yCaril	iCarly
gnFiidn eNom	Finding Nemo
scEiple	Eclipse
cmreAina odll	American Idol
rSat rsaW	Star Wars
ielcA ni doanedWrnl	Alice in Wonderland
tvAaar	Avatar
heT smipSsno	The Simpsons
myFial uyG	Family Guy
enlagTd	Tangled

Roman Numerals, p. 183

Super Bowl XLIV was the 44th Super Bowl.

2010 = MMX

Super Bowl XIX (19) was played in 1985.

Homework Tip: Decimals to Fractions, p. 184

0.4 = 2/5

0.75 = 3/4

0.9 = 9/10

By the Numbers, p. 185

```
            N  I  N  E  T  Y
                  I     W
            F     N     E  I  G  H  T
   T  H  I  R  T  E  E  N     N
   H  F     H           T
   R  T  H  I  R  T  Y  T  W  O
   E  E     R           W
S  E  V  E  N  T  Y  T  W  O
I     N     Y     W
X           O  N  E     F  O  U  R
   S  E  V  E  N     L     I
            E     V     V
            E  L  E  V  E  N
```

Word Whirl, p. 241

The answers are:
1. Maris, 2. Szabados, 3. Schaub, 4. Bradford,
5. Durant, 6. Taurasi, 7. Ingram, 8. Mickelson

¹M	A	R	I	²S	Z	A
⁵D	U	R	A	N	⁶T	B
R	⁸M	I	C	K	A	A
O	A	N		E	U	D
F	R	O	S	L	R	O
D	G	N	⁷I	S	A	³S
A	R	⁴B	U	A	H	C

Index

A

Accidents *See* Disasters
Adams, Abigail 270, 277
Adams, John 270, 282
Adams, John Quincy 270
Aeolian Wind Harp 134
Afghanistan 152
　map 148
　war (2001–) 6, 122, 323
Africa
　facts about 97
　history 94, 320–321
　map 150–151
African Americans
　historic figures/
　　events 112, 209, 231,
　　281–287, 296, 332,
　　333
Air Force Academy, U.S. 123
Airplanes *See* Aviation
Air pollution 76, 77, 82, 84
Airports, U.S. 295
Alabama
　facts about 292
　map 289
　origin of name 290
Alaska
　facts about 292
　largest city (land area) 256
　map 288
　national park 255
　origin of name 290
Albania 152
　map 146–147
Alchemy 203
Algeria 152
　map 150
Alice in Wonderland 15, 131
Allen, Benedict 95
Allergies 100
Amendments to U.S.
　Constitution 60, 259,
　286
American Idol (TV show) 11,
　129, 132, 193
American Indians *See*
　Native Americans
American Revolution (1775–
　1783) 120, 281, 329
Amoebas 207
Amundsen, Roald 95
Amusement parks 251
Ancient civilizations
　Africa 320
　Americas 279, 328

Asia 322
　calendars 56
　Europe 324–325
　Middle East 318
　numerals 183
　weights and measures 314
Andorra 152
　map 146
Angola 152
　map 151
Animals 22–33
　bats 27
　classifying 24
　deep sea life 32
　endangered species 30–31
　size/speed 26
　life span 27
　names for adults/babies/
　　groups 28
　parasites 25
　pets 28–29
　time line for 25
Annapolis (U.S. Naval
　Academy) 123
Anorexia 100
Antarctica 97, 145
Antigua and Barbuda 152
　map 143
Ants 22
April Fools' Day 58
Arbor Day, National 63
Arctic Ocean 97
Argentina 153
　map 145
Arizona
　facts about 292
　map 288
　national park 254
　origin of name 290
Arkansas
　facts about 293
　map 289
　origin of name 290
Armenia 153
　earthquake 68
　map 142
Armstrong, Neil 40, 284
Art 34–37
　museums 262
Arthropods 24
Arthur, Chester A. 273
Asia
　facts about 97
　history 94, 322–323
　map 148–149
Asian Americans, 190, 287

Asteroids 219
Asthma 100
Astrology 43
Astronauts 217, 218, 249, 284
Astronomy *See* Space
Atlantic Ocean 97
Australia
　energy production 72
　facts about 97, 153, 186
　history 327
　map 140
　Sydney Opera House 52
Austria 138, 153
　map 146
Automobiles
　electric cars 76
　hybrid cars 76, 249
　Model T Ford 248, 284
Auto racing 229
Avatar 15, 128
Aviation 63, 248–249
　disasters 70
Awards *See* Prizes and
　Contests
Azerbaijan 153
　map 148

B

Bahamas, The 153
　map 143
Bahrain 153
　map 148
Balloons and ballooning 247
Bangladesh 154
　map 149
Barbados 154
　map 143
Baseball 220, 230–231, 285,
　330
Basketball 20, 21, 232–233
Bastille Day 60
Bats (animals) 27
Belarus 154
　map 147
Belgium 138, 154
　map 146
Belize 154
　map 143
Bell, Alexander Graham 112
Benin 154
　map 150
Beyoncé 132
Bhutan 154
　map 149
Bible 196, 325

Bicycles and bicycle
     riding 220, 241, 247
Biden, Joe, 264
Bieber, Justin 16, 133
Bigelow, Kathryn 129
Bill of Rights, U.S. 259
Biology *See* Life science
Biomass energy 73–75
Biomes 78–79
Birthdays of
     celebrities 38–41
Black holes 209, 219
Blackwell, Elizabeth 332
Blizzard 312
Blume, Judy 45
Body systems 104–105
Boer War (1899) 321
Bohr, Niels 209
Bolívar, Simón 154, 329
Bolivia 154
     map 144
Bolt, Usain 26
Bonaparte, Napoleon 297,
     327
Books 44–49, 333
     awards 44
     children's authors 44–45
     e–books and e–readers 49
     movies based on 130–131
Bosnia and Herzegovina 155
     map 146
Boston Tea Party 281
Botswana 155
     map 151
Bradford, Sam 235, 236
Brain, human 104–105
Brazil 155
     energy consumption 72
     map 144
     Rio de Janeiro Summer
          Olympics (2016) 227
Brees, Drew 20, 234
Bridges 54–55
Brunei 155
     map 149
Bryant, Kobe 20, 232
Buchanan, James 272
Buddhism 196, 322
     holy days 199
Bugs *See* Insects
Buildings 50–55
Bulgaria 138, 155
     map 147
Bulimia 100
Burj Khalifa 6, 50, 176
Burkina Faso 155
     map 150
Burundi 155
     map 151

Bush, George H. W. 276
Bush, George W. 218, 268,
     276
Byzantine Empire 325

C

Cabinet of the United
     States 260
Calendar 56–63
     odd holidays 63
California
     Chavez, Cesar 287
     earthquakes 68, 161
     facts about 282, 293
     Hispanic Americans 191
     immigration 190
     map 288
     origin of name 290
Calories 100–103
Cambodia 155
     map 149
Cameroon 156
     map 150
Canada 156
     energy 72
     map 142
     Vancouver Winter
          Olympics
          (2010) 18–19,
          222–226
Canada Day 60
Cancer, Tropic of 96
Cape Verde 156
Capitals
     of nations 152–177
     of states 292–308
Capitol, U.S. 309
Capricorn, Tropic of 96
Carbohydrates 102
Careers
     computer industry 245
     energy industry 77
     fashion designer 89
     graphic designer 37
     storm chaser 71
     veterinarian 33
Carson, Rachel 209
Carter, Jimmy (James
     Earl) 192, 276
Carver, George
     Washington 209
Catherine the Great 327, 332
Cedar Point (amusement
     park) 251
Celebrities
     birthdays 38–41
     in the news 10–17
Cells (biology) 206
Celsius (centigrade)
     temperature 315

Census, U.S. 8, 189
Central African Republic 156
     map 150
Central America 328–329
     map 143
Ceres (dwarf planet) 210, 213
Chad 156
     map 150
Challenger disaster
     (1986) 217
Chanel, Coco 88
Chanukah *See* Hanukkah
Charles, Tina 21, 233
Chavez, Cesar 287
Chemical elements 202–203
Chemistry 64
Cherokee Indians 178, 179,
     282
Children
     authors for 44–45
     favorite sports 220
     health issues 100
     Kids' Choice Awards 193
     population 189
Chile 156
     earthquakes 68
     map 145
China 156
     area 186
     armed forces 122
     calendar 56
     earthquakes 68
     energy 72
     flood 71
     Forbidden City 53
     history 322–323
     immigrants from 190
     language most widely
          spoken 114
     map 149
     population 186–187
     tallest buildings 50
Chinese New Year 56, 57
Cholesterol 102
Christianity 196
     history 318, 325, 326
     holy days 198
Christmas 198
Chu, Steven 287
Cinco de Mayo 59
Circulatory system 104
Cities
     largest in United
          States 188, 292–308
     largest in world 187
     national capitals 152–177
     state capitals 292–308
     with tallest buildings 50, 256
Citizenship Day 61

Civil rights movement 231, 284, 286–287
Civil War, U.S. 120, 283, 286
Clark, William 92, 93
Cleary, Beverly 45
Cleopatra 332
Cleveland, Frances Folsom 273, 277
Cleveland, Grover 273
Clinton, Bill 276
Clinton, Hillary 264
Coal 74, 75
Coast Guard Academy, U.S. 123
Coins, U.S. 125
College sports
  basketball 21, 233
  football 236
Colombia 156
  immigrants from 190, 191
  map 144
  volcanic eruption 69
Colorado
  facts about 293
  map 288
  origin of name 290
Colors 36
Colosseum (Rome, Italy) 53
Columbia disaster (2003) 217
Columbus, Christopher 94, 95, 161, 171, 280, 328
Columbus Day 61
Comets 219
Comoros 157
  map 151
Compounds, chemical 203
Computers 242–245
  e–book readers 49
  Internet 242–245
  invention of 113
  terminology 243
  time line 242
Congo, Democratic Republic of the 157, 187
  map 150–151
Congo, Republic of the 157, 321
  map 151
Congress, U.S. 261–262, 309
Connecticut
  facts about 294
  map 289
  origin of name 290
Constitution Day 61
Constitution, U.S. 258–259, 282
Constitutional Convention 282

Contests *See* Prizes and Contests
Continents
  drift of 99
  facts about 97
  hottest and coldest places 315
  maps 140–151
Coolidge, Calvin 274
Copernicus, Nicolaus 202, 209
Coronado, Vásquez de 280
Cosmonauts 217
Costa Rica 157
  map 143
Côte d'Ivoire (Ivory Coast) 157
  map 150
Countries *See* Nations
Cousteau, Jacques 95
Crazy Horse 287
Creamer, Timothy 218
Crime 64–65
  court cases 65
Croatia 157
  map 146
Crosby, Sidney 19, 224, 238
Crusades (1096–1291) 326
Cuba 157
  immigrants from 190, 191
  map 143
Curie, Marie 209
Curie, Pierre 209
Currency *See* Money
Cyprus 138, 157
  map 148
Czech Republic 158
  map 146

D

D–Day 121
Dalai Lama 199
Dams 55, 74
Dancing with the Stars 11, 135
Darwin, Charles 176, 209
Delhi 187
De Soto, Hernando 94
Decimals 184
Declaration of Independence 281
Delaware
  facts about 294
  map 289
  origin of name 290
Democracy 138
Denali National Park 255

Denmark 138, 158
  map 146
Depp, Johnny 15, 129
Depression, economic *see* Great Depression
Deserts 79, 92
DeWyze, Lee 11, 129, 132
Diabetes 100
Diatoms 207
Dickens, Charles 48
Digestive system 104
Dinosaurs 201, 252, 301
Disasters 66–71
Disneyland (California/France/Japan) 250
Disney World *See* Walt Disney World
Djibouti 158
  map 150
DNA 64, 206, 207
Dollars (bills and coins) 125, 126
Dome of the Rock 53
Dominica 158
  map 143
Dominican Republic 158
  Hispanic Americans 191
  immigrants from 190
  map 143
Douglass, Frederick 287
Du Bois, W.E.B. 286
Dwarf planets 210, 213

E

Earth 210, 212
  earthquake production 68
  hemispheres of 96
  latitude and longitude 96
  science 200
  seasons 214
  structure of the 68, 98
Earth Day 58
Earthquakes 7, 68, 123, 329
East Timor *See* Timor–Leste
Eating disorders 100
Eclipses 211
Ecuador 158, 191
  map 144
Edison, Thomas 112
Egypt 158
  Cleopatra 332
  Great Pyramid 50
  hieroglyphics 318
  longest river 92
  map 150
  mythology 136–137
Einstein, Albert 209
Eisenhower, Dwight D. 275

Election 2008 264–269
  Electoral College and
    map 269
  president and vice
    president 264–265
  results of the
    election 266–267,
    269, 301
  voter eligibility 268
Election Day 62
Electricity 73–74, 112
Electronics 113
Elements, chemical 202–203
Elevators 51
Ellis Island 190
El Salvador 158
  immigrants from 190, 191
  map 143
Endangered species 30–31
Endocrine system 104
Energy 72–77
England *See* United Kingdom
English language 118–119
Entertainment
  Kids' Choice Awards 193
  movies and TV 128–131
Environment 78–85
  garbage and
    recycling 82–83
  global warming 84–85
  water pollution 81
Equator 96
Equatorial Guinea 159
  map 151
Erie Canal 283
Eris (plutoid) 210, 213
Eritrea 159
  map 150
Estonia 138, 159
  map 147
Ethiopia 159
  map 150
Euro 127, 138, 331
Europe 97
  history 92, 324–327
  maps 138, 146–147
European Union 127, 138
Everglades National
    Park 255
Evolution 209
Executive branch, U.S. 260
Exercise 100–101, 103
Explorers 94, 95, 280–281,
    328
Explosions 70
Eyesight 106

F

Faces and Places 6–21
Fahrenheit temperature 315
Fall (season) 61, 214
Family trees 39
Fashion 86–89
Fat, dietary 101–102
Father's Day 59
Federer, Roger 240
Field Museum 252
Fiji 159
  map 141
Fillmore, Millard 271
Final Fantasy (video
    game) 91
Finland 138, 159
  map 147
Fires 70
First ladies 270–276, 277–
    278
Fish 23, 24, 26, 28–29, 32
Flag Day 59
Flags
  of nations of world 152–
    177
  of United States 257
Florida
  Everglades 255
  facts about 280, 294
  Hispanic Americans 191
  immigration 190
  map 289
  origin of name 290
  population 190
Food
  nutrients, calories, and
    fat 100–102
  pyramid 101
  Spanish vocabulary 116–
    117
Football 20, 63, 183, 221,
    234–236
Ford, Betty 275, 278
Ford, Gerald R. 275
Ford, Henry 284
Forensics 64
Forests 78, 254–255
Fossil fuels 73, 74, 75, 76
Fourth of July *see*
    Independence Day, U.S.
Fractions 184
Frank, Anne 333
France 60, 138, 169
  cave art 34–35
  energy consumption 72
  Joan of Arc 332
  map 146
Franklin, Benjamin 63, 112,
    280

French and Indian War 280
French Revolution 326
Friendship Day 60

G

Gabon 159
  map 151
Galaxies 219
Gambia, The 160
  map 150
Games 90–91
Garbage 82–83
Garfield, James A. 273
Generations 42
Genes 206
Geography 92–99
  contest 194
  continents and oceans 97
  explorers 94–95
  globe 96
  largest/smallest
    countries 186
  national parks 254–255
  reading a map 93
Georgia (nation) 160
  map 148
Georgia (state)
  facts about 295
  map 289
  origin of name 290
Geothermal energy 73
Germany 138, 160, 333
  energy consumption 72
  map 146
Ghana 160
  map 150
Glass House
    (Connecticut) 52
Glee 10
Global warming *see*
    Greenhouse effect
Globe 96
Gold Rush 282
Golden Gate Bridge 54
Golf 237
Gorbachev, Mikhail 285
Gore, Al 192
Gossip Girl 87
Government, forms of 138
Graphic designer 37
Grand Canyon National
    Park 254
Grandparents' Day,
    National 61
Grant, Ulysses S. 272
Grasslands 79
Gravity 208
Great Britain *See* United
    Kingdom

Great Depression 284–285
Great Salt Lake 306
Great Seal of U.S. 257
Greece 138, 160
  ancient history 324
  map 147
  mythology 136–137
Greek language 119
Greenhouse effect 76, 78, 84–85
Greenland 92
  map 142
Greenwich meridian 96
Gregorian calendar 56
Grenada 160
  map 143
Groundhog Day 57
Guatemala 160
  immigrants from 190, 191
  map 143
Guggenheim Museum (Bilbao, Spain) 52
Guinea 160
  map 150
Guinea–Bissau 161
  map 150
Guyana 161
  map 144
Gymnastics 237

H

Hailstone (largest) 312
Haiti 161
  earthquake (2010) 7, 68, 123, 329
  map 143
Halley's Comet 219
Hall of Fame
  baseball 231
  basketball 232
  football 235
  hockey 238
Halloween 61
Hanukkah 198
Harding, Warren G. 274
Harrison, Benjamin 273
Harrison, William Henry 271
Harry Potter (books, movies) 45, 129, 131
Haumea (plutoid) 210, 213
Hawaii
  facts about 295
  map 288
  origin of name 290
Hawking, Stephen 209
Hayes, Rutherford B. 272
Health 100–107
  exercise 101–103
  human body 104–107

nutrition 100–102
senses 106–107
Health care reform law, U.S. (2010) 9, 285
Hearing 106
Heart, human 104–105
Heisman Trophy 236
Hemispheres of Earth 96
Henry, Joseph 209
Henson, Matthew 95
Herschel, William 213
Hinduism 197, 322
  holy days and festivals 199
Hispanic Americans 190, 191, 287
Hitler, Adolf 327
Hockey *See* Ice hockey
Holcomb, Steve 226
Holocaust Memorial Museum, U.S. 309
Homework Help 108–111
Honduras 161, 191
  map 143
Hong Kong 186
Hoover, Herbert 274, 296
Hoover, Lou Henry 274, 277
Hough, Derek 11, 135
House of Representatives, U.S. 261, 262
How to Train Your Dragon 13
Hudson, Henry 94, 281
Human body 104–107
  Spanish vocabulary 116–117
Human genome 206
Hungary 138, 161
  map 146
Hurricanes 66
Hussein, Saddam 285, 319
Hydroelectric power 73–75
Hydrogen fuel cells 76

I

Ice hockey 19, 224, 238
Iceland 161, 186
  geothermal energy 73
  map 146
Idaho
  facts about 295
  map 288
  origin of name 290
Illinois
  facts about 296
  immigration 190
  map 289
  origin of name 290

Immigration 190, 191
Immune system 105
Incinerators 82
Independence Day, U.S. 60
India 161, 322
  armed forces 122
  earthquakes 68
  energy 72
  immigrants from 190
  map 148
  population 186–187
  Taj Mahal 53
Indiana
  facts about 296
  map 289
  origin of name 290
Indianapolis 500 229
Indian Ocean 97
Indonesia 161
  earthquake 68
  energy production 72
  map 149
  volcanic eruptions 69
Infinity 182
Ingram, Mark 236
Insects 22, 23, 24, 25, 26, 27
Instruments, musical 134
Internet, research on the 111, 244
Inventions 112–113
Invertebrates 24, 32
Iowa
  facts about 296
  map 289
  origin of name 290
iPad 49, 242, 300
iPhone 112
Iran 162
  armed forces 122
  earthquakes 68
  energy production 72
  hostage crisis 285
  immigration from 190
  map 148
Iraq 162
  Iraq War (2003–) 122, 285, 319
  map 148
  Persian Gulf War (1991) 121
Ireland 138, 162
  map 146
Iron Man 2 12
Islam 171, 197, 318
  calendar 56
  holy days 198
  Sunnis and Shiites 197
Island, biggest 92

Islands of Adventure
  (Florida) 251
Israel 162
  history 319
  map 148
Italy 138, 162, 187
  map 146
  volcanic eruption 69

J

Jackson, Andrew 271
Jacksonville 294
Jamaica 162
  map 143
James, Kevin 193
Jamestown 281
Japan 162, 187, 285, 323
  earthquake 68
  energy consumption 72
  map 149
  volcanic eruption 69
Jay-Z 88, 193
Jefferson, Thomas 270, 305,
  309
Jefferson Memorial 309
Jemison, Mae 95
Jews and Judaism 197
  ancient Hebrews 318
  calendar 56
  Holocaust impact 121, 309
  holy days 198
  museums 309
  Palestine migration 319
Joan of Arc 332
Johnson, Andrew 272
Johnson, Lady Bird 275, 278
Johnson, Lyndon Baines 275,
  286
Jonas, Nick 17
Jordan 162
  map 148
Judicial branch, U.S. 263
Juneteenth 59
Jupiter (planet) 210
  exploration of 216, 218
  facts about 211, 212

K

Kansas
  facts about 297
  map 288–289
  origin of name 290
Karate Kid, The (2010) 14
Kazakhstan 163
  map 148
Keller, Helen 292
Kennedy, Jacqueline 275,
  278
Kennedy, John
  Fitzgerald 275, 284

Kennedy, Robert F. 284
Kentucky
  facts about 297
  map 289
  origin of name 290
Kenya 163
  map 150–151
Kepler, Johannes 209
Key, Francis Scott 63
Keys, Alicia 16
Khalifa Tower see Burj
  Khalifa
Kidneys 105
Kids' Choice Awards 193
Kindle 49, 113
King, Billie Jean 333
King, Coretta Scott 287
  book award 44
King Jr., Rev. Martin
  Luther 38, 57, 192, 284,
  286, 287
Kingsley, Mary Henrietta 95
Kiribati 163
  map 141
Koran 197, 318
Korea, North See North
  Korea
Korea, South See South
  Korea
Korean War (1950–1953) 121,
  285, 323
Kosovo 163
  map 148
Kuwait 163
  map 148
Kyrgyzstan 163
  map 148

L

Labor Day 61
Lakes 92, 174, 256, 301, 304,
  306
Landfills 82
Lange, Dorothea 35
Language 114–119
  animal words 28
  computer words 243
  early writing 318
  foreign words 115–117
  languages spoken in United
    States 114
  names of the months 56
  new words 118
  languages of nations 152–
    177
  similes 118
  words commonly
    confused 109
  world languages 114

Laos 164
  map 149
Lascaux 35
Latimer, Lewis 289
Latin roots 119
Latin America, history
  of 328–329
Latitude 96
Latvia 138, 164, 187
  Johnson-Sirleaf, Ellen 321
  map 147
Lautner, Taylor 13, 38, 193
Lava 69
Lebanon 164
  map 148
Legislative branch, U.S. 258,
  261
Lesotho 164
  map 151
Levers 205
Lewis, C.S. 45
Lewis, Meriwether 94, 95,
  283, 303
Liberia 164
  Johnson-Sirleaf, Ellen 321
  map 150
Library of Congress 309
Libya 164
  map 150
Liechtenstein 164
  map 146
Life science 200, 201, 206–
  207
Light 73, 74, 204
Lightning 204, 312
Lincoln, Abraham 57, 272,
  283, 305
Lincoln, Mary Todd 272, 277
Lincoln Memorial 309
Lindbergh, Charles 284
Literature See Books
Lithuania 138, 164
  map 147
Little League 220
Longitude 96
Looking back
  (2011/2012) 330–331
Los Angeles 188
Louisiana
  facts about 297
  Gulf oil spill (2010) 9, 81
  map 289
  origin of name 290
Louisiana Purchase 282
Lunar eclipses 211
Luxembourg 138, 165
  map 146
Lysacek, Evan 19

M

Maathai, Wangari 192
Macau 186
Macedonia 165
 map 147
Machines 205
Machu Picchu 330
Madagascar 165
 map 151
Madden NFL (video
 game) 91, 221
Madison, Dolley 120, 270,
 277
Madison, James 270, 282
Magellan, Ferdinand 94, 95
Magic Kingdom
 (Florida) 250
Magma 69
Magna Carta 326
Maine
 facts about 298
 map 289
 origin of name 290
Maine, U.S.S. (ship) 120
Makemake (plutoid) 210, 213
Malaria 25
Malawi 165
 map 151
Malaysia 165
 map 149
 tallest buildings 50
Malcolm X 286, 287
Maldives 165, 186
 map 148
Mali 165
 map 150
Malta 138, 165, 186
 map 146
Mammals 23–24, 26–27, 30
Mantle, Mickey 230
Maps
 continents and
  nations 140–151
 continents and oceans 97
 European Union 138
 plates of Earth 68
 reading of 93
 United States 143,
  288–289
 U.S. election results
  (2008) 269
 world languages 114
Maris, Roger 230
Mars (planet) 210
 exploration of 216, 218
 facts about 211, 212
Marshall, Thurgood 286
Marshall Islands 166
 map 141

Martin Luther King Jr.
 Day 57
Maryland
 facts about 280, 298
 map 289
 origin of name 290
Massachusetts
 facts about 281, 298
 immigration to 190
 map 289
 origin of name 290
Mauritania 166
 map 150
Mauritius 166
Mayflower 63
McCain, John 264, 266–267,
 269, 285
McCartney, Stella 88
McKinley, William 273
Measurements *See*
 Weights and Measures
Memorial Day 59
Mercator projection 96
Merchant Marine Academy,
 U.S. 123
Mercury (planet) 210
 exploration of 212, 216
 facts about 211, 212
Meridians of Earth 96
Merkel, Angela 333
Meteoroids 219
Meteorology
 meteorologists 71, 312
 see also Weather
Metric system 317
Metropolitan Museum of
 Art 252
Mexican–American War
 (1846–1848) 120, 282
Mexico 166
 history 328–329
 immigrants from 190, 191
 map 143
 volcanic eruption 69
Mexico City 187
Michelangelo 331
Michigan
 facts about 299
 map 289
 origin of name 290
Micronesia 166
 map 141
Middle East
 history 318–319
 map 148
Military 120–123
Milky Way 219
Miller, Bode 225
Mimivirus 207

Minerals (nutrition) 102
Minnesota
 facts about 299
 map 289
 origin of name 290
Minuit, Peter 281
Mississippi
 facts about 299
 map 289
 origin of name 290
Missouri
 facts about 300
 map 289
 origin of name 290
Missouri Compromise 283
Moldova 166
 map 147
Monaco 166, 186, 187
 map 146
Monarchy 138
Monet, Claude 35
Money 124–127
 dollar bill 126
 new U.S. coins 125
 richest people 124
 world currency 127
 youngest billionaires 124
Mongolia 166, 186
 map 149
Monroe Doctrine 283
Monroe, James 270
Montana
 facts about 300
 map 288
 origin of name 291
Montenegro 167
 map 147
Moon
 exploration of 215–218
 facts about 215, 284
 lunar eclipses 211
Moonbow 312
Moore, Gordon E. 113
Moore's law 113
Morocco 167
 map 150
Morrison, Toni 333
Mother Goose 63
Mother's Day 59
Mountains 79, 92, 256
Mount Everest 92
Movies and TV 128–131
 Kids' Choice Awards 193
 personalities 10–15
 popular TV shows 129
Mozambique 167
 map 151
Mumbai, India 186
Muscular system 105

Music and dance 132–135
dance classes 135
instruments 134
Kids' Choice Awards 193
personalities 16–17
Mussolini, Benito 327
Myanmar 167
map 149
Mythology 136–137

N

Names, popular given 42
Namibia 167, 186
map 151
NASCAR 229
National anthem, U.S. 63,
257
National Aquatic Center 52
National Archives 309
National parks,
U.S. 254–255, 256
National World War II
Memorial 309
Nations 138–177
energy producers and
users 72
immigrant birth–
countries 190, 191
languages 114–119, 152–
177
maps 140–151, 288–289
population 186–187
Native Americans 178–181
contributions 178
cultural areas 180
history 179, 279, 282, 283,
287, 293, 328
population 181
Natural resources *See*
Energy
Nauru 167, 186
map 141
Navajo Nation 178
Nebraska
facts about 300
map 288
origin of name 291
Nebulas 219
Nepal 167
map 148
tallest mountain 92
Neptune (planet) 210
exploration of 216
facts about 211, 213
Nervous system 104
Netherlands, The 138, 167
map 146
Nevada
facts about 301

map 288
origin of name 291
Newark (NJ) 187
New Deal 285
New Hampshire
facts about 301
map 289
origin of name 291
New Jersey
facts about 301
immigration 190
map 289
origin of name 291
New Mexico
facts about 302
Hispanic Americans 191
map 288
origin of name 291
UFO museum 253
Newport (RI) 305
Newseum 253
New Year's Day 57
New Year's Eve 62–63
New York (state)
disasters 66
facts about 281, 302
immigration 190–191
map 289
origin of name 291
population 188–190
New York City
facts about 302
population 188
World Trade Center
attack 70, 285, 330
New Zealand 168
map 141
Nicaragua 168
immigration from 190, 191
map 143
Nickelodeon Kids' Choice
Awards *see* Kids'
Choice Awards
Niger 168
map 150
Nigeria 162, 168
map 150
Nile River 92
Nintendo 90–91
Nixon, Richard 275, 285
Nobel Prizes 192
North America
facts about 97
history 94, 279, 328–329
map 142–143
North Carolina
facts about 302
map 289
origin of name 291

North Dakota
facts about 303
map 288
origin of name 291
North Korea 121, 122, 163,
323
map 149
North Pole 92, 95, 96
Norway 168
energy production 72
map 146
waterfall 92
Nuclear energy 71, 73–75
Numbers 182–185
in Spanish 117
Nutrition 100–102

O

Obama, Barack 7, 9, 192, 218,
264, 265, 266–267, 269,
276, 285, 287
Obama, Michelle 100, 193,
262, 276, 278
Obesity 100, 103
Oceania 97
Oceans 79, 97, 140–151
O'Connor, Sandra Day 285
Ohio
facts about 303
map 289
origin of name 291
Ohno, Apolo 225
Oil (fuel) 73–75, 306, 319
Oils (food) 101
Oil spill, Gulf of Mexico
(2010) 9, 81
Oklahoma
facts about 303
map 288–289
origin of name 291
Olympics 18–19, 222–227
Paralympics/Special
Olympics 228
Youth Olympics 227
Oman 168
map 148
Opium War (1839) 323
Orchestra, instruments
of 134
Oregon
facts about 304
map 288
origin of name 291
Ottoman Empire 319, 326

P

Pacific islands 140
Pacific Ocean 69, 97
Painting 34–35

Pakistan 122, 168
 earthquake 68
 immigration from 190
 map 148
Palau 169, 186
 map 141
Paleo–Indians 279
Paleontology *See* Science
Palestine 318, 319
Palmer, Keke 11
Panama 169
 map 143
Panama Canal 284
Paolini, Christopher 45
Papua New Guinea 169
 map 141
Paracelsus, Philippus
  Aureolus 203
Paraguay 169
 map 144–145
Paralympics 228
Parks 254–255, 256
Parks, Rosa 289
Paulsen, Gary 45
Pennsylvania
 facts about 304
 map 289
 origin of name 291
Percentages 184
Persian Gulf War (1991) 121,
  285, 319
Peru 169
 earthquake 68
 map 144
 mud slide 330
Pets 28, 29
Philadelphia (PA) 304
Philippines 169
 immigrants from 190
 landslide 71
 map 149
 volcanic eruption 69
Physical science 200, 202–
  205
Pierce, Franklin 272
Pilgrims 281
Pirates 172
Pizarro, Francisco 94
Planes *See* Aviation
Planets 210–213
Plants 23, 78–79, 200, 206
Pledge of Allegiance 257
Pluto (plutoid) 210, 213
Poland 138, 169
 map 146–147
Polk, James Knox 271
Polo, Marco 94
Ponce de León, Juan 280
*Poor Richard's
  Almanack* 280

Population 186–191
 cities 187, 188
 HIspanic Americans 191
 immigrants 190
 nations 152–177, 186–187
 Native Americans 181
 United States 188–191
Portugal 138, 169, 320, 328
 map 146
Postal abbreviations 292–
  308
Powell, Colin 286
Precipitation 80, 312
Prefixes 119, 182
President dollars 125
Presidents' Day 57
Presidents of United
   States 270–276
 cabinet departments 260
 first ladies 277–278
 death and succession 260
 election of 264–269
 powers and duties 265
 term of office 260
Prime numbers 182
Prizes and Contests 192–
  195
Proteins 102
Puerto Rico 191, 308
 map 143
Pulleys 205
Puzzles and quizzes
 answers to 334–336
 buildings 54
 energy 75
 movies and TV 131
 numbers 183, 184, 185
 sports 241

Q

Qatar 170
 map 148

R

Railroads *See* Trains
Rain forests 22, 78
Ramadan 198
Rankin, Jeannette 284
Reagan, Nancy 276, 278
Reagan, Ronald 276, 285
Recycling 83
Reference books 47
Religion 196–199
 major holy days 198–199
Reproductive system 105
Reptiles 23–24, 26, 28
Respiratory system 104
Revolutionary War *See*
  American Revolution

Rhode Island
 facts about 304
 map 289
 origin of name 291
Rice, Condoleezza 41, 286
Richest people 124
Ring of Fire (earthquakes,
  volcanoes) 69
Rivers 92
Robinson, Jackie 231, 285
Rochette, Joannie 226
Rocks 98
Roller coasters 251
Roma 171
Romania 138, 170
 map 147
Roman numerals 183
Rome, ancient 324–325
 Latin 119
 months 56
 mythology 136–137
Roosevelt, Eleanor 274,
  278
Roosevelt, Franklin
  Delano 274, 285
Roosevelt, Theodore 192,
  273, 299, 305
Rowling, J.K. 45, 131
Russia 170
 area 186
 armed forces 122
 Catherine the Great 327,
  332
 energy 72
 maps 147–149
 population 184
 Sochi Winter Olympics
  (2014) 227
 space exploration 216,
  217, 333
 Strategic Arms Reduction
  Treaty (START) 7
Rwanda 170, 321
 map 151

S

Sacagawea 179, 303
Safety online 243
Sahara Desert 92, 320
Saint Kitts and Nevis 170
 map 143
Saint Lucia 170
 map 143
Saint Vincent and the
  Grenadines 171
 map 143
Samoa 171
 map 141
San Marino 171, 186
 map 146

São Paulo, Brazil 187
São Tomé and Príncipe 171
　map 151
Satellites 219
Saturn (planet) 210, 212, 216
Saudi Arabia 171
　energy production 72
　map 148
Saund, Dalip Singh 287
Scherzinger, Nicole 11, 135
School segregation 284
Science 200–209
　chemical elements 202–203
　famous scientists 209
　questions and answers 208
Scientific method 201
Screws 205
Scuba diving 208
Sculpture 34
Sea organ 132
Seasons 214
Seattle (WA) 307
Senate, U.S. 261
Sendak, Maurice 130
Senegal 171
　map 150
Senses 106–107
September 11, 2001, terrorist attacks 70, 285, 330
Serbia 171
　map 147
Seychelles 172
Seyfried, Amanda 88
Shiite Muslims 197
Ships 63, 246–249
　disasters 70
Sierra Leone 172
　map 150
Signs and symbols
　chemical elements 202–203
　on maps 93
　U.S. emblems 125, 126, 257
Silk Road 322
Similes 118
Simpsons, The 128
Singapore 172, 186
　map 149
Skeletal system 105
Skin 107
Skyscrapers 6, 50–51
Slavery, abolition of 120, 259, 283, 286
Slave trade 281, 283, 286, 321, 328
Slovakia 172
　map 146

Slovenia 138, 172
　map 146
Smell, sense of 107
Smith, John 281, 328
Smithsonian Institution 252, 309
Snakes *see* Reptiles
Soccer 239
Social networking 242, 243
Social science 200
Solar eclipses 211
Solar power 73, 74
Solar system 210
　unmanned missions 216
Solomon Islands 172
　map 141
Somalia 172
　map 150
Sony PlayStation 91
Sotomayor, Sonia 287
Sound 204
South Africa, 173, 321
　map 151
South America
　facts about 97
　history 328–329
　map 144–145
South Carolina
　facts about 305
　map 289
　origin of name 291
South Dakota
　facts about 305
　map 288
　origin of name 291
South Korea 121, 122, 163, 323
　energy consumption 72
　immigrants from 190
　map 149
Soviet Union *See* Russia
Space 210–219
　astronauts/cosmonauts in 217, 218, 249, 284
　Columbia disaster 217
　Challenger disaster 217
　famous scientists 209
　space shuttle program 8
　unmanned probes 216
Spain 138, 173
　immigration from 191
　map 146
　rail disaster 70
Spanish (language) 114, 116–117
Spanish–American War (1898) 120, 283, 329
Special Olympics 228
Spelling Bee, National 194

Spiders 208
Sports 220–241
　auto racing 229
　baseball 220, 230–231, 330
　basketball 20, 21, 232–233
　football 20, 63, 183, 221, 234–236
　golf 237
　gymnastics 237
　ice hockey 19, 224, 238
　Olympics 18–19, 222–227, 331
　Paralympics/Special Olympics 228
　soccer 239
　tennis 21, 240
　X Games 241
Spring (season) 58, 214
Sri Lanka 173
　map 148
St. Patrick's Day 58
Stars
　galaxies 219
　Sun as star 210
Stars (people) *See* Faces and Places
"Star–Spangled Banner" 63, 257, 283
States of United States
　Electoral College votes 269
　facts about 292–308
　origins of names 290–291
　record temperatures 313
　representation in U.S. House 262
Stock car racing 229
Stone Arch Bridge 54
Storm chasers 71
Storms 66–67, 71
Strategic Arms Reduction Treaty (START) 7
Subways 248
Sudan 173, 321
　longest river 92
　map 150
Suffixes 119
Summer 59, 214
Sun 210
　distance from planets 212–213
　light and energy from 73, 74, 84
　solar eclipses 211
Sundogs 312
Sunni Muslims 197
Super Bowl 20, 63, 183, 221, 234, 235
Supreme Court, U.S. 263
　historic rulings 284, 286

Suriname 173, 186
  map 142
Swaziland 173
  map 151
Sweden 138, 173
  map 146
Swift, Taylor 133, 193
Switzerland 174
  map 146
Sydney Opera House 52
Symbols *See* Signs and
  symbols
Syria 174
  map 148
  wars 319

T

Taft, William Howard 274
Taiwan 174
  map 149
  tallest buildings 6, 50
Tajikistan 174
  map 148
Taj Mahal (India) 53
Tanzania 174
  map 151
Taste, sense of 107
Taylor, Zachary 271
Technology 242–245
Telegraph 112, 282
Telephones 112
Television *See* Movies and
  TV
Temperature 313, 315
Tennessee
  facts about 305
  map 289
  origin of name 291
Tennis 21, 240
Tereshkova, Valentina 217,
  333
Terrorism *See* September
  11, 2001, terrorist
  attacks
Tetris 90, 182
Texas
  facts about 306
  immigration 190, 191
  map 288–289
  Mexican War 120, 282
  origin of name 291
  tornadoes 67
Thailand 174
  map 149
Thanksgiving 62
Then and Now
  (2011/2012) 330–331
Tibet 92
  Dalai Lama 199
  map 148

Tidal waves *See* Tsunami
Tiffany, Louis Comfort 35
Timbuktu 320
Timor–Leste (East
  Timor) 174
  map 149
Titanic (ship) 331
Togo 175
  map 150
Tokyo 187
Tonga 175
  map 141
Torah 197
Tornadoes 67
Totalitarianism 138
Totem poles 181
Touch, sense of 107
Toy Story 3 14
"Trail of Tears" 282
Trains 247–249, 283
  disasters 70
Transcontinental
  railroad 248
Transportation 246–249
Travel 250–255
  national parks 254–255
  Wonders of the World 253
Trees 78, 79, 293
Trinidad and Tobago 175
  map 144
Tripitaka 196
Trojan War 137, 324
Tropics 96
True Jackson, VP 11
Truman, Harry S. 275, 300
Truth, Sojourner 332
Tsunami 69
Tubman, Harriet 332
Tundra 79
Tunisia 175
  map 150
Turkey 122, 175
  earthquake 68
  map 148
Turkmenistan 175
  map 148
Tuvalu 175, 186
  map 141
Twilight (books, movies) 13,
  129, 131, 193
Twitter 218, 242
Tyler, John 271

U

Uganda 176, 187
  map 151
Ukraine 176
  Chernobyl disaster 71
  map 147

Umami 100
Underwood, Carrie 17
United Arab Emirates 176
  map 148
  tallest building 6, 50
United Kingdom (Great
  Britain) 138, 176
  London Summer
    Olympics (2012) 227
  map 146
  war with America 281,
    283
United Nations 139
United States 176, 256–309
  capital of 309
  census 8, 189
  Constitution,
    U.S. 258–259
  earthquakes 68
  Election Day 62
  elections 264–269
  energy 72, 75
  flag 176, 257
  government 260–263
  Hispanic Americans 190,
    191
  history time line 279–285,
    328–329
  immigrants 190, 191
  languages spoken 114
  largest cities 188
  legal holidays 57–62
  maps 142–143, 288–289
  money 125, 126
  motto 257
  national anthem 257
  national parks 254–255,
    256
  national symbols 257
  population 186, 188–191,
    256
  presidents 270–276
  space exploration 8, 216,
    217, 218
  states, facts about 290–
    308
  wars and military 120–
    123, 280–285
Universal Studios
  (Florida) 251
University of Connecticut
  women's basketball
  team 21, 233
Uranium 73
Uranus (planet) 210, 213, 216
Urinary system 105
Uruguay 176
  map 145
Usher, 133

Utah
  facts about 306
  map 288
  origin of name 291
Uzbekistan 177
  map 148

V

Valentine's Day 57
Van Buren, Martin 271
Vanuatu 177
  map 141
Vatican City 177, 186
  map 146
Venezuela 177
  highest waterfall 92
  map 144
Venus (goddess) 136
Venus (planet) 210
  exploration of 216
  facts about 211, 212
Vermont
  facts about 306
  map 289
  origin of name 291
Verrazano (bridge) 256
Verrazano, Giovanni da 280
Vertebrates 23, 24
Veterinarian 33
Veterans Day 62
Vice presidents of the United
    States 260, 264, 265,
    270–276
  first Native American 179
Video games 90–91
Vietnam 177
  immigrants from 190
  map 149
Vietnam Veterans
    Memorial 309
Vietnam War 121, 284, 309,
    323
Virginia
  facts about 286, 307
  Jamestown 328
  map 289
  origin of name 291
Viruses (biological) 207
Viruses (computer) 243
Vitamins 102
Volcanoes 69
Volunteering 310–311
Vonn, Lindsey 18
Voting 259, 260, 268

W

Walking 101, 103
Wal–Mart 293
Walt Disney World
    (Florida) 250, 251

War of 1812 63, 120, 283
Washington (state)
  facts about 307
  hydroelectricity 73
  map 288
  origin of name 291
Washington, D.C. 282, 286,
    309
  map 289
Washington, George 57, 270,
    282, 305
Washington Monument 50,
    309
Water
  boiling and freezing points
      of 315
  energy from 73–75
  global warming 85
  hydrological cycle 80, 85
  pollution 81
  survival in freezing 208
  use and
      conservation 80–81
Water World (Colorado) 251
Waterfalls 92
Watergate scandal 285
Weather 312–313
  facts about 312
  map 312
  symbols 312
  temperatures 313, 315
  see also Disasters
Webster, Noah 63
Wedges 205
Weights and
    measures 314–317
West Point (U.S. Military
    Academy) 123
West Virginia
  facts about 307
  map 289
  origin of name 291
Wetlands 81
Wheels and axles 205
Where the Wild Things Are
    (book, movie) 130
White, Shaun 18, 225, 241
White House 260, 309
Wii, Nintendo 90–91
Williams, Jody 192, 333
Williams, Serena 21, 240
Wilson, Edith 274, 277
Wilson, Woodrow 192, 274
Wind
  energy 72–74
  hurricanes 66
  and skyscrapers 51
  tornadoes 67
Winter 62, 214

Winthrop, John 281
Wipeout 10
Wisconsin
  facts about 308
  map 289
  origin of name 291
Wizard of Oz, The 297
Women
  Equality Day, 60
  historic figures 287, 298,
      332–333
  military service
      memorial 309
  WNBA 233
  Women's Professional
      Soccer (WPS) 239
Wonders of the World 253
World currency 127
World History 318–333
  Africa 320–321
  Americas 328–329
  Asia 322–323
  Europe 324–327
  Middle East 318–319
World Trade Center (New
    York City) 70, 285, 330
World War I (1914–1918) 121,
    284, 319, 327
World War II (1939–1945) 86,
    121, 285, 323, 327
Wright Brothers (Orville and
    Wilbur) 63, 248
Wyoming
  facts about 308
  map 288
  origin of name 291
Yellowstone National
    Park 254, 255, 256

X

Xbox 90, 91
X Games 241

Y

Yellowstone National
    Park 254, 255, 256
  map 288
Yemen 177
  map 148
Yosemite National Park 254
  map 288
Youngest billionaires 124
Youth Olympics 227

Z

Zambia 177
  map 151
Zimbabwe 177
  map 151
Zodiac 43

Photo Credits

This product/publication includes images from Artville, Comstock, Corbis Royalty-Free, Corel Stock Photo Library, Digital Stock, Digital Vision, EyeWire Images, IndexOpen.com, iStockphoto, One Mile Up Inc., PhotoDisc, Rubberball Productions, and Shutterstock, which are protected by the copyright laws of the U.S., Canada, and elsewhere. Used under license.

FRONT COVER: AP Images: Evan Agostini (Justin Bieber); Bill Feig (Drew Brees); Akira Suemori (3D glasses). Newscom: Photoshot (Kim Yu-Na). **BACK COVER**: AP Images: Charles Sykes (Miranda Cosgrove). Newscom: La Nacion (iPad); ZUMA (Shaun White). The White House (Michelle Obama). **INTERIOR: Alamy**: Interfoto (Pong), 91. **AP Images**: 268, 333 (Frank); Bill Feig, 4 (Brees); Damian Dovarganes, 9 (top); Michael Becker/FOX/PictureGroup, 11 (*American Idol*); Jackie Johnston, 41 (Lin); Haraz N. Ghanbari, 100 (bottom); Kevin P. Casey, 124 (Gates); Douglas C. Pizac, 124 (Brin); Imaginechina, 124 (Yiu); Frank Micelotta/FOX/ PictureGroup, 129 (top), 132 (bottom); Michael Becker/PictureGroup, 133 (bottom); Ames Tribune, Nirmalendu Majumdar, 228 (bottom); San Antonio Express-News, Edward A. Ornelas, 233; Jim Prisching, 237 (bottom); Harry Harris, 333 (King). **Apple Inc.**: 112 (iPhone). **Ron Blunt Photography**: 52 (Glass House). **The Bridgeman Art Library International**: Pushkin Museum, Moscow, Russia, 3, 35 (Monet); Museum of Fine Arts, Houston, Texas, USA/Brown Foundation Accessions Endowment Fund, 35 (Tiffany). **Timothy Bryk**: 314 (1 yard). **Jimmy Carter Library and Museum**: 319 (top). **EA Mobile**: 3, 90 (*Tetris*). **EA Sports**: 91 (*Madden NFL 2010*). **Environmental Protection Agency**: 208–209 (background). **Courtesy of Meredith Evans**: 3, 89 (fashion sketch). **Everett Collection**: Carin Baer/© FOX, 10 (bottom); Francois Duhamel/©Paramount, 12; ©Paramount Pictures, 13 (top); ©Columbia Pictures, 14 (top); ©Buena Vista Pictures, 14 (bottom), 129 (bottom); ©Walt Disney Pictures, 15 (top), 130 (top); TM & Copyright ©20th Century Fox. All rights reserved, 15 (bottom), 128; Adam Orchon, 39 (Harris); Roth Stock, 40 (Gomez); Giovanni Rufino/© The CW, 87 (*Gossip Girl*); ©Warner Bros, 130 (bottom left); Jaap Buitendijk/©Warner Bros., 131 (top). **Gagarin Cosmonaut Training Center**: 218 (bottom). **Getty Images**: 7 (top), 20 (bottom); Rob Hoffman/JBE, 3, 17 (Jonas); Charles Crowell/Bloomberg, 6 (Burj Khalifa); Jewel Samad/AFP, 7 (bottom); John Moore, 9 (bottom); Adam Larkey/ABC, 11 (bottom), 135 (top); Morena Brengola, 16 (top); Michael Tullberg, 16 (bottom); Andy Lyons, 17 (bottom); Martin Bureau/AFP, 18 (top); Fabrice Coffrini/AFP, 18 (bottom); Harry How, 19 (top); Vncenzo/AFP, 19 (bottom); Tom Hauck, 20 (top); Christian Petersen, 20 (bottom), 232 (middle); Bill Frakes/Sports Illustrated, 21 (top); Findlay Kember/AFP, 21 (bottom); Gandee Vasan, 49 (top); Sony/Matt Cardy, 49 (bottom); New York Daily News, 64 (top); Carsten Peter/National Geographic, 71; Hulton Collection, 86 (1900s), 231; Frank A. Cezus, 87 (1970s); Roland Schoor/Time & Life Pictures, 88, (top); Mike Marsland/WireImage, 88 (middle); M. Caulfield/American Idol 2008, 132 (*American Idol* logo); Peter Read Miller/Sports Illustrated, 183; Kevin Winter/KCA, 193 (top); Jeff Kravitz/ FilmMagic, 193 (bottom); Tim Sloan/AFP, 199 (bottom); Gianluigi Guercia/AFP, 221 (top); Jeff Gross, 221 (bottom); Luis Acosta/AFP, 224; Cameron Spencer, 225 (top); Matthew Stockman, 225 (bottom), 226; Marcia Foletto/Globo, 227; Kevin C. Cox, 228 (top); NASCAR/Rusty Jarrett, 229 (top); Jonathan Ferrey, 229 (bottom); Chris McGrath, 230 (top); C&G Collections, 230 (Mantle & Maris); Ezra Shaw, 234; Jeff Zelevansky, 235; Tom Hauck, 236; Andrew Redington, 237 (middle); Jim McIsaac, 238; G. Newman Lowrance 239 (bottom left); Torsten Blackwood/AFP, 240; Doug Pensinger, 241; Cynthia Johnson/Time & Life Pictures, 286; Win McNamee, 311 (top); Nicolas Asfouri/AFP, 331 (bottom). **HarperCollins**: *Sounder* by William H. Armstrong, Cover Illustration Copyright © 1989 by Daniel Maffia. Used by Permission of HarperCollins Publishers, 46; *Gettysburg: The Graphic Novel,* by C. M. Butzer, HarperCollins Children's Books, 47; *Where the Wild Things Are* by Maurice Sendak, 130. **Henry Holt & Co.**: *Charles and Emma: The Darwins' Leap of Faith,* by Deborah Heiligman, 46. **Houghton Mifflin Harcourt**: *Alchemy and Meggy Swann* by Karen Cushman, Clarion Books, 44; *The Hobbit* by

349

J. R. R. Tolkien and *A Crooked Kind of Perfect* by Linda Urban, 46. **Infobase Publishing**: *How Astronauts Use Math,* 37. **The International Astronomical Union**: Martin Kornmesser, 210. **Dusso Janladde**: 251. **Lyndon B. Johnson Library**: Robert Knudsen, 278 (Johnson). **John F. Kennedy Library**: 278 (Kennedy). **Lausch Photography**: Ed Lausch, 311 (middle). **Library of Congress**: 270–276 (Washington-Clinton); LC-USZ62-93635, 35 (bottom); LC-DIG-ppmsc-01269, 38 (King); LC-USZ62-60242, 38 (Einstein); LC-USZ62-108565, 41 (Barton); LC-USZ61-694, 48; LC-USZ62-69629, 51 (right); LC-USW361-109, 86 (1940s); LC-USZ62-25351, 94; LC-USZC4-7503, 95; 120: LC-USZC4-2737 (American Revolution), LC-USZC4-6893 (War of 1812), LC-B8184-10086 (Civil War), LC-USZC4-3933 (Spanish-American War); LC-USZC4-3859, 121 (World War II); LC-B2- 5202-12, 190; 247: LC-USZC4-3266 (Stagecoach), LC-USZ62-43058 (Balloon), LC-D4-22602 (Steamboat); 277: LC-USZ62-56782 (Adams), LC-DIG-hec-00962 (Madison), LC-USZ62-15325 (Lincoln), LC-DIG-hec-22289 (Cleveland), LC-G432-0932 (Wilson), LC-USZ62-25811 DLC (Hoover); LC-USZC4-2019 DLC, 278 (Ford); 280: LC-DIG-pga-02388 (Columbus), LC-USZC4-12217 (New Amsterdam), LC-USZC2-2004 (Franklin); LC-H8-CT-C01-063-E, 281 (Declaration of Independence); 283: LC-USZC2-3796 (War of 1812), LC-USZC4-3365 (Fredericksburg), LC-DIG-stereo-1s00612 (train); LC-USZ62-86846, 285 (O'Connor); LC-USZ62-109426, 287 (Parks); LC-USZC4-6895, 326 (Luther); LC-DIG-hec-04921, 327 (Nicholas II); LC-DIG-pga-00710, 328 (Columbus); LC-USZ62-47764, 328 (Cortes); LC-USZ62-100275, 329 (Diaz); LC-USZ62-119343, 332 (Truth). **Tony Lipinski**: 311 (bottom). **Little, Brown Books for Young Readers**: *The Lion and the Mouse* by Jerry Pinkney, 44. **Maps .com**: 140–151, 288–289. **Naismith Basketball Hall of Fame**: 232 (bottom). **NASA**: 8 (top); 40 (Armstrong); 284 (Man on Moon); GSFC & NRDC, 85 (Polar cap); JPL/GSFC/Ames, 211 (Saturn Rings); JPL, 215 (Moon), 218 (Juno); NASA/Johns Hopkins University Applied Physics Laboratory/Southwest Research Institute, 216 (New Horizon); JPL-Calech/University of Arizona, 216 (Phoenix); Space Telescope Science Institute, 218–219 (Spiral); Johnson Space Center, 249 (Shuttle). **National Archives and Records Administration**: 121 (World War I); 178 (Code Talkers); 258 (Constitution); 261 (Congress); 282 (Constitutional Convention); 284 (School Segregation); 327 (Mussolini & Hitler). **Naval Air Engineering Station (NAES) Lakehurst**: 70. **Newscom**: PRNewsFoto/BBC, Edwin Giesbers, 3, 22 (frog); Chris Martinez/La Opinion, 3, 64 (bottom); ZUMA, 4, 135 (dancer), 124 (Helú), 135 (bottom), 222–223 (Olympic torch); Visions of America, 4, 123 (top); Photo Take Medical, 25 (tapeworm), 32 (tubeworm); Photoshot, 30; dbcstock, 32 (top); dpkpphotos/Ilyas Dean, 37 (designer); Debbie VanStory/iPhotoLive.com, 38 (Lautner); Mirrorpix, 39 (Fitzgerald); AFP Photo/Dimitar Dilkoff, 40 (White); Random House, 45 (top); WENN, 45 (bottom), 132 (top); AFP Photo/Eitan Abramovich, 68; Richard B. Levine, 76; Ahmad Elatab-Saleem Elatab/Splash News, 88 (bottom); AFP/Getty Images/Nicholas Roberts, 113 (bottom); Splash News/Bobby Martinez, 133 (top); AFP, 209 (Curies); Roger L. Wollenberg/ UPI, 234 (bottom); International Sports Images, 239 (Lilly); SHNS Courtesy of General Motors, 249 (Volt); UPI Photo/Pat Benic, 252 (top); Stock Connection, 252 (bottom); Black Star Photos/ Dennis Brack, 263; AFP Photo/Saul Loeb, 285 (Obama); Oe Rimkus Jr./Miami Herald, 331 (top); AFP Photo/Scanpix Norway-Solum Stian Lysberg, 333 (Williams). **Courtesy of NF Observatory**: 134. **NOAA**: 67. **Oakland Museum of California**: Andrew J. Russell Collection, 248 (Model T). **Obama-Biden Transition Project**: 192 (top). **Penguin Books for Young Readers**: *The House with the Clock in Its Walls* by John Bellairs, illustrated by Edward Gorey, 46. **Photofest**: ABC, 11 (top). **Ronald Reagan Presidential Library**: 278 (Reagan). **Franklin D. Roosevelt Library**: 278 (Roosevelt). **Martin Rowe**: 192 (bottom). **Russell Knightly Media**: 207 (bottom). **SECCHI, STEREO, NRL, NASA**: 4, 219 (comet). **David Shankbone**: 51 (Chrysler Building). **ShurTech Brands, LLC**: 195 (Duct Tape Prom Contest). **Stuttgart Chamber of Commerce**: 195 (Chick and Sophie Major Memorial Duck Calling Contest). **Kimberley French/© 2009 Summit Entertainment. All Rights Reserved**: 13 (bottom), 131 (*Eclipse*). **Edward A. Thomas**: 53 (Colosseum), 162 (Venice), 318 (Hieroglyphics). **Courtesy of Tuskegee University Archives**: 209 (Carver). **UN Photo**: Mark Garten, 321 (Johnson-Sirleaf). **U.S. Air Force**: 121 (Persian Gulf War); Airman 1st Class Laura Goodgame, 122 (Afghanistan). **U.S. Army**: Sgt. Jeffrey Alexander, 6 (Afghanistan). **U.S. Census Bureau**: Public Information Office, 8 (bottom), 189. **U.S. Department of Agriculture**: 101 (food pyramid). **U.S. Department of Defense**: Petty Officer 2nd Class Robert Whelan, U.S. Navy, 122 (Iraq War); Jim Garamone, 123 (bottom).

THE WORLD ALMANAC FOR KIDS 2011

#1 for Facts and Fun

》》 Amazing facts fill every page of The World Almanac for Kids.
Here are just a few...

What is the best-selling home video game of all time? **see page 90**

Where is the world's tallest building? **see page 50**

Why did all Major League Baseball players wear No. 42 on April 15, 2010? **see page 231**

Which rap star helped create the Rocawear clothing company? **see page 88**

When was the first Earth Day celebrated? **see page 58**

Where is London Bridge? **see page 292**

How many Americans have a reptile as a pet? **see page 28**

Where will the next Summer Olympics be held? **see page 227**

Who was the first woman to win an Academy Award for Best Director? **see page 129**

What First Lady was once a professional dancer? **see page 278**

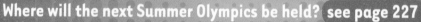